Beyond Testimony and Trauma

shared
ORAL & PUBLIC HISTORY

This series presents distinctive works that challenge conventional understandings of not only who speaks for history but also how history is spoken, and for whom. In an era when the possibilities for collaborative research and public engagement are almost limitless – when the term *history* can at once embrace deeply personal life stories and the broad scope of a public museum exhibit – the need to explore new methodological models and assess their ethical implications has never been so vital. This series, unique in its focus, provides the pivot for a transformative vision of historical practice.

Other volumes in the series:

According to Baba: A Collaborative Oral History of Sudbury's Ukrainian Community
STACEY ZEMBRZYCKI (2014)

Oral History at the Crossroads: Sharing Life Stories of Survival and Displacement
STEVEN HIGH (2014)

Beyond Testimony and Trauma

ORAL HISTORY IN THE AFTERMATH OF MASS VIOLENCE

Edited by Steven High

UBCPress · Vancouver · Toronto

25 24 23 22 21 20 19 18 17 16 15 5 4 3 2 1

Printed in Canada on FSC-certified ancient-forest-free paper (100% post-consumer recycled) that is processed chlorine- and acid-free.

Library and Archives Canada Cataloguing in Publication

Beyond testimony and trauma: oral history in the aftermath of mass violence / edited by Steven High.

(Shared, oral and public history)
Includes bibliographical references and index.
Issued in print and electronic formats.
ISBN 978-0-7748-2892-5 (bound). – ISBN 978-0-7748-2893-2 (pbk.). –
ISBN 978-0-7748-2894-9 (pdf). – ISBN 978-0-7748-2895-6 (epub)

1. Oral history. 2. Oral biography. 3. Victims. 4. Survival. I. High, Steven C., editor II. Series: Shared, oral & public history

D16.14.B49 2015 907.2 C2015-900356-3
C2015-900357-1

Canada

UBC Press gratefully acknowledges the financial support for our publishing program of the Government of Canada (through the Canada Book Fund), the Canada Council for the Arts, and the British Columbia Arts Council.

This book has been published with the help of a grant from the Canadian Federation for the Humanities and Social Sciences, through the Awards to Scholarly Publications Program, using funds provided by the Social Sciences and Humanities Research Council of Canada.

Printed and bound in Canada by Friesens
Set in DIN Round and Perpetua by Artegraphica Design Co. Ltd.
Text design: Sigrid Albert, StepUp Communications
Copy editor: Joanne Richardson
Proofreader: Lana Okerlund
Indexer: Cheryl Lemmens

UBC Press
The University of British Columbia
2029 West Mall
Vancouver, BC V6T 1Z2
www.ubcpress.ca

FOR MY DAUGHTER LEANNA

UBC Press is publishing three books based on insights from the Montreal Life Stories project. These are:

STEVEN HIGH
Oral History at the Crossroads: Sharing Life Stories of Survival and Displacement

STEVEN HIGH, ED.
Beyond Testimony and Trauma: Oral History in the Aftermath of Mass Violence

ELIZABETH MILLER, EDWARD LITTLE, AND STEVEN HIGH
Going Public: Participatory Approaches to Oral History, Documentary Media, and Theatre

HISTOIRES DE VIE MONTRÉAL
MONTREAL LIFE STORIES

oral history
Concordia University

Contents

Part 3: Acts of Composure and Framing

Acknowledgments

For the past seven years, I have been immersed in the Montreal Life Stories project, a major collaborative research initiative recording the life stories of Montrealers displaced by war, genocide, and other human rights violations. Funded under the Community-University Research Alliance (CURA) and Diffusion programs of Canada's Social Sciences and Humanities Research Council, the project culminated in an ambitious month-long program of public events in March 2012. Several thousand people attended the many live performances, screenings, launches, round-table discussions, workshops, inter-generational dialogues, audio walks, installations, and exhibitions, and an interdisciplinary conference entitled "Beyond Testimony and Trauma: Oral History in the Aftermath of Mass Violence." This edited collection originates in this conference. The program committee, consisting of Lisa Ndejuru, Henry Greenspan, and myself, hoped to consider the many ways that oral historians and others engage with life stories in the aftermath of mass violence, widely defined.

The conference committee benefitted from the assistance of a superb team of student and community-based assistants. Conference organizer Ozren Stambuk – an undergraduate student in history, did a great job. He was ably assisted by Kim Moore, Marie-Hélène Sauvé, Chandra Ky, Gracia Dyer Jalea, Phil Lichti, Caroline Kunzle, Neal Santamaria, and Nick Kanhai. As always, Magaly Sala and her team at Alternatives provided excellent simultaneous interpretation. Funding came from the Social Sciences and Humanities Research Council, Concordia University, and the Canada Research Chairs program. A visiting professorship at the Scottish Oral History Centre at Strathclyde University in Glasgow, immediately following the conference, enabled me to push this edited collection forward relatively quickly. The generosity of Arthur McIvor, also a contributor here, was truly remarkable.

Most of all, I would like to thank the twenty-one contributors to this volume. It was a wonderful group of people. I would particularly like to acknowledge Henry Greenspan, who kindly read and commented on all the chapters, writing one himself, as well as the book's afterword. His approach to interviewing continues to inspire many of us. I also want to thank Melissa Pitts, Darcy Cullen, and Holly Keller at UBC Press for their support and enthusiasm. Colette Stoeber once again served as an outstanding copy-editor before submission. Finally, I would like to thank my friends and colleagues in the Montreal Life Stories project whose generosity, passion, and insight has been a great inspiration to me. My part of the book is dedicated to my daughter Leanna.

Beyond Testimony and Trauma

Introduction

STEVEN HIGH

> My dad was a steel worker with Great Lakes Steel, a union man, put in his thirty years [...] I grew up in Southwest Detroit which is a predominantly blue-collar part of the city of Detroit. The factories were the prevalent workplace [...] As I grew up, I had hopes for college, but the factories were the lure, the money, the pay, the stability [...] We went in with high hopes, ambition, and we settled in. But as time wore on after five, ten years, we realized we had choices to make. As we started to marry and build our families, we knew then that this was a keeper. That we were gonna be part of this [...] Hired in, it was a whole new world to me. Working for GM, "business of businesses." We're partners, we're going to do this for life, this thirty-year ambition. So as time wore on, I chose to become a good worker. Be on time, come in everyday; build the product the way they wanted it to be built [...] I got married when I worked in the shop, we had a child, we moved out to the suburbs. The big dream was on. I bought the GM product, the car, the truck, the house in the suburbs, the new baby, the new furniture. And then [chuckles] the dream came crashing down.
>
> – Gabriel Solano[1]

It may seem strange to begin a volume on oral history in the aftermath of mass violence with the recollections of a Detroit autoworker as his story of forced economic displacement is not typically understood in these terms. We are much more accustomed to thinking of mass violence and survival in the context of war or atrocity crimes. But as this edited collection demonstrates, there is considerable value in stretching ourselves to make new connections and to revisit old assumptions. Survivor testimony has developed a conventional form and rhetoric. For the most part, survivors of mass violence are understood as either eyewitnesses to history or as people traumatized by it. Testimony and trauma are thus firmly embedded in legal and medical discourses. Survivor testimony has become familiar: indeed, ubiquitous. The contributors to this volume consider other ways to engage with survivors and their accounts. Particular emphasis is placed on collaborative approaches and the political and historical context in which survivors recount their experiences. What are the rightful claims of a more holistic or collaborative approach to survivors' retelling? What are the political and ethical implications of different ways of engaging survivors' accounts?

While the contributors to this collection respond to these questions in varying geographic and historical contexts, there is much continuity between the chapters. The underlying logic of recorded accounts is subject to examination throughout the collection. By being attentive to the form and structure of oral accounts, as well as to what they have to say directly about the past, we can deepen our engagement with survivors' remembered experiences. According to Julie Salverson, "a significant element in the encounter with testimony is the unexpectedness, the shock of the collision between the world of the listener and the world of the event."[2] The narrated life of Gabriel Solano is a case in point.

I first interviewed Gabriel in his Southwest Detroit home in February 1998, after he responded to my public appeal for plant shutdown stories. He had waited a long time to tell his story, so he jumped right in. Gabriel began working for General Motors in 1977, right out of high school. Like many in his blue-collar generation, he was not comfortable for long. The North American auto industry went through a period of crisis in the 1980s and 1990s, resulting in union concessions, mass layoffs, and factory closures. You can hear the disillusionment in Gabriel's voice as he recounts how fast his life unravelled:

> [The] pressure was on. "Do this, or we shut the shop down." Threats. The threats were coming. They were coming full force. I mean, they weren't hidden threats, they were open threats. "Do this, give us this, or it's your job." At which point we then became a workforce full of fear [...] The factory, GM, with their cut-throat mentality cared not one for us. We were just kicked to the curb. We were put out to the pasture to die off. Myself, personally, I couldn't believe it and I didn't want to believe it. After one year of being laid-off from '86, my marriage started to dissipate right in front of me. The pressures were immense, they were intense. We bought the house, we bought the vehicles, we had a brand new baby, and the pressure was on. It, it, eventually became too much for me and my wife and we divorced. At which point I became a bitter, a very, very bitter

> man. Everything that I'd worked for and trained for, I watched it fall away. I fell to the wayside, GM pushed us to the wayside, my marriage went to the wayside ... Well, it was a long and bitter layoff. Seven years, eight months to be exact. I survived it. I survived. And the reason that I survived was because I gave up on thinking that they would ever call me back. I had to let go of GM because GM sure in the hell let go of me.

After such a long wait, Gabriel was finally recalled to another GM plant, then another, and then another as one auto plant after another closed beneath him. Each time, Gabriel had to wait to be recalled and then started back at the bottom rung of the employment ladder. He no longer had the seniority to hold day shift as the company and union distinguished between corporate and plant seniority. This set workers apart and changed them. By the time that I interviewed Gabriel, he had closed three GM plants. After Fisher Guide in Southwest Detroit, he worked briefly at a Livonia trim shop and Pontiac's east plant before resurfacing at the west plant.

Plant shutdown veterans like Gabriel eventually came to identify themselves with their displacement. They were no longer simply autoworkers but something other. Transplanted workers in the area, who had considerable corporate seniority but no plant seniority, soon took to calling themselves the "I-75 Gypsies." Gabriel explained to me that these were the workers who had come off long layoffs, having closed GM plants up and down Interstate-75:

> We are the people who shut down plants up and down I-75, that's why we call ourselves the 75 Gypsies. We have no home plants. We're very hardened people. We're very thick-skinned, but we're also very good people because we've been to all the battles in the war called the automotive industry. And to meet one ... you'll meet the most wonderful person because at the facility I'm at, we're gypsies: the majority in our area, in our facility. There's like four or five hundred of us there and they stuck us all in damn near the same building. So, we're neat because everyone has a story. And they're beautiful stories. They're stories of hurt, of fear, of anger, of loss, of gain ... the whole rollercoaster ... We're taken in, but we're treated differently.

Told from the vantage point of a battle-hardened, yet still defiant, I-75 gypsy, Gabriel's account is cast in absurdist terms. The things he saw and experienced were often ridiculous, irrational, and even humorous in a perverse kind of way. I would like to relate a story he shared with me about the closing of his third plant. He was called in to work there only after the company announced its closure:

> So I get there and the foreman gave me this "you're here to do the job," and I mean, he's gung-ho and I'm looking at him like I just got a free ticket on the *Titanic*. It's already hit the iceberg, it's three-quarters sunk and you're telling me strike up the band? And I said, "Can life get any worse? And then I meet you?" So he, he reads me his riot act about what we have to do for this plant and it's gonna shut down in two weeks. Mind you, this is at Christmas time. And I'm like, is this real? It's real. So, you're absolutely right. Which way is the lifeboat? [Laughs] At which point I said I have to have fun with this. And I made it fun. I was around a bunch of workers who had never been to a plant closing and I had already closed two.

At this point in recounting his story, I interjected as Gabriel had not yet revealed the second closure to me. He forged ahead without skipping a beat:

> It was a Livonia trim shop. I was there briefly ... I think it was the *Lusitania* and then I got on the *Titanic*. So one got torpedoed and the other hit the iceberg. So I, I was rather enlightened because I had now become calloused and I understood what was going on. To watch some of these other workers, threatening to bring in guns. I hate everyone's mentality, it was understood: I seen, I felt it, I done it. Been there. Oh, there was one hell of an irony because it was Christmas time and I can remember this day so vividly 'cause I was taking notes because I wanted to feel this even farther down the road. So I took notes every day on how workers were acting. I mean the things that were done in there. They were horrendous ... the one day that I took notes, I can still remember them so vividly. "Attention, attention." And then they put out flyers, posters. "Free hot dogs. Pops. Popcorn in the cafeteria. Please come down!" But hey, I'll look at the freebies. So I go down there and I'm sitting in the corner and I'm writing down, I'm watching people and I'm writing this down. You can see the anger. You can see the hurt. You can see

> the anxiety. And you can see, most of all, the fear. That magic word: fear. They start playing Christmas music over the PA and I'm thinking, "Strike up the band, the *Titanic*'s going down." So we get in line and the plant manager and all of his colleagues passing [out] hot dogs and pop. They are so damn cheerful and they're taking pictures. So he hands me a hot dog. So I drop it on the floor. He says, "Oh, here's another one." So I throw it against the wall. He says, "Do you have attitude?" [Laughs] And I started laughing and I says, "It's ironic you should ask me that. Here you are shutting our plant down, putting us out of work. You're playing Christmas music. It's at Christmas time. I should be happier than a pig in you know what." And I said, "No! No! But this is what I think of your hot dog, this is what I think of your pop." So at which point they said, "Call security, we don't want him in here because he's disrupting the other employees." I says, "No, you don't have to call them. I'll leave. But I just want you to know how I feel and that's genuine. Been through a lot to have to do this but this is my respect for you, the same respect you're giving me." It was a hell of an irony. Christmas music, free hot dogs, plant closes at Christmas time. So, here I am on the *Titanic* and I'm thinking, "God, GM is just being too kind to me."

The incongruous juxtaposition of soon-to-be unemployed autoworkers being feted by their smiling managers is not something easily forgotten or forgiven. Philosopher Thomas Negel once suggested that, in order to recognize the absurd in our own lives, we have to see ourselves from the outside: to become estranged from our condition.[3] We see this occurring in Gabriel's repeated mention of having written down notes as these events unfolded. His detached amazement thus sets him apart from the other autoworkers waiting in line for their free hot dogs and pop. As he says, he had become "enlightened." But this is not simply an exercise in mass observation, as his subsequent act of rebellion attests.[4] Gabriel is clearly angry.

Gabriel's plant shutdown story is a tragic tale brimming with absurdity. The absurd is epitomized in Greek mythology by Sisyphus, who is condemned by the gods to roll a rock up a hill for an eternity. Once he arrives at the top, the rock rolls back down, and he has to start over again. It is all pointless, of course.[5] Writer Albert Camus, famous for

FIGURE 0.1 Gabriel Solano, photographed inside the ruined Fisher Guide plant in Southwest Detroit. 2004. *Photograph by David W. Lewis.*

his existential novels, believed that Sisyphus was an absurd hero because he continued to push the rock up the hill but mocked the gods who condemned him to this fate by doing so cheerfully. For Camus,

> If this myth is tragic, that is because its hero is conscious [...] Sisyphus, proletarian of the gods, powerless and rebellious, knows the whole extent of his misery: that is what he thinks of during his descent. The clairvoyance that was meant to be his torture crowns at the same time his victory. There is no fate that cannot be surmounted by scorn.[6]

One can see parallels in the interview with Gabriel Solano. The oft-repeated experience of factory closure, layoff, and recall is a similarly unending cycle of misery for Detroit autoworkers. Gabriel, like Sisyphus, thus conquers his cruel fate by heroically scorning it. There is a movement from silence to despair to rebellion in Gabriel's plant shutdown story: an awakening conscious.[7] The form and structure of his story is, in itself, a product of his experience of displacement.[8]

Naturally, my intention here is not to equate the fate of industrial workers to the slaughter of thousands or millions in Rwanda, Bosnia, Argentina, Cambodia, or Nazi-occupied Europe. Deindustrialization is devastating for those directly affected, but it is not genocide. My point is to show that acts of witness range across many sites of resistance to mass violence.[9] First-person narratives give us unique "glimpses into the lived interior" of forced displacement and its aftermath.[10] One of the legacies of mass violence and forced displacement, in all its varieties, is the emergence of new communities of activist survivors who form their own identities and institutions. In Ari Gandsman's chapter, for example, we see how the surviving "disappeared" in Argentina formed their own association to undertake its historical and judicial work. Elsewhere, groups of injured workers (Storey), genocide survivors (Sheftel and Zembrzycki), eugenics survivors (Wilson), and others do much the same work. Through this broad approach to mass violence, this collection responds to some of the criticisms of "wounded attachment" raised by sociologist Beverley Skeggs, who notes that "only some groups can articulate their identities through wound and pain," thereby "eclipsing structural inequality and suffering."[11]

This edited collection originates in the work of the Montreal Life Stories project, a six-year community-university research alliance that recorded the life stories of Montrealers displaced by war, genocide, and other human rights violations. University-based researchers worked collaboratively with survivors and their organizations, envisioning the project together and co-producing its many activities. Almost five hundred multi-session interviews were conducted, and the project produced a variety of online digital stories, animated and documentary films, radio programming, live performances, QR-coded audio portraits in metro cars, audio walks, art installations, pedagogical materials, and a museum exhibition.[12] In March 2012, we also organized an international conference entitled Beyond Testimony and Trauma: Oral History in the Aftermath of Mass Violence, which drew almost two hundred participants. Presenters explored a wide range of national and historical contexts using a variety of approaches. This collection emerged from this extended conversation, both in terms of the project and the conference itself.

Beyond Testimony and Trauma is also a product of the historiographical moment. The popularity of trauma research and psychoanalytic theory in the humanities and social sciences since the 1990s was tied to the rise of memory studies and the publication of Felman and Laub's *Testimony* in 1992 and the work of Cathy Caruth, published in 1995 and 1996. Soon, however, questions were raised about trauma theory. In 2001, Susannah Radstone and Katharine Hodgkin asserted that trauma theory was a "phenomenon begging analysis."[13] Radstone, in particular, expresses concern that the "usual cut and thrust of academic parrying and debate" was rendered "inappropriate" in the presence of human suffering.[14] She raises the possibility that trauma had "become a 'popular cultural script' in need of contextualization and analysis in its own right – a symptom, the cause of which needs to be sought elsewhere."[15] Since then, a growing number of scholars have questioned the uncritical and undifferentiated use of trauma in the study of mass violence. Our own efforts to go "beyond trauma" are therefore part of the wider rethinking occurring across the humanities and social sciences.

The thirteen chapters that follow are organized into three parts, each taking us beyond testimony and trauma in unique ways. We start with the political work of testimony. Too often, we understand testimony singularly as an individual act of witness, ignoring the contexts in which these first-person accounts are invited, recorded, heard, and diffused. Nor do we hear enough of their important place in social movements and within survivor communities themselves. Part 2 of the book takes us into the important memory work that is being conducted collaboratively by researchers and survivors. The emphasis here is on Henry Greenspan's notion of "sustained conversation" and "genuine dialogue."[16] Part 3 takes us into the internal logics of recorded oral narratives. Meaning can be found in the form and structure of the recorded narratives, and in the silences therein, as well as in what is actually said. We can therefore learn a great deal from reading oral accounts for the "symbols and logic embedded in them" rather than simply as sources of historical information.[17] Only then, according to historian Daniel James, can we "attend to their deeper meaning and do justice to the complexity found in the lives and historical experiences of those who recount them."[18] It is this complexity found in political context, sustained conversation, and deep listening that is the subject of this book.

The Political Work of Witness

War keeps coming back in narratives and memories as the most dramatic point of encounter between the personal and the public, between biography and history.

– Alessandro Portelli[19]

Part 1 of *Beyond Testimony and Trauma* comprises four chapters that explore the wider context of survivor recounting: its place and function within movements for social justice and within societies more generally. Interviewing for human rights purposes ranges from acts of "fact-finding" during or in the immediate aftermath of mass atrocities to the development of vast archives of conscience long after.[20] Truth and reconciliation processes have now occurred in many countries, including my own. As I write, Canada's Truth and Reconciliation Commission (TRC) is gathering the statements of thousands of Aboriginal survivors of residential schools.[21] The past twenty-five years have also seen large-scale testimony-gathering projects such as that of the Shoah Visual History Foundation. To some extent, the "ethical force" of these projects stems from the "accumulation of many stories."[22] But even taken individually, as Sidonie Smith and Julia Watson write, "Narratives of witness [...] make an urgent, immediate, and direct bid for attention and call the reader/listener to an ethical response through their affective appeals for recognition."[23]

What is interesting here, however, is the degree to which these large and ambitious projects encourage us to think of the large body of interviews as a whole or in terms of the individual survivor bearing witness. What we do not see as often is the survivor activism that often initiates these efforts or the central role of survivors in the projects themselves. Nor do we hear much about the survivor communities that form in the aftermath of mass violence as this occurs beyond the sight lines of the eyewitness to mass violence. Human rights discourse tends to privilege individual rights and to emphasize the innocence of the survivor. But when we listen more closely to human rights activists, we hear a subtle tension between the legal discourse of individual human rights and the language of collective political struggle for equality and social justice. Human rights discourse presents activists and social movements with a way to transcend domestic politics and long-established ideological divides, leveraging international support through a discourse of legality. This became evident in a series of interviews that I conducted in 2010 with visiting human rights activists from Latin America, Africa, and Asia.[24] I was struck by the frequency with which they corrected themselves during the interview after momentarily speaking of "student rights," "women's rights," or "disability rights." The growing importance of first-person accounts in North American social movements is similarly clear. The ACT UP oral history project with surviving members of the AIDS Coalition to Unleash Power in New York City comes immediately to mind.[25] This movement context provides us with an alternative political frame to individual eyewitness or trauma.

In Chapter 1, Ari Gandsman explores the work of survivors in post-dictatorship Argentina. Remembering mass violence in a post-conflict society is, of course, vastly different from remembering it as part of a diaspora. Gandsman's surviving "disappeared" struggle against the societal perception that they survived because they had collaborated. For some, they are morally suspect, compromised, or tainted. Only one in one hundred of the estimated thirty thousand who were disappeared by the military dictatorship between 1976 and 1983 survived. These survivors have faced hostile questioning and snide remarks ever since. In Argentina, moral authority rests in the families of those killed, such as the Mothers of the Plaza de Mayo. Survivors have therefore been politically marginalized, despite their key role in the criminal prosecution of the killers and torturers. A member of the Association of Ex-Detainees and Disappeared, for example, is quoted as saying: "We were pointed at, left to the side, treated like traitors and ghosts. There was no solidarity for us." Some survivors, however, do find solidarity with one another.

In Chapter 2, North Americans are reminded that mass violence is not just located somewhere else or sometime before but also in the here and now. Robert Storey specifically engages with the place of "accident stories" within the injured workers' movement. At present, in Canada, the everyday violence of capitalist labour processes leaves a worker seriously injured (requiring time off) every nineteen seconds, and each day three workers die from workplace accidents or disease. These workers are twice harmed, first by not being adequately protected at work against injury and then by a regime that turns "hurts into harms." Injury compensation is a "profoundly individualizing experience" as their claims are adjudicated strictly on a case-by-case basis.[26] The sharing of stories that is taking place between injured workers thus contributes to "new understandings" about their personal experiences, furthering political mobilization and resistance to changes in government policy as well as countering the shame and isolation felt by many injured workers. "Nobody should be going through this alone," says Alice (an injured worker).

Historians and other researchers have an important role to play in building solidarity within marginalized populations. In the context of the Injured Workers History Project, a community-university research alliance, Storey addresses the political potential of "gatherin' a little knowledge," with movement activists and leaders sharing not only personal stories within the movement but also historical knowledge. Storey speaks to how contact with the "long history" of injured workers provides a political framework within which injured workers may situate their experiences, a process that serves to politicize their understanding of their experience of injury. Both Gandsman's and Storey's activist-survivors formed groups to "work with these testimonies," filling in the blanks through additional historical research. This political framing stands as an alternative to the "preoccupation with the experience of loss and a privileging of trauma as a mode of knowledge," which "provides an essential yet limiting framework that fixes testimony within a discourse of loss and the tragic."[27] Pain and suffering need not be pathologized as an individual problem.

The politics of telling one's story changes when the context shifts from survivors sharing with one another to the telling of their stories to wider publics. Who controls the process is of fundamental importance. The ethics of learning from survivor accounts in the classroom is the subject of Chapter 3, co-authored by feminist educators Lisa Taylor, Marie-Jolie Rwigema, and Umwali Sollange. They are in the initial stages of a participatory action project that will result in community-led curriculum development for a Grade 11 course entitled "Genocide and Crimes against Humanity." Too often, they argue, Western audiences are only interested in the experiential stories of Rwandan genocide survivors and not their expertise – leaving control of interpretation in the hands of non-Africans. The naïve solicitation of autobiography, Salverson argues elsewhere, may "recycle scripts of melancholic loss" and reproduce "a form of cultural colonialism that is at the very least voyeuristic."[28] A similar point is made here when Taylor observes that "voracious empathy risks being an exercise in emotional tourism, an ahistorical, sentimentalized, and romanticized 'feeling good about feeling bad.'" This can amount to the "theft of pain." Public testimony, at least in North America, is often delivered in "highly formalized settings," whereas "insider practices" often take the form of informal "chit-chat testimonies," Sollange reminds us. Ultimately, they argue, the aspirations for survivor testimony to galvanize responses to end the violence "remain unattained and increasingly uncertain." Researchers and educators, by working collaboratively with survivor communities, need to "work through the demands of testimony" and to re-examine the "ways testimony is framed and used within genocide education."

In Chapter 4, the final chapter in this section, Rob Wilson explores the role of oral history in surviving a eugenics past. Canada's history of surgical sterilization of the "mentally defective" ended only in 1973 when British Columbia repealed its legislation a year after Alberta did so. Wilson's project, the Living Archives on Eugenics in Western Canada, yet another community-university research alliance, is working in partnership with eugenics survivors and human rights advocates to document this history through archival research and recorded interviews. The research project is very much understood as a political intervention and part of a wider effort to take back control and to break the silence. As Wilson writes: "It is not simply that survivor oral history has been omitted, forgotten, or neglected, as in other cases; rather, it is that survivor oral history has been presumed to be precluded by the putative nature of those deemed mentally deficient." We learn about the courage and determination of Leilani Muir, a eugenics survivor and Living Archives team member, who brought a lawsuit against the government – shining critical light on the forced sterilization of three thousand Canadians.

Working with Survivors

> Collaboration does not mean that we abandon our own stance, that we lose our "critical edge" as scholars. It does, however, challenge our power dynamics in the field.
>
> – Alicia J. Rouverol[29]

Part 2 of *Beyond Testimony and Trauma* shifts our perspective to the kinds of working-through that go on in the collaborative interview or workshop. Of course the interview has become a standard tool for many humanities and social science disciplines.[30] For some disciplines interviewing is almost banal, though it continues to encounter strong resistance in others.[31] After years of debate, survivor accounts are now largely accepted in historical writing about mass violence.[32] Their immediacy, according to Geoffrey H. Hartman, "burns through the 'cold storage' of history."[33] How researchers approach the interview, however, varies. Henry Greenspan and Sidney Bolkosky, for example, suggest that "a great deal of activity that looks like interviewing Holocaust survivors and calls itself interviewing Holocaust survivors may not, in fact, be interviewing Holocaust survivors."[34] In reality, they continue, "a genuine interview with a Holocaust survivor may be a relatively rare thing." For them, as for me, a good interview is a collaborative work space in which the interviewer and the interviewee wrestle with the past and its legacies.

The "democratic impulse" within oral history, always strong, finds expression in the four chapters contained in Part 2.[35] The contributors, which include Greenspan, demonstrate a strong commitment to working collaboratively with survivors. They speak in terms of "collaborative witnessing," "compassionate listening," and being true "partners in conversation." As Kathleen Blee suggests, the evidence of oral history is "embedded not only in narrative accounts but also in the process of interviewing."[36] It is therefore important to be reflexive in our interviewing practice.[37] However, the line between being self-aware and reflexive researchers and being self-indulgent is "fragile and blurred."[38] Joy Parr, for example, insists that oral historians have "taken refuge in methodology" when faced with ethically challenging situations.[39] Alessandro Portelli goes further when he cautions us that too much self-reflexivity can effectively erase our interview partners.[40]

If the sharing of our research stories is fraught, the contributors to this section reveal that, in working collaboratively with survivors, methodology and self-reflexivity become part of the conversation rather than a turning inward or away. There is perhaps no better way to begin this section than with Henry Greenspan's reflections on forty years of listening to and working with Holocaust survivors. His book, entitled *On Listening to Holocaust Survivors* and now in its second edition, has become indispensable to many of us in the field. Here, again, he encourages us to meet survivors as "genuine partners in conversation." His chapter finds some of the key concepts in genocide studies – such as testimony, trauma, and memory – to be wanting. Testimony, he writes, is ill-equipped to explain the many ways, and all the reasons, that survivors retell. For this reason, Greenspan prefers to speak of accounts or retelling. Trauma likewise subsumes a wide range of anguish.[41] In *On Listening*, for example, he writes that "trauma theories can be a distraction from the kinds of listening that the best interviews entail."[42] For its part, memory cannot quite capture "in the bones knowledge," he writes. He proposes knowledge as an alternative to memory, at least in cases in which people survived mass violence. Knowledge, he suggests, may be grounded in memories but it also includes their implications. In this sense, Greenspan argues that knowledge is the more fundamental category, equipping those survivors – in this part and the one before – to draw on what they have learned, share it, and use it as the basis of organizing change.

The contributors that follow share Greenspan's emphasis on sustaining the conversation beyond the confines of the formal interview. In Chapter 6, Carolyn Ellis (a qualitative researcher) and Jerry Rawicki (a Holocaust survivor) reflect on their collaborative life-writing practice. The co-authors introduce us to the notion of "collaborative witnessing" as an alternative to the usual practice of "bearing witness" in testimony-giving. Carolyn Ellis has been using interactive interviewing and "co-constructed narrative approaches" since the early 1990s. Working together, the co-authors "mutually analyze" Jerry Rawicki's remembered stories. For the purposes of this chapter, they focus on one story in particular, called "Get the Jew," which was developed into a literary short story. Here, for the first time, we get to read the story in its final polished form while also being able to read it as it appeared in the transcribed initial interview. The co-authors then reflect on how they got from one point to the other. Importantly, their collaboration continued during the analysis phase, resting on an ethic of friendship that did not draw a hard line between the personal and the professional.[43]

Friendship also underlies the contribution of Chris Patti, who, in Chapter 7, relates his deepening relationship with Sal Wainberg, a Tampa Bay–area Holocaust survivor. Patti speaks to the experience of the interview, the forged connection, and the sense of intimacy that sometimes resulted. Playing with form, the dialogical structure of Patti's piece highlights that this is a conversation. It is an authorial voice that we are still unaccustomed to hearing, at least in my disciplinary home in history. But it draws the reader into the conversation, creating a space of exchange and reflection. Although this is sometimes a messy business it is also a living process. A similar kind of dialogical work space was apparent in the previous chapter, and both chapters point to a longer continuum of practice in which the formal interview sessions are only a part of the process. Sharing and listening are thus not confined to formal "research" spaces, nor are they set apart from everyday life. Here, again, we see a desire, and even a commitment, to blur boundaries and to extend the conversation. In talking to Sal, Patti shows us the power of "compassionate listening."

In Chapter 8, we move away from the one-on-one interview and towards workshop environments. Much like Greenspan, Ellis, and Patti, Anna Sheftel and Stacey Zembrzycki work collaboratively with Holocaust survivors, but this time in the context of a series of workshops held with the survivor-speakers associated with the Montreal Holocaust Memorial Centre. These workshops occurred after the sustained interviewing of many of the speakers by members of the Montreal Life Stories project, including Sheftel and Zembrzycki.[44] The focus of the interviews and workshops was on the evolving practice of survivor-educators. What have they learned from going into classrooms week after week for years, sometimes decades, and telling their stories to school children and youth? What "worked" and what did not? Was there a "best practice"? These are questions that survivors themselves posed, but they are unfamiliar, and may even be destabilizing, as survivor testimony is supposed to be authentic and spontaneous. To broach these subjects, however, was to recognize the *expertise* of the survivor-educators who have been at the heart of Holocaust education for a generation. In the workshops, survivors spoke of "their personal experiences in one breath and the educational strategies they employ in another – the two went hand in hand."

Chapter 9 also explores the pedagogical strategies of using first-person accounts to educate North Americans about genocide, forced migration, and integration. The Mapping Memories project, part of Montreal Life Stories, worked with refugee youth. Over the course of a year, a small group of young people worked with Michele Luchs (an educator) and Elizabeth Miller (a digital media practitioner and filmmaker) in the production of an immersive bus tour of the city of Montreal. It was a bus tour like no other as the interior of the bus was transformed into an immersive storytelling space. Their stories were shared during the bus journey through a combination of pre-recorded scripted stories as well as spoken word and music. These stories of Palestine, Rwanda, and Zimbabwe were anchored in Montreal at a series of stops along the way. A book published and freely available online, entitled *Mapping Memories: Participatory Media, Place-Based Stories and Refugee Youth,* was subsequently launched.[45] The chapter published here focuses on the next stage of this multi-year collaboration: a tour of Montreal-area high schools by Léontine, Ayanda, and Stéphanie, three of the young team members. Here, with the testimonial act front-and-centre, we learn about the challenges and opportunities in participatory outreach. Taken together, the five chapters in this section reveal the collaborative potential in working with survivors of mass violence, but it requires time, flexibility, and a commitment to work together. As Henry Greenspan writes: "Pedestals quarantine as effectively as asylums."

Acts of Composure and Framing

> We compose our memories to make sense of our past and present lives. "Composure" is an aptly ambiguous term to describe the process of memory making. In one sense we compose or construct memories using the public languages and meanings of our culture. In another sense we compose memories that help us to feel relatively comfortable with our lives and identities, that give us a feeling of composure.
>
> – Alistair Thomson[46]

Part 3 of *Beyond Testimony and Trauma* focuses on the underlying logic of the recorded oral narratives. What is recorded during the interview is shaped by how people make sense of their past based on who they think they are and how they got that way.[47] The form and structure of the narrative, as well as its actual content and the silences in-between, thus become evidence for oral historians. These acts of self-composure, as Thomson explains, never occur in isolation. In narrating their lives, interviewees draw on "pre-existing storylines and ways of telling stories."[48] Our memories, however, become "risky and painful" if they "do not conform to the public norms of versions of the past."[49] As a result, these acts of composure are never fully formed or achieved as time continues to pass and change us.[50]

The interview, too, is an active process that frames what is said. Oral historians often speak of the "conversational narrative" that results from its question-and-answer format. To varying degrees, the interview is co-produced, but it is mediated by the interview frame of the researcher's project design, key questions, recruitment strategies, and very presence in the room. Catherine Baker's chapter, in particular, focuses on these "framing processes." As she notes, "All possible frames exist within certain configurations of power." Baker therefore conceives of the interview as a "struggle for the power to interpret and represent." This point may, she continues, prove "uncomfortable for oral historians, who often regard their work as participatory or emancipatory." In exploring composure and framing, the contributors to Part 3 reflect on agency and structure in oral history.

In Chapter 10, drawing upon oral testimonies of asbestos disease, Arthur McIvor examines violence and trauma found in workplace disease in the United Kingdom. Almost always fatal, asbestos-related cancers represent one of the clearest examples of the economic violence inherent in industrial production. Much of the scholarship, however, tends to focus on state policy or legal frameworks and not on workers themselves.[51] The chapter examines the stories of workers diagnosed with serious and terminal asbestos-related diseases, such as mesothelioma, documenting its impact on individuals and families and the political responses it generated, including the emergence of advocacy groups such as Clydeside Action on Asbestos in Glasgow. A fiercely independent working-class culture in Scotland, and economic insecurities, McIvor argues, contributed to a "high risk threshold culture." Outwardly, many faced their deteriorating health with stoicism and fatalism; inwardly, however, there was a great deal of anger and fear. According to Phyllis Craig, a welfare rights officer working for Clydeside Action: "I think the physical and mental go together; the mental is torment; that's the only word. It's torture. They have severe breathlessness to the point they feel they are suffocating. And they can't breathe. And the fear and anxiety brings it on more." Identity mutation is at the core of the chapter, as is the successful fight (in Scotland) for what is generally regarded as the most progressive compensation system in the world regarding asbestos-related diseases.

In Chapter 11, Catherine Baker considers a series of "framing processes" that determines what is in view and what is left unknown or unstated within the interview. The UK-based project in translation studies, Languages at War: Policies and Practices of Language Contacts in Conflict, of which she is a member, considers the mediation of the interviewing process. Baker interviewed former interpreters active during the international intervention in Bosnia-Herzegovina, and she examines the "interviewing frames" of language policy, working identities, collection strategies, and the choice of place names (e.g., Serb versus Croat). She is particularly interested in the moments when the border-crossing interpreters interviewed felt compelled to explain terminology or practice and when their own ethnicity was made visible or put into question. Normally, testimony takes the Yugoslav wars as its frame, but Baker attempts to shake this up and "transgress the form" by shifting the focus to the framing processes found in the production of knowledge.

The final two chapters in this collection find special significance in the structure of the oral narratives themselves. In Chapter 12, a dozen interviews with Sephardic Jews in Montreal are examined for what they tell us about the nature of their departure from Muslim lands. Specifically, Yolande Cohen, Martin Messika, and Sara Cohen Fournier explore the remembered stories of departure. In their research, they were quickly confronted by interviewees who did not see how their experiences fit within the project's title and, thus, its framing: Life Stories of Montrealers Displaced by War, Genocide and Other Human Rights Violations. Many Sephardic interviewees, particularly from Morocco, vehemently denied that they were forced to leave their homelands; therefore, they saw themselves as immigrants rather than as refugees or survivors. What is interesting here is that the collision with this particular interview frame prompted a great deal of discussion that further deepened the dialogue. The chapter thus explores these ambiguities. The phrase "stories of departure," rather than "stories of displacement," indicates the continued bond of affection that many interviewees still have with Morocco despite their being compelled to leave. This is a study of memory itself: of what is minimized, emphasized, overlooked, and forgotten.

A similar interest in the ways in which lived experience structures remembering can be found in Chapter 13. Here, Marie A. Pelletier considers the place of religion in the oral narrative of seventy-three-year-old Ven Runnath, who survived the Khmer Rouge and now lives in Montreal. Her strong religious faith offers Ven Runnath a framework for interpreting, or making sense, of her own experience. What is especially noteworthy is that she was Buddhist during the Khmer Rouge years and only later converted to Christianity. This is significant as Ven Runnath now relies heavily on Christian symbolism and imagery to tell her story. The entire chapter is thus dedicated to the narrated life of one individual. "To respect memory also means letting it organise the story," historian Luisa Passerini once wrote.[52]

FIGURE 0.2 and FIGURE 0.3 The *Nous sommes ici / We Are Here* exhibition at the Centre d'histoire de Montréal was one of the many outcomes of the Montreal Life Stories project. March 2012-April 2013. *Photographs by Denis-Carl Robidoux.*

Conclusion

The contributors to this volume help shake us out of the habitual ways of thinking about, and engaging, "testimony" and "trauma." The inclusion of "survivor" workers, of eugenics, and of others contributes to a rethinking of the issues, bringing together the directly targeted disposable and the structurally disposable. We began this introduction with the plant shutdown story of Gabriel Solano. In 2004, I returned to Detroit with photographer David Lewis to visually record some of the devastation caused by deindustrialization. I asked Gabriel if he would show us "his Detroit." The places he took us had special significance to him: the first factory in which he laboured, his father's steel mill, the ruined river boat that took his family for weekend getaways, among others. Our relationship to the ruined city was thus mediated by someone who had lived there all of his life. Far from being universal, the resulting images of industrial ruination were made that much more meaningful by their association with Gabriel, his family, and the stories that he shared with us. Since then, a large number of coffee-table books, films, and websites have featured the industrial ruins of Detroit. This has stirred considerable debate in the city about the politics and ethics of consuming (and profiting from) other people's loss and pain. Some have even called it "ruin porn."[53]

Similar kinds of concerns have arisen with respect to the interviewing of survivors of war, genocide, and other human rights violations. We risk "eroticizing injury," suggested Salverson, finding voyeuristic pleasure in seeing other people's pain.[54] Should we even be interviewing vulnerable people, on "ethical grounds," asks Joy Parr?[55] If so, how might we "retune" our practice in these instances? Vulnerability and distress can of course be found in any interview, regardless of what it is supposed to be about. One of my first interviews as an undergraduate student was with a woman who spoke at length about the sexual violence that she experienced as a child. She wanted it on the historical record, and so she volunteered to be interviewed for my hometown museum's "local history" project. Sometimes the risks are greatest when we encounter "difficult" or "risky" stories unexpectedly. As a result, I favour "retuning" our oral history practice across-the-board rather than simply in cases when groups identified as vulnerable are being interviewed. All of our interviewees are well served when we think things through in advance and when we forge collaborative relationships.

There are also connections to be made across seemingly disparate experiences. For example, when I shared a preliminary draft of this introduction with Henry Greenspan, who has been a bit of a mentor to me over the years, it sparked a series of recollections of his own. When he was starting out as a psychotherapist, he worked downriver from Detroit with a number of men from Chrysler, Republic Steel, and BASF, companies that had large plants located there. The BASF workers often referred to the factory as "Auschwitz," Greenspan remembered, both because they were aware of the company's role as one of the core parts of IG Farben/Auschwitz 3 and because that was how they saw their working conditions. Their black humour, a kind of humour often employed by Holocaust survivors, flooded back into Greenspan's mind when he read the excerpts from the interview with Gabriel Solano. He also recalled how one of his own interview partners, Reuben, would not move his store out of his "ruined" Detroit neighbourhood because it reminded him of that other ghetto, the one in Lodz: "Everything was boarded-up. And ruined."[56] Greenspan then reflected on how this might play into what it means to be a "survivor" in a more specifically American sense. The "aspiration to go 'beyond testimony,'" Greenspan writes in his afterword, so evident in this collection, "means to move toward useful and respectful partnership." Today, more than ever, I am convinced that an ethic of sharing is at the heart of oral history practice.

The chapters that follow will resonate with many readers, perhaps prompting the kinds of reflections that Greenspan shared with me. No two readings are the same, however. We engage with these pages in our own unique ways, finding connection with our own lives. I am the father of a severely disabled daughter, who can only speak with her eyes and her laughter, and Wilson's chapter on eugenics touched something deep inside me. Kyle, who also communicates non-verbally but can use text-to-voice software to speak (something my daughter Leanna will not be able to do), notes that the negative or ignorant opinions of some people do not matter: "those people do not know the real me." It may be naïve or wishful thinking on my part, but getting to know the "real me" of another human being is a big part of what oral history is about. In the encounter, if we are lucky, we also learn something more about ourselves.

Notes

1 Gabriel Solano, interviewed by author, 24 February 1998. This videotaped interview is archived at the Walter Reuther Library in Detroit, Michigan, and the Centre for Oral History and Digital Storytelling in Montreal, Quebec.

2 Julie Salverson, "Anxiety and Contact in Attending to a Play about Land Mines?" in *Critical Perspectives on Canadian Theatre in English* (Toronto: Playwrights Canada Press, 2010), 17: 80.

3 Thomas Nagel quoted in Jeffrey Gordon, "Nagel or Camus on the Absurd?" *Philosophy and Phenomenological Research* 45, 1 (1984): 15–28. In his study of Nigerian war literature, H. Oby Okolocha suggests that the absurd stems from the "dislocation of the mind." See "War and Absurdity: Viewing the Manifestations of Trauma in Uwem Akpan's 'Luxurious Hearses,'" in *Focus on Nigeria: Literature and Culture*, ed. Gordon Collier, 159–72 (New York: Rodopi, 2012), 160.

4 The mass observation project asked British residents to observe their everyday lives and inner worlds and report on them between 1937 and the early 1950s. For a fascinating study of nine mass observers in the Second World War, see James Hinton, *Nine Wartime Lives* (Oxford: Oxford University Press, 2010).

5 Michael Smith, "Is This All There Is?" *Journal of Ethics* 10 (2006): 79.

6 Albert Camus, *The Myth of Sisyphus* (New York: Knopf, 1957), 129.

7 Camus, for one, believed that rebellion arises "from the spectacle of the irrational coupled with an unjust and incomprehensible condition." See Albert Camus quoted in Harold A. Durfee, "Albert Camus and the Ethics of Rebellion," *Journal of Religion* 38, 1 (1958): 32.

8 For more on Gabriel and displaced industrial workers, see Steven High, *Industrial Sunset: The Making of North America's Rust Belt* (Toronto: University of Toronto Press, 2003); Steven High and David Lewis, *Corporate Wasteland: The Landscape and Memory of Deindustrialization* (Ithaca: Cornell University Press, 2007).

9 Sidonie Smith and Julia Watson, *Reading Autobiography: A Guide for Interpreting Life Narratives* (Minneapolis: University of Minnesota Press, 2010), 219.

10 Alistair Thomson, "Moving Stories: Oral History and Migration Studies," *Oral History* 27, 1 (1999): 26.

11 Beverley Skeggs, *Class, Self, Culture* (London: Routledge, 2004), 58.

12 For more on the Montreal Life Stories project, see Steven High, *Oral History at the Crossroads: Sharing Life Stories of Survival and Displacement* (Vancouver: UBC Press, 2014); Steven High, Edward Little, and Thi Ry Duong, eds., *Remembering Mass Violence: Oral History, Digital Media and*

Performance (Toronto: University of Toronto Press, 2013); Anna Sheftel and Stacey Zembrzycki, eds., *Oral History Off the Record: Toward an Ethnography of Practice* (New York: Palgrave-Macmillan, 2014).

13 Susannah Radstone, "Trauma and Screen Studies: Opening the Debate," *Screen* 42, 2 (2001): 188. See also Radstone's "Trauma Theory: Contexts, Politics, Ethics," *Paragraph* 30, 1 (2007): 9–29; and her "Reconceiving Binaries: The Limits of Memory," *History Workshop Journal* 59 (2005): 134–50.

14 Radstone, "Trauma and Screen Studies," 189.

15 Ibid.

16 Henry Greenspan, *On Listening to Holocaust Survivors: Beyond Testimony*, 2nd ed. (St. Paul: Paragon House, 2010).

17 Daniel James, *Doña María's Story: Life History, Memory, and Political Identity* (Durham: Duke University Press, 2000), 124.

18 Ibid.

19 Alessandro Portelli, *The Battle of Valle Giulia: Oral History and the Art of Dialogue* (Madison: University of Wisconsin, 1997), ix.

20 Kay Schaffer and Sidonie Smith, "Venues of Storytelling: The Circulation of Testimony in Human Rights Campaigns," *Life Writing* 1, 2 (2004): 3–26; Lawrence L. Langer, *Holocaust Testimonies: The Ruins of Memory* (New Haven: Yale University Press, 1991), 197.

21 See, for example, Naomi Angel, "Before Truth: The Labors of Testimony and the Canadian Truth and Reconciliation Commission," *Culture, Theory and Critique* 53, 2 (2012): 199–214. The South African TRC, for its part, gathered around twenty thousand statements during 1996–97. See Mark Saunders, *Ambiguities of Witnessing: Law and Literature in the Time of a Truth Commission* (Stanford University Press, 2007), 2–3. For Australia, see Rosanne Kennedy, "The Affective Work of Stolen Generations Testimony: From the Archives to the Classroom," *Biography* 27, 1 (2004): 48–77; and also, Shurlee Swain, Leonie Sheedy, and Cate O'Neill, "Responding to 'Forgotten Australians': Historians and the Legacy of Out-of-Home Care," *Journal of Australian Studies* 36, 1 (2012): 17–28.

22 Schaffer and Smith, "Venues of Storytelling," 6.

23 Sidonie Smith and Julia Watson, *Reading Autobiography: A Guide for Interpreting Life Narratives* (Minneapolis: University of Minnesota Press, 2010), 133.

24 These activists came to Montreal as part of a summer training course offered each year by Equitas, one of our partners. I conducted six interviews in June 2010 and wrote a reflection on them. This reflection is available in the Interviewer Reports File in the basecamp archive of the Montreal Life Stories project, Centre for Oral History and Digital Storytelling.

25 ACT UP Oral History Project, at www.actuporalhistory.org. See also Debra Levine, "Demonstrations of Care: The Act Up Oral Histories on Video," *GLQ: A Journal of Lesbian and Gay Studies* 16, 3 (2010): 441–44; Jim Hubbard, "Contemporary and Urgency: Differing Strategies of Filmmakers and Video Makers Confronting AIDS," *GLQ: A Journal of Lesbian and Gay Studies* 16, 3 (2010): 436–41; Roger Hallas, "Queer AIDS Media and the Question of the Archive," *GLQ: A Journal of Lesbian and Gay Studies* 16, 3 (2010): 431–35.

26 In his recent study of Harlan County, Kentucky, oral historian Alessandro Portelli observes that "Italian memories of poverty are dominated by anger, Appalachian narratives by shame." He continues: "Because poverty is related to shame, the response is an emphasis on pride: pride in having survived hardship, in being a hard worker, in the self-sufficiency and warmth of the family." A similar pattern can be found here. See Portelli, *They Say in Harlan County* (New York: Oxford University Press, 2010), 292.

27 Julie Salverson, "Change on Whose Terms? Testimony and an Erotics of Injury," *Theater* 31, 3 (2001): 122.

28 Julie Salverson, "Performing Emergency: Witnessing, Popular Theatre, and the Lie of the Literal," *Theatre Topics* 6, 2 (1996): 182; Salverson, "Change on Whose Terms?" 124.

29 Alicia J. Rouverol, "Collaborative Oral History in a Correctional Setting: Promise and Pitfalls," *Oral History Review* 30, 1 (2003): 63.

30 Bertrand Muller, "Archives orales et entretiens ethnographiques: Un débat entre Florence Descamps et Florence Weber," *Genèse* 62, 1 (2006): 93–109.

31 Philippe Joutard, *Ces Voix Que Nous Viennent du Passé* (Paris: Hachette, 1983), 7.

32 Nanci Adler, Selma Leydesdorff, Mary Chamberlain, and Leyla Neyzi, eds., *Memories of Mass Repression: Narrating Life Stories in the Aftermath of Atrocity* (New Brunswick: Transaction Publishers, 2011), ix.

33 Geoffrey H. Hartman, "Learning from Survivors: The Yale Testimony Project," *Holocaust and Genocide Studies* 9, 2 (1995): 197.

34 Henry Greenspan and Sidney Bolkosky, "When Is an Interview an Interview? Notes from Listening to Holocaust Survivors," *Poetics Today* 27, 2 (2006): 438–39.

35 Sherna Berger Gluck, "Reflections on Oral History in the New Millennium: Roundtable Comments," *Oral History* Review 26, 2 (1999): 8.

36 Kathleen Blee, "Evidence, Empathy and Ethics," in *The Oral History Reader*, 1st ed., ed. Robert Perks and Alistair Thomson, 322–31 (London: Routledge, 1998), 336.

37 Suzanne Day, "A Reflexive Lens: Exploring Dilemmas of Qualitative Methodology through the Concept of Reflexivity," *Qualitative Sociology Review* 8, 1 (2012): 60–85; Natasha S. Mauthner and Andrea Doucet, "Reflexive Accounts and Accounts of Reflexivity in Qualitative Data Analysis," *Sociology* 37, 3 (2003): 413–31.

38 Andrea Doucet, "'From Her Side of the Gossamer Wall(s): Reflexivity and Relational Knowing," *Qualitative Sociology* 31 (2008): 73–87.

39 Parr, "'Don't Speak for Me,'" 3.

40 Alessandro Portelli, *The Battle of Valle Giulia: Oral History and the Art of Dialogue* (Madison: University of Wisconsin Press, 1997), xiv.

41 According to Sean Field, a South African historian who has studied forced removal during the Apartheid era, trauma refers to "the rupturing of an individual's sense of internal and external worlds which leaves post-traumatic legacies such as dissociation, depression and hypersensitivity." See Sean Field, "Beyond Healing: Oral History and Regeneration," *Oral History* 34, 1 (2006): 31–42. To be traumatized, writes Cathy Caruth, is to "be possessed by an image or event." See Caruth, *Trauma: Explorations in Memory* (Baltimore: Johns Hopkins University Press, 1995), 4–5.

42 Greenspan, *On Listening,* 257.

43 Lisa M. Tillmann-Healy, "Friendship as Method," *Qualitative Inquiry* 9, 5 (2003): 729–49.

44 Anna Sheftel and Stacey Zembrzycki, "Only Human: A Reflection on the Ethical and Methodological Challenges of Working with 'Difficult' Stories," *Oral History Review* 37, 2 (2010), 191–214.

45 See http://www.mappingmemories.ca/book.

46 Alistair Thomson, *Anzac Memories: Living with the Legend* (Melbourne: Oxford University Press, 1994), 8.

47 Charlotte Linde, *Life Stories: The Creation of Coherence* (New York: Oxford University Press, 1993), 3.

48 Luisa Passerini, *Fascism in Popular Memory: The Cultural Experience of the Turin Working-Class* (Cambridge: Cambridge University Press, 1987), 8.

49 Thomson, *Anzac Memories.*

50 As Alessandro Portelli suggests, memory is an "active process" rather than a "passive depository of fact." See Alessandro Portelli, *The Death of Luigi Trastulli and Other Stories: Form and Meaning in Oral History* (Albany: State University of New York Press, 1991), 52.

51 Arthur McIvor, "Narratives from the Dusty Coalface: Evaluating Oral Evidence in Understanding Work and Health Culture in British Mining since the 1930s," paper presented to the European Social Science History Conference, Glasgow, Scotland, April 2012.

52 Passerini, *Fascism in Popular Memory*, 8.

53 Paul Mullins, "The Politics and Archaeology of 'Ruin Porn,'" on Archaeology and Material Culture blog at http://paulmullins.wordpress.com/2012/08/19/the-politics-and-archaeology-of-ruin-porn/.

54 Julie Salverson quoted in Nisha Sajnani, "The Implicated Witness: Towards a Relational Aesthetic in Drama Therapy," *Dramatherapy* 34, 1 (2012): 7.

55 Parr, "'Don't Speak for Me,'" 1.

56 Greenspan, *On Listening*, 31.

Part 1:
The Political Work of Witness

1 | The Ex-Disappeared in Post-Dictatorship Argentina

The Work of Testimony and Survivors at the Margins

ARI GANDSMAN

Jorge Luis Borges's short story "Theme of the Traitor and the Hero" is about a man conducting biographical research on his famous great-grandfather, a national hero of nineteenth-century Ireland. During the course of his research, he discovers that his great-grandfather was a traitor. He eventually decides to suppress this information in the book he writes. The story served as inspiration for Bernardo Bertolucci's 1970 film, *The Spider's Stratagem*. The film transfers the story to post–Second World War Italy and shifts the perspective to a man returning to the village of his birth, where his father is venerated as an anti-fascist martyr, the village hero who attempted to assassinate Mussolini and was killed in the process. The main character eventually discovers the hidden secret: his father was a traitor who betrayed his cause, whose companions, as a final gesture of goodwill, disguised their execution of him so that people would believe he was murdered during a foiled assassination attempt. Not only did this action enshrine the father as a hero in historical memory but it also galvanized support for the anti-fascist cause. The heroic myth thus becomes a lie in service of a truth (i.e., anti-fascism). Both the short story and film point to the indeterminacy of heroism, dissolving platonic ideals of the hero and its counterpart, the traitor.

That Borges, a political conservative distrustful of ideologies, would write such a story is not surprising. But I believe Borges is less interested in debunking the idea of heroism than in calling attention to the cultural production of historical truths, a critical examination of how national heroes are created and sustained. Lurking beneath surface histories are ironic inversions. Simple narratives conceal complex realities that are conveniently swept aside by the hero's death. In terms of mythopoesis, as Joseph Campbell famously observed, the hero must die.

But what of survivors? Within Argentine progressive political circles, the disappeared, those kidnapped and murdered by the military dictatorship that ruled between 1976 and 1983, are venerated as national heroes. Mainly leftist activists, they are viewed as having sacrificed their lives defending the country, resisting a murderous dictatorship that installed economic policies that increased foreign debt, decimated national industries, and culminated in the country's political and financial collapse in 2001. Of the estimated thirty thousand who disappeared during the dictatorship, very few of them (estimated to be less than 1 percent) survived. Survivors have played a key role in the post-dictatorship period by providing essential testimony to reconstruct what happened in the clandestine detention centres, where the disappeared were held captive, tortured, and eventually murdered. At the same time, however, their role is ambivalent. Their survival not only precluded them from becoming heroes but also led to their marginalization. In post-dictatorship Argentina, survivors have been questioned over their very survival. They are not key symbolic reference points, or "moral witnesses"; instead, family members of the disappeared came to occupy that role.

This chapter examines the marginalized role of survivors of forced disappearance in post-dictatorship Argentina. Although their testimonial work has been central in reconstructing what took place during the military dictatorship in terms of identifying perpetrators, I argue that survivors are marginalized figures within the human rights movement, playing mainly a pragmatic role in the human rights struggle. I trace this to questions that have been repeatedly raised about their survival, questions as to whether their survival was a product of complicity with the dictatorial regime. Tracing these questions to "grey zones" between survivors and perpetrators, I contrast this with the testimonial work of survivors that functions within a narrow legal framework, a goal-directed effort relating to the use value of testimony in pursuing justice against military perpetrators.

Survival and the Work of Testimony

The communications director of a human rights organization told me of a woman named Adriana who disappeared while pregnant. The majority of disappeared pregnant women were murdered; their newborn babies were handed over to be raised by military families. Yet Adriana was released with her baby after giving birth. "Why did they let them go?" I asked. "She asks herself the same thing," he responded, and later advised me, "Never ask a survivor how they survived." When I subsequently interviewed Adriana, in fact, she did not question her survival. She explained why the military acted the way it did and even why the military disappeared people with no political activities: it formed part of their method of terror.

If they took someone active in an armed organization, it may spread fear, but not that much, because most people had nothing to do with those organizations. If they took someone who was active in a political organization that was not armed, then people would be even more afraid. But if they took someone who was not involved in anything, it was even worse. It was all part of their strategy. It was all planned and thought out.

Adriana also explained why she survived when so many others died. In her view, survivors were released precisely in order to tell people what was taking place inside the clandestine concentration camps. Survivors would disseminate state terror. They would speak of the brutal torture and the executions they witnessed. If not for survivors' testimony, nobody would have known what was happening, and the military needed people to know what was taking place in order to spread terror. Adriana was one of the "lucky ones" arbitrarily chosen for this role.

After her release, she continually testified about her experience.[1] At the time of our interview, she estimated that she had testified on over twenty different occasions before various legal bodies, both in Argentina and abroad. Her testimony contributed to sending military perpetrators to prison. For example, she testified at the trial against the military leaders in the 1980s, and her testimony was chosen as one of the "representative" accounts in a subsequent book consisting of a compilation of testimonies. She was still testifying at the time of our interview: her testimony had recently contributed to sending a military doctor to prison for kidnapping a child of the disappeared and for falsifying her birth certificate.

I was baffled by her explanation. "The military released you so you would speak about what happened to you, but because you have been speaking about what happened to you, they have gone to prison?" My confusion unwittingly gave voice to a survivor's paradox. For Adriana, to speak about the terror was to fulfill the military's plan. However, the military did not anticipate that they would ever be held responsible for their actions and thus failed to foresee the role survivor testimony would play at the trials that would send them to prison. Acknowledging this paradox, Adriana explained: "It was the giant leap we had to take. In a way, we carried out the military's orders to tell what happened. But we told it from the opposite standpoint – not out of fear but in order to demand justice. They thought that we were going to be terrorized for the rest of our lives and that we would only be transmitters of horror rather than motors for demanding justice."

This involved a difficult personal process for Adriana. Initially, she did not speak about what happened to her not only because of her own terror but also because her family prevented her, wanting to protect her. With the arrival of democracy in 1983, she felt a need to speak. By that time, over six years had passed. Adriana met other survivors during the work of the National Commission on the Disappearance of Persons (CONADEP), which was formed in 1984 and compiled thousands of testimonies from survivors, witnesses, and family members of the disappeared. These survivors exchanged telephone numbers and eventually began meeting as a group. Adriana described the meetings as therapeutic, especially as it enabled her to connect with others who had gone through the same experience. In 1984, Adriana co-founded the Association of Ex-Detainees and Disappeared (hereafter referred to as the Ex-Disappeared) with a small group of survivors, an organization still active today.

Adriana first experienced the double bind of survival when she went to speak to family members still searching for their children, the Mothers of the Plaza de Mayo. The members of this group of mothers of disappeared children emerged during the dictatorship to challenge it and went on to become internationally renowned human rights activists. "It was hard to speak to the Mothers of the Plaza de Mayo. We had to fulfill the role that the military wanted and to tell them of all the suffering that their children went through." She also had to tell them that their disappeared children were not going to reappear. In the words of another survivor: "When survivors of the camps began to speak, accepting that their children were dead was beyond difficult, it was impossible. It created an atmosphere of rejection. We were pointed at, left to the side, treated like traitors and ghosts. There was no solidarity for us. Our lists were not touched; our testimonies ended up at the bottom of a box."[2]

Despite this difficulty, a deeply rooted feeling of responsibility motivated Adriana and others to speak about their experience. As Adriana tells me: "The role of testimony is fundamental. It's a moral and political obligation. If we don't speak about what happened, this work is impossible." The importance lies in the knowledge she has of what happened in the clandestine detention centres in Argentina in the 1970s, piecing together different survivor accounts in order to construct a cohesive historical account. "The role of the survivor in reconstructing what happened is fundamental in this genocide like in any other. Everything that is known about what happened in the concentration camps is known because of us."

Reconstructing the past as part of her testimonial work does not simply involve publicly speaking about her experience or testifying in trials. When we began our interview, I told her that I had already read an extremely long and detailed testimony of hers. "I don't have to tell it again," she sighed with relief, "fantastic." Her work went beyond the testimonial to include the "scientific" (Adriana was herself a physicist): "We felt we had an enormous responsibility not only to give testimony but also to work with these testimonies: to work scientifically, cross-checking dates and comparing information. We dedicated ourselves to this for many years. We compile information for each concentration camp. We take all the testimonies from one camp, we load all of the information, and compare each one."

The point of this testimonial work was to obtain the "complete view of what happened," a work Adriana considered "possible but very difficult." While forensic anthropologists, when examining the sites and remains of victims, apply scientific methods to reconstruct what happened, Adriana's organization works with testimonies. The difficulty was not only that not many survived and that not all survivors came forward to testify but also that everything was done clandestinely: the disappeared were imprisoned with their eyes blindfolded, and military torturers used code names and aliases.

What was striking in Adriana's approach to testimony was how she treated it at a remove from her own experience in order to look at it scientifically, as if in a laboratory. She approached it as if it were a puzzle in need of assembly. In this sense, I could understand her relief at not having to give her testimony over again during our interview, thus enabling us to talk seriously about how she envisioned her testimonial work as a human rights activist. This is not untypical of survivors in Argentina. Pilar Calveiro's *Poder y Desaparicion* (power and disappearance) (2001) is one of the most important analyses written about the Argentine dictatorship.[3] Citing the theoretical sources expected of such a work (Foucault, Arendt, Deleuze, Todorov), Calveiro provides a lucid but standard academic analysis of the forms of power exercised in the military's concentration camps. What makes the work remarkable is that Calveiro is writing about her own experience. Apart from the prologue, in which readers learn that Calveiro was disappeared for over a year in a concentration camp, the text contains only one other fleeting reference to this fact.[4] Writing about her own experience, she adopts the third person as a means of analytic detachment. One of the few precedents for such a work is Bruno Bettelheim's *Individual and Mass Behavior in Extreme Situations*, which is based on his own experience in concentration camps.[5] Calveiro's work indicates how Argentines, even direct victims of the dictatorship, are able to distance themselves from their own experience, a position generally seen as the product of an outsider status, not of a survivor.

The Marginalization of the Disappeared

The role of survivors like Adriana in reconstructing what took place in the concentration camps has been essential in the pursuit of justice against military perpetrators. Their testimonies have provided relatives with information about what happened to their family members after their disappearance. They have identified military criminals so that they could be brought to justice and have provided invaluable information about the detention centres in which the disappeared were held and tortured. They have been integral to the construction of what is known about the dictatorship.

Very few members of the military have provided accounts of what took place in the concentration camps. Most notable of these, Raúl Vilariño gave media interviews shortly after the fall of the dictatorship and spoke of the torture in the ESMA (Navy Petty-Officers School of Mechanics, the most notorious concentration camp in Argentina); Alfredo Scilingo admitted in *El Vuelo* to participating in one of the navy's "death flights" in which disappeared were drugged, flown out over the Río de la Plata (River Plate), and thrown out alive;[6] and Víctor Ibañez followed Scilingo's confessions with his account of the Campo de Mayo concentration camp.[7] Although the mainstream media terms them *arrepentidos* (regretful or remorseful), many have contested this designation, arguing that they would do the exact same thing again.[8] Survivors, in particular, do not trust them. In the words of survivor Miguel D'Agostino: "I only have confidence in the testimony of the victims. I don't consider anything they contribute to be valid."[9]

Yet, despite the fundamental role they have played as witnesses, the position of survivors in the human rights movement in Argentina has been ambivalent and mainly pragmatic. They are not leaders in the human rights struggle, the ones providing its moral force; rather, they are simply supporting actors. In the narrative of human rights, family members of the disappeared, like the Mothers of the Plaza de Mayo or the Grandmothers of the Plaza de Mayo, emerge as the principal protagonists. Survivors lack the influence and visibility of these family members of the disappeared. Argentine human rights organizations separate "directly affected groups" (i.e., those considered to be direct victims of the dictatorship) from "non-affected groups." The "directly affected" label is used to describe family-member organizations: the Mothers, the Grandmothers, and HIJOS (Sons and Daughters for Identity and Justice Against Oblivion and Silence). Yet survivors are rarely included as a "directly affected" group or a human rights group. Such omissions are frequent to the point at which one ex-disappeared told me that ex-disappeared had never been allowed to "reappear," that they were still fundamentally invisible and unrecognized.

Several explanations exist. The first concerns the double bind of survival that Adriana discusses above. But their marginalization is also part of a historical development. In the immediate aftermath of the dictatorship, survivors played a key role in investigations. After the convicted were pardoned and amnesty was given to everyone else, trials ceased in Argentina until the twenty-first century, when the pardons and amnesties were overturned by the government of Néstor Kirchner. During this period, family members organized around a general "culture of memory" – not linked to the memory of survivors but to a general memorialization of the disappeared – in order to keep the demand for justice present in the public space through continued protests. For the human rights movement and the political left, the disappeared came to represent the "best of their generation." If the disappeared represent the "best of the generation," what does this imply for those who survived?

"Argentina wouldn't be in this mess if the disappeared were here. They took the best of a generation," a human rights activist told me. The disappeared are a popular explanation for the country's economic, social, and political woes. As the argument goes, the dictatorship disappeared politically active young people who would have become Argentina's future leaders. These disappeared would have opposed the economically disastrous neoliberal reforms that were imposed upon the country during and after the dictatorship. A popular interpretation holds that the dictatorship eliminated the disappeared precisely so that the military's "economic plan" could be implemented. Without them, the country was left with a corrupt and subservient political leadership that triggered the country's economic downfall.

As the use of the word "generation" in "best of a generation" signifies, the disappeared are collectively identified as being from the same historical epoch: they were born in the 1950s and came of age in the late 1960s and early 1970s. They are defined by their youth. Statistics support this characterization: the vast majority of the disappeared were younger than thirty-five. According to CONADEP's numbers, 30 percent were over the age of thirty, and only 17 percent were over thirty-five.[10]

In the conventional narrative, radical youth culture (or counter-culture) is ultimately assimilated into the political mainstream.[11] Akin to Marx's observation that "the traditions of the dead generation weigh like a nightmare on the living," rebellious youth ultimately collapses under the weight of responsibility as children succumb to their parents' fate. In this trajectory, the ideals of youth are compromised by the contingencies and economic necessities that come with age. This narrative is commonly observed in North America and Europe, as hippie counter-culture matured into the "me generation," a yippie-to-yuppie transformation typified by the 1983 film *The Big Chill* and/or Jerry Rubin's journey from 1960s anti-establishment icon into 1980s Wall Street venture capitalist. The transformation of revolutionary idealism into cynical disillusionment is also a recurring motif of Latin American fiction. Carlos Fuentes' *The Death of Artemios Cruz* (1962), a landmark work, traces the titular protagonist's life course from idealistic hero of the Mexican revolution to ruthless and corrupt landowner.

But the disappeared (by virtue of their disappearance) did not live long enough to make any concessions. They are frozen in time at the moment of their disappearance, remaining outside of the aging process, with its concomitant responsibilities and wrinkles. Their eternal youth is preserved in the photographs that accompany the tributes, commemorations, and publications of family-member human rights organizations. Human rights commemorations are mainly structured around the display of photographic images of the disappeared.[12] The photographs are headshots, resembling school photographs. The first time I saw such images grouped together, my main impression was how young they looked.

Survivors, on the other hand, have aged. They have been left to deal with the traumatic consequences of what happened – not only their own torture at the hands of military leaders but also the deaths of many of their closest friends and companions. However, in human rights discourse, family members often speak as though survivors do not exist at all: "The voice of that generation is absent," one child of the disappeared declared in a talk.

The Testimony of Jorge Julio López

In 2006, following the upholding of the repeal of the pardons and amnesty laws, survivors regained public visibility when trials against military officers charged with crimes against humanity restarted. Miguel Etchecolatz was second to be prosecuted. Etchecolatz was commissioner general of the Buenos Aires provincial police during the dictatorship and was responsible for running twenty-one concentration camps. He had been sentenced to a twenty-three-year prison term in 1986 but was pardoned several years later. He was also a vocal and unapologetic defender of the dictatorship, even publishing a book justifying his actions.

In his 2006 trial, a key witness was Jorge Julio López, a seventy-six-year-old construction worker who had been disappeared. In his testimony, he described his disappearance and torture and the participation of Etchecolatz in the murders of two prisoners. On 19 September, Etchecolatz was found guilty for his role in the murders of six individuals in addition to the disappearance and torture of López and one other witness, Nilda Eloy. López and Eloy, together with Adriana's Ex-Disappeared, were the principal plaintiffs in the case. Two days before the verdict was announced, López vanished. Various theories for his disappearance were initially postulated. One was that post-traumatic shock combined with López's Parkinson's disease had resulted in temporary amnesia and induced a fugue-like state. Others speculated that López's fear of retribution following his testimony had prompted him to go into hiding. When López did not reappear after an extensive campaign to locate him, many people concluded that he must have been kidnapped. Described as his "second disappearance," it was seen as an effort to intimidate future witnesses in order to prevent them from testifying.

In this atmosphere of uncertainty, accusations and conspiracy theories circulated. The general belief was that ex-military and their supporters were responsible. Many assumed the Buenos Aires provincial police were involved. Some accused the government. A week after his disappearance, Hebe de Bonafini, the leader of one faction of the Mothers of the Plaza de Mayo and one of the more famous figures of Argentinean human rights, met with President Kirchner after their weekly protest march. During the meeting, she attributed the disappearance to "a large operation" carried out against the Kirchner government's human rights policy. She also cast doubts about López and implied that he was involved in the conspiracy, implicating him in his disappearance. "For us, he is not a typical disappeared. López was not an activist, and one should investigate his trajectory."[13] Her doubts about López had to do not only with his lack of political activism but also with the contention that, according to her: "[he] lives in a police neighbourhood, he has a brother who is a policeman, and his family doesn't say that he is disappeared, which is strange." She also stated that he was not "as key a witness as people [thought]."[14]

In follow-up statements to a radio station, Hebe de Bonafini continued to raise doubts about López and his disappearance: "He was a guy nobody liked. He was in isolation because his father was police commissioner and so he had a lot of privileges in prison." She then speculated that his second disappearance "could be a *maniobra* [a scheme]. He is a very intelligent guy. Turning up to testify could be part of the plan. These *maniobras* can be very well prepared and well organized."[15] In response to Bonafini's comments, the Ex-Disappeared stated: "We regret that Bonafini continues following the orders of those who committed genocide: 'Don't trust the survivors.'"[16]

The Grey Zones of Survival

A survivor was accused of being complicit with the military (the same people who kidnapped and tortured him). Why were survivors not trusted? As the Ex-Disappeared statement implies, Bonafini's accusation was not an isolated incident but the product of a larger historical discourse in which survivors who came forward to speak about what happened to them were treated with suspicion. As several survivors told me, a common question addressed to them is, "How did you survive?" – or, even more bluntly, "Why are you alive?" Parents of disappeared children asked such questions because they were suffering: they wanted to know why some people's children survived while theirs did not. This created a climate of suspicion and, at times, hostility. Just as many Argentines believed that the disappeared must have vanished for a "reason" (i.e., that they were terrorists), so they believed that a survivor's "re-appearance" also happened for a reason. The implication is that they survived because they collaborated with the armed forces.

Primo Levi's much used (and abused) concept of a "grey zone" was coined to describe the murky area between privilege and collaboration in concentration camps, although now it is largely used to refer to the blurred boundaries between perpetrators and victims. In *The Drowned and the Saved* (1989), Levi discusses "privileged" witnesses who "could avail themselves of a certainly better observatory." Acknowledging it to be a "delicate" subject, Levi points out that "those who acquired privilege for themselves by becoming subservient to the camp authority [...] did not bear witness at all, for obvious reasons, or left incomplete or distorted or totally false testimony."[17] For Levi, the best witnesses were "the very few who had the ability and the luck to attain a privileged observatory without bowing to compromises." Levi specifically identified political prisoners as having better chances of achieving this than Jews.[18]

In Argentina, one former disappeared who fits Levi's "privileged observer" category is Mario Villani. Villani spent four years disappeared in almost every major camp in Buenos Aires (five in total). His survival was a consequence of his utility. He acted, in his own words, as a *bricoleur*, repairing items for the military. Alluding to Primo Levi's concept, Villani states,

> It is a very unclear zone. There are no blacks and whites. They are all greys, different shades of grey. I was always very worried about what kind of grey area I was in. I am certain I did not take part in some things. I never participated in torture. I never interrogated anyone. I never collaborated in intelligence. There were kidnapped people who ended up kidnapping other kidnapped people. But what does collaboration or non-collaboration mean? Because if I am working to fix things, with this activity what I was doing was solving problems, or, rather, helping the camp to function. In some way, I was collaborating. On the other hand, I was collaborating to keep myself alive.[19]

By being useful to the military, he received "privileges." He was not kept blindfolded in solitary confinement in a small cell. Like Levi's "privileged witness," moving more freely, he was able to better observe what was happening and to identify military perpetrators and other disappeared. This made him a critical witness after his release, and he has testified on numerous occasions. However, providing services to the military made him feel like a collaborator. He was faced with one of his most difficult decisions when a torturer asked him to fix a broken *picana,* the electric cattle prod they used to torture prisoners. Villani refused despite the risk. Instead, they used an electric transformer, which was far worse than the *picana*. When he saw this, he fixed the *picana* but adjusted its current to be weaker than normal.[20]

No human rights activist would call Villani a collaborator. Accusations of collaboration are made against other survivors, however, and continue to circulate. What about those who fall on the "wrong side" of Villani's grey areas? Most alleged collaborators never testified. This is considered a sign of their guilt, and it results in another double bind. The act of testifying opens a person up to accusations of having survived through collaboration, but not testifying is also considered a sign of collaboration.

Miguel Ángel Lauletta is one of the more controversial collaborators. He was a member of the Montoneros organization, a left-wing militant organization that was targeted during the dictatorship. He disappeared in October 1976 and was taken to the ESMA. He was held until March 1979, released, kidnapped again for fifteen days, and released again. He did not testify before the National Commission on the Disappeared. His survival, at that point, was unknown. In fact, his name was featured on the commission's initial list of the disappeared (as someone permanently disappeared – that is, someone who is considered dead). Years later, he came forward after being identified. He claimed he was treated like any other prisoner in the ESMA: tortured and confined, kept bound and hooded in a cell. At the time of his disappearance, he had a wife and a young child. In his account, the military threatened them, and he chose to collaborate in order to save them and himself. He claims his collaboration was also triggered by torture. "I am a broken man. They broke me under torture."[21]

He admits that he gave information that led to the disappearance and deaths of five fellow Montoneros: "I chose between my wife and three-month-old daughter and those *compañeros*. It was my only option." Other survivors accuse him of betraying many more; they say he is responsible for the deaths of over seventy people. Lauletta claims it was someone else who betrayed these people. Survivors accuse him of collaborating "excessively" and "zealously" and of abandoning all principles in order to save himself. In the words of one survivor, "He was a guy who didn't have any qualms about bringing others down." Survivors also accuse him of collaborating with the military as a *marcador* (marker): someone who goes out into the streets with military units to identify individuals who are later disappeared. They accuse him of acting more like a member of the military than like a prisoner. "When they brought in a *chupado* [kidnapped person], he entered like a military official," one survivor recalls. Lauletta defended his actions by saying others did the same: "I was in the same situation as all of the survivors of the ESMA. I performed a task that was forced by circumstances."

Lauletta's complicity with the military was widely disseminated through ex-Montonero Miguel Bonasso's account of one individual's survival of the ESMA, *Recuerdo de la Muerte* (Memory of Death).[22] Published in 1984, this work remains one of the most important accounts of a survivor's experience inside the concentration camps. In it, Lauletta is portrayed as an eager collaborator who gains numerous privileges, even weekly home visits to his family. In one instance, he says to another prisoner, "I'd even hand over my best friend," and he drinks a toast to the death of a fellow Montonero, whom he had marked out to the military for disappearance. Lauletta denies this account.[23] The notoriety resulting from Bonasso's book made Lauletta a pariah figure. He was fired from one job and stopped taking classes at the University of Buenos Aires after students discovered his presence there. These events led him to finally speak publicly. Admitting collaboration, he also acknowledges a paradox of survival in the death camps – a paradox that is also voiced by many other survivors: "There are people that didn't break and they are alive. There are people that broke and they are dead." Even the journalist who interviewed Lauletta accused him of not being fully forthright. Lauletta responded that it was easy for those who had not been there to judge. The journalist concluded: "I don't know if surviving under those circumstances is the most important thing for a human being."[24]

Máximo Nicoletti, another former Montonero, is a far less guilt-ridden collaborator. Unlike Lauletta, Nicoletti remained unrepentant when, in 1994, he made his only public statement: "Guilt? What guilt? I didn't have any options. I had no way out. When I fell in the ESMA, I negotiated for my life, for my wife's life, and for my children's lives.

But this was a business and, like in all businesses, one has to give something in exchange. I always knew it would be this way so I gave up people."[25] Once captured, he became an open collaborator, identifying key locations and going out with military teams to identify people to kidnap.

He eventually became an intelligence agent for the navy and a close associate of its head, even teaching in a counter-terrorism school. Nicoletti defends himself by arguing that, once he decided to collaborate, he respected the agreement. Once released from the ESMA in 1979, he continued working in intelligence for the navy in Venezuela. In 1982, he was arrested in Spain, where it was alleged that he had been commissioned by the Argentine Navy to blow up a British warship in Gibraltar during the Falkland Islands War. In the 1990s, he became head of a *superbanda* (criminal gang) composed of former police, army, and intelligence agents as well as Humberto Fratella, another disappeared person who chose to collaborate with the military. The group was eventually captured after an armoured car robbery, and Nicoletti went to prison.

The Case of Silvia Tolchinsky

Contradicting other survivors, Nicoletti argued that the only way to survive in the ESMA was through open collaboration. In fact, the military deliberately attempted to force complicity among its victims. Some victims of torture and disappearance were forced to apply the *picana* to other prisoners. In the words of one survivor, the military "loved it when someone 'broke.' They used it to frighten, taunt, and divide us even more."[26] Other stories of collaboration raise an even more delicate issue: that of female prisoners who allegedly fell in love with their captors while disappeared.

Silvia Tolchinsky was a high-ranking Montonero, the personal secretary of the head of the organization. Her first husband was murdered by the military in 1978. Her brother and his wife and two other family members also disappeared. She was disappeared in September 1980 and spent almost two years in captivity. She was taken to the Argentine-Brazilian border by one of Argentina's most infamous torturers to identify any Montoneros attempting to secretly enter the country. She maintains that she did not identify anyone. After a year and a half in captivity, she met a civilian intelligence agent working for the army, Claudio Gustavo Scagliusi, the son of an Argentine general. The two fell in love. Presumably using his father's influence, Scagliusi intervened, and Tolchinsky was released. She subsequently escaped to Israel. A month later, Scagliusi quit his post and joined her there. They eventually moved to Barcelona where they married and had children.

Unlike other accused collaborators, Tolchinsky pursued justice against those responsible for her disappearance and gave testimony on several occasions. She was the key witness and plaintiff in a major human rights case in 2002, when Argentine federal court judge Claudio Bonadío challenged the country's amnesty laws. He ordered Leopold Galtieri, dictator when Tolchinsky was disappeared, to be placed in preventive custody along with twenty-six other military officers, including Scagliusi. A warrant was put out for his arrest and he was to be extradited to Argentina. Scagliusi was accused of being a spy in charge of the operation in which Tolchinsky disappeared. He denied the accusation. His most ardent defender was his wife, the primary witness and plaintiff in the case that led to his arrest. The media referred to him as a "torturer."[27] Charges against him were eventually dropped after the judge met with the couple in Spain.

In court, however, lawyers for the accused military officials cited Tolchinsky's relationship with Scagliusi and her supposed collaboration with the military as a means of challenging her testimony. Florencio Varela, a prominent lawyer who, before his death in 2006, represented thirty Argentine military and police charged with crimes against humanity, argued that Tolchinsky could not even be considered "disappeared" because she was "an active and interested collaborator for more than three years in the system to repress terrorism."[28] According to Varela, her disappearance was "simulated" so that "she wouldn't be discovered by her companions so as to escape their vengeance." Varela alleged that Tolchinsky only came forward to give an official account of her disappearance in 1994 in order to receive the economic reparations that the state was granting to the disappeared. Financial incentive, he argued, motivated her testimony. He later called Tolchinsky "the most active collaborator of the army leading to one of the greatest successes of the counterintelligence work in the war."[29] He said she gave ninety pages worth of logistical information about the group, including their political and union connections and internal structure. An accused military officer likewise called her a "snitch."[30] At the trial, family members of the disappeared made the same accusation against Tolchinsky. Among them was the wife of a disappeared person whom Tolchinsky, in her testimony, had identified as someone she saw in captivity.[31] She was the one who pushed for charges against Scagliusi. When I interviewed the mother of Tolchinsky's disappeared sister-in-law, she, too, accused Tolchinsky of collaboration.

Tolchinsky stands as an example of the ambivalent position of survivors who, even after pursuing justice against the military, are accused of collaboration both by the military and by family members of the victims. In interviews, Tolchinsky defends her relationship with Scagliusi: "Even in the deepest hell there are certain spaces of life that somehow come to the surface [...] Gustavo, from the first moment, in that context of torture, rebelled to relieve my suffering."[32] The idea that he "rebelled" to help "relieve her suffering" is repeated in almost every interview she has given. She said that his outrage over what he witnessed drove him to help her. Unlike military officers, he had no power. In this way, Tolchinsky claims, Scagliusi is "in some ways as much a victim as [herself]."[33]

Tolchinsky, now a psychologist, has been accused of evincing Stockholm syndrome, in which hostage sympathizes with captor. One commentator likened her relationship with Scagliusi to *The Night Porter,* the controversial 1974 Liliana Cavani film in which a concentration camp survivor, a decade after liberation, resumes her relationship with the SS officer who tortured and raped her.[34] Tolchinsky rejects this interpretation and argues that the reverse (i.e., Lima syndrome)[35] is the case: Scagliusi empathized with her rather than vice versa.[36] She points out that, when he left the country to be with her, he broke completely with his former life: "During these eighteen years, he has dedicated himself to trying to repair the devastating effects the dictatorship had on my family. He identifies with our suffering and our way of seeing the world."[37] As a key witness, Tolchinsky says that accusations of collaboration are attempts to discredit her testimony. Calling her a "traitor" or a "snitch" involves using the military's language against her: "We didn't choose it. They didn't let me choose. It transfers blame to the victim for their actions."[38] In her words, her story is the "product of Argentina's evil history."

Numerous survivors face similar allegations. Their survival is called into question and attributed to their status as "double agents." For example, in a statement made in 2006, Varela speaks of the numerous "falsifications" and "manipulations" of survivor testimonies while describing survivors as "repentant ex-terrorists who were collaborators."[39] In a 1998 interview Gabriela Cerruti conducted with navy officer Alfredo

Astiz, one of the most notorious Argentine military perpetrators, Astiz states: "If the majority of the survivors of the ESMA don't speak, it's because the majority of them were collaborators. We even considered ourselves sympathetic to each other, because you end up taking a liking to people with whom you live together with for many days. I personally respect some Montoneros. I ended up taking a liking to some of them."[40]

Astiz's comment may be in reference to "friends" like Nicoletti.

Perverse Intimacies

Most accounts of collaboration focus on the ESMA. More than five thousand people disappeared through its gates, and only a small minority of these came out alive. Many prisoners were held over long periods of time, during which perpetrators and victims co-existed in the same space. This resulted in the creation of perverse intimacies, illustrated, for example, in Astiz's comment (see above) that he "ended up taking a liking to" the people whom he had kidnapped, tortured, and killed.

Mario Villani recounts the disturbing relationships that emerged between disappeared and military torturers, a product of sharing confined quarters on a daily basis: "I have found myself at times speaking with a torturer, the same person who tortured me, not about torture but about his family, about his son's problems in school, that his son was getting bad grades and he didn't know what to do."[41] Villani speaks of a torturer nicknamed Sangre (Blood) who played chess with the disappeared. Sangre even brought his young daughter to the camp one day and introduced her to him.[42]

Although largely absent from testimonial discourse, perverse intimacies are recurring motifs in Argentine fictional representations of the concentration camps. One of Argentina's theatrical hits of 1990 was Eduardo Pavlovsky's *Paso de dos* (Pas de deux). Pavlovsky, a noted playwright and medical psychoanalyst who pioneered psychodrama therapy in Argentina, describes the work as a "love story" between a torturer and his female victim.[43] The play ends with the torturer strangling his victim to death. The title *Paso de dos* evokes complicity. Marguerite Feitlowitz calls it a "dance of death."[44] Although the play was largely lauded as an incisive critique of the ideology of the dictatorship, its eroticized violence was a source of controversy and it was accused of both voyeurism and sadomasochism (Pavlovsky played the torturer in its initial run). Pavlovsky's supporters point to his credentials as a committed left-wing intellectual who was forced to flee the country during the dictatorship. Further, it is pointed out that the play was inspired by real events.

Numerous stories of torturers who ended up in relationships with the women whom they tortured circulate in Argentina. Silvia Tolchinsky rejects the idea that this occurred in her case. Other stories, although difficult to corroborate, leave less room for doubt. Marta Bazán was a Montonera who had been disappeared in the ESMA. It is alleged that, under torture, she betrayed the location of her husband, who was subsequently disappeared and executed. Afterwards, she reputedly fell in love with Ruben Chamorro, a navy vice-admiral. They eventually married and she went with him to South Africa, where he advised the apartheid government on counter-insurgency methods.

What was the attraction these military men felt for their enemies? Late in the dictatorship, after most disappearances had already occurred, bored navy officers in the ESMA began taking women who had disappeared in this concentration camp out to expensive restaurants in Buenos Aires. They cleaned them up, dressed them, took them out to eat, and then brought them back. Munú Actis, a survivor of the ESMA, recounts the story of an officer named Jorge "El Tigre" Acosta, implicated in numerous dictatorship crimes.[45] Dining at a restaurant one night, she asked Acosta why he stayed at the ESMA at night instead of going home to his family. Reacting furiously to her question, he shouted, "Don't you realize that it's your fault that we don't want to go home?" He continued: "With you, we can talk about movies, the theatre, about anything. We can talk about politics. You know about raising children; you can play the guitar; you know how to handle a weapon! You know how to do everything! You are the women that we thought existed only in novels and movies, and it has destroyed our families! Because what are we going to do now with the women we have at home?"[46]

Acosta then proceeded to complain about the monotony of domestic life. Military culture in Argentina was traditionally hermetic. Many military men married women who were the daughters of other military men. They were raised to be obedient and submissive to their husbands. Men like Acosta were fascinated when confronted with women who had broken out of traditional gender roles. He continued: "What can I share with my wife? I go home on Saturday, and we talk about whether or not we'll go to the club on Sunday, whether to take the picnic basket or not take the picnic basket [...] That's what I share with my wife."[47]

Another military officer from the ESMA, Jorge Radice, a.k.a. Ruger, similarly commented on the appeal of "enemy" women. Radice married his prisoner Anita Dvantman and had three children with her. One prisoner heard him say: "She was a transgressor and I was aroused by her attitude. I had never met a woman like her. She knew about cinema, painting, politics, even tools."[48] Radice is also an unrepentant perpetrator. The testimony he gave at the trial against military leaders is notorious. When asked what he did in the military, he stated that his superiors pointed to a target and he pulled the trigger.[49] When Radice was called to testify in 1997 in an open case about the final destination of the disappeared, he only acknowledged participating in one instance of torture: his wife's. He subsequently argued that it should be expunged from the record for reasons of privacy.[50] His wife, meanwhile, was criticized for receiving economic compensation from the state as a victim of disappearance, money she would ostensibly share with her husband.

Such relationships have served as inspiration for other prominent literary representations of the dictatorship.[51] Liliana Heker's 1996 novel, *El Fin de la Historia* (The end of history), recounts the story of a student leader of the Communist Party who becomes a high-ranking Montonera. She is kidnapped and tortured but falls in love with her torturer, the same man who killed her husband, and ends up collaborating with the armed forces. She survives the ESMA and the two end up together. Like Pavlovsky's play, Heker's novel sparked controversy. ESMA survivor Graciela Daleo responded to it with the question: "Why do those who speak of the 1970s – except for a few exceptions – dedicate their pen to those the terror broke?"[52]

Despite Daleo's criticism, Heker's work was, like Pavlovsky's play, based on real events. The novel, told from the perspective of the protagonist's novelist friend, is largely autobiographical, based on the experiences of Heker's friend Mercedes Carazo, another survivor of the ESMA. According to some accounts, Carazo resisted inside the ESMA until her husband was killed. The military took her to see him while he was dying. According to survivors, this event profoundly changed her and she ended up falling in love with a navy officer named Antonio Pernías, the man who led the group that killed her husband. According to Daleo: "You always hope that she did not know that he was at the head of that operation. If not, you can't explain how she could love him. She said that she was in love with him. Not, you know, that she slept with him to save her life."[53] Heker concurs with Daleo, believing her feelings towards Pernías were influenced by the gratitude she felt towards him after he gave her back her infant child.[54] Carazo never gave testimony and only broke her silence in 1998 after her relationship with Pernías had ended. Daleo's criticism of Heker's novel is not over whether or not the events depicted in it actually took place;[55] rather, she questions how representative this story is and criticizes the fact that treason, betrayal, and collaboration are prominent motifs in narrative representations of what went on in the camps.[56] The point of Daleo's criticism is that this focus is part of the larger context in which survivors have been questioned for surviving. She says that she prefers to call attention to the "small resistances" that took place in the camps rather than collaboration.

What does "collaboration" mean after prolonged torture and the threat of death? Can it be called "collaboration"? To do so is to embrace the absolutist logic of that period of history. The Montoneros accused anyone who broke under torture of treason. They ordered people to resist until death or to take cyanide pills before they were captured. They assumed that anyone not killed after capture was a collaborator. Noted writer and journalist Rodolfo Walsh, a Montonero also murdered by the dictatorship, argued with the group over this matter. For him, collaboration provoked by torture could not be considered treason.[57]

Some people withstood torture and did not give information. As one survivor said, "I know that in my case I beat them because I didn't give them any information and nothing happened to me."[58] But few could withstand the cruelty of military torture, which included the *picana*, sexual torture, suffocation, and dismemberment by attack dogs.[59] In spite of this, the idea that those who "gave in" to torture were guilty of betrayal persists. Miguel Bonasso's 1990 autobiographical novel, *La memoria en donde ardía* (Memory where it was burning) tells the story of an exiled Argentine journalist who returns to his native country after eleven years in Mexico.[60] The protagonist becomes obsessed with finding out whether his disappeared lover revealed the location of the house where they were living after she was kidnapped by the military. When asked in an interview why the character was so obsessed with the subject of "betrayal," Bonasso answered, "Because he wanted to know if he could keep loving her or not, in accordance with a terrible, absolutist and, in a certain sense, romantic logic of the 1970s."[61]

What does it mean to hold as a "romantic" ideal a person who refuses to break under brutal torture? This forms part of the context in which survivors are questioned for having survived and are marginalized within the human rights movement. This has created an odd cleavage within testimonial discourse. On the one hand, fictionalized accounts of survivors emphasize grey zones and blurred perpetrator-victim boundaries; on the other hand, the testimonial work of survivors emphasizes pragmatic legal ends and clearly defined boundaries. Within this legalistic framework, in which survivor testimony exists to identify perpetrators and victims, a clear black-and-white dichotomous logic between perpetrators and victims must be maintained. Human rights and the pursuit of justice depend on clear identities.

The role of survivors in post-dictatorship Argentina has largely been confined by a narrow emphasis on their testimonial work. Trapped by the urgent need to pursue justice against military perpetrators – even during the 1980s and 1990s, when justice was not possible – they identified perpetrators and victims. Testimonies were largely linked to this pragmatic value and legal goal of sending perpetrators to prison. The terror and torture that survivors experienced in the clandestine camps had to be funnelled through this narrow legal framework. Survivors in this sense become the conduits of justice, with personal experience being secondary to a call for historic truth and justice. Within this formalized narrative, the disappeared are largely abstracted into a broad nebulous category in which they are treated as "innocent victims" – innocent of not only "terrorism" but also of political beliefs altogether.

Underneath this generalized discourse lie grey zones of ambivalences and ambiguities that highlight questions of complicity and betrayal. Since legal trials have restarted and all of this testimonial work can now be put to use in the manner in which it was intended, there is the possibility that survivor experience, in all of its multifaceted nuances and complexities, can finally be fully represented. It is not so much that these questions have not been answered, but they have only been raised in the relatively safe space of fictional or semi-fictionalized works about the dictatorship. There is still the feeling that, even three decades after the collapse of this dictatorship, survivors themselves have been unable to fully represent their experience. Perhaps only after legal justice against military perpetrators is achieved will this finally be possible.

Notes

1 Adriana died in 2010 after a lengthy battle with cancer. She was an extremely generous and valuable informant who not only warmly offered her time but also put me in contact with other key informants. This chapter is dedicated to her memory.

2 Marta Diana, *Mujeres guerrilleras: La militancia de los setenta en el testimonio de sus protagonistas femeninas* (Buenos Aires: Planeta, 1996), 52.

3 Pilar Calveiro, *Poder y desaparición: Los campos de concentración en Argentina* (Buenos Aires: Ediciones Colihue, 2001).

4 Ibid., 47.

5 Bruno Bettelheim, *Individual and Mass Behavior in Extreme Situations* (New York: Irvington, 1991 [1943]).

6 Horacio Verbitsky, *El Vuelo* (Buenos Aires: Planeta/Espejo de la Argentina, 1995).

7 Fernando Almiron, *Campo Santo: Los Asesinatos del Ejercito en Campo de Mayo: Testimonios del ex-sargento Víctor Ibañez* (Buenos Aires: Editorial 21 SRL, 1999).

8 Claudia Feld, "La construcción del 'arrepentimiento': Los ex represores en la television," *Entrepasados: Revista de historia* 10, 20/21 (2001): 35–54.

9 Taken from the "Memoria gráfica del Club Atlético" exposition at the Centro Cultural Recoleta, 5 March 2004.

10 CONADEP, *Nunca Mas: The Report of the Argentina National Commission of the Disappeared* (New York: Farrar Straus Giroux, 1986 [1984]), 285.

11 For example, Thomas Frank's *The Conquest of Cool: Business, Culture, Counterculture, and the Rise of Hip Consumerism* (Chicago: University of Chicago Press, 1997), discusses how 1960s counterculture images and slogans became co-opted by marketing and advertising campaigns of 1990s capitalism.

12 For example, Bonafini's *Mothers* construct a pyramid of photographs of the disappeared around the monument of the Plaza de Mayo, the centre of their march. The other family member groups carry a banner of photographs on their procession down the Avenida de Mayo to the Plaza.

13 *Página/12*, 29 September 2006.

14 Ibid.

15 *Clarín*, 29 September 2006.

16 The first and last quotes in this paragraph are from *Página/12*, 30 September 2006.

17 Primo Levi, *The Drowned and the Saved*, trans. Raymond Rosenthal (New York: Vintage Books, 1989 [1986]), 18.

18 Ibid.

19 Cited in Marguerite Feitlowitz, *A Lexicon of Terror* (New York: Oxford University Press, 1998), 82.

20 Ibid., 84.

21 This account is drawn from the lengthy interview he gave to journalist David Cox, editor of the *Buenos Aires Herald*, which appeared in the weekly magazine *La Maga,* 3 May 1995.

22 Miguel Bonasso, *Recuerdo de la muerte* (Buenos Aires: Planeta, 1984).

23 The film is *Papá Iván* (2004), directed by María Inés Roqué. In interviews, Roqué says she believes Lauletta was not involved in her father's disappearance.

24 *La Maga,* 3 May 1995.

25 *Gente*, 9 June 1994.

26 Andrés di Tella, "La vida privada en los campos de concentración," in *Historias de la vida privada en la Argentina,* Tomo III, *La Argentina entre multitudes y soledades*, ed. Fernando Devoto and Marta Madero, 78–106 (Buenos Aires: Tauras, 1999), 66.

27 *Clarín*, 31 January 2003.

28 Taken from legal document entitled "Incidente de apelación en autos Scagliusi, Claudio Gustavo por privación ilegal libertad personal" (C.Nac.Crim. y Correc. Fed., Sala II – 30/01/2003).

29 *Seprin*, "Texto desgrabado de la conferencia del Dr. Florencio Varela en AUNAR el 30 de Septiembre," at http://www.seprin.com/menu/notas6243.htm.

30 *Página/12*, 17 November 2002.

31 Inter Press Service News Agency, 26 September 2005, at http://www.ipslatam.net/print.asp?idnews=35259. Alegrini also identifies one other Montonero, who was a *marcadora.*

32 *Página/12*, 17 November 2002.

33 *La Capital,* 4 September 2001.

34 *El Mundo*, 8 September 2001.

35 Named after the Japanese Embassy hostage takeover in Peru, in which the Shining Path guerillas' sympathy for their hostages grew during the standoff.

36 *Página/12*, 17 November 2002.

37 Ibid.

38 *Página/12*, 30 September 2005.

39 Florencio Varela, "Florencio Varela sin miedo y sin tapujos, declaración de Florencio Varela y una introducción," *La botalla al mar*, 5 September 2006, at http://www.labotellaalmar.com/vercorreo_lector.php?id=1784.

40 *Tres Puntos*, 11 January 1998.

41 di Tella, "La vida privada," 85.

42 Ibid., 86.

43 Marguerite Feitlowitz, "A Dance of Death: Eduardo Pavlovsky's 'Paso de dos,'" *Drama Review* 35, 2 (1991): 60–73.

44 Ibid.

45 In another bizarre occurrence involving his prisoners, Acosta chose a number of the disappeared from ESMA to go out and celebrate with him in the streets of the city after Argentina won the 1978 World Cup.

46 Cited in Munú Actis, Cristina Aldini, Liliana Gardella, Miriam Lewin, and Elisa Tokar, *That Inferno: Conversations of Five Women Survivors of an Argentine Torture Camp* (Nashville: Vanderbilt University Press, 2006), 163.

47 Ibid.

48 di Tella, "La vida privada," 95.

49 *El Libro del Juicio*, Testimonios (Buenos Aires: Editorial Testigo, 1985).

50 Débora D'Antonio, "Controversial Images of Women during the Last Argentine Military Dictatorship (1976–1983)," *Journal of Latin American Cultural Studies* 13, 3 (2004): 375–96.

51 See also Marco Bechis's film *Garage Olimpo* (1999), one of the most powerful films made about the dictatorship. Patricia Sagastizábal's novel *A Secret for Julia* (2001) recounts the story of a woman who had a child after being raped in a concentration camp and encounters her rapist two decades later in England. Ariel Dorfman's play *Death and the Maiden* (1994) also deals with this topic but sets it in an unnamed South American country.

52 *Página/12*, 8 September 1996.

53 *Página/12*, 16 November 1998.

54 Ibid.

55 Daleo has criticized Carazo for "knowing more than she has told" and for not being completely forthright with investigations into the disappearances. See *Página/12*, 16 November 1998.

56 Rolo Diez's *Los compañeros* (2000) also addresses this subject. The topic of betrayal in representations of the dictatorship is the subject of a recent full-length literary analysis in Ana Longoni's *Traiciones* (Betrayals) (Buenos Aires: Norma, 2007).

57 Michael McCaughan, *True Crime: Rodolfo Walsh and the Role of the Intellectual in Latin American Politics* (London: Latin America Bureau, 2002).

58 Diana, *Mujeres guerrilleras*, 51.

59 See CONADEP, *Nunca Mas*; and Feitlowitz, *Lexicon of Terror,* for graphic descriptions of military torture.

60 Miguel Bonasso, *La memoria en donde ardía* (Buenos Aires: Ediciones Colihue, 1990).

61 *Página/12*, 5 November 2006.

2 | Pessimism of the Intellect, Optimism of the Will

Engaging with the "Testimony" of Injured Workers

ROBERT STOREY

On 19 December 1929, Antonio Gramsci wrote to his brother Carlo, thanking him for the "solicitude with which [he] carried out [Gramsci's] errands." Just over two years into a prison sentence that would last until six days before his death on 27 April 1937, Gramsci continued by expressing "surprise" at what we are left to surmise were signs of emotional disturbance in another brother, Nannaro: "The two of you were in the war, Nannaro in particular fought in the war under exceptional circumstances, as an underground mine-layer, hearing through the thin wall that separated his tunnel from the Austrian tunnel the enemies' work that was intended to hasten the explosion of his mine and so blow him up." Gramsci continued:

> It seems to me that under such conditions prolonged for years, and with such psychological experiences, a man should have reached the loftiest stage of stoic serenity and should have acquired such a profound conviction that man bears within himself the source of his own moral strength, that everything depends on him, on his will, on the iron coherence of the aims that he sets for himself and the means he adopts to realize them, that he will never again despair and lapse into vulgar, banal states of mind that are called pessimism and optimism. My state of mind synthesizes these two emotions and overcomes them: I'm a pessimist because of intelligence, but an optimist because of will."[1]

This quote raises many points of possible discussion; however, as the title of this chapter indicates, our interest is in the sentence: "I'm a pessimist because of intellect, but an optimist because of will." While Gramsci is not its original author,[2] over time these words have come to be associated with him. As we can glean from this extract from his prison letters, there was a close, even dialectical, relationship between the two states of mind in that the presence of the one automatically ignited the other. Applied to the realm of politics and political activity, Gramsci's corpus of writings and his activism tell us that he believed a comprehensive understanding of the political economy (including culture) of a given situation was the critical and necessary middle ground – the passageway – between the paralysis of intellectual pessimism and the activism required to overcome it.[3]

This chapter is an elucidation of this process as it has been undertaken by injured workers and others in the Ontario injured workers' movement, who together have taken on the task of constructing the passageway even as they are moving through it. It is a process that involves dealing with and moving through trauma. That is, if we follow Dominick LaCapra in defining trauma as "a disruptive experience that disarticulates the self and creates holes in existence ... [with] ... belated effects that are controlled only with difficulty and perhaps never fully mastered,"[4] then the experiences of the injured workers who have participated in this research study through giving their oral histories can unquestionably be classified as traumatic. Having an arm torn off when building foundations shift, or mangled by the unexpected release of powerful, steam-driven machinery, or watching more or less helplessly as chronic pain from repetitive motions slowly takes over one's body and fundamentally diminishes one's life are events and experiences that "disarticulate the self and create holes in existence." And, as the oral histories of these workers demonstrate, they are events and experiences that "are controlled with difficulty and perhaps never fully mastered."

However, as the oral histories also demonstrate, the conscious and concerted efforts at "political" education undertaken by leaders in the injured workers' movement – to assist injured workers in making the connections between their private troubles and public issues[5] – have in some instances served to alleviate the pessimism that engulfed many, if not most, of them. In this way, the experiences and political trajectories of injured workers are little different than that of other workers and/or members of subordinate groups who have moved from quiescence to challenging the rules, regulations, and ideas that keep them constrained practically, politically, and ideologically. However, one of the differences may be – and this is one of my central conclusions – that the shift from pessimism of the intellect to optimism of the will was fuelled by new understandings that sprang from the telling of their life stories, and, just as important, from their exposure to stories of how injured workers struggled successfully with the workers' compensation system. If injured workers could conquer their fears in the past, then they could do the same in the present.

Assault on the Worker

Doug Cowles was born in Hamilton and has spent most of his life there. He did not like school very much and was "kicked out halfway through nine and … went to work" at a chrome plating company in Stoney Creek. There was, he said, "a lot of heavy lifting, a lot of heavy work, a lot of steady work. It was enjoyable. Spent a lot of hours. A lot of overtime." He worked there for two and one-half years and then moved to Dofasco, at the time Hamilton's second largest integrated steel maker, where he worked in the coke ovens for a year. "Couldn't get off the coke ovens," he related. "I lost 50 pounds in about 10 months. So, I found a good way to dieting. And, I thought, well, I'd like to have something left of me so I had to leave."[6]

He moved across the street to Hamilton's largest steelmaker, the Steel Company of Canada – Stelco – where, after refusing a job in the coke ovens, he was assigned a job in maintenance driving a truck.

> In 1977, I had an injury. I was loading the truck. The truck was loaded. I was strapping. I was chaining sheets down which sat on three-by-three's, and I was running down the road with them. So, I was strapping them down tight, the chains, and they had just tried saving binders and chains because outside truckers were coming along taking chains and binders. They were losing quite a few. But they decided we'll save some. We'll take the hooks off the chains, on the binders, and we'll weld the binders to the chains and we'll weld the chains to the rails through a three-by-eight bar. Well, three-by-eight bar, it doesn't make any difference how thick, the bars when they bend, they break. And it came off, threw me off the truck backwards, my right foot slipped, went underneath, my toes went underneath a load of sheets, and as I come off the truck, I come off the truck backwards, this way, didn't hit the ground, just hung from one leg. My leg should've broken. My back would've been probably a lot

> better, but it didn't. So now I've put up with my back since 1977. [In] 1987 I was, again they decided to save about eighteen dollars. And because we were hooking up and dismantling the trailers all the time, the safety bar inside the fifth wheel was removed, and I lost the trailer with the eighty-seven thousand pounds and the tractor went airborne and when it came down ejected the seat and ejected me into the roof of the cab and that destroyed my neck.[7]

Cowles worked at Stelco for twenty-five years, the last five in office jobs he did not care for – as he said: "I liked being active. I don't like being inside. I don't like sitting watching T.V. Not my cup of tea." He also did not like living with the chronic pain in his neck and back stemming from the accidents. He lamented his "lost" marriage and two other relationships. "It's not very easy trying to find relationships and making relationships go when you're not working," he told me: "But, you just can't keep living with people, and they have a hard time trying to adjust because they don't know what pain, chronic pain, what you have to put up with. Lack of sleep at night. Up and down. Different ways of doing things. So, life is totally different but you make the best of it and do the best you can. I think that's the history."[8]

I use Doug Cowles's story as a way to introduce the complexities of workplace accidents and injury. I employ it as well because it provides an entry point into the larger issue of the everyday, the "normal," violence of capitalist labour processes – what three Canadian researchers have termed an "assault on the worker."[9] With this term, these researchers are referring to the fact that the number of workplace accidents that are recorded nationally each year in Canada reaches into the hundreds of thousands – indeed, it recently topped the 1 million mark. The reports on these accidents inform us that in Canada a worker is injured every nine seconds. Further, accidents resulting in time away from work – the more serious – occur every nineteen seconds. Finally, and more tragically, we know from these reports that, every day, three workers die from workplace accidents and diseases.

Researchers who study occupational health and safety and workers' compensation question why these numbers do not warrant the same public profile as injury and death from, for example, automobile accidents or cigarette smoking, and they are quick to point out that even these staggering numbers significantly underestimate the real extent of workplace-related injury and death. Indeed, Canadian and American researchers have highlighted the many and varied obstacles that stand in the path of workers' filing compensation claims.[10] Before the arrival of post-Fordist labour processes and precarious forms of employment, workers typically did not report workplace accidents, either because they did not believe the associated injury called for such attention or because they did not know their rights. While the greater presence of unions in that period usually meant that unionized workers were more likely to know their rights than non-unionized workers, there was still no automatic relationship between accidents and reporting. And if membership in a union did not make such information – and, importantly, advocacy – available, workers in non-union workplaces were greatly disadvantaged with respect to both knowing their rights to workers' compensation and having some type of support for their claims.

Arguably, with the arrival and ongoing consolidation of "flexible" workplaces – with their characteristic precarious forms of employment – this situation is even more problematic. Indeed, as Wayne Lewchuk and his colleagues show in a comprehensive study of the health effects of "working without commitments,"[11] the job and the "long arm of the job" have enduring effects on the health of workers. These new (at least for North America) employment relationships are not likely to fall under the current occupational health and safety and workers' compensation laws, thereby adding to the large, but largely unknown, percentage of workers who are not covered by either health and safety or workers' compensation laws.[12]

Clearly, the shifting dynamics of workplace production (i.e., from producing goods to selling things) has not resulted in safer and healthier workplaces. Quite simply, the official statistics – not to mention the unrecorded accidents and the recently climbing number of abandoned claims – tell us quite a different tale: that employers continue, as David Harvey points out, to use workers' bodies "as an accumulation strategy."[13]

What does this mean? In Harvey's words, the raison d'être of work organization under capitalism – whether in a steel plant, a fast food restaurant, or a clothing store in a mall – is to extend and intensify the working day for ever-increasing production and the maximization of capital accumulation. As in Marx's time, one of the chief products of using workers – really using workers' bodies – as an accumulation strategy is accident and injury. In other words, capitalist labour processes are intrinsically violent. Doug Cowles's story affirms this theoretical point and this everyday reality. So, too, does the experience of Michael Ladouceur. Just twenty years old with six months' experience on the job, Ladouceur was hard at work at 2:00 AM when an "L-clamp" on a hand-powered lifting device he was operating slipped off the end of a ten-ton steel slab.

> MIKE: Yes, I put the L-clamp underneath the steel plate. I lifted the plate up about waist level, the L-clamp shot out and it hit me right between the eyes and went a half-inch into my skull. Knocked me back a couple steps, I banged the back of my head against a concrete block wall, fell forward, smacked my head against the cement floor and then I was in a coma for thirty-two days.
>
> ROBERT: Oh my God!
>
> MIKE: And the labourer, there was two guys in the shop when I had my accident. There was supposed to be three guys, and me, but there was only two and me because the one guy called in sick. And the guy at the back of the shop, he couldn't come to see what happened when the steel plate fell and hit the floor. They heard a bang and they didn't know what, what's going on. So the guy at the back of the shop couldn't come because he was running the Blanchard grinder, and the guy at the front of the shop he was a labourer. He heard the steel plate fall and he came wondering what's going on and he couldn't see me. So he walked around the steel plate and found me lying in a pool of my blood. And he ran to the nearest phone and called the paramedics. That explains my story there.[14]

There is much to think about from this signal moment in Ladouceur's life. First, I highlight the level of violence of the accident: the repeated smashing of his head, the pool of blood, his heart stopping for six to eight minutes after the accident, and, months later, his taking an overdose of pills when he could no longer deal with his depression. Second, we see that, at the time of the accident, Ladouceur had little or no control over the labour process. Because his shift was short a person, he had to do the job of the missing worker. Only his employer had the authority to call in another worker. If Ladouceur had had this authority, or if he had known that he had the right to refuse unsafe work, this accident might never have happened.

To reiterate and emphasize, violence lurks, and is a regular occurrence, in capitalist workplaces. As Suroopa Mukherjee writes in another context, at work "the body is a site of contestation."[15] To be sure, some workplaces are more hazardous and potentially more unhealthy than others. The 1885 Occupational Health and Safety Law in Ontario, and in other Canadian provinces, was a "Factory Act" that exclusively targeted the "dangerous trades," such as the steel mills, iron foundries, and potteries.[16] The "modern" workmen's compensation laws of the early twentieth century had a similar regulatory stamp as they, too, were largely restricted to the prototypical industrial workplace.[17]

But, this does not mean – nor was it ever the case – that working in offices and shops or in the streets was completely safe and healthy. In fact, among the injured workers who participated in this study, the largest number had been injured in jobs typically understood to be safer than working in a steel mill, an auto plant, down a coal mine, or in the woods. Eunice Lucas, for instance, was driving a Transit Windsor bus westward at University and Sunset:

> EUNICE: You know, if you drive, you're always scanning, and I scanned and I could tell the one car that was in front was not going to stop at the stop sign the speed he was going. So, I, literally, I was up off the seat, and like this on the steering wheel, trying to get the bus to stop. It didn't work. He hit, he ran through a stop sign and he hit the front of the bus, right in front of the door.
>
> ROBERT: So, on the passenger side?
>
> EUNICE: Right, passenger side. Passenger side, yup. He walked away. I've seen him a couple of times since the accident, and he's fine, unless it doesn't show, like the injuries don't show on me. He might be injured too. It just doesn't show. He got out the car, he said, "I just didn't see you," and honestly the motor of his car was almost on his lap, that's how hard he hit. And he caused almost twenty-thousand dollars' damage to the bus. As far as I know nobody on the bus was hurt. Nobody made out paperwork or anything. I was the only one that was hurt, which is okay. If I knew somebody got hurt on the bus, I would really feel, you know, they're my responsibility to keep them safe, and if they got hurt I would've failed. But it was all good.
>
> ROBERT: It doesn't sound like it's all good. You got injured.
>
> EUNICE: I get mad at them, Transit Windsor. At that time post-traumatic stress disorder did not work. Like, I was told,

> "No, that wasn't for that injury." It was thoracic outlet syndrome I have for that injury. And it was within an hour, half an hour after the accident, I could not move my head. It was just straight-forward. If I wanted to turn, I'd have to go like this in order to look.[18]

In a very insightful study, Ellen MacEachen and her colleagues show the physical, emotional, and psychological effects on injured workers of delaying compensation and treatment (i.e., they move from "hurt to harm").[19] Eunice's contention that her injury was both physical and emotional/psychological clashed with her employer's belief that it was solely physical – a belief that caused her great anxiety and that resulted in her returning to work seven months after the accident (long before she felt fully ready).

> ROBERT: And you continued to work? Is that what happened?
>
> EUNICE: Well, until 1989, where I saw a lady's head get run over by a van at work. [Nervous laughter.] It's not fun. If I didn't have psychological problems before that, I sure did after that. I gotta tell ya. I tried being stubborn. I tried working through it. It was, I believe, it was the Thursday before the Labour Day weekend and I tried to work through it. I think maybe two or three weeks ... I came in hot all the time, "hot" meaning that you're early, and you can't come in hot. You can come in late with the bus, you can't come in hot. And I came in hot, and the steward was there, and the steward was one of the good guys, one of our good off-suits. He came in and he said, "I've got to talk to you about your timing." The poor guy, I blew up at him. I couldn't, I couldn't do it anymore. And he said: "I think you'd better go see the doctor. Go take time off, go see the doctor." And he wrote it up for me, another angel on my site. So I did. At the end of my morning shift I went to the doctor, and I went off work, because it was no good. Every time I turned the corner, I thought I was going to see her again. My hands would get a grip like this. After I saw her head get run over for the next couple weeks I saw a motorcycle accident. The guy, he was making a left-hand turn, had lots of space, but the guy accelerated coming this way, and hit him. He got up from the accident limping. If you're limping after the accident, you're in big trouble because you have adrenaline going. I finished. I went up to the

> West End and I came back down and I told the police I saw the accident. And I wrote notes in my calendar of what I saw and I gave the police my name and address and that. And they got a hold of me a few months later, and asked me questions. Thank goodness I put notes in there, because he had a, he was a quad.[20]

Again, if we follow LaCapra's definition of trauma, then the hurt to harm that came to encompass Eunice's life is an example of it. It also exemplifies the experience of a Toronto woman, Cathy, who, in 1995, began to suffer from carpal tunnel syndrome:

> CATHY: And then I was injured again, my back in 1998, 1999, and 2000, lifting one of my patients from the shower and dressing him. And then I reinjured myself in 1999 taking my patient's dog out for a walk. I injured my shoulder.
>
> IWHP: Have your injuries affected your ability to work?
>
> CATHY: Well yes, I am not supposed to do any lifting, no repetitive. With my back I cannot do the bending, standing too long. And the pain I have to go through some days, most days, anyways ... My last job, I had to shower people, lift them, feed them, do their housework, do the laundry, do their shopping, take their pets out, all personal care. People I worked for were in wheelchairs so my hands and legs had to do all their work, what they couldn't do. And, there was a lot of lifting.[21]

Cathy's injuries brought her into contact with the Workers' Compensation Board. Only a few days after her shoulder injury, her adjudicator was on the telephone asking her when she was going to return to work. Cathy ended up going to see a psychiatrist. It is not clear from her story whether this happened before or after she "took a whole bunch of pills and ended up in the hospital because [she] got so depressed." Taking an overdose of pills, however, was not what she found most upsetting; rather, what most upset her was that the compensation board "case manager" told her doctor about the incident before she had a chance to do so. What also enflamed her was the fact that the same case manager sent her confidential medical files by courier to her home, where they were left on her doorstep. "And that's not right," she said, "because anyone going by could pick that up."[22]

There are, then, many meanings to the phrase "assault on the worker." At the most fundamental theoretical and day-to-day empirical levels, it means that the "normal" organization of work creates conditions within which hundreds of thousands of Canadian workers get injured sufficiently enough to file a workers' compensation claim. A second meaning can be found in the aftermath of this workplace violence. Looking at Michael Ladouceur's narrative, we read: "That explains my story there." By this phrase he means his life. The moment the L-clamp slipped off the ten-ton steel slab and smashed into his forehead was the moment his life – his story – changed forever. His family gathered behind him, but he "lost" his fiancée and he forgets things quickly and therefore cannot work. Eunice Lucas cannot work either – she is worried about what she will see at every turn of a corner. The same holds true for Cathy, who finds herself unable to work and, in some ways, has been unable to overcome the humiliation she felt because of her treatment by Workers' Compensation Board officials.[23]

Most, if not all, of the injured workers who participated in this research have a similar story to tell. In line with research findings on the stigmatization of injured workers,[24] Doug, Michael, Eunice, and Cathy each spoke about abusive officials who viewed them as fakers, cheaters, malingerers, frauds, and criminals. This message is strikingly similar to the story Frank Figlia told a legislative standing committee looking into workers' compensation reform in 1983.

> We immigrants know how to build houses, tunnels, roads, bridges, schools and churches. These things have been built with our hands, with much sweat and blood. Now, I have lost my future, my dreams, my enjoyment [...] To be injured is very bad. You suffer in many ways, trouble in the family, in society, humiliation, pushed by the WCB to go around like a gypsy to find work and, at the same time, receive humiliation because they don't find work [...] We have given everything to this country. We ask for our right we earned, to live as a Canadian, with right and dignity.[25]

The overall impact of these social, cultural, economic, political, and institutional forces is evident: even as injured workers struggled against these forces – within their families, communities, workplaces, the workers' compensation system, and the government – they felt diminished and alone. In those instances in which the injury inhibits or prevents easy bodily movement and intellectual engagement, the gradual result is isolation and disappearance. In the case of visible physical impairment, it means ostracism. It can also mean never being able to regain your life.

Activism and Oral History

A statement to the effect that activism is bred and nurtured by political education is far from novel. Indeed, it has a long and controversial history – the latter stemming primarily from its close association with the issue of leadership.[26] Yet, as would seem obvious, there can be no social movements without leaders. Leaders gather the resources considered so essential by resource movement theorists. Leaders create, as much as they react to, the political opportunities considered so important by political opportunity theorists. Leaders socially construct and frame the issues they hope will draw in members and supporters and resonate with the wider public and the targets of their causes.[27] Finally, leaders – and here I am referring to leaders at all levels, including Belinda Robnett's "bridge" leaders[28] – perform the crucial tasks of political education wherein collective identities are added to individual identities in preparation for collective action. With respect to this last and seminal leadership role, it is difficult to see how it could be otherwise. As George Lukas writes in his classic text, *History and Class Consciousness*, because of the "prevailing disunity, the differing degrees of clarity and depth to be found in the consciousness of different individuals, groups and strata," someone, or some group, has to raise the "consciousness of the emancipatory subject as a whole until self-emancipation is possible."[29]

Why this all too abbreviated foray into the muck and mire of leadership? Quite simply, because the subtle complexities surrounding leadership and political education pervade this moment in the history of the injured workers' movement. The rise and consolidation of neoliberal economic and political forces in the realm of workers' compensation have been able to overturn long-term policies, regulations, and aspects of the law to the point at which we are seeing a paradigmatic shift – a shift that is exemplified in, among other things, the change in the name of the act (from Workers' Compensation Act to Workplace Safety and Insurance Act); the disappearance from the letterhead of the motto "Justice Speedily and Humanely Rendered"; the appointment of a president and chief executive officer whose banking and actuarial backgrounds are important reference points on his resume; and a contract with this individual, signed by the ruling Liberal government, that holds out the carrot of a sizable annual bonus if he succeeds in cutting costs.

The principal task facing the members of the injured workers' movement is to confront these formidable challenges. The question is: How do they do it? To answer this question we face the issues of (1) remaking the injured workers' movement and (2) leadership and political education. And, for the purposes of this chapter, we look not only to the role of oral history as a political dynamic between the principal participants but also to the larger role of "history" in the political education of injured workers. Or, to put it within the framework of this collection, we ask: How has research into the condition and history of injured workers been used to engage them?

As a first response to these questions it is important to note the arguments oral historians make regarding the relationship between oral history and advocacy, and the central, even inspirational, place of "history" in consciousness raising and political education. One of the more profound statements for this latter position originates in the Popular Memory Group at Birmingham's Centre for Contemporary Cultural Studies:

> History – in particular popular memory – is a stake in the constant struggle for hegemony [...] [A] sense of history [...] is one means by which an organic social group acquires knowledge of its collective struggles, and becomes capable of a wider transformative role in the society. It is the means by which we may become self-conscious about the formation of our own common-sense beliefs, those that we appropriate from our immediate social and cultural milieu. These beliefs have a history and are also produced in determinate processes. The point is to recover their "inventory," not in the manner of the folklorist who wants to preserve quaint ways for modernity, but in order that, their origin known, they may be *consciously* adopted, rejected or modified. In this way a popular historiography, especially, a history of the commonest forms of consciousness is a necessary aspect of the struggle for a better world.[30]

These thoughts find reinforcement in Michael Frisch's understanding of this relationship: "It is history [...] that can provide the basis for shared re-imagination of how the past connects to the present, and the possibilities this vantage suggests for the future."[31]

To be clear, these writers are not referring to a reading of "history" in general – although there is no reason to think that reading something about the First World War, for example, will not result in the reader making a personal or revelatory connection between what she/he reads and her/his own history. Rather, they are referring to the oral histories that are most akin to the experiences of the people, individuals, workers, and so on who are being studied/interviewed. In other words, according to the proponents of this view, the oral history process itself can generate awareness and new forms of consciousness about the themes and underlying processes being brought to light during the conversations. Linda Shopes, for example, writes that there is no inherent reason that oral histories should lead oral historians to rethink their assumptions, "but, as a person narrates a life story and as the account wends its way through the accumulated details of a life story, social categories are exploded: the subject becomes an actor in simultaneous, multiple roles that do not conform to easy generalizations."[32] Alessandro Portelli goes a step further when he writes that it is okay, even desirable, to "use the 'fact' of the interview as an opportunity to stimulate others, as well as ourselves, to a higher degree of self-scrutiny and self-awareness [...] Political work is for change and all of these changes are highly political."[33]

Some of the same claims are made with specific regard to oral history and occupational health and safety. In their study of dust disease in the British coal mining industry, Arthur McIvor and Ronald Johnston state that "oral history testimony illuminate[d] the intimate relationship between employment and the body, and connected to this, the many and varied ways those holding power in the workplace – the employers, managers and supervisors, exploited those lacking such powers." According to these authors, oral testimony also allowed them to identify the presence and persistence of an "individualistic, competitive, machismo work culture in the pits" that militated against achieving better working conditions.[34] But it is Suroopa Mukherjee who makes perhaps the most forceful claims for the importance of oral history within the realm of occupational health and safety. In a truly remarkable study that traces the efforts of women to gain recognition of, and compensation for, ill health and deaths in the wake of the industrial disaster in Bhophal, India, in December 1994, Mukherjee places oral history – the testimonials of these women – in a pivotal position in terms of "allowing them to participate in the recovery and reconstruction of their experience." This is a process, she states, that is "especially useful in recreating a traumatic experience, by using empathy and compassion to evoke subjective states of heart and mind."[35]

As Mukherjee describes the paths taken to hold accountable both the Indian state and Union Carbide (the American owner of the plant in Bhopal, where the lethal gas was emitted), she shows how the women struggled against powerful actors who adamantly rejected the responsibility for the "accident" and its tragic aftermath and who, in fact, worked diligently to shift culpability from "institutions to the individual." Indeed, Mukherjee argues that state and private interests worked assiduously hand-in-hand to discredit, marginalize, and erase any and all individuals or groups who believed they were to blame. According to Mukherjee, oral history became the vital mode of understanding how the "unprecedented levels of violence and suffering that [were] unleashed by the processes of marginalization and erasure [...] [affected] the day to day lives of ordinary people." Oral history performed this difficult but necessary task by "penetrat[ing] that all-important space where historical events link up with people's stories."[36] Phrased somewhat differently, for Mukherjee oral history opened up the possibilities for these women to develop and use their sociological imaginations, or their abilities to link their private troubles with public issues.

Pessimism of the Intellect, Optimism of the Will

These are large claims for the emancipatory powers of oral history. However, as with the assertions made by the Popular Memory Group – who, Lynn Abrams writes, were "under no illusions about the difficulties of translating oral history practice into popular consciousness and political change"[37] – Mukherjee is emphatic that

> simply bringing in the voices of the oppressed people is not enough to present social reality. That can happen only by shifting attention away from merely personal experience which is narrated as a good story [...] A big part of education is making connections. When connections are made people realize that what is happening is not an aberration but the rule. But political education has to change into political action [...] We realized that without collective pressure nobody was going to listen to us.[38]

Leaders within the injured workers' movement have always understood the personal and political value of stories.[39] In the early 1980s, a critical component of their strategies to oppose proposed changes to the Workmen's Compensation Act involved the appearance of injured workers before the Legislative Committee charged with shaping a "White Paper" into legislative form. One of these injured workers was Frank Figlia, the immigrant Italian construction worker whose testimony we heard above, who demanded the "right we earned, to live as a Canadian, with right and dignity." Figlia was not the only injured worker to appear before this committee. Gerbina DiMichele spoke despairingly of her compensation benefits being cut off because the board officials thought her injuries were all in her head. "Some of its in my head," DiMichele stated: "But, take a more active look [...] at this discrimination. Look at the proper rehabilitation [...] [and] retrain people in decent jobs rather than forcing us to knock on doors like beggars, or to treat us like welfare cases, which we are not." According to Rosario Agosta, committee members could "never believe how an injured worker can feel to be out of the workforce. You feel destroyed by society, you feel like nothing in the family. The wife has to shoulder everything and run the house. The children, they have to stop school to help the family. So, everybody gets nervous."[40]

While it is not known for certain, it is highly likely that Figlia, DiMichele, and Agosta were among the more than three thousand injured workers and supporters who, on 1 June 1983, forced a meeting of this standing committee to move down the street, from its usual government-building meeting room to the grounds of Queen's Park. Once there, committee members were obliged to listen to the injured workers and their supporters into the afternoon as they aired their grievances and offered their suggestions for change.[41]

So there is a history of injured worker testimonials appearing before government and workers' compensation officialdom. There is also a history – echoing Mukherjee's admonition, "we realized that without collective pressure nobody was going to listen to us" – of injured workers having to make themselves visible. According to Phil Biggin, the president of the Union of Injured Workers for most of its thirty-odd years of existence, injured workers would not have achieved anything had they not been constantly standing in front of, and sometimes going into, the legislature and the building that housed the Ministry of Labour or protesting on the sidewalk in front of the Workers' Compensation Board headquarters in downtown Toronto.[42] It is this history that is presently an integral part of the political education being offered to injured workers. And it is here, finally, that we can situate the oral histories of the injured workers undertaken by the Injured Workers' History Project (IWHP).

Begun ten years ago, the research for this project was quickly brought under the guidance of a committee composed of injured workers, injured worker advocates from two legal aid clinics (which, since their inception in the 1970s, have specialized in helping injured workers with their compensations claims and appeals), and myself. There was an initial flurry of IWHP interviews with injured workers; however, as I was the only one among the group with any interviewing experience, the results of these interviews were mixed. A year or so later the IWHP became slightly more formalized when an injured worker, Sabrina Pacini, became a paid, part-time co-chair (I was the other co-chair) thanks to a successful Social Sciences and Humanities Research Council–Community University Research Alliance (CURA) application.

Carried out under the name Research Action Alliance on the Consequences of Work Injury (RAACWI), this injured worker–academic research collaboration evolved principally out of the frustration injured workers' movement leaders felt regarding what they perceived to be both a paucity of research on injured workers and the weaknesses and biases of existing research. Covering the themes of legislation, financial security, health and well-being, and history and political movements, injured workers and injured worker advocates worked alongside academics and institutionally based researchers on various studies. These focused, for example, on stigma; on how hurts can turn into harms through delays in treatment and decisions made on the basis of cutting costs; on how front-line Workers' Compensation Board employees perceive injured workers; on the impact of injury and disability on marriages and family/social life; and on poverty. Furthermore, under the auspices of the IWHP, we looked at issues, themes, and developments relating to the history of the injured workers' movement in Ontario.[43]

The IWHP has used the history it has collected – from oral histories to provincial government and Workers' Compensation Board archival records – in ways designed to promote the political education of injured workers. Before I gauge that impact, however, I must note the significant effects of "gatherin' a little knowledge" on leaders and long-time activists associated with the IWHP. Quite simply, these leaders and activists have been the key actors in taking the history being collected and fashioning it into forms that could be used for the education/mobilization of injured workers. To be sure, it is not the "history" alone that accounts for their activities over the course of the IWHP: their long-standing commitment to the struggles of injured workers is unquestionably the prime mover. However, their involvement in the items listed below suggests a heightened interest precipitated by the ongoing collection of new archival and secondary materials and, more important, at least for a couple of years, the oral history interviews they conducted with injured workers and the oral history interviews I conducted with them. As John McKinnon, an injured worker advocate, phrased it: "Playing with the theme 'their only power was moral,' I would say that our growing knowledge of history has reinforced the moral authority or our appreciation or analysis of the present day injustice."[44]

For each of the past seven years, these activists have been central to the creation and dissemination of IWHP "bulletins" that, in popular language, discuss and analyze current issues in both present and historical contexts. These bulletins have been widely disseminated in the injured worker and trade union communities and are posted on a website dedicated to promoting "better treatment for injured workers by their employers, governments, and workers' compensation systems."[45] In addition to the bulletins, the IWHP created a play using the actual words found in the 1910–13 Royal Commission into workmen's compensation headed by Ontario chief justice Sir William Meredith.[46] As it happened, the first performance of the play took place at the September 2008 founding conference of "Active History."[47] Over these years, the IWHP also developed a PowerPoint slideshow on the history of the injured workers' movement that I presented at meetings of injured workers and union conferences. Initially focused on the 1960s to the 1980s, the content and breadth of the slide show deepened and expanded on both sides of this period: at present, it stretches from the 1880s to the current day. As importantly, the slideshow entitled "Their Only Power Was Moral: A History of Injured Workers in Ontario, 1900-2010" has been transformed into a video and been shown at numerous injured worker and union meetings, forums, and conferences.

Both the play and the video are integral parts of a second major injured workers' initiative under RAACWI: the Injured Workers' Speakers School (IWSS). Two members of IWHP, Marion Endicott and Orlando Buonastella, both legal clinic injured worker advocates, along with Steve Mantis and Kate Lushington, have been the principal architects of the design and ongoing refinement of the IWSS. As Endicott writes:

> A number of years ago, principally at Orlando's initiative, we began an injured workers' history school at the clinic. The purpose of the school was to encourage the discouraged to become activists ("to go from venting to convincing") and to assist injured worker activists to become leaders [...] The main components of the course were: to learn the founding principles of what workers had won (in worker's compensation) and the social context of industrial/social unrest at the time (burgeoning socialism in this

> case); to understand the forces at work historically – the view of organized labour, the view of the manufacturers; to look at the purposes of the system; to see how they fared through time – looking at the ongoing thread of the contesting force of labour and capital with absolutely remarkable documents that we review together in the class that show the manufacturer view in its bold, anti-worker stance that persists almost unchanged through the decades.[48]

As Endicott writes, the history school was such a "big hit" with injured workers that, at the prodding of Steve Mantis, an injured worker activist in Thunder Bay, they added a speakers' course modelled after a "Toastmaster's" class he had taken. After presenting this a few times, Endicott continues, "the idea came of merging the two and we have been putting on this merged version for about four years":

> The flow of this merged course is to have both elements of history and speaking right from the start, but to be very loaded with the history at the beginning, with gradual increasing of speaking and reducing history, so that at the end it is almost purely speaking (with the history embedded in the speeches now!) [...] I should say that the speeches that this class develops are ones for injured workers to tell their own story and to do so in a way that makes an impact and which broadens it to make a point about the system itself in a compelling way.

According to Endicott, then, as with injured workers' groups formed over the past twenty years, the express purpose of the IWSS is to educate injured workers about the intricacies and the politics of the Workers' Compensation Board and the system as a whole, and to develop new activists and new leaders.

This is also how Orlando Buonastella understands its purpose. Remembering that the first course is the speakers' school modelled after Mantis's "Toastmaster's" class, Buonastella writes that the "second includes the history and principles of WC, the history of the injured workers' movement and how injured workers can work, fight and win by engaging in common activities for their interest. The purpose was not only to be able to speak about the self, but about the 'we'":

> They have seen the change that happens when they attend a meeting [...] They no longer feel isolated. They are amazed that it was

> not always so, that the way it is is not inevitable, that change is possible, that they do not have to feel awful about themselves, et cetera. They also like to laugh and re-discover the smile and the sense of humour they know they have.[49]

Buonastella's comment about the "we" is a particularly telling point that deserves some elaboration. Because workers' compensation claims are adjudicated on a case-by-case basis, with surprisingly little reference to precedent (except in claims and appeals that involve occupational diseases), injured workers, of necessity, become extremely knowledgable about how the many and convoluted aspects of the system apply to their claim. They learn – quickly – what materials are required and what they must say, even how to say it, if they want their claims to meet the known, and the ever-changing unknown, obstacles in the adjudication and appeals processes.

As the oral histories inform us, even for those who take the utmost care with their claims, there can be delays originating from other sources: for example, employers or doctors failing to file the necessary forms, a change in adjudicators, changes in physical or emotional-psychological conditions (requiring medical reassessment), the backlog of appeals hearings. Each of these possible points of delay further individuate what is already a profoundly individualizing experience. It is not surprising, therefore, that injured workers get discouraged, depressed, and, in most cases, focus almost exclusively on their own claims and their personal circumstances.

This is the state of mind of many injured workers when they finally come upon someone who can/will help them. They have, in most cases, been fighting the system alone, and, though they remain adamant that their accident and injury stories are truthful, their experiences with their employers, and especially the workers' compensation system, leave them despondent about their futures. This can be understood as pessimism of the intellect. As we can infer from the comments by Endicott and Buonastella above, moving injured workers from this pessimism of the intellect to an optimism of the will is the over-riding purpose of the courses, presentations, and protest rallies that they organize. In Gramscian terms, the course is a part of the educational/political process that moves injured workers along the path from "common" to "good sense" – from an "incoherent set of generally held assumptions and beliefs common to any given society" to "practical, empirical common sense, that is to say, common sense devoid of its contradictory, wayward elements and rendered into a systematic and coherent view."[50] As Gramsci writes:

> Critical understanding of self takes place [...] through a struggle of political "hegemonies" and of opposing directions, first in the ethical field and then in that of politics proper, in order to arrive at the working out at a higher level of one's own conception of reality. Consciousness of being part of a particular hegemonic force (that is to say, political consciousness) is the first stage towards a further progressive self-consciousness in which theory and practice will finally be one.[51]

In light of this, the question now becomes: Have these leaders, educators – "organic intellectuals," again in the Gramscian sense – been successful in shifting injured workers from "common" to "good" sense? A smaller question, albeit germane to the theme of this chapter, is as follows: If injured workers have travelled this path from "common" to "good" sense – from private troubles to public issues – what role, if any, has the "history" produced by the IWHP played?

Unlike Suroopa Mukherjee, I can make no firm claims that the oral histories carried out for this research have had any direct impact on the activism of individual injured workers. Nor can I, in the manner of Linda Shopes, recall any instance in which the account of an injured worker "exploded" social categories and she/he "became [an] actor in simultaneous, multiple roles that do not conform to easy generalizations." That said, through my ten-year engagement with the injured workers' movement, I, like Mukherjee and other researchers, have witnessed injured workers, whose oral histories we captured, become activists. And, during that time, I have also witnessed the "history" that they learned and that they are making become a significant component of their identities as injured workers – or, to put it in Mukherjee's terms, I have seen their personal needs and empowerment become linked with the cause of justice. This is certainly how Alice, who had a painful and debilitating repetitive strain injury from working for years in a poorly designed office environment, understood her continued participation in an injured workers' support group.

> ROBERT: Well, a final question, or we'll see where it goes. You've been through the system. You've fought it. In a sense have beaten it. At least you survived it. Why are you here? Why are you amongst this group of injured workers?

ALICE: That's a good question. I, I believe, first of all, I think because I've been through so much that ... I believe that injured workers really need a place to go, of support, so that they're not alone, so that they don't have to go through what I went through in isolation. What I went through, you know, not knowing. Like you said, "Why didn't you say anything to WSIB? Why didn't you say anything to your employer?" I didn't think I really, like, I really didn't know my rights, you know? ... It wasn't until I got together with the other injured workers. That one that, you know, she told me about the software. The other one who said, go back, sit at your desk, what are they going to do, kick you out? ... So it was through talking to these injured workers that, you know, why are each of us suffering in isolation, you know? We should be joining together because there's so many of us, you know? I go buy fruits at the vegetable stand, and the poor woman there, you know, doesn't hardly have, she needs all kinds of dental work, tells me her husband's, you know, out of a job because he's injured, you know? He's going through what I went through, you know? Like, we should not be going through this alone. That's why I'm here. Nobody should be going through this alone.[52]

Alice's "history" has many parallels among injured worker activists, both short and long term. Tom Noble, one of the latter, was injured in 1976 when a co-worker at Great Lakes Forging in Windsor hit him in the back with a steel bar that he was removing from an oven. "Broke two of my discs in my lower back," Noble stated: "He broke the L4, S1 and L5. Then I went back to work after that, on my own. I took a job for Hargreaves Security and I got hit on the highway, the expressway ... I got hit [while I was sitting in my truck] at eighty miles per hour. Rear-ended. Broke my neck and back. So, that ended the work."[53] After this second injury Noble got involved in the Windsor local of the Union of Injured Workers, at one point serving as its president. He became involved because "I knew that I wasn't alone in this ballgame, right. I can't play the game by myself. I had to ask other people to play."

There is more to Noble's activism than the realization that the struggle must be a collective one: he also had a historical, legal, political analysis. Two or three years prior to our interview, he was in Hamilton undergoing a medical reassessment ordered by the Workers'

Compensation Board. During the two months that he was there he learned about Sir William Meredith. Noble told me:

> You've got to understand the Board was set up by Meredith. Nineteen fourteen. They've got to go back to that situation and start understanding. Take care of the injured worker. Their job is to take care of the injured worker. Meredith, and that was law back then, and it should be law today. Because, you know, that went to court [...] Workers give up the rights of suing the plant, of suing them. They gave up those rights to get fair compensation, and this and that.

Sir William Meredith's role in the fashioning of Ontario's first "modern" workers' compensation law is far from common knowledge. It is, however, part of the curriculum of the course given in the IWSS. It is also part of Karl Crevar's extensive knowledge about workers' compensation. Crevar is a resident of Hamilton and a long-time president of the Ontario Network of Injured Workers Groups (ONIWG). When Noble was in Hamilton for his medical reassessment, he learned about Meredith in conversations with Crevar. On the topic of injured workers giving up their right to sue their employer in exchange for compensation, Crevar lamented:

> People gave up the right to the courts in order to get fair compensation. That still has to apply today, you know? When you give up your rights, that still has to apply today. You've given up your rights to go and sue your employer in exchange for fair compensation. What's happened over the years, and it's been proven, where you've had Royal Commissions that have reviewed, you know, up-to-date kind of stuff, what's really happening to workers, are they being fairly compensated or not? In two occasions that I know, the last two Royal Commissions [...] concluded that changes were needed to increase benefits, not to decrease. They saw something happening that shouldn't have been happening, and they said, "Hey, these are our recommendations." So, what you've seen is a wholesale shift from what it was originally designed to do, that being comp, during Meredith's time.[54]

As a long-time injured worker activist, Crevar's familiarity with Meredith is not recent. However, Crevar's understanding of Meredith's role has deepened through his attending the course offered by IWSS. Such knowledge of the history of injured workers has also encouraged Alan Noel, a union health and safety and workers' compensation activist, to make things better by "being proactive and making our voices heard." According to him, "We've got to be jumping up and screaming because we're getting screwed." Noel, who had experienced an IWSS presentation two years before his interview, was adamant:

> I think the message is really important, and I think injured workers, not just injured workers that aren't working any more, but injured workers that are working, they should know their roots, and they should know what's happened through the years, and it's really important [...] I've read a lot of the history of injured workers and what's happened, but a lot of people don't associate that there's a whole bunch of people out there that have been screwed and know how they got there, you know, as far as injured workers in the province.[55]

Conclusion

At a recent injured workers meeting there was some discussion of what each of us was doing. My response was that I was working on an article on injured workers and political education and leadership. After I offered the title of the article – this chapter – an injured worker retorted: "It is more like from pessimism to optimism to pessimism." While reflective of her particularly difficult situation, there is no question that these are extremely hard times for injured workers in Ontario – and, by all accounts, in other provinces, states, and elsewhere around the world. The rise and consolidation of neoliberalism has emboldened employers – capital – not only to take back past gains but also to change the paradigm from injured workers' rights, to compensation benefits, to benefits only to those who are deemed to be sufficiently deserving. This is tantamount to the welfarization of workers' compensation – a status that injured workers have refused since Sir William Meredith's time. The very recent appointment of Conservative MPP Elizabeth Witmer as the new chair of the Workplace Safety and Insurance Board is a telling sign of what troubles injured workers about the current system. As minister of labour in the Mike Harris Conservative government, Witmer was responsible for introducing and overseeing the passage of Bill 99 through the legislature. As mentioned briefly earlier,

Bill 99 not only changed the name of the act but also cut benefits, privatized rehabilitation services, lowered employer assessment rates, provided substantial financial rebates to employers with supposedly good health and safety records, and, in a number of other ways, went about preparing the path to the privatization of the entire workers' compensation system. It is not surprising then that injured workers saw her appointment by the ruling Liberal government as indicative of a renewed disdain for them.

There are no easy words that will alleviate the concerns of injured workers. Nor are there any quick fixes. But, as I outline earlier in this chapter, injured workers have been here before. In the 1960s and early 1970s most injured workers suffered their conditions within the private confines of their own homes. By the mid-1970s, with the UIW established and making its presence felt on the streets of Toronto and other Ontario cities, that situation had been transformed. Through their actions, they forced the Workmen's Compensation Board to open the files of injured workers so that they could know what was being said and written about them by compensation board officials and doctors. In the mid-1980s they defeated government plans to eliminate life-time pensions for workers with permanent disabilities; they won an annual cost-of-living increase; and they secured the establishment of an independent appeals tribunal.[56]

I was not a part of this birth and evolution of the injured workers' movement. However, the knowledge gathered from this research project has brought its history out of the past. In this way it addresses Terry Eagleton's mournful observation that "the absence of memories of collective, and effective, political action [...] has warped so many contemporary cultural ideas out of shape. There is a historical vortex at the centre of our thought which drags it out true." More specifically, this "gathering of a little knowledge," as Portelli phrases it,[57] now stretches back to Sir William Meredith's time, and injured workers are increasingly aware that he believed that they needed to be treated "fairly" – that full justice, "not half measures," needed to be ensured via the law.[58]

This is how this research engages with injured workers. It enables them, simultaneously, to uncover, learn, and use their history to, in Orlando Buonastella's words, contest the official and dominant discourses whose purpose it is to demonize and erase them.[59] They are engaging in the remaking of the injured workers' movement, and, in so doing, they are becoming – have become – a hybrid of what Linda Shopes calls "citizens-scholars-activists," that is, individuals who, by virtue of their activism "in a community over a period of time [...,] have the opportunities to develop networks, the political insights, the credibility that may enable [...] research to be useful in a process of social change."[60] They are, in Gramsci's words, "organic intellectuals" in the making.[61]

If this is indeed what is taking place, it is a significant development in the history of the injured workers' movement. During the rise and growth of the injured workers' movement in the 1970s and 1980s, most of its "members" and active participants were overwhelmingly recent immigrant male construction and industrial workers of Italian and southern European descent. There was a specific conjuncture that made this configuration understandable. During the postwar economic boom, these men, when they arrived in Canada, were channelled into the most hazardous and dangerous sectors and industries – concurrently the epicentres of an accelerating number of accidents and injuries and incubators for a host of occupational diseases. This was also the time, of course, of widespread social upheaval, exemplified in the emerging women's, anti-racist, environmental, and student and anti-war movements. It was a complex and volatile mix, and, as we are now aware, it was also the moment when economic and political elites in advanced capitalist countries began to coalesce under the banner of neoliberalism to devise strategies that would, over the next two decades, turn workplaces upside down in terms of their technical and social relations, all the while continuing to injure and kill workers at alarming rates.

While the numbers of injured workers today are unsettlingly similar to those of the 1960s and 1970s, the injured worker is not. Next to the male Italian and Portuguese construction worker we find the female Chinese textile or restaurant worker, the Iranian schoolteacher, the Mexican or Jamaican farm worker. In short, the demographics are dramatically different. More significantly for injured worker leaders, so are the backgrounds, understandings, beliefs, opinions, experiences, hopes, and dreams of these women and men who have been injured, as were those before them, "through no fault of their own."

The oral histories give life to these differences. But they also reveal what needs to be done, which can be assessed through asking the following question: What level of analysis can address this multiplicity of issues and individual circumstance? One response would be – and it is not designed to avoid the question – that the content will evolve out of the dialectic between leadership and membership. Marx writes: "Theory is capable of gripping the masses as soon as it demonstrates *ad hominem*, and it demonstrates *ad hominem* as soon as it becomes radical. To be radical is to grasp the root of the matter."[62] The theory that demonstrates ad hominem with regard to the injured workers' movement will need to be broader than it was in earlier periods. As we have just outlined, capitalist forms of production have changed, calling forth different workers with different kinds of injuries. Moreover, the theory – and practice – will have to incorporate the material and the cultural as expressed in the bridging of the lived realities of class, gender, and race. In saying this, injured workers' movement leaders should not, as is the academic fashion, invoke the holy trinity and then proceed to omit "class." In important respects, class is the common denominator when analyzing the system of workers' compensation. As Grant Duncan writes, "Workers' compensation is an instrument of government, serving the economic and political objectives of minimizing a cause of industrial conflict and maximizing capital accumulation, while simultaneously managing the conduct of the injured worker."[63]

Radical theory in this moment is a theory that highlights the links between private troubles and public issues within class and across gender and race. As John Sanbonmatsu writes: "Today our task is more difficult: we must show how perceptual structures make the various structures of *power* as such comprehensible. *Our task is to reveal the workings of capitalism*, but also to disocclude the structures of racist consciousness and to bring to light the occluded, naturalized habitus, or structuring structures, of patriarchy and so on."[64]

These are large tasks for the present and future leaders of the injured workers' movement, tasks that theorists of "postmodern" social movements have consciously eschewed but that we must theoretically and practically entertain. As David Harvey writes, "the net effect" of the theoretical fragmentation that has accompanied postmodern theory and identity politics has been to "limit our vision of the possible."[65] It has also, according to Harvey, instilled fears of personal and collective change. "No one," Harvey states, "can hope to change the world without changing themselves."[66] But where, he asks, in this day "in which routine, by virtue of its comfort and security, can mask the ways in which the jarring prospects of transformative change must be in the long run confronted," is the courage of our minds to come from? His answer:

> The lesson is clear: until we [...] know the courage of our minds and are prepared to take an equally speculative plunge into some

> unknown, we too will continue to be the objects of historical geography [...] rather than active subjects, consciously pushing human possibilities to their limits. What Marx called "the real movement" that will abolish "the existing state of things" is always there for the making and for the taking. That is what gaining the courage of our minds is all about.[67]

Injured workers are gaining the courage of their minds even as I write.

Notes

1 Antonio Gramsci, *Letters from Prison*, ed. Frank Rosengarten (New York: Columbia University Press, 1994), 1: 299.

2 According to Rosengarten, Gramsci adopted this phrase from Romain Rolland, who had written, "What I especially love in [Raymond] Lefebvre is this intimate alliance – which for me makes the true man – of pessimism of the intelligence, which penetrates every illusion, and optimism of the will." See Gramsci, *Letters from Prison*, 300. "Pessimism of the intelligence, optimism of the will" was also employed as the masthead for *L'Ordine Nuovo,* a socialist weekly that Gramsci helped found in Turin in 1919.

3 There are a great many books on Gramsci, a testament to his widespread influence. One of the better collections of his writings can be found in David Forgacs, ed., *The Antonio Gramsci Reader: Selected Writings, 1916–1935* (New York: New York University Press, 1999). See also Quintin Hoare and Geoffrey Nowel Smith, *Selections from the Prison Notebooks of Antonio Gramsci* (New York: International Publishers, 1971). On Gramsci's political theory, see Peter D. Thomas, *The Gramscian Moment: Philosophy, Hegemony and Marxism* (Haymarket Books: Chicago, 2009). For a sustained attempt to apply Gramsci's ideas to the Canadian context, see Ian McKay, "Canada as a Long Liberal Revolution: On Writing the History of Actually Existing Canadian Liberalisms, 1840s-1940s," in *Liberalism and Hegemony: Debating the Canadian Liberal Revolution,* ed. Jean-Francois Constant and Michel Ducharme, 347–452 (Toronto: University of Toronto Press, 2009).

4 Dominick LaCapra, *Writing History, Writing Trauma* (Baltimore: Johns Hopkins University Press, 2001), 41. See also Jeffrey C. Alexander, *Trauma: A Social Theory* (Cambridge: Polity Press, 2012).

5 This phrase is used a number of times throughout the chapter. It is taken from C. Wright Mills, *The Sociological Imagination* (Oxford: Oxford University Press, 1999).

6 Doug Cowles, interviewed by author, 19 October 2009.

7 Ibid.

8 Ibid.

9 Charles E. Reasons, Lois L. Ross, and Craig Paterson, *Assault on the Worker: Occupational Health and Safety in Canada* (Toronto: Butterworths, 1981).

10 Harry S. Shannon and Graham S. Lowe, "How Many Injured Workers Do Not File Claims for Workers' Compensation Benefits?" *American Journal of Industrial Medicine* 42 (2002): 467–73; Lenore S. Azaroff, Michael B. Lax, Charles Levenstein, and David H. Wagman, "Wounding the Messenger: The New Economy Makes Occupational Health Indicators Too Good to Be True," *International Journal of Health Services* 34, 2 (2004): 271–303.

11 Wayne Lewchuk, Marlea Clarke, and Alice de Wolfe, *Working without Commitments: The Health Effects of Precarious Employment* (Montreal and Kingston: McGill-Queen's University Press, 2011). A classic sociological statement on the effects of the job outside the workplace is Martin Meissner's "The Long Arm of the Job: A Study of Work and Leisure," *Industrial Relations* 10, 3 (1971): 239–60.

12 We do not have research on this topic for Canada. For a more general accounting, see Michael Quinlan and Claire Mayhew, "Precarious Employment and Workers' Compensation," *International Journal of Law and Psychiatry* 22, 5–6 (1999): 491–520.

13 David Harvey, "The Body as an Accumulation Strategy," *Environment and Planning D: Society and Space* 16, 4 (1988): 401–21. See also Carol Wolkowitz, *Bodies at Work* (London: Sage, 2006).

14 Michael Ladouceur, interviewed by author, 8 July 2009.

15 Suroopa Mukherjee, *Surviving Bhopal: Dancing Bodies, Written Texts, and Oral Testimonials of Women in the Wake of an Industrial Disaster* (New York: Palgrave, 2010), 7.

16 Eric Tucker, *Administering Danger in the Workplace: The Law and Politics of Occupational Health and Safety in Ontario, 1850–1914* (Toronto: University of Toronto Press, 1990).

17 Richard C.B. Risk, "'This Nuisance of Legislation': The Origins of Workers' Compensation in Ontario," in *Essays In The History of Canadian Law*, vol. 2, ed. D.H. Flaherty, 418–91 (Toronto: University of Toronto Press, 1981); Michael Piva, "The Workmen's Compensation Movement in Ontario," *Ontario History*, 67 (1975): 39–56; Eric Tucker, "The Law of Employers' Liability in Ontario: The Search for a Theory," *Osgoode Hall Law Journal* 22, 2 (1981): 212–80.

18 Eunice Lucas, interviewed by author, 7 July 2009.

19 Ellen MacEachen, Sue Ferrier, Agnieszka Kosny, and Lori Chambers, "A Deliberation on 'Hurt versus Harm' Logic in Early-Return-to-Work Policy," *Policy and Practice in Health and Safety* 5, 2 (2007): 41–62.

20 Lucas interview.

21 "Cathy," interviewed by author, 13 September 2004. "Cathy" is a pseudonym.

22 Ibid.

23 Another meaning can be found in the violence that often characterizes relations between workers and managements and the state (e.g., when police are brought in to tame picket lines or enforce court rulings). For two analyses of this type of violence, see Reinhold Kramer and Tom Mitchell, *When the State Trembled: How A. J. Andrews and the Citizen's Committee Broke the Winnipeg General Strike* (Toronto: University of Toronto Press, 2010); and Scott Thorn, "Violence and Capital: Workers' Self-Defence and the War at Giant Mine" (MA thesis, McMaster University, 2011).

24 Lee Strunin and Leslie I. Bodin, "The Workers' Compensation System: Friend or Foe?" *American Journal of Industrial Medicine* 45 (2004): 338–45; Katherine Lippel, "Workers Describe the Effect of the Workers' Compensation Process on Their Health: A Quebec Study," *International Journal of Law and Psychiatry* 30, 4–5 (2007): 427–43.

25 Quoted in John Deverell, "Give Us a Future, Injured Workers Plead," *Toronto Star*, 23 September 1982.

26 For a delineation of the controversies surrounding leadership and political education, see Colin Barker, Alan Johnson, and Michael Lavalette, "Leadership Matters: An Introduction," in *Leadership and Social Movements*, ed. Colin Barker, Alan Johnson, and Michael Lavalette, 1–23 (Manchester: Manchester University Press, 2001). See also John Sonbanmatsu, *The Postmodern Prince: Critical Theory, Left Strategy, and the Making of a New Political Subject* (New York: Monthly Review Press, 2004).

27 Each of these points refers to the differing orientations of the dominant social movement theories. For applications and innovations useful to the study of the injured workers' movement, see Doug McAdam, Sidney Tarrow, and Charles Tilly, *Dynamics of Contention* (Cambridge: Cambridge University Press, 2001); Sidney Tarrow, *Power in Movement: Social Movements and Contentious Politics* (Cambridge: Cambridge University Press, 2011); Deborah B. Gould, *Moving Politics: Emotion and ACT UP's Fight against Aids* (Chicago: Chicago University Press, 2009); Alf Gunvald Nilsen, "'The Authors and the Actors of Their Own Drama': Towards a Marxist Theory of Social Movements," *Capital and Class* 33, 99 (2009): 109–39.

28 Belinda Robnett, *How Long How Long? African-American Women in the Struggle for Civil Rights* (New York: Oxford University Press, 1997).

29 George Lukas, *History and Class Consciousness: Studies in Marxist Dialectics* (London: Merlin Press, 1971), 322.

30 Quoted in Lynn Abrams, *Oral History Theory* (London: Routledge, 2010), 157–58 (emphasis in original).

31 Ibid., 167.

32 Karen Olson and Linda Shopes, "Crossing Boundaries, Building Bridges: Doing Oral History among Working-Class Women and Men," in *Women's Words: The Feminist Practice of Oral History*, ed. Sherna Berger Gluck and Daphne Patai (New York: Routledge, 1991), 193.

33 Alessandro Portelli, "Research as an Experiment in Equality," in *The Death of Luigi Trastulli and Other Stories: Form and Meaning in Oral History* (Albany: State University of New York Press, 1991), 44.

34 Arthur McIvor and Ronald Johnston, *Miners' Lung: A History of Dust Disease in British Coal Mining* (Aldershot: Ashgate, 2007): 13–14. For oral histories of the dangers of work as experienced by workers and felt by family members, see Mike Heffernan, *Rig: An Oral History of the Ocean Ranger Disaster* (St. John's: Creative Publishers, 2009); Carol A.B. Giesen, *Coal Miners' Wives: Portraits of Endurance* (Lexington: University Press of Kentucky, 1995); Svetlana Alexievich, *Voices from Chernobyl* (New York: Picador, 2006).

35 Mukherjee, *Surviving Bhopal*, 8.

36 Ibid., 114.

37 Abrams, *Oral History Theory*, 158.

38 Mukherjee, *Surviving Bhopal*, 115. For other examples of how political education transformed the lives of those involved, see Kathleen M. Coll, *Remaking Citizenship: Latina Immigrants and New American Politics* (Stanford: Stanford University Press, 2010); Serena Cosgrove, *Leadership from the Margins: Women and Civil Society Organizations in Argentina, Chile, and El Salvador* (New Brunswick: Rutgers University Press, 2010).

39 For theoretical treatments of stories and storytelling, see Shari Stone-Mediatore, *Reading across Borders: Storytelling and Knowledges of Resistance* (New York: Palgrave, 2003); Francesca Polletta, *It Was Like a Fever: Storytelling in Protest and Politics* (Chicago: University of Chicago Press, 2006).

40 Ibid.

41 Robert Storey, "'Their Only Power Was Moral:' The Injured Workers' Movement in Toronto, 1970–1985," *Histoire Sociale/Social History* 41, 81 (2008): 99–131.

42 Phil Biggin, interviewed by author, 14 August 2003.

43 For a listing of the activities and projects associated with RAACWI, see the website at www.consequencesofworkinjury.ca.

44 John McKinnon, correspondence with author, 22 October 2012.

45 The bulletins can be found on the RAACWI website. They can also be found at www.injuredworkersonline.org.

46 Sir William Meredith's Royal Commission ended with his drafting a workmen's compensation act that, while vehemently opposed by representatives of the Canadian Manufacturers' Association, nevertheless was passed into law almost intact. Meredith's *Final Report,* published 31 October 1913, was a firm statement and defence of his findings and recommendations. The bases of his findings have, over time, crystallized into the "Meredith Principles" with, not surprisingly, different groups having quite divergent interpretations of what the principles are and what they mean. Injured worker groups are in the initial stages of planning an international conference on the state of workers' compensation, the start date of which will coincide with the hundredth anniversary of the publication of Meredith's *Final Report.*

47 Information on Active History can be found at www.activehistory.ca.

48 Marion Endicott to Orlando Buonastella, 3 March 2012.

49 Orlando Buonastella, communication with author, 25 May 2012.

50 Quoted in Peter Mayo, *Gramsci, Freire and Adult Education: Possibilities for Transformative Action* (London: Zed Books, 1999), 52. While Buonastella, Endicott, and Mantis consciously developed the history of workers' compensation course, it is fair to say that the students' enthusiasm for the "history" part of the course was, initially, somewhat surprising. Inadvertently, they found what other adult educators have found: that, in C. Wright Mills' terms, linking personal biography with related larger social/political issues is a crucial component of the process of politicization. See Mills, *Sociological Imagination;* see also Coll, *Remaking Citizenship.*

51 Hoare and Smith, *Selections*, 333.

52 "Alice" interview.

53 Thomas Noble, interviewed by author, 7 July 2009.

54 Karl Crevar, interviewed by author, 8 September 2009.

55 Alan Noel, interviewed by Sabrina Pacini, 11 October 2005.

56 For an analysis of this period, see Storey, "Their Only Power"; Robert Storey, "Social Assistance or a Workers' Right: Workmen's Compensation and the Struggle of Injured Workers in Ontario, 1970–1985," *Studies in Political Economy* 78 (2006): 67–91.

57 Alessandro Portelli, *The Battle of Valle Giulia: Oral History and the Art of Dialogue* (Madison: University of Wisconsin Press, 1997).

58 Sir William Meredith, *Final Report on Laws relating to the liability of employers to make compensation to their employees for injuries received in the course of*

their employment which are in force in other countries, and as to how far such laws are found to work satisfactorily (Toronto, 1913).

59 Over the past few years some small measure of change was made within the WSIB regarding its role in stigmatizing injured workers. However, those changes were achieved with a senior administration that was perceived to be more sympathetic than the present one. Hence, it remains to be seen what will happen with the proposed changes in form and attitudes. For an analysis of the "demonization" of the British working class along similar lines, see Owen Jones, *Chavs: The Demonization of the British Working Class* (London: Verso, 2011).

60 Shopes, "Crossing Boundaries," 201.

61 For a good analysis of this concept and how it relates to the role of intellectuals more generally, see Thomas, *Gramscian Moment*, 385–436.

62 Karl Marx, *A Contribution to the Critique of Hegel's Philosophy of Right*, ed., Joseph O'Malley (Cambridge: Cambridge University Press, 1970), at www.marxists.org/archive/marx/works/1843/critique-hpr/intro.htm.

63 Grant Duncan, "Workers' Compensation and the Governance of Pain," *Economy and Society* 32, 3 (2003): 454.

64 Sonbanmatsu, *Postmodern Prince*, 199 (emphasis in original).

65 David Harvey, *Spaces of Hope* (Berkeley: University of California Press, 2000), 237.

66 Ibid., 235.

67 Ibid., 255.

3 | The Ethics of Learning from Rwandan Survivor Communities

Critical Reflexivity and the Politics of Knowledge Production in Genocide Education

LISA TAYLOR | UMWALI SOLLANGE | MARIE-JOLIE RWIGEMA

This chapter traces some of the key tensions and questions at stake when history, human rights, and global citizenship education seek to "learn from" the diverse forms of knowledge and collective memory (including testimony) of genocide survivor communities.[1] We are particularly interested in the ethical implications and epistemic challenges that occur when schools and survivor and stakeholder communities seek to build relationships of reciprocity and meaningful collaboration in the teaching and study of the 1994 Rwandan genocide against the Tutsis.[2]

The discussion below responds to one of this collection's main concerns: we live in an "age of testimony,"[3] and yet the aspirations implicit in testimony's articulation and study – documenting atrocities, holding perpetrators accountable, provoking practices of witnessing, and coming to terms that might bear upon our conduct as collective inheritors, thus galvanizing responses that might bring an end to such violence – remain unattained and increasingly uncertain. Questions of representation become increasingly salient in an era characterized by a crisis of witnessing,[4] "second-hand witnessing,"[5] and "post-memory."[6] In our digitally connected global village, we increasingly find ourselves witnesses not to the original violence but, rather, to the witness's testimonial account or popular, literary, or journalistic representations. We believe that questions of representation and mediation raise particular ethical and pedagogical challenges that are of interest to education pertaining to the 1994 Rwandan genocide: they demand that we examine the ways in which testimony is framed and used within genocide education. In pedagogical terms, we believe the crisis in witnessing demands that educators develop pedagogies designed to support students in learning from an expanded range of testimonial sources through embodied, reflexive, and critical engagement.[7]

Our research takes an approach to the study of genocide that frames testimony within relationships that involve partnership, accountability, and reciprocity with survivor communities. This interest arises from a feminist, anti-colonial, and postcolonial understanding that processes of knowledge construction – of documenting, representing, studying, and teaching about genocide – are not separate from but, rather, integral to the historical power relations that foster the conditions of genocide. In other words, historians or students of history are never objective, neutral, or outside these power relations: they are separate from neither the object of study nor the institutional processes of constructing and defining that object within larger knowledge formations of academic or popular history. In our research, we assume that studying and teaching about genocide participates in a larger process of *narration* that positions different knowers and knowledge traditions within a hierarchy that establishes epistemic validity and academic authority. As Edward Said argues, "The power to narrate, or to block other narratives from forming or emerging, is very important to culture and imperialism, and constitutes one of the main connections between them."[8] Said's and other postcolonial theorists' critiques have launched an ongoing debate within historiography concerning what has been a predominantly Eurocentric narration of world history, which, Robert Young argues, silences or reduces and commodifies incommensurable indigenous epistemologies.[9] This Eurocentrism takes many forms, including the "intellectual colonialism" identified by Cynthia Callison in Western historiography's implicit cultural evolutionism, which defines literacy as a measure of civilization and denies the validity of oral history.[10] Spivak uses the term "epistemic violence" to refer to the hierarchies of knowledge and speakers that have been established by colonialism and that have functioned to set the differential terms on which colonized speakers can even be heard.[11]

It is a central premise of our research, then, that studying and teaching about the Rwandan genocide are inseparable from larger academic processes of narrating the genocide and from the ongoing colonial power relationship between Eurocentric and African knowledge traditions and knowers. While there is a growing body of work that examines the racialized and imperial power relations that construct hierarchies of authority between differently positioned speakers within the fields of Rwandan genocide commemoration and cultural representation (including reportage, documentaries, films, novels, theatre, and visual art),[12] this critical assessment has yet to extend itself to the examination of academic production and education.

These concerns inform our central questions: What kinds of power relations inform knowledge construction (specifically, the construction of authority and expertise) within educational initiatives whose aim is to learn from contested histories and communal memories of mass atrocity framed within a larger project of human rights, civic, and global education?[13] Simply put, who articulates the lessons of the 1994 Rwandan genocide and how does this happen? How are key stakeholders – particularly survivor communities – positioned in this process? How are diverse shared forms of knowledge that have been shaped through histories of trauma and genocide (e.g., oral history, music, literature, and artistic or healing practices as well as academic study within survivor communities) produced, represented, and engaged as objects of study? How is such knowledge shaped by institutional processes of selecting, organizing, publishing, and teaching curriculum, by curricular goals and the presumed normative student of human rights and/or peace education? In other words, what are the ethics of studying accounts of the suffering of others as a vehicle for developing what is constructed as "global citizenship"?[14] How do curricular choices address and position learners, structure particular relationships to the people/events being studied, and condition orientations towards listening and learning?[15] More urgently, what resources and exercises might support teachers in practising critical reflexivity and judgment in curriculum selection, development, and pedagogy in ways that centre the communities of expertise and multidisciplinary memory of Rwandan Canadians? What approaches might build accountable, action-oriented, and responsive relationships with survivor communities? These questions sketch the dimensions of the task before us as educators: it is the task of learning from diverse "ways of knowing" and practices of commemoration in such a way as to build a "transactional public sphere."[16]

This concern for issues of representation and authority – the politics of knowledge production within genocide studies and education – has direct implications for our own research, which seeks to shift the terms on which Rwandan survivor communities are included in genocide studies and education. We first describe this project and then draw out these implications.

We are in the early stages of a participatory action research project in community-led curriculum development for a ground-breaking Grade 11 world studies course in genocide education entitled "Genocide and Crimes against Humanity."[17] This will involve gathering, systematizing, and analyzing diverse forms of knowledge and collective memory within Rwandan-Canadian communities – a process that will serve as the basis of meaningful community intervention and collaboration in teaching about the 1994 Rwandan genocide against the Tutsis. Specifically, the project aims to support Rwandan-Canadian communities and Toronto District School Board teachers in developing classroom resources and pedagogy for courses that examine the 1994 Rwandan genocide. Two central concerns drive our inquiry: first, we want to include key stakeholders as partners in developing curriculum in a way that is both equitable and accountable to the diverse communities served by schools; second, we want to examine how the fields of anti-racist/social justice education and genocide education might mutually refine and critically inform reflexive pedagogical practice.

We are currently engaged in the initial stage of the project and have developed a research and pedagogical framework for teachers who are also researchers. These researchers will collaborate with Rwandan community members to bring a range of community-produced resources into the classroom in ways that seek to learn *from* and not simply *about* survivors.[18] We have documented our development process and a series of teacher workshops in order to lay the groundwork for the next stage: researching, with teachers, the use of community-based resources and testimony in Grade 11 classrooms.

We have come to this project from very different positions of access and expertise. Umwali Sollange and Marie-Jolie Rwigema are members of the Rwandan community in Toronto and have been active as equity educators and organizers in community processes of healing and commemoration. In response to a growing body of academic and popular discourse (journalism, documentary and dramatic films, books, academic texts, conferences) about the 1994 Rwandan genocide produced largely by non-Rwandans, Sollange and Rwigema collaborated with several other Rwandan community members to create a documentary that situates/places the voices of Rwandan genocide survivors as central in articulating an experientially grounded analysis of the genocide, its effects, and the politics of knowledge production surrounding it.[19] This collaboration in community knowledge production extended to encompass a community-school partnership in genocide education through the inclusion of Lisa Taylor, who brought a history of practice in feminist anti-racist action research and anti-discriminatory pedagogies, the latter being specifically focused on pedagogies of witnessing and remembrance.

As feminist educators we see the process of creating a collaborative research design as a process of knowledge production – one that expresses the power dynamics of differential access and authority that we have identified as the heart of the challenge of genocide education.[20] We have documented this process through an auto-ethnographic investigation that analyzes transcriptions of meetings and journals that contain the reflections of individual researchers. In this chapter, then, we present one tool that we have developed as part of this process. It is an exercise in feminist-situated knowledge,[21] the aim of which is to take seriously the ways that colonial power relations always already structure our collaboration, unequally positioning each of us as knowers and speakers.[22] Specifically, we each examine the role, stakes, and aspirations of testimony as we have observed them in our own lives, and we assess how this shapes our approach to witnessing. This demands that we each articulate and situate the embodied experiential knowledge we bring from emotional, familial, community, cultural, and institutional traditions of knowing.[23] This exercise draws from feminist methodologies of "memory work"[24] as well as from indigenous research methodologies and oral history.[25] In particular, these traditions inform our methodological vigilance as we actively examine and work against gendered and racialized dichotomies that can be constructed between different categories of knowledge and knowers, categories that position differently located knowers either as holders of limited, local knowledge, feeling, or experience, or as masters of objective analysis and theory.[26] Thus, our project in this chapter is prescriptive. Our central object of inquiry – understanding and proposing interventions into the politics of knowledge production in genocide education – guides the auto-ethnographic study of our own processes of knowledge production as differentially positioned researchers.

In the three sections below, we bring three distinct voices into conversation, each of us writing not only from her disciplinary and embodied location as researcher and educator but also from a feminist tradition of self-location and critical reflexivity. Rwigema reflects on her experience as a witness to testimony in her family and community contexts, seeing these as forms of community healing, "a dialogue in the process of survival." She highlights the risks of commodifying testimony when survivors are peripheral to how their accounts are framed and used. She examines the learning initiated when survivors set the terms of listening, as evinced in her documentary *The Rwandan Genocide as Told by Its Historian-Survivors.*[27] Sollange considers testimonial practices that build collective, intergenerational memory. She compares the particular conditions of testimony and remembrance practices within survivor communities with the challenges of sharing testimony with outsiders who bring their own desires, imaginaries, and limited contextual knowledge to the interaction. This grounds her call for pedagogies to support critically reflexive, embodied learning that addresses the context and relationships involved in the act of listening. Taylor conducts a family archaeology of testimony as silence, leakages, and proxies in intergenerational relationships burdened with the legacies of historical violence and complicity. She argues that anti-racist and social justice pedagogies bring critical tools for taking stock, helping to prepare us for active practices of collective witnessing and inhabiting the relationships underpinning the unique event of testimony.

We present and analyze these conversations as pedagogical activities aimed at supporting educators and learners as they prepare to witness testimony across relationships structured by power and memory. We extrapolate from them some implications for curriculum and pedagogy that would be beneficial to students in Canadian schools who are seeking to learn from Rwandan-Canadian survivor communities in critically self-reflexive ways – ways that foster self-implication, relationship-building, and transformative remembrance.[28]

In Conversation: Marie-Jolie Rwigema

My Relationship to Testimony

Testimonies have been ever-present throughout my life. Although I do not remember the first moment in which I heard a "testimony," I do hold a living archive of testimony-memories in my mind and heart. Since my childhood, I've heard my mother's testimonies of surviving massacres directed against Tutsi in Rwanda in 1959. I've also heard her testimonies of her life as a refugee in Idi Amin's Uganda and our family's experience as refugees living in Ethiopia during Mengistu Haile Mariams's "Red Terror." In 1994, I remember my twelve-year-old self watching my mother as she watched the slaughter of her family and her people, aired through the nightly news on our television set in Vancouver. Since 1994, I've heard many testimonies about the genocide in people's homes and in more formal settings, such as annual commemoration events hosted by Rwandan community organizations in Vancouver and Toronto.

Today, I watch my mother continue to grieve and to channel her grief into song, prayer, and reaching out to others. Over the years, I've watched her encourage survivors to talk about what they saw and what they lived as a process of healing. In my own way, though differently positioned than my mother in Rwandan communities (she being an elder/mother figure and me being more of a "Canadian" young person), I have also been engaged in testimonial, commemorative community work. Initially, I was involved as a facilitator with Hope for Rwanda's Children Fund in a photo-voice project with young survivors in Kigali, Rwanda, in 2001. More recently, I've worked with testimony as the director of the documentary film *The Rwandan Genocide as Told by Its Historian-Survivors,*[29] and I am currently working with Umwali Sollange and Lisa Taylor in collaboration with TDSB teachers in an attempt to think through ways to teach about the Rwandan genocide in Toronto secondary schools. As part of my own process of grieving and making sense of the genocide and its impact on myself, friends, family, and community, I've also chosen to pursue a doctorate in social work and to take clinical training in therapeutic counselling as ways of enhancing my understanding and activism.

Problematic Uses of Testimony I Have Observed

In my understanding, testimony aims not only to communicate the experience of violence but also to change its conditions, including the power relationships that make violence possible (relationships that are in themselves a form of violence). This points to what emerges as a central issue in *The Rwandan Genocide as Told by Its Historian-Survivors*:[30] in this documentary, the survivors repeatedly problematize uses of testimony they have observed in the study and commemoration of the Rwandan genocide – uses that reinforce rather than transform racialized relations of power, expertise, and authority. Of greatest concern to these survivors are the patterns they have observed in research and commemoration in which different groups are positioned as the testifier (the one embodying and expressing lived experience of suffering) or as the expert (the one analyzing and theorizing the other's experience of suffering, and then making recommendations to decision makers).

In the above documentary Ntare Sharangabo argues, for example, that survivors are constantly "pushed back to the element of emotion," as if they have no intellect.[31] Similarly, Karera maintains that this relegation of survivors to the non-academic realm of emotion constitutes a "colonial continuity" in which "Africans have never been considered historians, intellectuals, politicians" or individuals with any type of agency.[32] Post- and anti-colonial theorists argue that the use of testimony and story within colonial processes of knowledge production reproduces and reifies Africans as embodied sufferers[33] – sufferers whose testimony is used by non-African experts (positioned as intellectual, expert, saviour, and decision maker) to fight/argue/legislate for democracy/justice/social change on the former's behalf. According to Rwililiza, a translator in Jean Hatzfeld's edited volumes on survivors and perpetrators in Rwanda, the impact of this is to marginalize the knowledge and role of survivors in post-conflict projects:

> I see today that there is an uneasiness in talking about the survivors, even among Rwandans, even among Tutsis. I think that everyone would like the survivors to relinquish the genocide, in a way. As if people wanted them to leave the task of dealing with it to others, who have never been in direct danger of being sliced up by a machete. As if we were from now on somewhat superfluous [...] We survivors, we are growing more like strangers in our own land – which we have never left – than all the foreigners and expatriates who consider us so anxiously.[34]

To some extent, Rwililiza may be referring to the discomfort felt by Rwandans and others when encountering the "disturbing memory" embodied by survivors, a memory they would prefer to forget.[35] Regardless of intention, the consequence of this silencing is that it is non-survivors who assume the tasks of "dealing with" the genocide: this includes making sense of the genocide; extrapolating the implications of this analysis for projects of justice, reconciliation, commemoration, and healing; and drawing lessons for future generations.

These analyses imply that the failure of testimony is rooted in the reality that those who are most likely to be violated as subjects of mass violence are structurally those least likely to have access to "voice,"[36] to the institutional authority and resources to transform the systems unjustly affecting them. Simply stated, physical violence operates hand in hand with epistemic violence. These survivors provide a grave critique of testimonial practices that prescribe the survivor's role solely as providing evidence: what is eclipsed in such practices is the fact that survivors are often also intellectuals, historians, politicians, and knowledge producers who are interested in sharing much more than their trauma – that is, they are interested in "doing" knowledge, not simply in sharing it.[37]

This is a vital insight to bring to the study of the Rwandan genocide, an area in which, as Hron argues, the field of experts (especially academic knowledge producers) is dominated by non-Rwandans.[38] When Rwandans appear often as witnesses but rarely as authors/filmmakers there is a real risk that testimony may become an emotional commodity provided by the racialized survivor of violence for use in the academic and non-profit marketplace.[39] It provides the expert (academic, humanitarian worker, author, filmmaker) with moral and intellectual authority,[40] "cultural introspection and self-invention,"[41] and often economic rewards while, paradoxically, silencing and disempowering the survivor.[42] This process has been described as the "theft of pain,"[43] "epistemic violence,"[44] "producing speechlessness,"[45] "silencing the Other,"[46] and the "spectacle of the dead African body."[47] Theorists such as Heike Härting argue that current representational practices regarding the Rwandan genocide are "complicit in the reproduction of humanitarianist capital":[48] in the growing economy of humanitarianism, good will cannot blind us to clear-eyed questions of who benefits and how.

Potential for Productive, Ethical Uses of Testimony

In my own experience, the process of creating the documentary *The Rwandan Genocide as Told by Its Historian-Survivors* (hereafter *Rwandan Genocide*) offers an exemplary case of using testimony in ethical, meaningful, accountable, and action-responsive ways.[49] The documentary was principally created as a response to the very large and growing body of films and academic/journalistic texts created about the Rwandan genocide. The members of the collective who created the film all shared the concern that so much academic and cultural production about the Rwandan genocide was being created by non-Rwandans, much of it reflecting the perspectives and interests not of survivors and the dead but of the non-Rwandan and non-survivor creators and audiences.

Notably absent from so many attempts to theorize, learn lessons from, or share stories about the genocide is what feminist and participatory researchers identify as the question of reciprocity – that is, the question of how a particular text benefits Rwandan survivors. This concern is raised by Sherene Razack in her analysis of two films – *Shake Hands with the Devil*[50] and *Ghosts of Rwanda*[51] – that use the experiences of Canadian peacekeepers as an entry and end point to understanding the genocide (both films are used as educational resources). Razack argues that, by excluding Rwandan analyses and knowledge production, such films imply that "understanding what has happened in Rwanda is a human thing, devoid of historical specificity, devoid, in fact, of Rwandans."[52] When survivors are not needed to understand the lessons of the genocide – when their role is solely to provide evidence that it occurred – one might reasonably wonder why anyone would feel accountable to them when we study, teach, and learn about the genocide.

I want to stress that the distinctive difference between my documentary project and those mentioned above was that the entire process and content were and remain directly accountable to the individual survivors who provided the testimony of their lived experience of violence. Within this context of production, what emerged was a film in which survivors are positioned not simply as victims telling their stories of survival but also as educators, theorists, analysts, and social change agents who overtly demand accountability, responsibility, and responsiveness from the viewer. This is relevant to understanding the audience responses I have observed on several occasions when screening *Rwandan Genocide*. Audience questions and comments tend to begin a conversation with survivors (in direct response to their thoughts/feelings/knowledge and interests) rather than with non-Rwandan experts or protagonists. At the same time, I observe audiences addressing survivors as knowledge holders rather than as objects of pity. I would argue that the speaking positions claimed by the survivor historians in *Rwandan Genocide* set the terms of the learning relationships into which audiences are invited.

This example suggests, then, that testimony will be most effective in creating change if it is survivors who direct the uses to which their testimonies are put. In the very instance of claiming voice and authority, a colonial relationship is unsettled: their position as victim is transformed, and the process of social change begins.

In Conversation: Umwali Sollange

My Relationships to Testimony

I want to distinguish the ways I have experienced Rwandans passing on memory and honouring the dead from what, within European juridical and philosophical traditions, has come to be termed "testimony" (particularly our contemporary notions of this term as they have been shaped by post-Holocaust trials, literature, philosophy, psychoanalytic theory, and education).

In my experience, family, friends, and community members have shared stories of atrocities they have witnessed or survived in very informal ways – ways that are woven into the fabric of everyday conversation. These stories and memories arrive unannounced and incidentally, almost unexpectedly (at least for the listeners). One person might begin telling a story or proverb with "once upon a time" (*cyera habaye ho*) to tell, not a traditional proverb, but an account of his or her own escape from one of the massacres that formed the decades-long build-up to 1994 (or a story of a family member who did or did not survive). This remembering is interspersed with joking and laughter and the flow of everyday, intimate family conversation. The stories told are familiar – we might have heard them once or many times – and the protagonists are family or community members whom we know as whole, complex beings. The point is that testimony and remembrance as I have experienced them are a part of everyday conversation: they are not set apart with formality or ceremony.

Moreover, the hardships and suffering described in these stories are not distant, unfathomable, or shockingly outside the limits of our imagination or awareness. Without essentializing, I wish to make the point that, as a community, we are accustomed to hardship: death is a part of living. Telling stories of violence, like telling stories of life and love and strength, is a means by which older community and family members pass on a common heritage. For those of us listening, this is how we learned the cultural values of our community: we learned what it means to lose a loved one, how to console the survivors for their loss, how to stay grounded and strong as a community, and how to survive with tears and laughter. It was through listening to these stories of atrocity and survival that we developed a shared set of memories and understandings, cultural norms, and values. It was also through taking up these memories that we affirmed our relationships to ourselves, to our family members both present and dead, close and distant.

Problematic Uses of Testimony I Have Observed

I want to distinguish these "insider" practices from what I have become familiar with in North America: practices of testimony delivered to strangers or people outside the family and community. These audiences have little historical and cultural understanding through which to contextualize the stories or to understand the people in them as three-dimensional human beings. I say this not to argue that testimony is possible or valuable only within a survivor community but, rather, simply to recognize the different conditions and the challenges raised.

When I (or other Rwandans) speak in Canada of the 1994 genocide, I feel that I am providing testimony that is being delivered and received in highly formalized settings, set apart from the business of everyday living in a context that feels rarified, distant, and cold. When talking about the genocide in these forums, I feel the weight of the hush of an outside audience's desire to hear only of suffering and atrocity. I worry about the desire for shock value in these settings. I'm conscious that the atrocities of which we speak are not heard in a vacuum but alongside daily TV and video game images of war and carnage, often involving racialized populations and villains. A plethora of dead and violated racialized bodies float easily and accessibly through popular culture. How do these influence the ways Canadians – with neither the personal nor the historical context to approach individuals as three-dimensional beings and to understand the complex forces feeding this violence (forces in which we as listeners are *all* implicated) – hear these stories? How does it influence the ways they do or do not put themselves in the picture?

I'm trying to emphasize the importance of context and the kinds of relationships that context structures. In the context of Rwandan community and ancestral memory practices, the knowledge contained within testimony was not individual but collective. I'm conscious that in academic settings knowledge becomes commodified as it is the basis of individual advancement and evaluation. In such institutions, many Rwandans have found their stories being cited by those who claim authorship, those to whom the wisdom contained in these stories comes to be credited.

Likewise, in contexts that define roles and identities according to rigid "us" and "them" binaries, even apparently well-intentioned practices of listening enact a kind of symbolic violence that I, as an invited speaker, have felt quite viscerally. When framed by juridical discourse and evidentiary agendas, testimony implicitly creates a giver and a receiver, establishing an existential and epistemic distance and hierarchy. This dynamic tacitly creates a performer out of the speaker and an audience out of the listener; the audience becomes a distant observer whose mere listening validates the knowledge shared. For example, in my experience as a guest speaker in elementary or high schools across the greater Toronto area, children and youth were keen listeners and their questions were innocent, but I experienced an emptiness after sharing my stories. I felt like an academic performer talking about a world issue but without the authority of a teacher; I seemed to be an object of study for the students. Even with this apparently well-intentioned and caring audience, there was still a noticeable absence of any understanding of the emotional cost of sharing, especially when it comes to sharing traumatic stories. The audience's responses often seemed inappropriate, re-victimizing me as the speaker. The feelings of emptiness, helplessness, hopelessness, guilt, fascination, pity, or romanticization that seemed to circulate during these events suggested to me that students were engaging with me more as a symbol than as a fellow human being, educator, or neighbour.

On other occasions, I have found myself drawn into more impromptu testimonial interactions in which I am asked to share my story as a Rwandan with no consideration of the content or repercussions of this practice. I call these "chitchat testimonies": they seem informal, casual, and conversational in a way that presumes intimacy and easy access. On such occasions, when I am asked about my background and I mention Rwanda, I immediately get that deep, sympathetic look that is followed by the question: "When did you come to Canada?" When I respond that I arrived in 1998, regardless of whether I am on the bus, on the street, or at a grocery store, people begin to engage me in my trauma as a Rwandan. I am always left feeling strangely disturbed and violated by the casualness of the inquiry, the ease with which this boundary of intimacy is crossed and subsequently dropped. In these interactions, what strikes me most powerfully is the ways I experienced ostensibly innocent, curious questions as violating my personal space, my boundaries, and, with neither notice nor permission, invading my very core. This stance of naiveté positions me as a victim and reduces my experiential knowledge to mere evidence. The apparently well-intended questions work to simplify and to categorize complex experiences. My testimony becomes a confirmation of an issue or incident within a binary frame: it is either a success story or the confirmation of an atrocity. This distorts the nuance of historical experience: in testimony, there is no good or bad; we have all lost something, albeit differently.

Potential for Productive, Ethical Uses of Testimony

I have highlighted the particular conditions of testimony and remembrance practices within survivor communities as I experienced them (and their significance for me as a member of this community), and I have contrasted these with the challenges of sharing testimony with outsiders who bring their own desires, investments, imaginaries, and limited contextual knowledge to the interaction. I do this not to suggest that testimony should be delivered and received in the same way in different cases but, rather, to alert us, as educators, to the challenges arising from very different contexts and conditions.

What does this mean for the ways that I would hope the larger global community would receive and value the expertise and wisdom gleaned from traumatic histories of the 1994 genocide as told by survivor communities? I now try to offer some guidelines.

I believe that we need to begin ethical practices of listening by rethinking and restructuring the implicit dynamics within testimony: Manichaean binaries of absolute evil or absolute innocence do implicit violence to the multiple dynamics within each account. We need to seek complexity, not simplicity. It is my experience and estimation that testimony is a personal experience that one shares in order to connect with other human beings. Each connection is unique, and the receiver of the account has an obligation to hold this interaction with respect, to focus on the testifier and her or his well-being (what I call "mindful listening"),[53] and to reflect on where or how she or he is implicated. It is an opportunity to go on a journey that tests our ability as human beings to be present to and for each other.

The practices of witnessing I envision would approach those testifying with respect as knowledge producers. This implies framing testimonies and personal accounts as valid sources of analysis that can contribute to the comprehension of an issue/topic. Experiential knowledge cannot be trumped by theory or other practices of knowledge acquisition. To give a full picture, all sources and forms of knowing need to be received with mutual respect.

This approach implies recognizing the power dynamics involved in the practice of testimony – the relationships presumed, the agendas that frame the interaction, and the outcomes for different stakeholders. As a member of a survivor community, I am not interested in looking to the audience for sympathy, salvation, or the opportunity to become a poster child for the campaign of the month. This position is disempowering, is condescending, and perpetuates stereotypes. Over the years, I have shifted from sharing details about personal experience to addressing social issues in a context that asks audience members to reflexively examine their own implication in all forms of violence and injustice: historical and contemporary, distant and local. Ideally, my testimony would receive the same respect, value, and reaction as would that of the white body next to me, and it would be able to inform policy, legislation, and academic discourse. My sharing would bring communities and individuals together and build bridges across class, race, ability, ethnicity, language, socio-economic status, citizenship, and other barriers.

Ultimately, ethical practices of witnessing demand that listeners honour the dead by integrating and embodying the lessons gleaned from survival and loss and applying these to their current socio-economic, political, environmental, and cultural lives. True allies begin by building the strength to recognize and challenge each other in terms of their implication in immediate and local relations of injustice, violence, and power. Embodiment requires constant questioning and presence in our immediate context of lived relations.

In Conversation: Lisa Taylor

My Relationships to Testimony

My earliest experiences of testimony were of its silences, its leakages, and its proxies. My mother grew up during the Second World War in Austria within a family that, like so many, lived a continuum from passive to (on the part of certain members) explicit support of the regime. In Austrian schools, the silence concerning the Holocaust was complete.[54] She moved to Canada as soon as she reached adulthood in order to leave behind painful family relationships. In time, in this very different context, she came to learn much more about the Holocaust than had been allowed to surface in Austria. In our household, however, it was stories of domestic, intimate traumas and intergenerational suffering that erupted and seeped down to me as testimony in a way that almost precluded links to broader historical relations of complicity or implication.

Only as my teaching and activism encouraged me to think about discrimination as intersecting systems, and only as I increasingly turned to racialized feminist and Jewish post-Holocaust authors, scholars, and educators in my own learning, did I begin, with mounting urgency, to seek out testimony that excavated these silences. My search has been driven by a need to understand the ongoing histories of colonization and mass and systemic violence from which I continue to benefit in the material, social, and psychological conditions of my own life. These are marginalized histories that must engage in ongoing struggles to gain or maintain differently precarious institutional footholds – histories that have different institutional "levers of sustainability."[55] They demand reflexive practices of pricking one's ears to unmarked silences, both in official accounts and in the institutionally trained habits of interpretation and "structures of feeling" I bring as a listener.[56] Eventually, the urge to probe institutional silences spilled into my personal inheritances. As I've pressed within my family to hear testimony of this intergenerational domestic history of inflicted suffering and loss, I've come to see it as inextricable from larger historical forces of political and cultural violence, as a leakage from the fault lines of an "unmasterable past."[57] This has led me back to seek out testimony of Holocaust survivors as a means of understanding the complex burden I inherit from a family and cultural history of complicity. I have also come to recognize the very different obligations of witnessing and conditions within which these personal and cultural memories are taken up by those of us who live in the shadow of the Holocaust. I understand that I am differently – and in some ways better – supported in prying open this silence than are members of generations closer to that particular violence.

Problematic Uses of Testimony I Have Observed

Of course, there is a pedagogical aspiration at the heart of testimony: the hope that something is learned by the witness and that what is learned might lead to actions and vigilance that would deter the recurrence of such violence. I have observed a growing use of testimony in formal and informal educational settings, uses that raise a number of pedagogical concerns for me about the different conditions and practices of testimony: What is presumed to be learned, by whom, from whom, for whom? Whose sense of history and whose agendas implicitly structure how testimony is selected, presented, and received? What affective dynamics are disavowed, indulged, consoled, or considered in institutional settings?

Umwali and Marie-Jolie have, in generous conversations, urged me to recognize that, before that familiar and suspect rush to pedagogy, I should first examine questions of learning, beginning with my own. They have pushed me to consider the ways different people are taught to see their relationship to testimony (and, by extension, to violence) and the ways these perceived relationships are structured. Umwali's description of "chitchat testimony" and well-intended voyeurism prompt me to explore the ways I have been taught to see mass violence as something distant, archaic, foreign: these include the ways I have been insulated by intergenerational silences, by the domestication and filtering of collective memory through the prism of family traumas, and also by a racially segregated society and colonial Canadian discourses of terra nullius and white settler innocence.

In my family, intergenerational memory of the quotidian social and psychological breakdowns, accommodations, and complicities with fascist and wartime governance was truncated, deposited on the other side of the Atlantic far from the American dream of a fresh start in a virgin land. My generation was raised within the bubble of a mythic white settler colonial First-World utopia, insulated by personal and national narratives of strategic amnesia. More than amnesia, this was *an amnesia of a suppression*, a double cultural loss, as Jane Jacobs suggests.[58] Years of ethnic cleansing in Austrian society and institutional regimes of silence left my mother with few conscious memories of the Holocaust and its violations to pass down: she witnessed no precipitously vacated neighbours' apartments or unexplained empty desks at school. For her, family traumas lent a visceral affinity to New World narratives of a therapeutic break from the Old World with its festering histories of conflict, colonial narratives of escape to a young, innocent society of unlimited potential for reinvention.

This particular family foreclosure of memory found resonance with late capitalist, consumerist North American cultures of solipsism and hostility to memory,[59] insulated within a global context of a widening North/South (and settler/indigenous) gulf between "our" security and "their" unrelenting wars, "our" prosperity and "their" vicious exploitation, "our" technological convenience and consumption and "their" apparent backwardness, "our" human rights record and "their" context of disenfranchisement and popular struggles.[60]

What this auto-ethnographic archaeology raises for me is the question of how I have been raised within insulating family and continental hegemonic cultures to approach testimony of mass violence as something shocking and foreign. The silences in my inherited relationships to the Holocaust and to the ongoing colonization of this land mean that I have learned to hear the violence of which testimony tells as *the violence of others*, as an unprecedented and almost unimaginable knowledge. Testimony of horrific violence seems to rip the liberal democratic fabric of Canadian society. The racial and economic segregation of my national and global communities works to isolate me from face-to-face relationships with those affected by systemic violence within which I am implicated and of which I am a beneficiary.

The consequence of this structured relation is that, when I seek out testimonial and documentary accounts, my action could easily be framed within a congratulatory discourse of courage, commitment to social justice, or generosity simply for pushing back against the affordances of my cultural context and positionality. It feels brave, almost edifying, to listen to testimony. Once I do, I experience knowledge of mass violence and trauma as something unfamiliar and vastly distant from my everyday lived relationships of white bourgeois civility and political stability.[61] Even as I consciously resist liberal rhetorics of generosity and empathy; as I attend to the reality of systemic violence and the violence of perpetrators, bystanders, and beneficiaries in particular; even as I try to listen with "open heart and mind," the fact that I have lived a life that so rarely (if ever) required me to think about mass violence means that I approach this practice of witnessing as a relatively wide-eyed initiate struggling to learn skills in their very practice.

All of this reinforces my position as innocent, un-implicated, and separate from this violence, untouched and somehow *inherently nonviolent in character*. Equally significant, the enormity of the suffering I witness will never inhabit my life as it does those of the survivors. My practice of facing this loss and implicating myself in the structural conditions that continuously feed such violence will always be a *conscious* practice: this is not my family's loss. While these are indeed, in a non-presumptuous sense, *my* dead – while my obligation to them is even greater than that of their survivors – these ties binding me must be made continuously visible and are not the thick, sensuous, emotional web of love and kinship.

I say this not to argue for the impossibility of a careful use of many tools (including empathy) to build and extend dialogue between communities into the uncomfortable, transformative territory of cosmopolitan response-ability[62] and covenantal practices of witnessing.[63] Rather than as a pretext to foreclose the demands of critical reflexivity or claim licence for indifference, I want to examine the contrasts between Marie-Jolie's, Umwali's, and my own experiences of witnessing in order to take seriously the very different conditions within which our relations to witnessing are structured. These very different conditions have direct implications when we turn our attention to pedagogy.

Potential for Productive, Ethical Uses of Testimony

My interest in the structural and psychic landscapes within which I am continuously positioned to see myself in particular ways and relationships – as an untouched bystander, an un-implicated, sympathetic listener to testimony of the *violence of others* – is spurred by my hopeful scepticism regarding educational uses of testimony.[64] That is, I understand testimonial-driven pedagogies of social change – pedagogies that ask learners to face and make sense of hearing the impact of social, political, and economic violence – as staging a demand for a particular form of listening. This is a practice of listening that opens them to the possibility of remaking one's relation to others and, by extension, remaking meaning and remaking the self. For subjects who have been raised to understand themselves as having no relation to violence (or strictly belated relations of sympathy for those affected), forging a relationship to the historical and contemporary roots and mechanisms of violence contradicts foundational self-images: it involves engaging knowledge that is outside the frames through which they apprehend themselves and their relation to the world around them. Ellsworth explains this another way: "In order to learn something new, as in previously unthought, we must lose that part of ourselves whose identity depends on not thinking that thought ... that depends on not being the kind of person who entertains such thoughts or understands such thoughts."[65]

Something becomes profoundly and irreparably unsettled and off-kilter when I listen to face-to-face testimony of survivors of the Holocaust, of the colonization of the Americas, or of the Rwandan genocide if this testimony addresses me as someone *implicated and not merely sympathetic* to this injustice and suffering. When "I didn't know" is not accepted as an end point but engaged as a prompt to a series of "why" and "how" questions. When ignorance is not equated with innocence but problematized as a stance of insistent non-relation, a stubborn refusal of relation. There is a shift from "I didn't know" to "How have I been taught to not-know and what forms of ongoing violence does this not-knowing facilitate?" to "What else do I not-know? How am I invested in not-knowing? From what does not-knowing protect me? Is the rush to empathy a form of not-knowing?" I have been acculturated to approach testimony ready to empathize, an emotion substantially problematized by educational theorists.[66] Freud argues that empathy is a projected fantasy – one in which I see myself in the circumstances of the other, allowing me to judge their actions to the extent that these diverge from the fantasy of what I would or would not have done.[67] Roger Simon argues that this voracious empathy risks being an exercise in emotional tourism, an ahistorical, sentimentalized, and romanticized "feeling good about feeling bad."[68]

Rather than now feeling bad about feeling good about feeling bad – an endless exercise recentring my own pain – I turn to Todd, who proposes a pedagogy that approaches these expressions of guilt as a "symptom of a susceptibility to social responsibility,"[69] reflecting the emotional labour of seeking to implicate oneself and to build a responsible relation to another's suffering. This is not to deny that susceptibility triggers psychic defences; rather, it is to underline the libidinal volatility and unpredictability of learners' responses to educators' uses of testimony, to press us, as educators, to ask ourselves tougher questions about the conditions within which we introduce testimony in the classroom and the shapes and paths we imagine that learning from such testimony might take. It is to ask what kinds of preparation, conditions, supports, conceptual vocabulary, relationships, and community might allow someone to sit face-to-face with the demands of testimony, to take the risk of "transforming [oneself] without knowing whom [one] will become."[70]

Deborah Britzman proposes the term "difficult knowledge" to refer to the kind of insight that can emerge when knowledge that is normally kept outside the bounds of the "thinkable" is introduced into the conscious attention of a learner, contradicting valued self-images (particularly the image of oneself as a coherent, good person).[71] Thinking the unthinkable makes demands upon learners that tap into longer psychic and social histories of conflict; learners may react by resisting, retreating into familiar beliefs, or rushing to simplistic responses.[72] The challenge of pedagogy as it is being clarified in the discussions among Marie-Jolie, Umwali, and myself is to hold open a space for learners' emotional and critical labour of *working through* the demands of testimony, resisting the impulse to consume another's pain or recentre one's own. This work of remaking oneself *in relation to* ongoing historical systems of violence and inequity – the work of staying answerable to those affected by systemic violence in which I am implicated or from which I broadly benefit – takes time and self-observation.[73]

In the process of this reflection, I've become conscious that probing and bearing public witness to inherited ongoing histories of violence involves telling stories – our own but also those of others or stories that involve others. Much of the sense of who I am and how I relate to the world is shaped by the silences and stories, the family cultures and psychological susceptibilities, I inherit. As a consequence, I need to carve my path of reflection and self-examination through these inherited stories in order to move into action: But are family stories mine to tell and put into the public sphere? Was that the understanding when they were passed down to me? Am I being self-indulgent in this examination, recentring my privileged experience? Where is the line between self-indulgence and taking responsibility for understanding and dealing with the forces that have shaped me as an actor in the world?

The fact that so many questions and feelings surge through my exploration of these small, domestic histories shaped by historical forces gives me insight into Umwali's experience of the violation implicit in the casualness of "chitchat" requests for testimony. Our relationship to history is never casual, and we do a disservice to that history in treating it as such.

I hope this exercise develops habits in me that influence the ways in which I listen to the testimony of others, not just in terms of seeing myself as un-implicated but also in terms of giving me a language with which to understand the relationships and stakes in someone's act of testifying to me.

Conclusion

A series of insights and proposals emerges from our above autoethnographic excavations, insights that bear upon the project of genocide education and oral history, in particular with reference to the 1994 Rwandan genocide. We note a certain common ground between many of these proposals and the guidelines for practice of shared authority[74] that are intrinsic to the collaborative work of oral history.[75] This includes a practice of knowledge co-construction that is based on a sustained relationship of ongoing dialogue, mutual respect, trust, and concern or care for the other's well-being (not a relationship of contractual exchange or one-way benefit). It implies a method that problematizes and actively works against hierarchies of knowledge and knowers: this involves setting the academic authority of the researcher (based on training and claims to distance) alongside the *equally valuable and irreplaceable* epistemic privilege,[76] thick contextual cultural knowledge ("insider knowledge"), and embodied experiential knowledge and interpretive resources of the subject of life history or testimony.[77] Miller, for example, defends the position that oral traditions provide access to emic knowledge about a past event, one that can coexist with other forms of knowledge as equally reliable in order to build a more complete understanding.[78] Practices of shared authority also insist that the subject of life history or testimony should enjoy equal recognition and benefit from, and have equal control over, the process of research, authorship, and defining the purpose/audiences and dissemination of the life history. Finally, such a practice of oral history seeks out a broad spectrum of resources, media, and divergent voices, and it privileges voices systematically marginalized within academic and societal institutions; it recognizes that all knowledge is enriched by an emotional, embodied dimension of the experience of remembering and documenting history as a dense contextual web of heterogeneous meaning.

Rwigema and Umwali write above of the thick web of meaning within which survivor communities learn, heal, and build agency from the loss and suffering that systemic violence inflicts. We describe a knowledge ecology within which individual sense-making is inextricable from collective memory and lived relationships in survivor communities. Such contextualized, embodied, relational learning could not be replicated in educational initiatives. This is particularly the case in our racially and economically segregated world, which insulates one's awareness of differently positioned learners. Pedagogically, this means we can never presume that simply listening to testimony is automatically transformative of the relations of violence to which it bears witness. Testimony brings no guarantees, particularly in an age of ubiquitous *second-hand* testimony mediated by the very relations of power and epistemic violence it marks. This means that naïve practices of listening to testimony – as well-intended as they may be – can re-entrench colonial dichotomies and hierarchies if listeners do not prepare for this practice by first investigating their own complex, mediated, and re-membered relationships to violence. As educators and historians committed to the call of testimony – "Never again" – we need to understand the particular challenges of educational projects that seek to foster practices of listening and learning among "outsiders" who bring their own desires, investments, imaginaries, insulations, and limited contextual knowledge to the gift of testimony.

Sollange and Rwigema also raise urgent concerns about how diverse non-academic collective knowledge forms – shaped through histories of trauma and genocide (e.g., oral history, media, artistic, or healing practices) – come to be framed, produced, represented, commodified, and engaged as an object of study, and the ways the survivors come to be marginalized in this process. Sollange posits that ethical listening means honouring survivors and the dead by approaching violence not as something distant or foreign but, rather, as something local and immediate in one's life. Rwigema argues that only when survivors direct the uses of their testimony and the kinds of listening relationships into which audiences are invited will testimony start to chip away at the forms of violence it decries. An instructive approach to the power relations of preserving community forms of knowledge is provided by archives of the Sto:lō people: "We don't transfer ownership – it's not our [archive's] ownership. It still belongs to the person." This highlights a commitment to not alienating or appropriating knowledge to interests and agendas external to the community unless they are specifically gifted to someone.[79]

In our project, we are exploring pedagogical strategies – such as the exercise presented above – that start from this recognition that learning from testimony is a profoundly embodied practice imbricated within systemic, community, personal, and psychosocial relationships and histories. We believe that the methods of feminist oral history and autoethnography have much to offer such a pedagogy.

Classroom adaptations might involve students' exploring the ways their and their families' lives have been and continue to be shaped by violence. This involves tracing a broad, complex array of these relationships – including relationships of silence, denial, misrecognition, and disavowal – and generating a vocabulary that students might use to articulate new understandings of violence that lead to paths of action (beyond empathy or pity). This exercise begins with the explicit recognition that there exists a range of relationships that *always already* bind each of us in different ways to the 1994 Rwandan genocide. Particularly when hearing of the genocide for the first time, it can be shocking to consider the possibility that one can be in a relationship of which one feels entirely unaware. Different learners may have always believed such extremes of violence have "nothing to do with me." Based on this recognition, educators might ask students to brainstorm and mind-map different relationships between themselves and the form of violence, the event, or the communities under study; examples noted could be accompanied by a short explanation to their peers. Facilitators can offer personal examples of relationships of which they are aware – relationships of shared humanity, implication, reciprocity, inheritance, or participation in other examples of systemic violence (the most obvious example of the latter being our relation to this colonized land on which we live).

As Taylor articulates above, it is our hope that the experience of investigating one's own and family histories, memories, and inheritances – an experience demanding emotional, critical, and ethical forms of making sense – might prepare learners to listen to the testimony of others not as "not-knowing," un-implicated bystanders but, rather, as members of a complex range of relationships, including the relationship of accountability initiated through the gift of testimony. In our collaboration, Rwigema and Sollange have insisted that testimony be understood as a gift that inaugurates a relationship of answerability and ongoing care. Richard Daly, an anthropologist who gave expert opinion in the 1997 *Delgamuukw v. British Columbia* Supreme Court ruling, also characterizes the presentation of Aboriginal oral history in court as a "gift of knowledge": "I submit that the plaintiffs and their experts deployed their respective gifts in the *Delgamuukw* case. They sought to gift the public with particular knowledge and information, and to give what is at the core of all gifts, namely, idea and relationships."[80] Donald, Glanfield, and Sterenberg remind us of the Latin root of the word "authority" – "augere," or "making grow" – and encourage us as researchers to seek "generative relationships" by "embracing our vulnerabilities and deliberately deciding not to reside in the shadows of authority."[81] The work of pedagogy lies in preparing learners to receive a gift that inaugurates relationships interwoven with both vulnerability and accountability.

Considering the dynamics of testimony from a clinical perspective, Dori Laub argues that testimony does not transmit information.[82] It is this "transmission" approach to testimony within the instrumentalist agendas of historiography and education that is of primary concern to us, particularly when pursued in the absence of a critical analysis of the racialized relations of knowledge production, circulation, and acquisition. Rather than transmitting information, testimony "make[s] something happen," namely, a crisis of meaning, self-integrity, and language.[83] It is in the unique event of testimony – in the detritus of fractured knowledge and selves triggered by this unique crisis – that the listener is called upon to bear witness to these multiple crises. The listener witnesses both the testimony offered and her/his own practice of listening;[84] she/he witnesses both the effects of this knowledge on her/himself and the relationships that are forged in this gift (relationships binding her/him not only to the testifier but also to other actors in the historical trauma being related). These are interminable and ongoing practices of attending to the relationships activated and forged in testimony, and observing what these relationships imply in our daily lived experience as learners, researchers, educators, social actors, and neighbours.

Notes

Lisa Taylor: I wish to dedicate my work in this chapter to the loving memory of Roger I. Simon, cherished educator and mentor. I realized in the editing that he is a principal interlocutor in this work, as he implicitly has been in so many areas of my life. In his generous example, I've begun to sense what it might mean to take our debt and inheritance seriously, to love this world as Hannah Arendt proposed. In my teaching, research, and moments of ethical reflection and aspiration, I will always be in conversation with him.

1 Deborah Britzman, *Lost Subjects, Contested Objects: Toward a Psychoanalytic Inquiry of Learning* (Albany: SUNY Press, 1998).

2 We give primacy to the designation "the Rwandan genocide against Tutsi" in recognition of the reality of discourses of denial and revisionism (i.e., the propagation of theories of "double genocide" and outright denials that the 1994 genocide was primarily aimed at decimating the Tutsi population of Rwanda). Nonetheless, we recognize that those targeted for massacre extended beyond ethnic lines to include those identified as sympathizers, traitors, or internal threats. We use a range of terms, including "1994 Rwandan genocide" and "Rwandan genocide."

3 Shoshana Felman, *Testimony: Crises of Witnessing in Literature, Psychoanalysis and History* (London: Routledge, 1991), 105.

4 Ibid.

5 Michael F. Bernard-Donnais, book review of *The Belated Witness: Literature, Testimony, and the Questions of Holocaust Survival* and *Testimony after Catastrophe: Narrating Traumas of Political Violence, Comparative Literature Studies* 44, 3 (2007): 340–45.

6 Marianne Hirsch, "The Generation of Postmemory," *Poetics Today* 29, 1 (2008): 103–28.

7 Roger I. Simon, *The Touch of the Past: Remembrance, Learning, and Ethics* (New York: Palgrave Macmillan, 2005).

8 Edward Said, *Orientalism* (New York: Pantheon Press, 1978).

9 Robert J.C. Young, *White Mythologies: Writing History and the West* (London: Routledge, 1990 [2004]).

10 Cynthia Callison, "Appropriation of Aboriginal Oral Narratives," *UBC Law Review,* special issue (1995): 165–81.

11 Gayatri Chakravorty Spivak, "Can the Subaltern Speak?" In *Marxism and the Interpretation of Culture*, ed. Cary Nelson and Lawrence Grossberg, 271–313 (London: Macmillan, 1988).

12 Audrey Small, "Tierno Monenembo: Morality, Mockery and the Rwandan Genocide," *Forum for Modern Language Studies* 42, 2 (2006): 201–11; Alfred Ndahiro and Privat Rutzibwa, *Hotel Rwanda ou Le Genocide des Tutsis vu par Hollywood* (Paris: L'Harmattan, 2008); Robert Bromley, "After Such Knowledge, What Forgiveness?: Cultural Representations of Reconciliation in Rwanda," *French Cultural Studies,* 20, 2 (2009): 181–96; Alexandre Dauge-Roth, *Writing and Filming the Genocide of the Tutsis in Rwanda: Dismembering and Remembering Traumatic History* (Lanham, MD: Rowman and Littlefield, 2010); Rangira Gallimore and Chantal Kalisa, *Dix ans après: Réflexions sur le génocide rwandais* (Paris: L'Harmattan, 2005); Nicholas Marzoff, "Invisible Again: Rwanda and Representation after Genocide," *African Arts* 38, 3 (2005): 36–39, 86–96.

13 Britzman, *Lost Subjects.*

14 We gesture here to important critiques of global citizenship education (GCE) such as those provided by Pashby, who argues that even critical approaches to GCE construct the subject and object of learning and agency within colonialist imaginaries and ways of knowing. See Karen Pashby, "The Stephen Lewis Foundation's Grandmothers-to-Grandmothers Campaign: A Model for Critical Global Citizenship Learning?" *Critical Literacy, Theories and Practices* 3, 1 (2009): 59–70. See also Lisa K. Taylor, "Beyond Paternalism: Global Education with Preservice Teachers as a Practice of Implication," in *Postcolonial Perspectives on Global Citizenship Education,* ed. Vanessa de Oliveira Andreotti and Lynn Mario T.M. de Souza, 177–99 (London: Routledge, 2011).

15 Roger I. Simon, "Towards a Hopeful Practice of Worrying: The Problematics of Listening and the Educational Responsibilities of the IRSTRC," in *Reconciling Canada*, ed. Pauline Wakeham and Jennifer Henderson (Toronto: University of Toronto Press, 2013).

16 Ibid.

17 Toronto District School Board, *TDSB Ontario Ministry of Education Approved Proposal for a Locally Developed Course: CHG38 Genocide and Crimes against Humanity (Course Profile)* (Toronto, 2008); Toronto District School Board, *Report of the Genocide Curriculum Review Committee* (Toronto, 2009).

18 Britzman, *Lost Subjects.*

19 Marie-Jolie Rwigema, Axelle Karera, Natacha Nsabimana, Ntare Sharangabo, and Umwali Sollange Sauter, *The Rwandan Genocide as Told by*

Its Historian-Survivors (videotape), dir. Marie-Jolie Rwigema (Toronto: Kabazaire Productions, 2009).

20 These issues have been explored within the practice of oral history, particularly in debates about shared authority. We find instructive the practices of shared authority proposed by Michael Frisch in 1990 and 2003. These are explored within the university-community project Montreal Life Stories and in the 2009 special issue of the *Journal of Canadian Studies*, edited by Steven High.

21 Sandra Harding, *The Feminist Standpoint Theory Reader: Intellectual and Political Controversies* (London: Routledge, 2004).

22 Linda Alcoff, "The Problem of Speaking for Others," in *Who Can Speak? Authority and Critical Identity*, ed. Judith Roof and Robin Wiegman, 97–119 (Chicago: University of Illinois Press, 1995).

23 We're inspired by the exemplary model of reflexive memory work that many researchers have undertaken among themselves in order to challenge what they identify as the "colonial logic" of educational research in indigenous communities. See Dwayne Donald, Florence Glanfield, and Gladys Sterenberg, "Living Ethically within Conflicts of Colonial Authority and Relationality," *Journal of the Canadian Association for Curriculum Studies* 10, 1 (2012): 53–77.

24 Sherna Gluck and Daphne Patai, eds., *Women's Words: The Feminist Practice of Oral History* (London: Routledge and Kegan Paul, 1991); Frigga Haug, *Beyond Female Masochism: Memory-Work and Politics* (London: Verso, 1992); Annette Kuhn, *Family Secrets: An Act of Memory and Imagination* (London: Verso, 1995); Patti Lather, *Getting Smart: Feminist Research and Pedagogy with/in the Postmodern* (New York: Routledge, 1991); Susannah Radstone, "Memory Studies: For and Against," *Memory Studies* 1, 3 (2008): 31–39.

25 Miller points out, for example, that one of the limitations of the ways historians are trained in this discipline is that "oral history is second best, it's used to fill gaps, substitute for other information, even though it's golden." See Bruce Miller, *Oral History on Trial: Recognizing Aboriginal Narratives in the Courts* (Vancouver: UBC Press, 2011), 73. See also Michael Frisch, *A Shared Authority: Essays on the Craft and Meaning of Oral and Public History* (Albany: State University New York Press, 1990); Henry Greenspan, *On Listening to Holocaust Survivors: Recounting and Life History* (New York: Praeger, 1998); Steven High, ed., "Special Issue on Sharing Authority: Building Community University Research Alliances Using Oral History, Digital Storytelling and Engaged Scholarship," *Journal of Canadian Studies* 43, 1 (2009); Alessandro Portelli, "What Makes Oral History Different," in *The Oral History Reader*, 2nd ed., ed. Robert Perks and Alistair Thomson, 32–42 (New York: Routledge, 2006); Alistair Thomson, ed., "Special Issue on Sharing Authority: Oral History and the Collaborative Process," *Oral History Review,* 30, 1 (2003).

26 Suresh Canagarajah, "Reconstructing Local Knowledge," *Journal of Language, Identity and Education* 1, 4 (2002): 243–59.

27 Rwigema, *Rwandan Genocide.*

28 Roger I. Simon, Sharon Rosenberg, and Claudia Eppert, eds., *Between Hope and Despair: Pedagogy and the Remembrance of Historical Trauma* (Lanham, MD: Rowman and Littlefield, 2000).

29 Rwigema, *Rwandan Genocide.*

30 Ibid.

31 Sharangabo in Rwigema, *Rwandan Genocide.*

32 Karera in Rwigema, *Rwandan Genocide.*

33 Heike Härting, "Global Humanitarianism, Race and the Spectacle of the African Corpse in Current Western Representations of the Rwandan Genocide," *Comparative Studies of South Asia, Africa and the Middle East* 28, 1 (2008): 61–77; Sherene Razack, "Peacekeeping as International White Supremacy," in *Political Violence and Human Security in the Post 911 World,* ed. Chika Obiya and Kuroki Hidemotsu, 19–50 (Osaka: The Japan Centre for Area Studies National Museum of Ethnology, 2006); Sherene Razack, "Stealing the Pain of Others: Reflections on Canadian Humanitarian Responses," *Review of Education, Pedagogy, and Cultural Studies* 29 (2007): 375–94.

34 Dauge-Roth, *Writing and Filming*, 9.

35 Ibid.

36 I use the term "voice" in scare quotes: I recognize this term as necessary even as it has been problematized by feminist scholars; "voice" is not a simple possession or transparent representation that people can be presumed to "have" or "not have," that others can "give" to the "voiceless." For more, see Alcoff, "Problem of Speaking"; Mary Bryson and Suzanne de Castell, "En/gendering Equity: On Some Paradoxical Consequences of Institutionalized Programmes of Emancipation, *Educational Theory* 43, 3 (1993): 341–55; Chandra Mohanty, "On Race and Voice: Challenges for Liberal Education in the 1990s," *Cultural Critique* 14 (1990): 179–208; Gayatri C. Spivak, "Can the Subaltern Speak?" in *Marxism and the Interpretation of Culture*, ed. Cary Nelson and Lawrence Grossberg, 271–313 (London: Macmillan, 1988).

37 Rwigema, *Rwandan Genocide.*

38 Madelaine Hron, "Gukora and Itsembatsemba: The 'Ordinary Killers' in Jean Hatzfeld's Machete Season," *Research in African Literatures* 42, 2 (2011): 125–46.

39 Rwigema, *Rwandan Genocide.*

40 Razack, "Peacekeeping"; Razack, "Stealing the Pain."

41 Härting, "Global Humanitarianism."

42 Liisa Malkki, "Speechless Emissaries: Refugees, Humanitarianism and Dehistoricization," *Cultural Anthropology* 11, 3 (1996): 377–404.

43 Razack, "Stealing the Pain."

44 Spivak, "Can the Subaltern Speak?"

45 Malkki, "Speechless Emissaries."

46 Trihn T. Minh-ha, *Woman, Native, Other* (Bloomington: Indiana University Press, 1989).

47 Härting, "Global Humanitarianism."

48 Ibid., 61.

49 Rwigema, *Rwandan Genocide.*

50 Roger Spottiswoode, *Shake Hands with the Devil* (Toronto: White Pines Productions, 2007).

51 Greg Barker, *Ghosts of Rwanda* (Public Broadcasting Service, 2004).

52 Razack, "Stealing the Pain," 384.

53 There are important parallels between my vision of "mindful listening" and the practice of "deep listening" proposed by Lisa Ndejeru. See Lisa Ndejeru, "Shared Authority as Deep Listening and Sharing the Load," *Journal of Canadian Studies* 43, 1 (2009): 5–11.

54 Eva Kovacs, "Innocent Culprits – Silent Communities: On the Europeanisation of the Memory of the Shoah in Austria," *Totalitarian Movements and Political Religions* 9, 2/3 (2008): 225–36.

55 Ndejeru, "Shared Authority," 8.

56 Raymond Williams, *Marxism and Literature* (Oxford: Oxford University Press, 1977).

57 C.S. Maier, *The Unmasterable Past: Holocaust and German National Identity* (Cambridge, MA: Harvard University Press, 1988).

58 Jane Jacobs, *Dark Age Ahead* (New York: Random House, 2004).

59 Toni Morrison, *Playing in the Dark: Whiteness and the Literary Imagination* (Cambridge, MA: Harvard University Press, 1992).

60 I recognize that these are sweeping characterizations of broad, monolithic categories of North versus South, settler versus indigenous. My gesture here is towards the trends of neo-imperial late capitalist globalization and the patterns of polarization in wealth, power, and well-being they trace.

61 David Theo Goldberg, *The Threat of Race: Reflections on Racial Neoliberalism* (Malden, MA: Wiley-Blackwell, 2008); Sherene Razack, *Casting Out: The Eviction of Muslims from Western Law and Politics* (Toronto: University of Toronto Press, 2008).

62 Sharon Todd, *Toward an Imperfect Education: Facing Humanity, Rethinking Cosmopolitanism* (Boulder: Paradigm, 2009).

63 Simon, "Towards a Hopeful Practice."

64 Ibid.

65 Elizabeth Ellsworth, *Teaching Positions: Difference, Pedagogy, and the Power of Address* (New York: Teachers College Press, 2005), 89.

66 Megan Boler, "The Risks of Empathy: Interrogating Multiculturalism's Gaze," in *Feeling Power: Emotions and Education*, ed. Megan Boler, 155–74 (New York: Routledge, 1999); Britzman, *Lost Subjects,* 83–84; Simon, "Towards a Hopeful Practice"; Todd, *Toward an Imperfect Education.*

67 Britzman, *Lost Subjects,* 83–84.

68 Simon, "Towards a Hopeful Practice."

69 Todd, *Toward An Imperfect Education,* 98–113

70 Ibid., 139.

71 Britzman, *Lost Subjects,* 83–84.

72 Alice Pitt and Deborah Britzman, "Speculations on Qualities of Difficult Knowledge in Teaching and Learning: An Experiment in Psychoanalytic Research," *International Journal of Qualitative Studies in Education* 16, 6 (2003): 756.

73 I describe an exercise in working through resistance in learning in Lisa Taylor, "Against the Tide: Working with and against the Affective Flows of Resistance in Social and Global Justice Learning." *Critical Literacy: Theories and Practices* 7, 2 (2013): 58–68.

74 Frisch, *Shared Authority.*

75 High, "Sharing Authority."

76 Uma Narayan, "Essence of Culture and a Sense of History: A Feminist Critique of Cultural Essentialism," in *Decentering the Center*, ed. Uma Narayan and Sandra Harding, 80–100 (Bloomington: Indiana University Press, 2000).

77 Indeed, the concerns animating our project are grounded in a profound scepticism regarding the expert/survivor binary and the hierarchies of knowledge this underpins. These essentialist binaries fuel reductive framings of "insiders," including the colonial construct of "native informants." See Shahnaz Khan, "Reconfiguring Native Informing in the Global Age," *Signs: Journal of Women in Culture and Society* 30, 4 (2004): 2017–35.

78 Miller, *Oral History on Trial,* 49–51.

79 Cited in ibid., 69.

80 Cited in ibid., 6.

81 Donald et al., "Living Ethically," 68–69.

82 Dori Laub, "Bearing Witness, or the Vicissitudes of Listening," in *Testimony: Crises of Witnessing in Literature, Psychoanalysis, and History*, ed. Shoshana Felman and Dori Laub, 57–74 (New York: Routledge, 1992).

83 Ibid., 53.

84 Ibid., 58.

4 | The Role of Oral History in Surviving a Eugenic Past

ROBERT A. WILSON

Introduction: Stories We (Might) Tell

Sarah Polley's brilliant film, *Stories We Tell* (2012), opens with a quote read by Polley's father, Michael Polley, and drawn from Margaret Atwood's *Alias Grace*:

> When you are in the middle of a story it isn't a story at all, but only a confusion; a dark roaring, a blindness, a wreckage of shattered glass and splintered wood; like a house in a whirlwind, or else a boat crushed by the icebergs or swept over the rapids, and all aboard powerless to stop it. It's only afterwards that it becomes anything like a story at all. When you're telling it, to yourself or to someone else.[1]

Middles are muddles, and it is only by telling a story that we move beyond this muddled middle to achieve "anything like a story at all."

While the words themselves suggest a stark contrast between "confusions" and "*real* stories," the film itself does much to undermine that contrast. Stories, as they are told "to yourself or someone else," strive to make, and often succeed in making, sense of what would otherwise be a confusion, a confusion about history, about circumstances, about what happened. But the very tellings of those stories can themselves be confusions, or – put with perhaps less hyperbole – they can be the source of much that is confusing or puzzling. Confusion might persist throughout the telling of a story and not just while one is in the middle of the telling of it.

Polley's very personal exploration of her own family history, one focused lovingly on her mother and driven by ongoing curiosity and speculation about the circumstances of Polley's birth, is a story told through interviews with Polley's siblings, her father, and close friends and associates of her mother; the story told also draws from many hours of home movie footage of the central protagonists in the story.

Part of what the performance of the quotation from Atwood adds to the framing of this particular story is the sense that the story to be told here is one that is told collaboratively, piecemeal, and with twists and turns over time and across tellers. It is a story told not simply by Polley herself but also by her father (whose reading from a script that of unknown origin for much of the film both confirms and contradicts much of what others have to say about "the story") as well as by other family members and friends.

As a family story centred on a larger-than-life personality, one exploring rumour and speculation about a sensitive and intimate matter in a family's history, there is a sense in which the story that Polley wants to convey can only be told collaboratively and with a kind of shared authority that has been acknowledged as critical to the most engaging work in oral history. But that remains simply an optional extra for many other stories we tell, and have told, about ourselves that revolve around the same kinds of sensitive and intimate matters that lie at the heart of Polley's film.

One such story is the story of eugenics in Canada, a story that we may well be in the middle of telling. That story – "history" some would feel more comfortable with – is not well known among Canadians and has been told chiefly by two kinds of authorities. On the one hand, it has been told by historians and other academics interested primarily in reproductive control, the history of medicine, case law, mental illness, or Canadian history; on the other, it has been told by journalists, filmmakers, and others creating a story for popular audiences via the corresponding media.[2]

While occasionally those most intimately affected by the history of Canadian eugenics have been interviewed by both academics and the media, the story of eugenics in Canada, unlike the story that Polley tells, has been told for the most part without a sharing of narrative authority between these storytellers and the greatest group of those affected: people who have survived the eugenic past to be more than the subhumanized "mental defectives" they were held to be. Indeed, part of this subhumanization is the assumption that those institutionalized, sterilized, and stigmatized in the name of eugenics were not capable of telling their own story, either in part or in full, as they were deemed to lack the basic capacity to contribute directly to the story we tell about eugenics. In this respect, it is not simply that survivor oral history has been omitted, forgotten, or neglected, as in other cases; rather, it is that survivor oral history has been presumed to be precluded by the putative nature of those deemed mentally deficient.

It is against this background that I want to take up the role of oral history in the story we tell about eugenics in Canada. I suggest that, despite the fact that the history of eugenics in Canada is necessarily part of the larger history of eugenics, there is a special role for oral history to play in the telling of this story, a role that promises to shift us from the muddled middle of the story. Not only has the testimony of eugenics survivors already played perhaps the most important role in revealing much about the practice of eugenics in Canada, but the willingness and ability of survivors to share their own oral histories makes the situation in western Canada almost unique. Conversely, I also discuss the role that oral history plays in "surviving a eugenic past," trading on the ambiguity of this phrase to reflect both on the survivorship of those who have been viewed as subhuman via some kind of eugenic lens and on the collective legacy with which Canada's eugenic past presents us.

Discovering Canadian Eugenics

Although "eugenics" may be a term readily recognized by academics and professionals, many among those who form a part of Emily Murphy's "upper crust" of Canadian society are surprised when they learn that Canada itself has had quite an extensive involvement with eugenics – an involvement that goes beyond mere ideas and proposals.[3] This discovery can be made in a variety of contexts: during a university class in philosophy at the University of Alberta, while attending a public outreach lecture on the "new eugenics," or through web surfing blogs such as *What Sorts of People Should There Be?*, or in engaging with the ongoing conversations generated by the Facebook group "Eugenics Exposed."[4]

The emotional reaction to this discovery about a hidden part of one's own cultural history often shifts from surprise to the unease associated with more negatively tinged emotions, such as shock, shame, or even disgust, particularly as the outlines of the history of eugenics in Canada, especially in western Canada, are sketched. Such outlines can be traced from eugenics considered as some kind of abstract ideology to the more tangible testimony of those with lived experience of eugenic institutionalization, sterilization, and stigmatization. Consider four steps in this kind of transition in characterizations of the story of Canadian eugenics.

Transitional Steps in Exploring the Story of Canadian Eugenics

Ideas

The term "eugenics" was coined by Sir Francis Galton in 1883, though Galton's first eugenic work appeared in a pair of articles in *Macmillan's Magazine* in 1865 in a study of intergenerational patterns of professional accomplishment in English upper- and upper-middle-class families. Over the next forty years, in the vast majority of countries in Europe and North America, the term "eugenics" came to partially structure wide-ranging public and professional discussions about criminality, disease, euthanasia, immigration, child development and welfare, poverty, medical intervention and treatment, schooling, marriage, and sexual behaviour.[5] Eugenics became a social movement during this time, one that appealed to science in the service of human improvement by aiming systematically to raise the quality of human populations – whether locally, nationally, or internationally – over intergenerational time. As such, eugenics was interwoven with government regulation of health, including mental health, sometimes under the headings of "social hygiene," "mental hygiene," and "human betterment," and was often advocated by many of the leading social progressives of the time.[6]

One way to so improve the quality of human populations over generations would be to promote ideas and policies that aimed to ensure *every* person's potential to produce and raise children with at least as much "quality" as their parents. Many public health measures, such as reducing the amount of lead in home and school environments that would likely negatively affect developmental processes, are of this nature. That was not, however, the way of human betterment favoured predominantly within the eugenics movement. Instead, eugenicists typically followed Galton and emphasized that quality was not equally distributed in the kinds of human populations that are regulated by governmental policies and jurisdictional legislation. More specifically, they tended to think of such populations as being composed of *kinds of people*, with some kinds being of higher quality than others. The goal set within the eugenics movement was thus to increase the proportion of higher-quality people in future generations. This was to be achieved by advocating ideas, laws, policies, and practices either that aimed to maximize the reproduction of higher-quality people (positive eugenics) or that aimed to minimalize the reproduction of lower-quality people (negative eugenics).

Introduced into societies with a history of racism and colonialism, eugenic ideas were often formulated with respect to the kinds of people picked out by racial or ethnic groups, with some such groups deemed to be superior, others of inferior, quality. This directed social policies concerning the geographical boundaries of national populations (such as immigration policies) as well as those focused on ethnic and cultural groups already within those boundaries (such as Aboriginal and Native peoples). As eugenics movements established institutional bases in particular regions and countries, they typically came to focus their gaze on a putatively underlying menace to society – that posed by the "feeble-minded" or the "mentally deficient."[7]

Canada was no exception to this general trend. Influenced by the formation of eugenics societies amidst concerns about the "menace of the feeble-minded" in both Great Britain and the United States, both provincial and nation-wide initiatives in the second decade of the twentieth century propelled eugenic ideas into Canadian professional and public policy circles. In 1913, the Ontario government's newly created position of "inspector of the feeble-minded" was filled by Dr. Helen MacMurchy, who became a vocal advocate of eugenics, based on her view that growing social problems, such as alcoholism, venereal disease, and tuberculosis, stemmed from the rise of mental deficiency as expressed in her popular 1920 book *The Almosts: A Study of the Feeble-Minded*. The Canadian National Committee for Mental Health, founded in 1918, reflected that same sentiment, and over the first years of its existence provided expert advice as requested by the western provinces of Manitoba, Alberta, and British Columbia on the relationship between such social problems and mental deficiency.[8]

Legislation

Although immigration policy is one major area in which eugenic ideas exerted themselves in the first quarter of the twentieth century in North America, it was eugenic sterilization legislation in the United States, beginning with an Indiana statute passed in 1907, that was to have the most impact on the lives of vulnerable individuals in Canada. By 1914, when Harry Laughlin of the Eugenics Records Office at Cold Spring Harbor introduced a "model eugenic sterilization law," eugenic sterilization legislation had been passed in twelve states in the United States. Over the next thirty years, an additional twenty-one states would follow suit.[9]

The American precedent was influential in the 1920s in the western provinces as they sought to translate advice and direction concerning the putative dangers of the feeble-minded into legislation and public policy. Legislation authorizing and regulating the practice of eugenic sterilization was introduced into the legislature in the Province of Alberta in 1927, being passed there in 1928, and in the Province of British Columbia in 1933. These were the only two provinces in Canada to pass such legislation, which was repealed only in 1972 and 1973, respectively. The Sexual Sterilization Act of Alberta was amended in 1937 to explicitly distinguish between mentally deficient and psychotic residents of institutions and to remove the need for consent from the former with regard to sterilization; further amendments in 1942 broadened the range of conditions that could form the basis for eugenic sterilization, explicitly including epileptics and those with Huntington's chorea and those suffering from neurosyphilis.

Practices

Over the forty-four years it was law, the Sexual Sterilization Act of Alberta led to the approved sterilization of almost three thousand Canadians, a number that requires some brief explanation to convey what it says about the reach of eugenics in western Canada. First, that act underwrote ongoing practices of sterilization at rates that were among the highest in North America and that continued at relatively high rates until the repeal of the Sexual Sterilization Act of Alberta by the newly elected government led by Peter Lougheed. Second, those high rates continued well into the 1950s and 1960s, a time by which, even in jurisdictions in which eugenic legislation persisted, the practice of eugenic sterilization had been largely reduced or stopped altogether. Third, the board that approved such sterilizations, informally known as the "Eugenics Board," approved over forty-eight hundred sterilizations, rarely rejecting an application for sterilization from institutional authorities and representatives.[10]

Even following the repeal of the Sexual Sterilization Act of Alberta in 1972, very little was known about the practice of eugenic sterilization in Alberta and British Columbia. The substantial but still radically incomplete knowledge that we now have about eugenic practices more generally, at least in Alberta, came in the wake of the actions of one survivor of eugenic sterilization, Leilani Muir, more than twenty years later.[11]

Judicial Action

In a landmark legal case concluded in 1996, Leilani Muir successfully sued the Province of Alberta for wrongful confinement and sterilization as a resident of the Provincial Training School (PTS) in Red Deer, Alberta. This lawsuit uncovered much about the eugenic past in Alberta. The discoveries made here relied, in part, on the personal memories of those, like Leilani, who lived through that past as residents of "training schools" for those deemed "feeble-minded" or "mentally deficient." Leilani's courage in launching legal action against the Province of Alberta, and her determination to see that action through to its conclusion over a number of years, resulted in a novel kind of witnessing of the history of eugenics in Canada. In Leilani's case, this witnessing came from someone wrongfully deemed mentally defective, wrongfully classed as a "moron," and wrongfully subjected as a young teenager (without her knowledge) to eugenic sterilization.[12]

Among the evidence that this legal case generated were indications that the testing of those admitted to the school as mental defectives, and the subsequent processes that led to their sterilizations, departed markedly from both the requirements of the Sexual Sterilization Act of Alberta itself and the scientific and procedural norms of the day. In her judgment in the case, Madam Justice Veit wrote: "The circumstances of Ms Muir's sterilization were so high-handed and so contemptuous of the statutory authority to effect sterilization, and were undertaken in an atmosphere that so little respected Ms Muir's human dignity that the community's, and the court's[,] sense of decency is offended."[13] In uncovering the details of those circumstances, much was revealed about how, in general, eugenics operated over an extended period in Alberta's history, and it rapidly became clear that Leilani's treatment was far from exceptional. In the wake of this legal action, over seven hundred individuals began the process of launching similar legal actions for wrongful confinement and sterilization in the Province of Alberta.

Nearly all of these actions were settled by the Province of Alberta, but only after the Klein government had made an initial decision to oppose those actions, leading to a several-year period in which the kind of first-person testimony and witnessing that Leilani was able to provide began to be elicited from many individuals. Despite much variation in their personal circumstances and aptitudes, many of these people who had been institutionalized, sterilized, and stigmatized via the eugenics movement that generated the Sexual Sterilization Act of

Alberta were like Leilani in that they had a story not just to be told but also to tell. Like Leilani, many of them did not know anything approximating the full story of their own histories when they began this process; they were often very much in the middle of their own stories (at least with regard to this aspect of them).

Living Archives on Eugenics and Survivorship

The four-step transition in the story of Canadian eugenics should, of course, be taken with at least a grain of salt when seen as an attempt to provide a historiographical overview of the direction taken by the story of eugenics in Canada. I am not a trained historian, let alone one versed deeply enough in the ways of history to "do historiography." What the history I allude to above presents us with, however, is a chain of events and eventualities that creates an opportunity to tell the story of eugenics, at least in Alberta, in a manner that incorporates a role for oral history that is rare, if not unique, in histories of eugenics.[14]

In Canada, as elsewhere, eugenic ideology was translated into an active social movement that gave rise to legislation, social policy, and ongoing practices of institutionalization, sterilization, and stigmatization. However, unlike in other places and at other times, many of the people who were socially excluded and marginalized by eugenic ideas, laws, and practices in Canada in ways that supposed that they could not tell a story not only are *able* to do so but also are, with various degrees of circumspection and enthusiasm, *willing* to do so. The idea that their stories – however difficult they may be to tell and however difficult they may be to hear – are integral to whatever story is told about eugenics in Canada has been central to the Living Archives on Eugenics in Western Canada project. It is very much a community-university initiative that strongly emphasizes a shared authority model of the practice of oral history construction and that strives to incorporate both eugenic survivors, and community members who most readily identify with those survivors, as tellers of the broader story that the project aims to tell about eugenics in western Canada.[15]

The most obvious form this shared authority model takes is in the opportunity it provides for eugenics survivors to tell their stories, to have them recorded, and to create avenues for them to be retold through recordings. Before turning to these stories, however, I want to illustrate some ways in which the project embraces the ideal of shared authority that go beyond the individual stories of survivors of a eugenic past and that speak to the idea of a *living archives* on eugenics. I focus on two examples. The first of these concerns artistic responses to eugenics, the second concerns the stories of people who parent, or are considering parenting, in a society that continues to systematically discriminate against those with disabilities.

In October 2011, several summer interns who had worked with the Living Archives on Eugenics in Western Canada project the preceding summer rounded out their internships by organizing and hosting an art exhibition entitled the Collective Memory Project: Responses to Eugenics in Alberta. Curated by Anne Pasek, a graduating undergraduate major in art history and visual culture, this exhibition featured the work of thirteen artists whose submissions were the culmination of a larger community-focused project led by Anne. The Collective Memory Project involved soliciting art work from community members in general, engaging interested artists in conversations about eugenics (and supplying information that some of them would otherwise lack), and providing studio space and opportunities for potential contributors to explore their own responses to eugenics over an extended period of time during the late summer and early fall of 2011. Responses came from artists with disabilities, from recent immigrants to Canada, from residential school survivors, and from women whose ongoing institutional experiences formed the basis for a shared sense of social marginalization with those from past generations. Eleven of the thirteen artists whose work was represented in the exhibition were women, and the majority of those submitting were not professional artists.[16]

Foremost among these submissions were artistic responses received as a result of the Collective Memory Project's community outreach to those who were incarcerated in Edmonton-area prisons and who felt a particular identification with those who had survived a eugenic past. Many of these artists were women of Aboriginal heritage, and their artworks often evoked a feeling of social segregation and exclusion from family life that created continuities between past and present. Although their circumstances limited the extent to which they could be more fully involved in the Collective Memory Project – as attending artists, as speakers, as participants in the opening of the exhibition itself – their artworks proved to be among the most powerful in terms of the responses they elicited from viewers.

The Collective Memory Project also included a walk-and-talk with artist Kay Burns, drawing on her collaborative performance art piece, *Perambulate*. Struck by the fact that there are a number of Edmonton landmarks named in honour of leaders whose advocacy of eugenics is typically unregistered or forgotten as part of their legacy for and influence on Canadian society, Kay led groups of participants through Louise McKinney Park in the summer of 2011. Along with other members of the Famous Five – the five women who successfully fought for the full political recognition of Canadian women in the case commonly referred to as "The Persons Case" – McKinney was a vocal advocate for eugenics. The walk through a familiar public space provided the leisure to absorb and reflect on what, for many participants, was new information about McKinney, and the walk itself ended with a ceremonial renaming of the bridge connecting McKinney Park to the downtown side of the river as the Leilani Muir Footbridge. The Collective Memory Project provided the opportunity to revisit and reflect on Kay's *Perambulate*, to see and hear about the documentation of the original event, and to participate in a communal reclamation of public space that was evocative of a eugenic past. One of the special features of this opportunity involved walking with sterilization survivors, something that allowed for the kind of informal sharing of experiences that often occurs in a common public space.[17]

Because of their putative cognitive and other disabilities, sterilization survivors were denied the opportunity to parent and to form their own families. While those parenting in circumstances of disability today are presented with choices that were not available to survivors of sterilization, these choices are very much constrained and influenced by the eugenic past. For this reason, issues concerning parenting and disability are integral to the project's being conceived as one working to sustain a "living archives" of the history of eugenics in western Canada. This is especially so for community partners, such as the Alberta Association for Community Living and Neighborhood Bridges, whose day-to-day advocacy work with and for members of the disability community often concerns parenting and disability.[18]

A person with a disability in contemporary Canadian society faces systematic barriers to parenting that often reflect, and in some cases are a continuation of, the kind of views of "intelligent parenting" and cognitive disability that dominated the eugenics movement. For that reason, the stories of those parenting with disability form an important part of the story of eugenics in western Canada to which the Living Archives project sees itself as contributing. While such stories are not testimonials from survivors of the period during which eugenic sterilization was legally practised in Alberta and British Columbia, they often convey experiences with child welfare services and legal, educational, and medical agencies that reflect a view of their own subhuman status and misgivings about their ability to parent adequately. The similarity here to views of people who were deemed feeble-minded or mentally defective and were thus sterilized during the middle half of the twentieth century invites reflection on the story we tell about eugenics in Canada, reflection informed by interviews, public panel discussions, and working group conversations in which the lived experience of those parenting with disability speaks for itself.[19]

The link between the eugenic past and contemporary technology and reproduction extends beyond the realm of actual and ascribed disability to that in which there is the mere possibility of disability. Any Canadian who makes parenting decisions, including the decision of whether to be a parent, does so within contemporary medical and social contexts that differentially value foetuses, infants, and children deemed to have actual or even merely likely disabilities. For example, foetuses are routinely screened in Canada in pregnant women over thirty-five for Trisomy 21 – the presence of an additional chromosome, in part or in whole, on chromosome 21 that correlates with Down Syndrome. In 2007, a Society of Obstetricians and Gynaecologists of Canada working group recommended that this screening extend to all pregnant women, given that the majority of children born with Down Syndrome were born to mothers under thirty-five. In the United States, the vast majority of foetuses found to have Trisomy 21 are aborted – despite the fact that only a small minority of the infants and children that such foetuses would have become would have been likely to manifest severe or life-threatening symptoms.[20]

Survivorship for the Subhuman

As touched on earlier, Leilani Muir's legal case against the Province of Alberta and the cases that were settled out of court in its wake have revealed much that, previously, had been virtually unknown about the history of eugenics in western Canada. This includes aspects of day-to-day life for those residing in institutions such as the Provincial Training School of Alberta in Red Deer. It also includes facts about the treatment of children in these institutions – treatment that many find deeply disturbing. Paramount among these facts was the use of bare "quiet rooms" in which residents could be left in relative isolation for days or weeks and, during this time, the apparently extensive psychotropic experimentation on children deemed mentally deficient or psychotic. Especially striking in Leilani's court case was the revelation of a number of cases in Alberta during the 1950s and 1960s in which testicular tissue was unnecessarily removed during eugenic castrations (not simply sterilizations via vasectomies) performed on males with Down Syndrome, tissue that was then used for experimental research purposes.[21]

The cumulative documentation of Alberta's eugenic past suggested practices that not only violated the spirit and letter of the Sexual Sterilization Act itself but that also involved systematic disregard for persons who found themselves at governmental institutions for the feebleminded and mentally ill. Madame Justice Veit's statement in Leilani's case – "the community's, and the court's[,] sense of decency is offended" – could be readily extended to characterize the likely response that both community and court would have had to the treatment of many other eugenics survivors in western Canada.

Like other oral histories, those of people institutionalized, sterilized, and stigmatized by Alberta's eugenic enthusiasm convey something both of what life was like in the past (in their case, in government-run institutions such as the Provincial Training School) and of what life is like having survived a traumatic past (in this case, a eugenic past). Apart from the distinctive content provided by survivor standpoints, the resulting narratives are notable for being coherent, partial, and personally reflective stories from those thought incapable of this kind of narration. Here the restoration of full humanity that narrative brings counters both the dehumanization caused by traumatic episodes and events and the subhumanization of people whose putative reasoning deficits excluded them from an important part of family life and was the basis for their extended segregation from the rest of society. That restoration also helps to build some sense of community feeling among survivors, both with one another and with others participating in a common project. Since today's popular views of cognitive disability share much with those of the middle half of the twentieth century, people who have, or are assumed to have, cognitive disabilities continue to confront subhumanizing attitudes and policies. For these reasons, oral history has a special role to play in the story we tell about eugenics in Canada.

Stories Being Told

Living Archives only began recording interviews with sterilization survivors and with those parenting or considering parenting in circumstances of disability in the second half of 2012. Our approach to recording these stories has been cautious in that we are especially sensitive both to the vulnerabilities of all those whom we interview and to our affiliation with a university that had been directly involved in the practice of eugenics in Alberta.

A key component of our approach to oral history is to work, at least primarily and in the first instance, with individuals who have a high level of comfort with their own story and who have both antecedent and developing trustful relationships with other team members. Such individuals have often become their own advocates, and, as with participants in other oral history projects, such as Montreal Life Stories, they tend to view the process of constructing their own narratives in a positive light.

The process of story construction is coordinated by Nicola Fairbrother of Neighborhood Bridges, a key partnering organization of the Living Archive project and one that has extensive outreach in the local disability community. While we aim to produce stories that are video-recorded and that can be shared in a fully public way, our co-participatory method also allows for the construction of audio-only and restricted-viewing stories. To date, Nicola has conducted nearly all of the small number of interviews and has been the only team member present for them, apart from videographer Jordan Miller. While the process of story construction continues, we can convey some sense of the stories that are beginning to emerge. I focus on three video stories that have now been completed. The first two are stories told by sterilization survivors who are now in their sixties; the third is a story told by a much younger person, and it reflects on his own experiences with disability and parenting.

Early in his story, Roy Skoreyko tells us that he's now retired and enjoys what he does, adding, with a laugh, that he "has a life." He then reflects on some of his experiences at the Provincial Training School, now called the Michener Centre:

> The first day that I moved into Michener Centre, I was about ten years old. My parents dropped me off there, and man it was so

> hard for me to leave my family. All they did was give me some other clothes. I couldn't wear my regular clothes; they gave me jeans and all that, and a shirt. And they would just drag you and put you in your day room there. [...] And we all had to line up to the dining room to eat, lined up to go take a shower. When you lined up to take a shower, you had to walk down the hallway, no clothes on at all, and people could see you. [...] It was scary, 'cause the doors were always locked. And they just went like this [moves hands together] [...] and they always had a key, to lock the dayroom doors, lock the dormitory doors where people would go to sleep [...] Some of us were scared to say anything, scared for our lives. And I have seen some of the people there that there were tooken [*sic*] into this little room by themselves. No clothes on, and all there was just [...] there was no sink, all there was was just a mattress on the floor, and there was no bed, no bed at all. You had no clothes on. And you could see, they had these thick, thick glass windows, but you still could see people walking around in there. And you would be locked in there.

Beginning with his feelings about being "dropped off," Roy moves quickly to say how clearly he remembers the regimentation of life at Michener – how he was clothed, the lining up, the locked doors, the "quiet rooms," his nakedness, being seen by others. Returning later in his story to talk about his ongoing, positive relationship with his parents while he was at Michener – including visits home, his reluctance to return to Michener, and his discussions with them later in life about his sterilization – Roy ends his story by reflecting on disability and his pride in how far society has come. Of his sterilization, Roy simply says: "I feel offence and a little bit disappointed that that was done. You know, they took control of our body, and they did it, and they didn't ask us. There was a lot of things that went on there that, you know, shouldn't have."

The second story is that of Glen George Sinclair. Glen, who is soft-spoken, tells his story by sharing with Nicola photograph albums and material from his legal case file. For Glen, as for other sterilization survivors, while the photograph album prompts many personal memories, the legal file contains information (from institutional and other government authorities) about his life that, for many years, had remained unknown to him. Glen has spent much time reading and reflecting on this "information." Shrugging, Glen characterizes society's attitude towards those resident at the Provincial Training School as follows: "Lock 'em up, throw the key away. Like I didn't really have any purpose in life." He goes on to talk about being ordered around "like a dog" while resident at the school.

Despite their brevity, Glen's comments on the documents contained in the legal file are powerful, especially when juxtaposed with their visual presence in the video story. Part of what Glen, Roy, and other survivors grapple with are the views expressed about them in these documents and, in turn, the broader societal attitudes towards the "mentally deficient" that they convey. Glen does not need to say much in order to convey the absurdity and wrongfulness of his labelling and subsequent subhumanizing. His visual presence in telling his story provides an immediate, direct, and re-humanizing connection to anyone listening to and watching him.

The third story is not that of a sterilization survivor but, rather, someone more than a generation younger than Roy and Glen – someone whose reflections resonate with much of what survivors have to say about family life and disability. Kyle communicates non-verbally. His story is presented via photographs and music, and he uses text-to-voice software to present a verbal narrative. Kyle's story focuses on his positive views of his family and friends, his work with children at the Glenrose Hospital, his status as a role model for children (especially given his own history), and his views of the rights and responsibilities of parenting. After saying, "I know that I am not ready to start a family right now," Kyle notes what a big commitment this would be. He then turns to the views of others:

> I am sure that some people would react poorly if I became a parent. But those people do not know the real me, so their opinions do not matter. I have every right to be a parent. I am a good person who knows how to love. No one can tell me otherwise and I would fight for the right if somebody told me I couldn't have children.

Kyle then lists some of the things that he would need help with, and some that he would not need help with, once he is ready to start a family. Kyle's story concludes with a short reflection on government intervention and an affirmation of his right to parent: "I don't think that the government would let me keep my child. But like I said before, I would fight for my rights to make sure I keep my child. The government has no right to tell me that I am not fit to be a parent."

Like the other two stories highlighted above, Kyle's story focuses on what he thinks is important to express both about himself and his views. In constructing these stories, each storyteller has authorial control through active participation in the extensive editing and re-editing of his story as well as the opportunity to give, re-give, and retract consent to the story that evolves throughout the process.

Although all three stories are told in distinctive ways and convey much about the unique personalities of each of the storytellers, as I hope even this brief look at them suggests, they overlap and contrast in rich and provocative ways. For example, the conclusion to Roy's story shares a strong sense of disability activism with Kyle's story, while Glen's reflections on how he was treated convey more of a sense of a personal injury, one that was, as Glen acknowledges, shared with many others but is nonetheless very much his own. Glen's and Roy's stories both bring out some of the fears, humiliation, and sense of day-to-day trepidation that were part of institutional life, whether brought about by being paraded through hallways naked (as in Roy's case) or by feeling that the institution's attitude towards them was "lock 'em up, throw the key away" (as in Glen's case).

Conclusion

The year 2012 marked the fortieth anniversary of the repeal of the Sexual Sterilization Act of Alberta, while 2013 marked the fortieth anniversary of the repeal of the corresponding legislation in British Columbia (it was eighty-five years since it had been introduced). As works on the history of eugenics make clear – and as the emerging stories of those whose lives were radically changed by eugenic ideas, policies, and laws make vivid – for those who survived it, there is much more to eugenics than sterilization and its aftermath.

The stories that survivors are starting to tell both compensate for the paucity of accessible documentation on the history of eugenics in western Canada and redress some of the biases of academic history and philosophical reflection conducted in the absence of personal experience. Enabling survivors to move beyond the middle of their own stories is one way in which oral history can be of value. And moving Canadians beyond the middle of the collective story of the history of eugenics in western Canada is one way in which the Living Archives project can be of value.

Notes

1 *Stories We Tell*, dir. Sarah Polley, prod. Anita Lee and Silva Basmajian (National Film Board of Canada, 2012); Margaret Atwood, *Alias Grace* (Toronto: McClelland and Stewart, 1996).

2 For general academic works, see Carolyn Strange and Jennifer A. Stephen, "Eugenics in Canada: A Checkered History, 1850s-1990s," in *The Oxford Handbook of the History of Eugenics*, ed. Alison Bashford and Philippa Levine, 523–38 (New York: Oxford University Press, 2010); Angus McLaren, *Our Own Master Race: Eugenics in Canada, 1885–1945* (Toronto: McClelland and Stewart, 1990); and Erika Dyck, *Facing the History of Eugenics: Reproduction, Sterilization and the Politics of Choice in 20th-Century Alberta* (Toronto: University of Toronto Press, 2013). For a more popular recent work, see Jane Harris-Zsovan, *Eugenics and the Firewall: Canada's Nasty Little Secret* (Winnipeg: J. Gordon Shillingford Publishing, 2010). The most common access point to this history is perhaps *The Sterilization of Leilani Muir*, dir. Glynis Whiting, prod. Graydon McCrea (National Film Board of Canada, 1996).

3 Emily Murphy was a strong advocate of eugenics, and her advocacy here was extensive. As part of that, Murphy wrote a regular column in the *Vancouver Sun* newspaper under the name "Janey Canuck"; the article "Should the Unfit Wed?" published on 10 September 1932, used "upper crust" in this way.

4 Mention of these three particular venues is deliberate. With regard to the first venue, following 1996 revelations about the operations of Alberta's Eugenics Board – a board chaired for most of its history by the founding chair of the Department of Philosophy and Psychology, John M. MacEachran, who is also the longest-serving provost of the university – a report issued within the Department of Philosophy, the "MacEachran Report," recommended both the removal of honours associated with MacEachran's name and the incorporation of the history of eugenics in Alberta into philosophy courses. The second venue, the *What Sorts* blog, established in 2007, played an important role in raising awareness about the history of eugenics within the context of a broader discussion of the question "What sorts of people should there be?" (www.whatsortsof people.wordpress.com), and contains over one thousand posts searchable by category and tags. The third venue, "Eugenics Exposed," is a closed Facebook group that arose from the activism of people parenting in the context of disability and has become instrumental in helping to inform and organize parents both about the eugenic past and ongoing practices that devalue the lives of vulnerable individuals, especially children.

5 For the introduction of the term "eugenics," see Sir Francis Galton, *Inquiries into Human Faculty and Its Development* (London: J.M. Dent,

1883); for Galton's earliest thought on heritability in this vein, see his two-part "Hereditary Talent and Character," *Macmillan's Magazine* 12 (1865): 157–66, 318–27.

6 For recent coverage of the eugenics movement across national contexts, see Alison Bashford and Philippa Levine, eds., *The Oxford Handbook of the History of Eugenics* (New York: Oxford University Press, 2010). For encyclopaedia-style entries on the movement with a focus on North America, see Ruth C. Engs, *The Eugenics Movement: An Encyclopedia* (Westport, CT: Greenwood Press, 2005). And for a sense of the range of academic work on eugenics, see David Cullen, "Back to the Future: Eugenics – A Bibliographical Essay," *Public Historian* 29, 3 (2007): 163–75.

7 This focus on the feeble-minded was not universal, however, and there is more to be said about the kinds of people targeted by eugenic policies in various contexts, such as nationalism. See, for example, Marius Turda, *Modernism and Eugenics* (London: Palgrave Macmillan, 2010). On mental deficiency and feeble-mindedness in the context of the United Kingdom, see Mathew Thomson, *The Problem of Mental Deficiency: Eugenics, Democracy, and Social Policy in Britain c. 1870–1959* (Oxford: Oxford University Press, 1998).

8 See Strange and Stephen, "Eugenics in Canada"; and McLaren, *Our Own Master Race*. See also Helen MacMurchy, *The Almosts: A Study of the Feeble-Minded* (Boston: Houghton-Mifflin, 1920).

9 See Paul Lombardo, "Eugenics Laws Restricting Immigration," 2001, an essay in the Eugenics Archive, at http://www.eugenicsarchive.org/html/eugenics/essay9text.html. See also the essays in Lombardo's collection, *A Century of Eugenics in America: From the Indiana Experiment to the Human Genome Era* (Bloomington: Indiana University Press, 2011).

10 The most reliable statistical analyses here can be found in Jana Grekul, Harvey Krahn, and David Odynak, "Sterilizing the 'Feeble-Minded': Eugenics in Alberta, Canada, 1929–1972," *Journal of Historical Sociology* 17, 4 (2004): 358–84.

11 The repeal generated a handful of analyses of and reflections on the history of eugenics in Alberta. See, for example, Timothy J. Christian, "The Mentally Ill and Human Rights in Alberta: A Study of the Alberta Sexual Sterilization Act" (Faculty of Law, University of Alberta, 1974); Bernard M. Dickens, "Eugenic Recognition in Canadian Law," *Osgoode Hall Law Journal* 13 (1975), 547–77; and Terry L. Chapman, "The Early Eugenics Movement in Western Canada," *Alberta History* 25 (1977): 9–17.

12 See *Muir v. The Queen in Right of Alberta* (1996), 132 D.L.R. (4th) 695–762. This case is the focus of *The Sterilization of Leilani Muir* (National Film Board).

13 *Muir v. The Queen,* clause [3] of the summary. The Veit judgment has provided both scholars and the public with important information about both Leilani's circumstances and general practices in Alberta. See also Deborah C. Park and John P. Radford, "From the Case Files: Reconstructing a History of Involuntary Sterilization," *Disability and Society* 13 (1998), 317–42; and D. Wahlsten, "Leilani Muir vs. the Philosopher King: Eugenics on Trial in Alberta," *Genetica* 99 (1997): 185–98. For Leilani's extensive autobiographical reflections, see her memoir, *A Whisper Past: Childless after Eugenic Sterilization in Alberta* (Victoria, BC: Friesen Press); see also http://eugenicsarchive.ca/discover/our-stories for a shorter video narrative of Leilani's own story.

14 As should also be clear, I am here very much focused on eugenic sterilization in Canada performed under the authorization of explicitly eugenic legislation. For discussion of some types of sterilizations performed beyond such authority, see Karen Stote, "An Act of Genocide: Eugenics, Indian Policy, and the Sterilization of Aboriginal Women in Canada" (PhD diss., University of New Brunswick, 2012).

15 See the project website www.eugenicsarchive.ca. The full video narratives from which the excerpts are taken in "Stories Being Told" below can be found at http://eugenicsarchive.ca/discover/our-stories.

16 The Collective Memory Project: Responses to Eugenics in Alberta, exhibition, Faculty of Extension Gallery, Edmonton, Alberta, 23 October – 23 November 2011. See also photos of the event at http://www.flickr.com/photos/uaextension/sets/72157627990812162/; Anne Pasek's chapbook for the exhibition; and the coverage of the event in the twenty-minute highlight video, *Alberta Eugenics Awareness Week 2011,* available on Vimeo at http://vimeo.com/39613954 and on YouTube at http://www.youtube.com/watch?v=iaKQeIfiZq4 as well as at the project website.

17 On *Perambulate*, see http://www.nlac.ca/feature/kay.htm; for Leilani Muir's own reflection on the October 2012 event, see http://leilanimuir.ca/266.

18 See http://www.aacl.org/ for the Alberta Association for Community Living (AACL), and http://www.neighborhoodbridges.ca/ for Neighborhood Bridges. On the history of the sterilization of people with cognitive and other developmental disabilities, see Ellen Brantlinger, *Sterilization of People with Mental Disabilities: Issues, Perspectives, and Cases* (Westport, CT: Auburn House, 1995).

19 On the voices of those who have lived through institutionalization in Alberta, see *Hear My Voice: Stories Told by Albertans with Developmental Disabilities Who Were Once Institutionalized* (Edmonton: AACL, 2006). For a recorded community dialogue on parenting with disability, see "In

Pursuit of Human Perfection, Defining Who Is Worthy of Life, University of Alberta," 23 October 2008, http://whatsorts.net/events/events-PursuingPerfection.htm, which was jointly sponsored by the What Sorts Network and the AACL as part of the national series "A Matter of Diversity," held in celebration of the fiftieth anniversary of the Canadian Association for Community Living. This is also available as a series of twelve short videos at the YouTube eugenicsarchive channel at www.youtube.com/watch?v=vUOJCCZS1yI&list=PL0ED50290AE0B6C52.

20 On the Canadian recommendation, see A. Summers, S. Langlois, P. Wyatt, and R.D. Wilson, "Prenatal Screening for Fetal Aneuploidy: SOGC Clinical Practice Guidelines, No. 187," *Journal of Obstetrics and Gynaecology Canada* 29 (2007): 146–61.

21 Part of what is truly disturbing here is that males with Down Syndrome are already reproductively sterile, and they were known to be during this time. Another part of what is so disturbing lies in the discretion of the Eugenics Board to, in effect, grant permission for tissue removal for medical experimentation, clearly exceeding the authority it had been given by the Sexual Sterilization Act of Alberta. See Madam Justice Veit's judgment in *Muir v. The Queen,* 695–762; and *Sterilization of Leilani Muir.*

Part 2:
Working with Survivors

5 | From Testimony to Recounting

Reflections from Forty Years of Listening to Holocaust Survivors

HENRY GREENSPAN

Coming to Terms

No terms have loomed larger within discussions of surviving genocide and mass violence than "testimony," "trauma," and "memory." They are the three permanent members of the Security Council of Discourse on Catastrophe. No wonder so many academic conferences are entitled some combination of them – Trauma, Testimony, and Memory; Memory, Testimony, and Trauma – I remember enough math to know there are six permutations. They adorn the names of journals, of disciplines, and of subdisciplines. Projects, programs, and whole careers are founded upon them.

These terms stand for vitally important phenomena. But as the foundational terms for the work we do – the automatic "go-to" words – they are all problematic. Indeed, I believe they are the wrong terms: not because they are imprecise but because, employed most usefully, their meaning *is* precise. They are *too* specific to be foundational, and making them so dilutes their particular meaning even while it distracts us from the complexity that they are intended to represent.[1]

So, for example, when used to cover all the ways and all the reasons that survivors retell, "testimony" loses meaning. For war crimes trials or narrowly focused documentary studies, "testimony" is the right term – getting as close as possible to a definitive account of what a witness witnessed – unadorned by extensive reflection or "hearsay" and at least relatively unchanging over time and in response to different questions, questioners, and circumstances. As such, testimony is one important genre of retelling, necessary and entirely appropriate in specific contexts. But, among the various forms of survivors' recounting, it is rare, just as it is rare in the ways all of us share experiences and reflections. Testimony as a genre is governed by the conceit (how else could you run a trial?) that particular contexts and interlocutors do not significantly influence how and what a survivor retells; that survivors' accounts do not have many versions; and that survivors do not interweave layers of reflection and questions (including self-questioning) within factual recital – all of which they do.

In my own work, I have preferred "accounts" – or the gerunds "recounting" or "retelling" – to refer to what survivors convey, with "testimony" being, again, one subset.[2] Rather than connoting fixed and finished declarations that witnesses "give" and others "gather," "accounts" leaves more room for all that is contingent, reflexive, and creative in survivors' retelling. Likewise, while "testimony" suggests a monologue that need only be elicited, "retelling" makes room for the complex dialogue in which survivors' accounts most typically emerge.[3] Agi Rubin, a Holocaust survivor who has been my friend and collaborator for many years, said of her own most fondly remembered interviews: "One thought sparks another, and then another, that I may not have even known I had. This is the part that is so gratifying. Whatever I imagine I'm teaching, I'm learning at the same moment. We're learning together."[4] Interviews thus experienced are informative, even transformative, for both partners in the conversation. And even this brief description of "learning together" suggests the difference between retelling understood as *inherently* dialogic versus "giving" or "getting a testimony" in the usual sense. Indeed, within the usual paradigm of testimonial bearing witness – "this I believe" or "this I experienced" – Agi's notion of interviews as opportunities for "learning together" is almost unimaginable. Once again, it reflects a different genre, with different attendant conventions, assumptions, and purposes.

Similarly, when used to stand for *all* the agonies that survivors endure, "trauma," extraordinarily important in itself, loses specificity.[5] This is not the place to discuss particular trauma theories. But virtually all theorists agree that trauma entails helplessness in the face of overwhelming terror leading to paralyzed shock – physiological as well as psychological – from which there is sometimes no return. Susan Brison – a theorist who herself experienced severe trauma – aptly summarizes the consensus among psychologists: "A traumatic event is one in which a person feels utterly helpless in the face of a force that is perceived to be life-threatening. The immediate psychological responses to such trauma include terror, loss of control, and intense fear of annihilation."[6]

Trauma is obviously horrific enough. But it does not subsume all the anguish that survivors have known: abandonment, isolation, desolation, degradation, humiliation, all the physical agonies (e.g., deprivation, hunger, exposure) not perceived as immediately life-threatening, helplessness to help others (often central in survivors' accounts), and – above all – loss and grief, which is what being a survivor of genocide means most literally: "I'm still here. While my loved ones, my friends, my community, and most of my people are not." Strangely, but understandably, what is most often missing when non-survivors imagine the "death camps" is the dead.[7] We never knew them or saw them. They never made up our world. Innocent Rwililiza, a survivor of the Rwandan genocide, notes that those who were murdered are at the core of survivors' remembrance but are mostly invisible to non-survivors: "They are dead to the living, but they have never disappeared for the survivors."[8] Agi Rubin once insisted to me, "You have to see the individuals before they became victims." Except through mostly anonymous photographs, however, we do *not* see them.[9] By contrast, the "traumatized survivor" is immediately before us.

But are not loss and all the rest related to trauma? Of course, in life, and certainly in mental life, everything is "related." But we cannot begin to fathom the complexity of those relationships, and how they play out in particular lives, without starting with careful and relevant distinctions. More fundamentally, invoking *all* the deaths that survivors know (by whatever name) simply does not make sense, or makes only superficial sense, apart from survivors' seemingly impossible ongoing lives. It is precisely that irreducible multiplicity that is most difficult to grasp – as much for survivors as for the rest of us. Again, Agi Rubin:

> We survivors are a bundle of contradictions. We push away the past, and we are drawn back to it. When we are here, we are also there. And when we are there, we are also here [...] So there are many strands at once. It is not that our joys are not real. They are entirely real. It is just that they never exist simply by themselves. They are always also in reference to something else.[10]

And again, more starkly, Innocent Rwililiza:

> For someone who did not experience it, there is before, during, and after the genocide, and it's all a life being lived in different ways. For us, there is before, during, and after, but they are three different lives, and they have broken apart forever [...]

> The survivors tend not to believe that they are truly alive anymore – in other words, that they're still the same people they were before, and in a way, that's a little how they keep going.[11]

Most of the survivors I know are "jugglers" (although that is also too facile a metaphor). "There is more than one world in this world," more than one survivor has told me. "The life I was made to live is gone," Agi once reflected: "I am alive, in another life." Survivors have many "life stories," which include the ones that are gone, and no psychologically convincing way (including through "narrative") of putting them together.[12] And so the "life story" approach that has become so common in oral history may be inherently misleading in the context of lives such as these. Even more inadequate are the dichotomies that tend to frame discussion of survivors – trauma *or* resilience, injured *or* well, dissociated *or* integrated. Such binary formulations do not serve our understanding and, as a result, they *dis*-serve survivors.[13]

And finally "memory": How can "memory" be problematic? Because it is not only memories that haunt most survivors but, often more essentially, *knowledge* – in-the-bones knowledge, knowledge founded in memories but not reducible to them. Knowledge brings questions. Leon, also a survivor of Auschwitz, said of his retelling:

> A mere recital of names, dates, and places would violate the essence of my experience of the Holocaust; it would rob it of what is most important. Because it touches on *all* our philosophic questions, *all* questions of purpose, of justice, of God. Is a world that permits Auschwitz a proper place to raise a family? Should there even *be* a future? And how does one begin to approach it? How do you even describe it, in any meaningful way?[14]

Reflections like Leon's would not be welcome in a war crimes trial, and, of course, Leon would be briefed to avoid such "irrelevant" directions. But Leon is not offering "testimony," he is not evincing "trauma" or "resilience," he is not reciting names, dates, and places – although he is fully capable of doing so. Here, however, he is raising questions – questions not only for himself, but for all of us, to engage *with* him together.

This chapter is, above all, about engaging questions *with* survivors: a collaborative approach that I and others have been developing for many years and of which there are many examples in other chapters of this volume. Still, working collaboratively with survivors has been exceedingly rare. Before discussing additional examples, and saying more about collaboration in general, it is worth revisiting a couple of earlier moments: one from the history of my own involvement in this work, and one from the wider history of engaging survivors.

"The Survivors Are All Dying"

The first time I interviewed a Holocaust survivor at length, it was by accident. In 1971, my first good job after college was as a research assistant for a psychologist studying "moral judgment" – how people think about issues of justice, fairness, ethical obligation in general. My own primary responsibility was to interview "subjects" based on a series of canned moral dilemmas.

By chance, one of my first interviewees was a Holocaust survivor. I did not know that until he asked, a half-hour into the interview, "Would you like to hear some *real* moral dilemmas?" Of course. And so he recalled decisions such as whether to escape the ghetto to join the partisans or to stay to help his family; and later, in Auschwitz, the ethics of stealing bread and of how to handle those who did.

Foretelling my work to come – multiple interviews with the same survivors over months, and with some people, over many years – what should have been a one- or two-hour interview became a full day. Beyond memories and reflections, the survivor also told me that I was the "first American" (meaning born in the United States) with whom he had spoken in depth about the war. I was to hear this often in the 1970s. It still amazes me now.

By 1975, I made the decision to write a dissertation about Holocaust survivors – specifically, about *how* they retell, aiming for the richest possible understanding of survivors' construction of accounts that will be both tellable by them and, to whatever degree, hearable by their listeners. And so I wrote a proposal emphasizing retelling as a complex action and interaction – "testimony as a verb," as I came to call it.[15]

The would-be members of my doctoral committee were cordial, but they were not supportive. The first three professors I approached said essentially the same two things: first, "All the work about Holocaust survivors has already been done; there is no reason to repeat it"; second – usually preceded by "anyway" – "The survivors are all dying." They recommended that I work with people who would be around for a while, perhaps the children of survivors.

Nineteen seventy-five: "All the work on survivors has been done; and, anyway, the survivors are all dying." Extraordinary assertions, and worthy of our reflection. The first presumption, of course, was countered just a few years later: the "explosion" (as it is usually called) of interest in the Holocaust and its survivors in the late 1970s, which led to the majority of the conferences, museums, archives, and academic studies that we have today.[16] That was to come. In 1975, I mainly had the survivor who told me I was the "first American" with whom he had spoken and the professors who told me there was nothing new to say.

"The survivors are all dying." As it turns out, the survivors I first interviewed in those years were mostly around fifty, about a decade-and-a-half younger than I am now. I hope that I am not on the edge of demise. They surely were not. Of the survivors I initially interviewed in the 1970s, roughly half are still alive today, generally doing well, almost forty years after they were supposed to be "all dying."

In any event, the professors were not unique. Also in 1975, a psychiatrist and expert on what was then called the "concentration camp syndrome" wrote the same. "Their melancholy tale is almost told," he reflected about survivors. Like my would-be committee, he suggested that the time had come to focus on survivors' children. Ironically, the psychiatrist himself, sixty-one in 1975, died in 2011, after thirty-five more years of active professional life.[17]

Clearly, then, my experience in graduate school reflected a broader phenomenon, no doubt with many explanations. Perhaps it was just too difficult *not* to identify survivors with the Holocaust itself – symbols of the horror – especially as it reached most of us (and still reaches most of us) through the ever-repeated newsreels of the liberated camps. Skeletons, naked, vacant, literally immersed in a sea of corpses: How could the survivors not *also* be dead – as, in some respects, they were? It was simply uncanny to imagine that they could go on living. Even more, that their lives could, in any genuine way, resemble our own.

Referring to the impact of the newsreels, Agi Rubin exclaimed: "We were ashamed, we were *made* to feel ashamed! I'm fine, Joe. *That's* not me! How are *you*?!"[18] In general, such assurances did not help. Jack Goldman recalls:

> I was always uncomfortable when people would expect me to be the emaciated, depressed survivor every minute of my day. "Oh, you look so well," they would say, surprised that a year after liberation I no longer weighed eighty pounds, as I did when the Americans rescued me. And having a dull job, and loving music, I used to whistle or hum a tune, without even knowing

> what I was humming, or what the tune was, and people would say, "How can you whistle after all you've gone through?" Such questions seemed so ridiculous to me.[19]

Perhaps ridiculous, but a way we often respond to people whose experiences, for us, signify death – for example, chemotherapy patients or people with profound disabilities. Even as we may celebrate their "triumph of the human spirit," they frighten us profoundly.[20]

Indeed, a triumphalist rhetoric did join the melancholic one in the 1980s – survivors not as dead but as "celebrants of life," "heroic witnesses," "redeemers of the human spirit." Once the most alien of men and women, survivors suddenly became the most representative. But the discourse of ghosts, guilt, and (now) trauma, trauma, trauma has not gone away. More essentially, pedestals quarantine as effectively as asylums. Holocaust survivor Ruth Kluger writes: "Beware of the kind of awe which easily turns into its opposite, disgust. We like to keep the objects of both emotions at arm's length, in instinctive revulsion."[21] Whichever discourse we invoke to discuss survivors – celebratory or psychiatric – eulogies remain far more common than conversation; last words rather than first.[22] Again, Kluger about her listeners in general: "If they did listen, it was in a certain pose, an attitude assumed for this special occasion; it was not as partners in a conversation, but as if I had imposed on them and they were graciously indulging me."[23]

Partners in a Conversation

The notion of meeting survivors as "partners in a conversation" seems an obvious one. And yet, as I have suggested, collaborative engagement has been rare in projects involving survivors. More typically, we simply know *from* survivors – "gathering their testimony" – or know *about* them, using their accounts as "raw material" from which to construct theories and generalizations in the study and after the fact. What has been left out is knowing *with* survivors – "learning together" as Agi Rubin puts it.[24] Indeed, I suggest that the very idea of "knowing *with*" survivors strikes many, especially among scholars, as strange, even threatening in a particular kind of way. This resistance, almost visceral, to collaborative work is itself worthy of analysis, and I return to it at the end of this chapter.

Here, it is worth describing a precedent to collaborative approaches that goes back to one of the earliest projects involving recording survivors' accounts. David Boder was an American psychologist, an immigrant from Russia well before the war, who travelled to Europe to record interviews with roughly one hundred survivors as well as with bystanders and others between July and September 1946.[25] He has been described by some as the first to gather survivor accounts and thus as the forefather of projects that were initiated decades later.

The reality is more complex and more interesting. By the time of Boder's work, there were already enormous testimony archives. The largest of these, created by historical commissions set up throughout Poland and occupied Germany, were organized mainly by survivors themselves. Much revisited in recent scholarship, the historical commissions had gathered ten to twenty thousand accounts in various forms by 1947, dwarfing Boder's hundred-plus.[26]

Gathering artefacts as well as eyewitness accounts, the historical commissions' primary goal was the widest possible documentation of the destruction. Boder had a different aim. As a psychologist, he was interested in the ways that retelling catastrophe might be mediated by personality and reflected in language. Although he later abandoned the practice, he initially asked most of his interviewees to take a Thematic Apperception Test (TAT), a projective psychological test similar to the famous Rorschach.

Boder's project thus differed from both the historical commissions and the large videotestimony archives that were to come. Still, there are connections with the latter. Rather than using free writing or note-taking, which the historical commissions employed, Boder was the first to electronically record his interviews. He used a wire recorder, which he considered the best technology then available. Over time, his scientific mission also became one of advocacy. He was well aware that the 1945 newsreel images did not match the survivors he was meeting, especially the young. Increasingly, he aimed to substitute their voices and stories for the presumptions that he knew dominated perceptions of "Displaced Persons" in the United States.[27]

That said, he was not entirely comfortable with the changes provoked by his own experience. Academic and scientific respectability had its own claims, and Boder was no iconoclast. While, retrospectively, he suggested that he followed the same essential protocol throughout his two months of interviewing, it takes a closer look – which Alan Rosen has provided – to understand Boder's evolution. As noted, the TAT was dropped early on. Boder seems to have viewed it as mostly beside the point. More essentially, his work was initially anchored in a near juridical testimony model: that witnesses should tell only what they personally saw or experienced and avoid "hearsay" and wider reflection. Only in this way, Boder believed, could survivors' accounts be both convincing and, by the standards of the times, scientifically useful. The concept obviously has a certain nobility, and, as noted, it is a necessary conceit for some purposes. Still, Boder discovered that, within his own interviews, it was unsustainable.

As Rosen describes, Boder's interviews with Abraham Kimmelman were a watershed.[28] Even in 1946, then nineteen-year-old Kimmelman did not hesitate to present himself to the American professor, three times his age, as a co-investigator. In an opening statement that he asked be "on the record," Abe (I have come to know him) insisted that, no matter how many survivors Boder interviewed, none could present things as they "really were." Abe then proceeded to provide as detailed an account as Boder received, moving between particular episodes and reflection about their ethical significance, including the nature of human nature itself. As the interviews progress, Boder does not steer Kimmelman away from such reflection. Indeed, he appears to have become transfixed. Kimmelman's interview lasted more than twice as long as any of Boder's others, was the only interview that went beyond one session, and even then it was unfinished. Boder and Abe made plans to continue their conversation when Boder returned to Geneva a few weeks later. In his personal notes, Boder expresses regret when, in the end, his itinerary did not allow that further meeting.

On one level, Boder's Kimmelman interviews demonstrate what all interviewers know: that there are always certain people who will emerge as special participants. As I have described, interviewing may not be a science, but there is no avoiding chemistry.[29] More broadly, the Kimmelman interviews catalyzed a process of improvisation and experimentation in Boder's work that continued. While he tried different forms, and had varying results, his project was never the same again.[30]

Boder's capacity to learn from experience was perhaps best expressed in an interchange with Abe that has been cited by many. It comes near the close of the selection from the Kimmelman interviews included in Boder's 1949 book, *I Did Not Interview the Dead*.[31] Alan Rosen puts the same excerpt at the end of his own book on Boder himself:[32]

> KIMMELMAN: I want to ask you a question. You are a professor of psychology?
>
> BODER: Yes…

KIMMELMAN: Are the psychologists so advanced that they *really* know human nature so well. Do they *really* have a picture of man's various qualities? Do they really understand the human qualities so well?

BODER: Absolutely, no.

KIMMELMAN: You are entirely right. I didn't ask you simply because I wanted to know, because I knew this already. I just wanted to hear it from you. After all that I have seen, I know that we know nothing yet.

Learning Together

We know everything, said my professors in 1975. We know nothing, said Abe Kimmelman in 1946, and Boder qualifiedly agreed. There could hardly be more polarized perspectives.

From the perspective of the present, we would certainly be inclined to take the Boder/Kimmelman side. Not as an endorsement of nihilism, of course, but as an affirmation of how easy it is to oversimplify and how challenging it is – intellectually, ethically, and personally – not to. Mass destruction *begets* the temptation to stop short. In the face of its realities, and especially its images, what else is there to know? It is not easy to sustain the conviction that there is *everything* to know.

The relationship between Boder and Kimmelman has long held a special place in my own work as a psychologist and interviewer. Their virtual compulsion towards multiple interviews is part of it. Equally important is the glimpse into a collaborative process as it emerged in real time. Kimmelman *insists* on a collaboration that excludes nothing from discussion, including the core premises of the project itself. Boder is responsive and personally engaged, but he does not simply give in. As their dialogue continues, he pushes back:

BODER: Excuse me, Abe. You are a very fine young man, but you should never argue about things you really don't know [...] psychologists never claim that they have ascertained *everything* [...] How could a psychologist know what would happen under Hitler? Isn't that so?[33]

Kimmelman bides his time. He suggests that he and Boder defer that discussion until their mutually planned third meeting, which, sadly, never happened. For the moment, they "agree to disagree."

Kimmelman's particular style is very much his own – and still is, as will become apparent. But there is nothing unique about survivors breaking the frame of conventional testimony. Given opportunity and time, they almost always do. Even in single interviews, retelling particular episodes interweaves with reflections about the possibility of retelling at all – as it did for Kimmelman and for virtually every survivor with whom I have spoken over nearly forty years. As suggested by Leon's reflections, questions of meaning, philosophy, and theology are also ubiquitous in interviews with survivors. Survivors also commonly speak of the psychological impact of their experiences – even when the interviewer is not (like Boder or myself) a psychologist. Typically, psychological issues are both interesting to survivors themselves and, as survivors have learned, almost always of interest to their listeners. Thus, although we almost universally think of interviews with survivors as projects in oral history – and most large projects invoke the label "oral history" to describe what they do – the reality is that they are no less "oral philosophy," "oral narratology," "oral psychology," and more. Like "testimony," "oral history" is also a term of habit and may similarly be misleading as the foundational way to describe the process and content of survivors' retelling.[34]

That said, oral history itself has widened its focus over the years, increasingly engaging perspectives from ethnography, literature, communications, psychology, and beyond.[35] Within my own work, I would note aspects of my practice that were particularly influenced by psychology and, in particular, by my being a clinical psychologist.

There is, first, the use of multiple interviews. As I have described many times, it never occurred to me that most of my interviews with survivors would be limited to single sessions, and very few of them have been.[36] In the 1970s, psychiatrist Robert Coles was a particularly important model for me – especially his elucidating how racism and desegregation shaped the awareness of children in the American South.[37] Coles's acute sensitivity to detail and imagery – as well as to how very large (political, social, and historical) things can be illuminated by things seemingly psychological, private, and "small" – were an inspiration. His approach suggested that a clinician's sustained attentiveness could complement the "slow and careful work" of the civil rights activists and organizers with whom Coles also worked.[38]

While my interviews with survivors were not part of any therapy, my training as a therapist made it natural for me to assume that significant communications take time and trust to emerge – particularly the kind of trust that depends on two people having the experience of working specifically with each other. In the language of therapy, such a "working alliance" between participants is the foundation and prerequisite of everything else that might develop between them.[39] I assumed the same kind of sustained acquaintance and commitment to working together would be required in interviews with Holocaust survivors.

As it happened, most of the survivors I interviewed in the early years shared that assumption. Almost none of them anticipated we would only meet once, even though one-time interviews became the model in virtually all the "testimony" projects that developed later. In any event, most survivors suggested some version of "come back next week; we'll talk again; we'll talk some more." And so we did – over months, years, and, in a few instances, decades. The multiple-interview approach, a cornerstone of collaborative work, was thus itself developed collaboratively. Like so much else, it emerged *between* survivors and myself.[40]

Multiple interviews are a foundation of collaborative work both because of the "working alliance" facilitated by sustained acquaintance and because later interviews make it possible to test developing understanding. And, indeed, I often returned to parts of earlier interviews in subsequent ones. This has been most literally expressed in my bringing excerpts from earlier meetings to later meetings – especially easy to do with audiotape – so that the survivor and I could think about them together. Perhaps more than any other aspect of my approach, I believe this opportunity to work together over specific excerpts grounded interpretive collaboration – literally, labouring *with* – more generally.[41]

Here, too, my psychotherapist's habits played an essential role. Indeed, in the psychodynamic (essentially psychoanalytic) tradition in which I was trained, understanding attained by the therapist alone was not considered "interpretation" at all but, rather, "conjecture." Only within the therapeutic dialogue, and within the thick context of multiple revisions and permutations, could conjecture properly become interpretation.[42] Of course, this is always a question of degree. Even within therapy, any interpretation is considered a "working hypothesis" that may be revised, and sometimes fully overturned, later in the process. In interviewing, too, no interpretation can be more than a hypothesis, always subject to potential refinement and revision.

As follows from this discussion, I have also believed that deploying survivors' recounting in brief, illustrative bits easily blinds us to the evolving personal and interpersonal contexts within which it is constructed. Thus, I typically present survivors not as excerpts from "testimony" but, rather, as particular people whose retelling cannot be separated from their wider individual life histories. Presenting survivors as individuals with whom readers also become acquainted (through one's writing) also runs counter to conventional practice – both in work concerning survivors and in much of oral history more generally.[43]

It happens that David Boder also followed a modified life history approach, writing about the people he interviewed in a genre that he called "topical autobiographies" – long chapters, each of which focuses upon the retelling of a particular interviewee. Boder's approach reflected both the convention of "case histories" in psychoanalysis and the "study of lives" tradition in personality psychology.[44] Interestingly, Boder also did not call his interviews "testimonies," even though the Yiddish equivalent of testimony was one of the terms employed by the contemporaneous historical commissions. Rosen notes that Boder "did not use the term '*testimony*,' but rather referred to the DP interviews as narratives, reports, personal histories and documents, stories, and even 'tales.'"[45] As I argue later in this chapter regarding collaborative interpretation, Boder also believed that the most compelling generalizations are precisely those that *require* – rather than reduce – different individual perspectives: the careful piecing together of a "mosaic," as he described it to Kimmelman.[46]

With all of this in mind, then, the Boder-Kimmelman exchange represents less a precursor to later projects than a road – perhaps just the suggestion of a road – mostly not taken. Still, other chapters in this volume present exceptions. Different as each project is, there is much they share: interviews are part of sustained relationships that go far beyond formal recording; the authors are acutely sensitive to both the complementarities and differences between their own priorities and those of their partners; the entire process of collaboration is understood to be evolving and unpredictable – a "voyage of discovery" for both participants, as I have described it elsewhere.[47] In work like this, we come a very long way from the one-stop, one-way model of "gathering a testimony." The creative improvisation that Boder stumbled into – partly because he could not resist it – has become, in these projects, a necessary and cherished part of method.

Such improvisation, however, is not cherished more generally. Indeed, over the years I have learned that conventional ways of engaging survivors have become so taken-for-granted that it is difficult to persuade people that there *can* be any other option. This is particularly so within history and literary studies, which have dominated work related to "testimony."

I return to this issue at the end of the chapter. Here, I discuss two additional examples of sustained collaborative work precisely because they are situated both within, and against, conventional historiography and literary study. What becomes striking, I believe, is how profoundly collaborative engagement can enhance the yield of both – and in parallel ways.

Beyond Testimony

Like Abe Kimmelman, Helen (a.k.a. "Zippi") Tichauer was also one of the survivors David Boder interviewed in 1946. She was on one of the first transports of Slovakian Jewish women taken to Auschwitz in 1942 and, thus, among the first Jewish prisoners in Auschwitz. What she endured was horrific enough. But her skills as a graphic artist provided her access to the names and numbers of registered prisoners because she inscribed those numbers on tags sewn onto prisoners' uniforms. She thus had a unique perspective on the wider organization and development of the camp. She is also a "natural" documentarian and, consequently, a survivor who has had a particular affinity with Holocaust historians. Historians also rely on "chemistry" as they find (and are found by) key informants.

For all of these reasons, a group of historians associated with the United States Holocaust Memorial Museum's Office of Oral History had established sustained relationships with Zippi over many years. In 2011, Jürgen Matthäus, one of the museum's senior historians, published *Approaching an Auschwitz Survivor*, a unique collection in which five different historians write about the process and fruits of their long collaborations with Zippi.[48] It is an exceptionally informative work – both because of the history it retells and, most pertinent to this chapter, because of what it suggests about the collaborative process itself.

Like other contributors, Atina Grossmann vividly describes her work with Zippi. Zippi's stories, Grossmann writes, were "transmitted over a period of several years":

> At first during visits to her New York apartment, darkened against the sun that hurt her almost blind eyes and overflowing with the

> books and papers of her private Holocaust archive, and then in numerous long telephone conversations (somehow we often called each other just when I was on my way to the airport for yet another conference) [...] [And they] always both reinforced and subverted what I was uncovering in other sources. Further complicating the relationship between history and testimony, or, as I suspect Zippi would prefer, between history as understood by the historian and history as transmitted by the eyewitness, is the circumstance that even my best efforts to convey Zippi's (sometimes utterly against the grain) challenges to my research findings are of course my renditions of what she told me – frequently (especially more recently) not during anything resembling formal interviews (or oral histories) but on the phone, with me frantically scribbling notes on whatever pieces of paper happened to be available.[49]

Like contributors to the present volume, Grossmann is exquisitely sensitive to the differences as well as the complementarities between herself and Zippi with regard to privilege (e.g., who writes what is published), perspective, and long-range purpose. Awareness of that complexity only adds to our understanding of the multiple dimensions of their collaboration: conversations over "several years," initiated by *either* survivor or scholar, in person or by phone, recorded and scribbled, scheduled and on the fly (literally) – a constantly creative, improvisatory, and evolving process. Once again, in work like this we are on a different methodological planet from the one-time, video-framed, relatively contained (by studio or living room) and brief (usually two to three hours) encounters that we have come to associate with "gathering survivor testimony."

By the time Grossmann wrote her chapter, she had been talking with Zippi for five years. Other contributors to the Matthäus volume had collaborated with Zippi over fifteen years. While all such partnerships rest on a mutual commitment to working together, they do *not* (as Grossmann makes so clear) rest on agreement. Indeed, it is precisely sustained and respectful engagement that makes *dis*agreement possible, useful, and recognizable as such. A text may be challenging, but it cannot directly tell you (on the way to the airport) whether it thinks you get it and in what specific ways. Likewise, accounts as texts (gathered by someone else) more easily elide or conceal. While one may be able, in essence, to guess what issues are avoided in an archived testimony, that is a world away from what one learns by attempting – in multiple ways, over multiple conversations, eye-to-eye – to ask about them.

While Grossmann's interviews with Zippi began as eliciting memories – itself a subtle craft – by the time of the description cited here they were actively (in Grossmann's phrase) "sparring."[50] Far from surrendering or even tabling her hard-won historian's knowledge, Grossmann brings that knowledge directly *into* her conversations with Zippi – citing other sources and findings, especially her own. Of course, it is a subtle dance, which always depends, among other things, on the nature of the relationship and one's sense of one's partner. One does not pursue every question in the same way or with the same persistence. Meanwhile, survivors do their own assessing. "You study me, and I study you," said Victor, a Treblinka survivor about whom I have written much.[51] Victor's comment could stand as an epigram for every interview that has ever been done.

Work of this kind, then, has nothing to do with sentimentalizing "the witness" or "giving survivors voice" (an extraordinarily patronizing notion). It is, rather, the hard work of working hard together. Of some of the *most* challenging phases in her work with Zippi, Grossmann writes, "I ask more questions, listen more carefully, and realize that perhaps the stories are not contradictory but complementary, limning the same place and situation with different perspectives [...] part of an excruciatingly complicated story [...] that needs to be told in as layered (multilingual even) a fashion as possible."[52] Sometimes, collaborative work goes nowhere. Sometimes, participants can only "agree to disagree" (*where* may itself be informative and would never have emerged *without* their sustained dialogue). Sometimes, the most inclusive generalizations are precisely those that emerge from differences. As we might say it in everyday conversation: "You see it this way, I see it another. But aren't we talking about different aspects on the same thing ('limning the same place and situation') at another level?" It is precisely the differences in perspective that reveal the "other level." Their juxtaposition puts whatever "same issue" – and its complexity – *into* perspective.[53]

The publication of the Matthäus collection was a significant event because, as I have emphasized, collaborative work with Holocaust survivors has been rare. Relatedly, the project brought together top-notch historians in association with the United States Holocaust Memorial Museum – not a "marginal" context. Personally, I found much in its chapters that complemented my own collaborative efforts and, in its way, a return to the possibilities suggested by Boder's work so many years ago. And so I describe one additional example.

Abe Pasternak is one of the survivors I have known since my initial interviews in the 1970s. Like the partnerships described in other chapters, our relationship has extended far beyond formal interviews – friendship, consulting on his anticipated class visits and other public talks, and discussing a range of other topics of mutual interest. Like Abe Kimmelman, Abe Pasternak is a memorable "character," but in a different way. He is less critic than searcher, with a unique capacity to read his listeners and to push them to search as well. Early on in our relationship, he pushed me as follows: "So, Hank, you're a psychologist. So do you think the survivors are all crazy?" I treaded water. After a few beats, Abe came to my rescue: "*Of course*, we're crazy! You'd have to be *crazy* to go through something like that and not be crazy!" If experiences like this do not teach a young interviewer/psychologist the advantages of "knowing with," then nothing will.[54]

Over all these years, I have spoken with Abe about the Holocaust many times, just as I have heard him speak in a range of other contexts. I have thus heard many versions of his recounting and seen the ways it changes in response to what he has learned "works" both for him and for his audience – a process of self-editing of which Abe is very much aware. While there are times when Abe is caught up in memory and his "story" seems to tell itself, his recounting is also creative and contingent, responsive to specific contexts and specific listeners. My experience has been that Abe's creative agency in retelling is typical of Holocaust survivors – including those who seem most haunted by the destruction.[55]

Against the background of long acquaintance with Abe and the permutations of his retelling, I have discussed Lawrence Langer's interpretation of a particular excerpt from a 1984 interview with Abe archived in Yale's Fortunoff collection.[56] Langer's interpretation was of special interest to me because, over the years, I had heard Abe retell multiple versions of the episode as well as his own interpretation of its significance (including why he retells it). So here was the chance to directly juxtapose interpretation based on a single archived "testimony" with interpretation emerging from sustained acquaintance and collaboration.

The excerpt comes from Abe's discussion of the initial "selection" at Auschwitz. His parents were sent to one side, with those doomed to be gassed immediately (which Abe, of course, did not know), while Abe, along with an older and younger brother, were sent to the other.

Abe recalls sending his "kid brother" to be with their parents. "Little did I know I sent him to the crematorium," Abe reflects in the 1984 interview.[57] In that context, he expresses considerable guilt over his action. It is Abe's guilt – even more specifically his saying, "I feel like I killed him" – that is Langer's focus.[58]

As part of his analysis, Langer notes that Abe, in taking so much responsibility himself, does not blame fate, God, or the perpetrators themselves. That is generally true in the 1984 interview, which was all Langer had to consult, but it is absolutely not true in earlier versions of the episode as Abe had retold it to me. Indeed, in those earlier interviews Abe *does* "blame God," if ambivalently, and describes having done so for years. In a 1979 recounting of the same memory, Abe mentions his guilt, but he also reflects that his blaming himself for his little brother's death is "ridiculous."[59] There was thus a clear evolution towards the 1984 version of Abe's account, knowledge of which, obviously, requires familiarity with Abe's earlier retelling.

Based on only the 1984 interview, Langer argues that, notwithstanding its genuine anguish, guilt helps Abe make "moral sense" of the amoral "inner chaos" he actually remembers: "He prefers to accept the possibility of his own blame [...] rather than embrace the law of systematic caprice that governed the selection process."[60] Blaming himself thus restores, even at Abe's own expense, a sense of meaningful moral choice to a world in which, for victims, there was none.

Langer's interpretation is compelling within the material to which he had access, but it does not square with Abe's earlier retelling or with Abe's wider reflections on guilt's significance. Indeed, Abe suggests that the story of his guilt, which had become increasingly salient in his retelling, had at least as much to do with helping *us*, his listeners, make sense of the "chaos." He reflects:

> People don't want to listen to the, the – how do I describe the – corpses that were lying around there, like, like, like garbage. Or the stench [...] They can't understand, they can't relate to, the terror, the smell, the chaos, the dead bodies all around. How can they relate to that?! But *this* [his expression of guilt] they can relate to. I noticed that [...] Yes, I noticed that. *This* they related to.[61]

While Langer suggests that guilt helps *Abe* make sense of the terror, stench, and chaos, Abe himself suggests that retelling guilt is mainly for *our* benefit – or at least for the benefit of conveying *something*: "This they can relate to."

How do we square the two interpretations? There is no need to make a definitive choice; they are not mutually exclusive. But, just as for Grossmann and Zippi, there is no question that Abe's own perspective opens the way to a more complicated, layered, even multilingual story. Whether or not such complexity is desirable depends on one's purposes. But there is also no question that we could attain it far more often than conventional ways of engaging "testimony" generally allow.

In light of all this, I concluded:

> We cannot do without the perspectives of those, like Langer, who have probed survivors' accounts most deeply. But we also cannot do without survivors' own reflections on who they are, what they retell, and why. We cannot do without knowing where a particular fragment of recounting (especially one insistently repeated) sits within the rest that that survivor has to retell. We cannot do without knowing about the multiple versions of an account and its development over time. We also need to know about listeners' expectations of survivors, and survivors' perceptions of those expectations, as each recounter determines what will be hearable by their listeners and tellable by them.[62]

As listeners, we have generally been unaware of that dynamic, active, and interactive process. I argue that our ignorance has come at a cost.

Conclusion

Every way of engaging survivors has benefits as well as costs, promise as well as limitations. Not every project lends itself to the kind of collaboration described here and in other chapters of this volume. Not every interview pair will have the inclination, time, personal chemistry, and at least minimal mutuality of commitment (which does not mean identity of purpose) to make "knowing with" possible. Still, it has been my own conviction, as it is of other contributors to this collection, that a great deal more collaborative work could be done than has been done, particularly in the arena of Holocaust and genocide survivors. It is worth at least briefly suggesting why that approach has been so seldom pursued.

The primary disciplines that have been involved with gathering and interpreting survivor accounts – history and literary studies – rarely engage recounters directly. Unlike psychology, and branches of anthropology and sociology, history and literary studies are overwhelmingly concerned with writing – documents and texts – not speech. There is an interesting converse phenomenon: a tendency, especially among text-centred literary critics, to celebrate the presumed "immediacy" and "spontaneity" of oral retelling (usually as preserved on videotape) relative to accounts that are written. "We quite literally watch the narrator organize his testimony," James Young writes: "[Witness] is quite literally made before our eyes."[63] Lawrence Langer similarly notes: "Oral survivor testimony unfolds before our eyes and ears, we are present at the invention of what, when we speak of written texts, we call style. What is style, Jonathan Swift reminds us, but the search for proper words in proper places?"[64] As the example of Abe's retelling suggests, however, we are very rarely "present at the invention" of a survivor's "style"; rather, both the form and content of retelling evolve over years, co-exist in multiple versions, and are honed in response to different audiences and circumstances. When we talk with survivors directly – precisely what we *cannot* do with texts – they can often tell us how and why.

The much-discussed issues of interpretive authority are obviously at the core of responses to collaborative approaches. As other chapters in this volume relay, there are, indeed, always complex methodological and ethical issues within actual practice.[65] Atina Grossmann, for example, brings everything to the table in her formal and informal conversations with Zippi, even while remaining exquisitely sensitive to privileges (e.g., control over describing the process and results of their collaboration) that are not equally divided. Once again, different projects and different participant pairs will create their own division of the labour in collaborative work. And the only "authority" truly surrendered is *exclusive* authority: scholars having the *only* interpretive word that practically matters or, conversely, the suggestion that anything less means "giving *everything*" to "non-professionals." The latter argument, of course, is purely "straw man."

All of this suggests what many call the "messiness" of collaborative work: ethical dilemmas that are often unpredictable; the patience required on all sides, either to yield productive results or to conclude there are none to be had; and, most obviously, the complexity of human relationships themselves – all potential conflicts, as well as complementarities, presumed. Such work is, rightfully, not to everyone's taste and need not be everyone's pursuit. This chapter obviously aims to make the case for the virtues of collaborative work. But its wider argument concerns our need to think more self-consciously about the costs and benefits of *whatever* approach we pursue.[66]

These, then, are some of the general factors that militate against knowing founded in sustained collaborative engagement. There are also issues that pertain specifically to survivors of atrocity: those, as Ruth Kluger describes, whom we have particular reasons to keep "at arm's length" rather than meet as "partners in a conversation." Virtually every Holocaust survivor I have interviewed has eventually commented on the various ways that others keep them at ritual distance. Agi Rubin insists: "I am *not* a quote-unquote 'Survivor' with a capital 'S' [...] I always feel that turning us into Survivors makes us unreal again. Like the people in the newsreels, our loved ones, we also become creatures from another planet."[67] In a 2004 interview for the United States Holocaust Memorial Museum, Abe Kimmelman commented on the current trend in psychology to document Holocaust survivors' "resilience" – trauma's happy flipside – and his response to an invitation to be part of such a study.

> I said, "You want to meet me, you're welcome. I just want you to know that if the plan is that you write about me, that 'this is a man who has been through the circles of hell and has remained a normal person, and built a family, and he has children,' then I'll pass." [...] What does this have to do with an allegedly deep inquiry into the Holocaust? "There, you see, the people were in the Holocaust, and they stayed normal." That, of course, is only beneficial to those who need a patronizing approach to this issue, although they are not aware of it.[68]

"Patronizing" is, indeed, a common way to keep people "at arm's length." It implies no shortage of talk and speculation *about* them. But that, once again, has nothing to do with sustained talk *with* them.

I would suggest that, even now, after all these years, the notion of meeting survivors as genuine partners in conversation continues to seem somehow strange, even uncanny. Are we still, as Agi suggests, inhibited by "the newsreels"? "How can we learn *with* them after all they've gone through?" Some years ago, Professor Werner Weinberg, who is also a survivor, reflected about his colleagues' response to him in a traditional academic context:

> In the course of time my role as a survivor became well structured. It was almost as if I had specialized in the field of "survivorship" in addition to my official academic discipline [...] I began, with honest self-irony, to refer to myself as the "survivor-in-residence." Strangely, this seldom evoked mirth.[69]

If humour has something to do with providing candid and liberating perspective, we seem to struggle for it here.

It is obviously too late to redo most of the ways we have engaged Holocaust survivors. Still, I hope that this chapter and those that immediately follow leave us chastened. If it is too late to redo, it is not too late to rethink. There is no single way gathering Holocaust survivors' accounts had to be. And there is no single way gathering the accounts of others, who have gone through different hells, has to be.

Indeed, it is my sense that contexts other than the Holocaust are now most likely to yield truly innovative work. It is relevant to revisit Umwali Sollange's reflections on resistance to collaborative partnership:

> My experience of when I or other Rwandans speak of the 1994 genocide in Canada is often that of testimony delivered and received in highly formalized settings, set apart from the business of everyday living in a context that feels rarified, distant, and cold. [...] Likewise, in contexts that define roles and identities in rigid binaries of "us" and "them," even apparently well-intentioned practices of listening enact a kind of symbolic violence that I, as an invited speaker, have felt quite viscerally [...] For example, in my experience as a guest speaker in elementary or high schools across the greater Toronto area, children and youth were keen listeners and their questions were innocent, but I experienced an emptiness after sharing my stories. I felt like an academic performer talking about a world issue but without the authority of a teacher; I seemed to be an object of study for the students. [...] The feelings of emptiness, helplessness, hopelessness, guilt, fascination, pity, or romanticization that seemed to circulate within these events suggested to me that students were engaging with me more as a symbol than as a fellow human being, educator, or neighbour.[70]

Ruth Kluger or Abe Kimmelman or Werner Weinberg could not have said it better.

Notes

1 Of course, every term potentially "overgeneralizes" – that is what concepts do. The test is a pragmatic one: what is revealed, and what is obscured, in using a term in any particular way.

2 See, for example, Henry Greenspan, *On Listening to Holocaust Survivors: Beyond Testimony* (St. Paul, MN: Paragon, 2010), 1–7. The text above is a second and expanded edition of *On Listening to Holocaust Survivors: Recounting and Life History* (Westport, CT: Praeger, 1998). For the sake of simplicity, I have only cited from the second edition for this chapter.

3 This is not to say that testimony does not require listeners – without some faith in that possibility, survivors do not recount at all. And it is certainly true that every interview is "co-constructed" to the extent that two people are usually involved. But "co-construction" can mean very different things – from one-time "eliciting" to active and sustained exploration. Given the variety in actual interview practice, invoking "co-construction" does not tell us much.

4 Agi Rubin and Henry Greenspan, *Reflections: Auschwitz, Memory and a Life Recreated* (St. Paul, MN: Paragon, 2006), 219–20.

5 Long before more recent controversies surrounding the diagnosis of "post-traumatic stress disorder" and its applications, clinicians have worried about the inflated use of the concept of trauma more generally. Thus, as early as 1967, Anna Freud wrote that the over-use of "trauma" would "in the course of time, lead inevitably to a blurring of meaning and finally to abandonment and loss of a valuable concept." Cited in Henry Krystal, *Integration and Self-Healing: Affect, Trauma, Alexithymia* (New York: Routledge, 2009), 140. As an example of how all-inclusive the use of "trauma" has become, a student with whom I recently met for academic advising scanned my office bookshelf and said, "I see you are interested in trauma." After she left, I looked through the shelves. While there were many titles that concerned the histories of genocides, not a single one included the word "trauma." (She also was not aware that I am a psychologist!)

6 Susan Brison, *Aftermath: Violence and the Remaking of a Self* (Princeton, NJ: Princeton University Press, 2002), 38. Henry Krystal similarly defines the core of trauma as "surrender to what one experiences as an unbearable situation with no escape, no exit." See Krystal, *Integration and Self-Healing*, 154. It will be noted that both Brison and Krystal emphasize that it is the traumatized person's assessment ("feeling," "perception," "experience") of the situation as inescapable and lethal that makes it traumatic. No situation in itself, no matter how horrific, is *necessarily* traumatic as these writers understand the term, although it is obvious that some are horrific enough that virtually anyone immersed in them will experience some version of trauma.

7 I have tested this notion with my own students many times. When imagining themselves in the camps – as we all inevitably do – they often describe feeling terror or hopelessness, seeing barbed wire or chimneys, and the like. But they virtually never mention seeing dead people. Indeed, they rarely mention other people at all, with the occasional exception of immediate family. Relatedly, one unanticipated consequence of the contemporary habit of subsuming mass murder under "trauma" is that, effectively, it makes the dead go away. Trauma almost always refers to the impact of catastrophe on those who did *not* die.

8 In Jean Hatzfeld, *The Antelope's Strategy: Living in Rwanda after the Genocide* (New York: Farrar, Straus, and Giroux, 2009), 107.

9 As I emphasize further on, mass graves and anonymous corpses filmed at liberation *are* very much part of our images of the destruction. But this, of course, is not seeing "the individuals before they became victims" – or even during the Holocaust itself.

10 Rubin and Greenspan, *Reflections*, 105–6.

11 In Jean Hatzfeld, *Life Laid Bare: The Survivors in Rwanda Speak* (New York: Other Press, 2006), 117.

12 I have long taken issue with the commonly held notion that retelling trauma "as a narrative" aids "healing," at least among Holocaust survivors. Rather, engagement with an interested listener is far more significant, whether one's account is an "integrated narrative" or not. See, for example, Greenspan, *On Listening*, 270–72. I return to this issue in the Afterword.

13 See Taylor, Rwigema, and Sollange (Chapter 3, this volume).

14 Henry Greenspan, "Beyond Testimony," *Past Forward: The Digest of the USC Shoah Foundation Institute for Visual History and Education* (Autumn 2010): 11.

15 See, for example, Henry Greenspan, "Survivors' Accounts," in *The Oxford Handbook of Holocaust Studies*, ed. Peter Hayes and John Roth, 414–27 (New York: Oxford University Press, 2011).

16 Greenspan, *On Listening*, 59–73.

17 Paul Chodoff, "Psychotherapy of the Survivor," in *Survivors, Victims, and Perpetrators: Essays on the Nazi Holocaust*, ed. Joel E. Dimsdale, 205–18 (Washington, DC: Hemisphere Publishing Company, 1980), 216.

18 Greenspan, *On Listening*, 57.

19 Sylvia Rothchild, *Voices from the Holocaust* (New York: New American Library, 1981), 373.

20 See Henry Greenspan, "On Testimony, Legacy, and the Problem of Helplessness in History," *Holocaust Studies: A Journal of Culture and History* 13, 1 (2007): 48–49; and Greenspan, *On Listening*, 283.

21 Ruth Kluger, *Still Alive: A Holocaust Girlhood Remembered* (New York: Feminist Press, 2001), 94.

22 See Greenspan, *On Listening*, 63–71.

23 Kluger, *Still Alive*, 94.

24 Greenspan, *On Listening*, 217–19.

25 Alan Rosen, *The Wonder of Their Voices: The 1946 Holocaust Interviews of David Boder* (New York: Oxford, 2010). Most of my discussion on Boder that follows in this section is indebted to Rosen's excellent, detailed study. I minimize references unless they document particularly important issues.

26 See Henry Greenspan, *The Awakening of Memory: Survivor Testimony in the First Years after the Holocaust, and Today* (Washington, DC: United States Holocaust Memorial Museum, Occasional Paper of the Center for Advanced Holocaust Studies, 2001); and Laura Jockusch, *Collect and Record: Jewish Holocaust Documentation in Early Postwar Europe* (Oxford: Oxford University Press, 2012). Jockusch's volume is, by far, the most thorough study of the historical commissions.

27 In the Introduction to *I Did Not Interview the Dead* (Urbana: University of Illinois Press, 1949), Boder's first book on his interviews, he writes pointedly: "The displaced persons, in spite of their sorry state today, are not riffraff, not the scum of the earth, not the poor devils who suffer because they don't know their rights, not idlers who declaim that the world owes them a living. They are uprooted people" (xviii).

28 See Rosen, *Wonder*, 77–83, on the significance of the Kimmelman interviews. In 1946, Kimmelman went by the German spelling, "Kimmelmann" and is thus named in Rosen's book. Today, he lives in Israel and goes by "Kimmelman" in English. For the sake of simplicity, I use the current spelling throughout.

29 See Greenspan, *On Listening*, 233–34, on "chemistry" and the question of whether that yields selective bias in interview-based projects.

30 About the legacy of the Kimmelman interviews, Rosen writes, "Boder was now primed to experiment with new forms of narration." Rosen, *Wonder*, 83.

31 David Boder, *I Did Not Interview*, 126–27. Boder uses pseudonyms for his interviewees, Kimmelman's being "Abe Mohnblum." The title of the Kimmelman chapter is "What Is Man?" – very much in the spirit of Leon or, for that matter, Primo Levi, whose original English title of *Survival in Auschwitz* was *If This Is a Man*.

32 Rosen, *Wonder*, 230.

33 Boder, *I Did Not Interview*, 127.

34 Greenspan, *On Listening*, xiii.

35 It is relevant that, as much as documentary history remained central, even the historical commissions established during the first years after liberation followed a methodology that included folklore, anthropology, and psychology. See Jockusch, *Collect and Record*, especially 89–104.

36 Ibid., 1–3.

37 Especially influential was Robert Coles, *Children of Crisis: A Study of Courage and Fear* (Boston: Atlantic-Little-Brown, 1967).

38 The expression "slow and careful work" comes from Charles Payne, *I've Got the Light of Freedom: The Organizing Tradition and the Mississippi Freedom Struggle* (Berkeley: University of California Press, 1995), 136.

39 The concept of the therapeutic alliance is most fully explicated in Ralph Greenson, *The Technique and Practice of Psychoanalysis* (New York: International Universities Press, 1967).

40 I often cite Agi Rubin's saying to me: "For remembering, I need your questions, the spark of conversation, fully to bring it out. Then memories take their shape and find their words. They emerge between us." See Greenspan and Rubin, *Reflections*, xviii. It is my impression that truly engaging the concept of "the between" – particularly as the locus of phenomena like memories – has been one of the impediments to acceptance of collaborative work.

41 I should note that it was usually (but not always) me who suggested what excerpts to revisit – the kind of inevitable negotiating of agenda that is part of collaborative work.

42 The distinction between conjecture and interpretation is well articulated in Charles Brenner, *Psychoanalytic Technique and Psychic Conflict* (New York: International Universities Press, 1976), 35–58. Regarding the psychoanalytic approach in general, Michael Maccoby summarizes it by saying that, in psychoanalysis, the patient becomes a necessary "co-investigator." See Michael Maccoby, *The Gamesman* (New York: Bantam, 1976), 32.

43 As always, there are important exceptions. Daniel James's *Doña María's Story: Life History, Memory, and Political Identity* (Durham, NC: Duke University Press, 2001) may be the best known. It is often assumed that attention to individual biographies makes collective portraits impossible. I argue against this assumption in *On Listening*, 77–113.

44 Rosen, *Wonder*, 178–82.

45 Ibid., 12 (emphasis in original). The historical commissions employed a number of terms to describe eyewitness accounts, including, as noted, the equivalent of testimony. Laura Jockusch, who is expert on this subject, summarizes: "What I found is that the most common term for 'testimony' at the time was the Yiddish *gviyes-eydes*, derived from the Hebrew *gviat-edut*. The biblical Hebrew word *edut* has multilayered legal

and theological connotations as 'witness,' 'testimony,' 'evidence.' For example in Ex. 25: 16, 21–22, the scripture is referred to as a 'testimony' of God's deeds." (personal communication, 5 June 2011). To return to Ruth Kluger's phrase, giving testimony or bearing witness clearly is a "special occasion" – and appropriately so. And it is also, once again, a very different and more particular mode of retelling than the kind of collaborative partnership towards which Kimmelman was pushing Boder.

46 Rosen, *Wonder*, 78–79.

47 Rubin and Greenspan, *Reflections*, 217–20.

48 Jürgen Matthäus, ed., *Approaching an Auschwitz Survivor: Holocaust Testimony and Its Transformations* (New York: Oxford University Press, 2009).

49 Atina Grossmann, "Living On: Remembering Feldafing," in *Approaching an Auschwitz Survivor: Holocaust Testimony and its Transformations*, ed. Jürgen Matthäus, 73–94 (New York: Oxford University Press, 2009), 75.

50 Ibid., 81.

51 Greenspan, *On Listening*, 213.

52 Grossmann, "Living On," 82–83.

53 I have tried to exemplify the method of juxtaposition – and its difference from thinking of generalizing as the search for "lowest common denominators" – in Greenspan, *On Listening*, 77–113.

54 I have often thought of this episode with Abe as my own "Kimmelman moment."

55 Compare Anna Sheftel and Stacey Zembrzycki (Chapter 8, this volume). In my own work I have often quoted Leon's description of his retelling: "It is *not* a story. It has to be *made* a story. In order to convey it. And with all the frustration that that implies. Because, at best, you compromise. You compromise" (Greenspan, *On Listening*, 3). By definition, whatever is a "compromise" can change – and often does.

A guiding assumption of "trauma studies" is that truly traumatic memories are relatively unchanging and persist independent of creative agency until "integrated." This is a very complex issue. I would only suggest that, while certain sensory memories associated with terror (especially smells and sounds) may have such an independent life, they rarely encompass an entire episode or scene. Even when revisited by such memories, therefore, survivors are most typically able to construct narratives, including changing narratives, "around" or "beside" them. To that extent, creative agency in retelling is neither inhibited by such traumatic memories nor does it "integrate" them; rather, what is most typical is their co-existence.

56 The fullest analysis of Abe's retelling, his own interpretation of his motives, and that of Langer is in Greenspan, *On Listening*, 238–48.

57 The 1984 interview was conducted by Professor Sidney Bolkosky and is part of the Voice Vision Holocaust Oral History Archive. The recording was donated to the Fortunoff Archive at Yale, where Lawrence Langer found it. It can be viewed online at http://holocaust.umd.umich.edu/pasternak/.

58 A much more detailed description of the evolution of Abe's retelling, and the differences between Abe's own interpretations and Langer's, can be found in Greenspan, *On Listening*, 238–48.

59 Ibid., 242–44.

60 Lawrence Langer, *Holocaust Testimonies: The Ruins of Memory* (New Haven, CT: Yale University Press, 1991), 186–87.

61 Greenspan, *On Listening*, 244–45.

62 Ibid., 247.

63 James Young, *Writing and Rewriting the Holocaust: Witness and the Consequences of Interpretation* (Bloomington: Indiana University Press, 1988), 161.

64 Langer, *Holocaust Testimonies*, 5.

65 The literature on what is variously called "shared inquiry," "sharing authority," or simply some version of "collaboration" has become enormous. Many key works are referenced in other chapters in this volume, so I will only mention a forthcoming collection that takes many of these issues to new levels of sensitivity and depth: Anna Sheftel and Stacey Zembrzycki, eds., *Oral History off the Record: Toward an Ethnography of Practice* (New York: Palgrave, 2013).

66 In an interesting recent article, Caroline Wake makes the case that it is precisely the *absence* of the "complications, implications and responsibilities" present in direct engagement with survivors that is one of the benefits of engagement through recorded "testimonies." This is a point worthy of consideration, but only when juxtaposed with the potentialities *present* in direct engagement – and especially in the collaborative approach I have emphasized – and is impossible at a remove. As I have reiterated, how one weighs limits and benefits will also vary for different projects, different purposes, different survivors, and different interview pairs. See Caroline Wake, "Regarding the Recording: The Viewer of Video Testimony, the Complexity of Copresence and the Possibility of Tertiary Witnessing," *History and Memory* 25 1 (2013): 111–44.

67 Rubin and Greenspan, *Reflections*, 198. Some of my students wondered whether, when there are no longer survivors with whom to meet directly, they will become like "unicorns" – semi-mythological beings.

68 Interview with Avraham Kimmelman, conducted in Israel on 6 May 2005, *United States Holocaust Memorial Museum*, Record Group–50.562*0009.

69 Werner Weinberg, *Self-Portrait of a Holocaust Survivor* (Jefferson, NC: McFarland and Company, 1985), 13.

70 Taylor, Rwigema, and Sollange (Chapter 3, this volume).

6 | Collaborative Witnessing and Sharing Authority in Conversations with Holocaust Survivors

CAROLYN ELLIS | JERRY RAWICKI

"Death was not the problem; survival was," is Jerry's reply when I ask him, "Did you think about death during the Holocaust?" His answer piques my interest, and a long conversation ensues about how he escaped the Nazi killing machine as a young boy living in the Warsaw Ghetto. In his stories, Jerry repeatedly asserts how "lucky" he was, and I am continually impressed by the ingenuity he showed under pressure.

In this chapter, we describe the collaborative witnessing process that Jerry Rawicki and I employed as we co-constructed and mutually analyzed stories about how he survived during critical moments when his life was in danger. Our goal is to build on the burgeoning interest in sharing authority in oral history[1] and to respond to Linda Shopes's call to show and reflect on how this cooperation works in practice.[2] We focus on the process Jerry and I used to write one of these stories together, emphasizing the opportunities and difficulties that emerged in our collaboration. In the first part, we relate the story in its final form, composed as a literary work intended to draw readers in to feel the experience, consider its meanings and implications, and retell it to others. After this representation, we present a transcript of the story as Jerry told it in our first interview. A second transcript then demonstrates how we began to construct the details of the story together. A third transcript segment includes a portion of a session in which we collaboratively analyzed the meaning of the story, focusing on the role of luck and agency in how Jerry managed to survive. From this and other sessions, we compose a coherent conversation that delves further into the moral of the story. We end the chapter by returning to the complexities of what it means to share authority in collaborative relationships.

Collaborative Narrators

At twelve years old, Jerry Rawicki was deported from Plock, Poland, to a ghetto in the small town of Bodzentyn, Poland. He and his sister escaped Bodzentyn, taking considerable risks as they hid in the forests and then passed as non-Jewish on public transportation. They made their way to Warsaw, where Jerry rejoined his father in the Warsaw Ghetto and his sister lived as a Gentile in the City. From the age of fourteen to sixteen, Jerry acted as a courier between the Jewish resistance and Polish underground. After surviving the Warsaw Ghetto uprising in 1943, he passed as a Roman Catholic in Poland for the remainder of the war and then moved to the United States in February 1949, where he married and became an optician. Now eighty-five years old, he has a passion for talking and thinking about the Holocaust, both from a historical and a personal point of view.[3]

I, Carolyn, am an ethnographer interested in storytelling, in particular stories about loss, trauma, and grief. Educated as a sociologist, I started out doing community ethnography. After a number of personal losses, I turned my attention to writing auto-ethnographically about what happened to me as a way to understand experiences of loss sociologically and also to add concrete, lived, emotional experiences to the study of social life.[4] Working at the intersection of humanities and social science, I do research as a communication scholar and ethnographer who keeps field notes on her own experiences in interaction with others, and I express my efforts in stories, using scenes, dialogue, character development, and plot. I seek to write stories that invite readers to "experience the experience" – to feel the feelings conveyed, retell the story to others, and respond with stories of their own. My goal is to open up conversation about the story's content and the moral issues it raises.

Since 1990, I have worked collaboratively with participants, using interactive interviewing and co-constructed narrative approaches. These methods encourage researchers and participants – one and the same – to examine and write their stories together, telling and examining their emotional experiences in the events depicted as well as in the research process.[5] In the project described here, I bring these narrative and ethnographic approaches to my study with Holocaust survivors. My intent is to work collaboratively with them, focusing on their lives, honouring the interactional context that we share as co-narrators, and showcasing the evocative power of their stories.

I met Jerry in March 2009 when I worked with the University of South Florida (USF) Holocaust and Genocide Center and the Florida Holocaust Museum to interview forty-five survivors living in the Tampa Bay area. The interviews were digitized, and transcripts and audio are available on the USF Libraries website.[6] Early in this interviewing process, I made arrangements to continue meeting with several survivors who showed interest in continuing to talk about their experiences. This group included Jerry, with whom I had conducted an initial four-hour interview. I was impressed with how deeply Jerry considered my questions and the emotionality and insight with which he told his stories. A bonus was that he had written and published a novel and several creative nonfiction pieces.[7]

Jerry and I have been talking and writing together for more than three years. We have recorded more than a dozen sessions thus far and plan to record many more. We have co-authored one short story and two articles, both of the latter containing short stories and commentary about survival.[8] These stories involve months of daily back and forth editing, commenting, and decision making as we figure out how best to convey his experience and gain insight into its meaning.

Collaborative Witnessing

We call this methodological approach "collaborative witnessing." This effort has been influenced during the last thirty years by qualitative researchers, feminists, and others writing from a postmodern sensibility,[9] and it has much in common with the development of a collaborative and multiple interview process in oral history in which researcher and survivor share authority.[10] Henry Greenspan, a pioneer in this approach with Holocaust survivors, spent several decades talking and writing with the same narrators. He describes an interview as "knowing with," a "particular kind of collaborative conversation: one in which two people work together to gain their best possible understanding of the experiences and reflections of one of them, the interviewee."[11] In his book with Agi Rubin, Greenspan notes that, though the story told and its insights are "entirely Agi's," the "retelling itself came to life, as Agi said, 'between us.'"[12]

Focusing on how context and relationship affect the stories created in interaction during interviews, we also intersect the work of those interviewing survivors, such as Greenspan and Dori Laub, who caution against separating or distancing ourselves (the listeners) from survivors

FIGURE 6.1 Jerry and Carolyn working together. *Photograph courtesy of Carolyn Ellis.*

(the tellers). Greenspan, for example, talks of the importance of being "*in*": "*in* the process, *in* the rhythm, *in* the details and their potential significance."[13] Collaborative witnessing connects the roles of storyteller and listener so that both come to be narrators together, to know and tell *with* each other in mutual engagement of hearts and minds joined in long-term relationships and dialogic exchange. This approach encourages survivors to take greater ownership of the interpretation and meaning of their testimony, and interviewers to have greater latitude for improvisation, questioning, and engagement with survivors and their stories.

As a collaborative witness, I view my time with survivors as intimate, multifaceted, and incremental. Sometimes our conversations are light and easy, as relationships sometimes are, and less formal than traditional interviews. Sometimes we talk further about an incident described in the original archived interview. Sometimes we talk about how the Holocaust affected their lives after liberation. We talk about memory and forgetting, the impact storytelling has on their emotions, their anger and sorrow, their thoughts of forgiveness and feelings of revenge. As we laugh, cry, and rage together, chaos and rupture appear alongside narrative coherence; self-reflection intersects storytelling about the events that occurred.

We do not only sit and talk. We share meals and attend Holocaust events. We meet with other survivors or family members. We e-mail throughout the week, and pass books, articles, and videotapes back and forth that we then discuss on e-mail or in person. In these multiple contexts, we become comfortable talking about and listening to the intricacies of traumas and deep feelings. Although I always arrive with camera and audio recorder, sometimes they remain packed in their cases. Survivors (like Jerry) and I want and need unrecorded time to break out of our roles of researcher and researched, to explore intimate topics and the pain they might not want recorded, to discuss topics outside the Holocaust, and to become friends who share our current life experiences.

As a researcher, I play an active role in the stories that are told by survivors in terms of the questions I ask, the verbal and emotional responses I give, and my body language. Thus, in all the original interviews, the filming crew set up two cameras: one focused on the survivor and one that includes the survivor and interviewer in the frame, so that the interactive space and responses of the interviewer might also be observed. In follow-up conversations, the relationship that forms between a survivor and researcher and the history we share affects stories told. Sometimes stories are generated that may not have been remembered and told before. I believe, like Rubin, in the context of working with Greenspan, that memory can be stimulated and "born in conversation." Rubin continues: "For remembering, I need your questions, the spark of conversation, fully to bring it out. Then memories take their shape and find their words. They emerge between us."[14] Stories and memories constructed in conversations with people in developed relationships are different in form and content from those told in one-shot interviews, in which one person, usually a stranger, asks questions and the survivor answers.

Collaboration also takes place during the analysis part of the process. I feel that nobody has deeper insight into what the stories mean than those who experienced them. Thus I resist separating the story analyzers (the academics) from the storytellers (the survivors), as has typically been done. Instead, I engage survivors in conversations about what their stories mean to them, and I discuss how I interpret the stories as well. As Greenspan notes, in an interview that is "cooking," "much of the interpreting takes place *within* the conversation."[15]

Collaborative witnessing requires developing deep, trusting, and open relationships with survivors. I feel called to be a secondary witness, to assist in the telling and meaning making, to listen intimately and to respond from my heart. That is the only way I know to comfort survivors when their memories are "too terrifying to remember in isolation" and too painful to be endured alone.[16]

Always the well-being of survivors is as important as my project; their well-being *is* my project. Thus, I let survivors determine the pace and how deeply we explore, and I have no plans to "exit the field" as long as they desire and are able to converse with me. I believe it is my responsibility to do everything I can so as not to do harm. I take it seriously when survivors say they want to experience attentive patience, gentleness, protection, care, even love when they give testimony.[17] Though I believe these sessions provide some of those comforts, I am also aware that sometimes remembering and telling bring to the present the pain and misery of loss and trauma. I am committed to being with survivors emotionally and relationally as a compassionate witness, listener, and recorder, maintaining, as I do, an awareness of the effect these discussions are having on them *and* on me.[18]

Collaborative witnessing involves researching with an "ethic of friendship," which, as Tillmann-Healy says, "means that although we employ traditional forms of data gathering...our primary procedures are those we use to build and sustain friendship: conversation, everyday involvement, compassion, giving, and vulnerability."[19] Thus, as collaborative interviewers we can expect similar demands and dynamics as those we experience in friendships: time and energy to nurture the relationship; issues with emotional investment, such as disappointment and hurt; matters of confidentiality and loyalty; and difficulties in and from being critical.

Likewise, difficulties might stem from the collaboration itself. For example, two narrators with different histories and experiences might differ in what they want to tell and how, as well as in the audiences they speak to, their goals, and the meaning they see in stories. These differences might be addressed through discussion and by including multivoiced narratives, where possible. Working through these issues might also strengthen the work and engage participants in deep memory, thick descriptions, and complex analysis.

I believe that being aware of these differences assisted Jerry and me to tell the best story we could, one that provides occasion to contemplate survival during the Holocaust. The product of many collaborative sessions, the story that follows is told by Jerry in the present tense, though he is looking back at his experiences. We tell it this way to invite readers to enter, feel, and think about what happened.

"Get the Jew": Jerry's Story

It is early morning and I am fortunate to be marching with a labour group through the gate of the Warsaw Ghetto, the only way to get out of the ghetto. I say "fortunate" because it is much better to be on the outside doing anything, even the heavy work sanctioned by the Germans, than stuck behind those walls, where people are starving and dying on the streets. The air feels fresh, not stale like the suffocating ghetto air permeated with death.

"Today seems like a good day to separate from the group," I tell myself. The word has gone out that the gate is "playing," which means someone has been able to bribe the German guards, who now pay little attention to us as we exit the ghetto.

Once we are on the Polish side, the next obstacle is the Polish police, who watch us as we march along the route to our work place. They too do not seem to be concentrating on us. They are not necessarily our friends, but perhaps some of them are human enough that they don't want to do us harm. Or maybe they just don't want to be bothered today. Or perhaps someone bribed them as well. My "reading" better be right; otherwise I will be in deep trouble when I pull away from the group and make a dash for "freedom." The police will arrest me on the spot and I'll be turned over to the Germans. I keep my eyes on the police, ready to change my plan quickly. Cautiously I slip my Jewish Star armband from my sleeve and hide it in my hand. It is supposed to be sewn on, but I have unstitched mine so that I can remove and attach it easily. Being caught without a band is punishable by death.

I position myself at the edge of the marching column so that I can make contact with the locals waiting outside the gate to do "business" with us ghetto Jews. As soon as we're out of the gate, the Polish locals surround us. They grab at the "merchandise" – everything from woollen socks to jewels – they know we have brought out for barter. We rip the smuggled items from under our clothes and frantically exchange them for food – sometimes eggs, meat, or lox – anything we can strap under our clothes to bring back to the ghetto after work that day.

As we continue marching to the work site, I cautiously separate myself from the group, slip my armband into my pocket, and mingle with the bartering crowd. I sigh a deep breath of relief. The separation is now complete. I have transitioned from my role of a Jew bartering with Gentiles into a Gentile bartering with Jews. Now comes the hard part: the threat from blackmailers who might be lurking, trying to catch me, a sitting duck, because that's what I am outside the ghetto – a vulnerable, defenceless sitting duck.

I move through the crowd that surrounds us. As I do, I feign boredom. "Hell with these dirty Jews," I say, as though I am fed up and don't want to barter anymore with them. Then I move away quickly.

Once among the crowd, I walk slowly and calmly. I'm free: free, that is, until I have to meet the work group and return to the ghetto at the end of the day. I'm free, that is, if no blackmailers, or *szmalcownik*, have seen me leave the group. I can't appear frightened; but I can't help glancing back. I know I can be turned in by a blackmailer and killed on the spot, but to get to the Polish side of Warsaw as a Gentile is worth the risk. Now I can interact "normally" with the Poles and go about my business. Still I have to be very cautious because somebody may have seen me leave the group and followed me.

Once outside the ghetto, I often have assignments from the Jewish underground, such as to deliver communications that must not fall into the wrong hands. Sometimes I become a smuggler of people, too, young children whose parents have arranged to get them out of the ghetto to be hidden by someone on the Polish side. Blackmailers assume that if I risked passing as a Gentile I must have something important to do. Their goal is to figure out what I am up to and catch me at it, so they can blackmail me. All they have to do is threaten to turn me in and they have me at their mercy and can take whatever goods I have on me. Of even greater value to them is to follow me and blackmail people I've led them to. Finding well-to-do Jews in hiding outside the ghetto is a bonanza because the blackmailers can make large sums of money by threatening to turn them in. But it isn't always just money they are after. Sometimes they try to catch us for sport or because they hate Jews so intensely.

Today, my job is to bring back food from the market for the people in the ghetto, and I clutch the money they have given me to make purchases.

Suddenly a big man approaches me. Something about his movements makes me tense up and change directions. I don't know why. After all, my non-Jewish features should help me blend into the crowds of Poles in the streets of Warsaw. I think I am safe when suddenly I sense his menacing presence. I turn and see him about twenty to thirty feet behind me, following my every move. To get away, I change directions, first slowly then frantically. With the sense of a stalked animal, I know he is a *szmalcownik*. Sadly, I know that a blackmailer, like a hungry carnivore closing in on his kill, will recognize a Jew.

My evading tactics fail. I hear the dreaded blood curdling "*Tam Żyd leci! Tam Żyd leci!*" (A Jew is running there! A Jew is running there!). Other voices join the pursuit, and I take off running as fast as my small and wiry fifteen-year-old body will move. Though I know I can outrun the big man, I am afraid I can't outrun what suddenly has become a full-blown chase. As I zigzag through the crowded streets, I am mindful that the stupefied pedestrians gawking at the bedlam might trip me or in some other way help the big man catch me. I run on anyway, since this is my only hope. Breathless now, I suddenly extend my hand forward, pointing and screaming: "A Jew is running there! A Jew is running there! Get the Jew!"

"*Gdzie?*" (Where?) The befuddled pedestrians take off running beside me. So now a small group is running down the street, with the big blackmailer way behind us.

At the top of my lungs I yell, "*Tam Żyd leci!*" (A Jew's running there!) still pointing in the direction we are headed.

"Get the Jew," reverberates around me as I slow down and duck into a courtyard. As I had hoped, the courtyard let out to another street and to safety. I try to compose myself, slow my breathing back to normal, and crawl into a cocoon of anonymity in hopes of living another day.

Co-Constructing the Story

To construct the story above, we started with the story Jerry narrated about this experience during our first formal, videotaped interview. Within a longer chronological narrative about life before, during, and after the Holocaust, he described this event quickly without much descriptive detail or opportunity for revision. In this more traditional "teller-and-listener" context, Jerry narrated the following.

JR: And some of these *szcmalcowniki*, these people, these blackmailers – they had, you know, hawk eyes; they knew exactly what was going on. And on one or two occasions, I thought I was safe and they approached me. One – on certain occasions, I gave him the few things that I had and they let me go. One time somebody spotted me, and I start running away and he says, "Hey, there's a Jew over there!" And right away there was three or four guys, because there were more than one. You know, there's very unfortunate things, because anti-Semitism was great. Warsaw – there was a war going on, people needed money. The combination of two made these blackmailers – you know, very active.

And remember that I told you that my training track and field helped? I started to run. I almost kept – I kept well ahead of them, but they were almost coming closer to me, and they were yelling, "There's a Jew running! Jew running!" And I kept saying the same thing. "There is a Jew over there!"

CE: Oh, that's wonderful!

JR: And I slowed down a little bit, and some of them, as they ran past me, say, "Where, where, where?" I say, "There right around the corner." [Laughs.]

CE: [Laughs.] Oh, that's wonderful!

JR: Yeah, I was very slick.

CE: Wow. Wow.[20]

I was immediately taken by this story because of Jerry's cleverness and quick thinking in getting out of the jam he was in as well as because of the passion and enthusiasm with which he told it. He smiled, laughed, and pointed exuberantly with his index finger when he demonstrated how he led the crowd towards where the imaginary Jew was running. We laughed together, as I uttered, "Wow. Wow," and the expression on my face – and on his – was one of delight. Then when he finished, he sighed and looked as though he were holding back tears, which portrayed the strong feeling this story engendered in him.

So why retell this story? While the original telling is powerful in and of itself, I wanted to reconstruct it with Jerry as a coherent, stand-alone story, worthy of analysis in its own right. I feared this brief but telling episode would get lost within a four-hour video and lengthy transcript. I wondered how many people would actually watch or read it in its entirety, and if those who did would recognize the importance of this episode, told so quickly within the dramatic events of Jerry's life in the ghetto. Moreover, I was struck by how cunningly Jerry had survived, and I wanted readers to get a glimpse of the dialectics of agency and luck so vividly present in this story.

Through the many conversational sessions that followed and in the many revised versions we constructed of the story, I asked questions and Jerry recalled more details and emotions. When he could not remember specific details, we did our best to fill in missing particulars by talking about what might have been the case and how a similar scene had played out at another time. Always we sought to stay as close to the truth of Jerry's memory of these events as we could. With the benefit of thinking and rethinking, writing and rewriting, we were able to recast this episode into a short story that readers could remember and retell, thus keeping it alive long after Jerry would be around to tell it himself.

I include here a small portion of one of our sessions during which we worked on the details of this story together.

CE: Okay, now describe that situation.

JR: Well, when he yells "the Jew," you have to understand, as I say, it was a very unusual scene, you know, for anybody to looking to running [*sic*] after somebody and people were – some of these bystanders pedestrians looked at me and they say, "oh, he's, he's running." So they could have very well apprehended me.

CE: Okay so … you saw the blackmailer and you started running.

JR: I saw the blackmailer, I presumed it was a blackmailer because he he says, "Hey, there's a Jew running."

CE: He said that. Okay, "there's a Jew running," okay…

JR: So the pedestrians…

CE: So you keep running then? [Talk over each other.]

JR: So I keep running, and I run, and the pedestrians stop and they look at me, you know. So they could have very well come to his help and tripped me or stopped me or something. So I … when they looked at me and say "here's a Jew running," and some of them kept running with me…

CE: [Laughs and claps.] I love this story. I love it so. Then what happened?

JR: And some of them … as I said I was very fast, and in this particular instance this is when I had about three or four people running with me. And I kept yelling, "there … is a Jew," and they say, "where, where, where." And I say, "over there," you know. And all of the sudden I was getting a little bit tired and I let them go ahead of me. The other guy was still behind me but I ducked into a – there were buildings in Poland that had courtyards – so I ran into one of the courtyards and the courtyards sometimes … had an entry from both streets and

CE: You hoped this one did.

JR: Oh, yeah, I got away, yeah.

CE: So you ran in and out the other side?

JR: Yeah, while they were running, he probably, he might … because there were so many people running. There was four or five people running that he might have at that time, I don't know whether he, maybe he got out of breath and all that.

CE: What did he look like, do you remember?

JR: No, I don't. You know I did, the only thing that I realized as he was after me is when he yelled because I was … I wasn't running to begin with. I talked to myself. I was very calm and collected and I start walking just like the others did … But he saw me from far away and say [*sic*] "hey there's a Jew here." And that's then I start running and say, "Where, where, where"… and with the people. That's why …

CE: Do you remember what you were supposed to be doing that day?

JR: I was supposed to go somewhere, you know, either deliver the letter or something, you know, a message or see somebody or, you know, but

CE: And then do you remember what happened after that?

JR: I just, I just went

CE: Did you go about your business?

JR: Oh, yes, yes, yeah ...[21]

After several similar sessions, I composed a version of the episode, one of eight stories that we wrote together in a two-year period. I e-mailed questions to Jerry and he responded by e-mail, and I then added new elements. Finally, I sent him a rough draft of the story. During one face-to-face session, I worked with him on using Microsoft Word's track changes. Though this process continued to frustrate him, he did manage to send track changes by e-mail. At first Jerry was hesitant to make changes in the texts that I wrote, but as time went on he began to make more comments and suggestions. Finally, when I had what I thought was a complete draft, I sent him a hard copy and he then mailed me typed out comments, which he seemed to be more comfortable with than making track changes.

Jerry wasn't the only one who was hesitant about how to respond. At first, I was reluctant to reject any of Jerry's changes. After all, it was his story. Soon, though, I saw that Jerry would let me know what really mattered to him, especially if he felt that what I said failed to match his memory of his experience. For example, we went over and over how he bartered with the Polish people and separated himself from the other Jews in the workgroup until he felt that our descriptions captured the process. Once I knew he would stand up for his position, I then became braver about trying to write the best story I could from what he and I talked about, revising it as it seemed appropriate.

Given that this was a collaborative process, one might wonder why I wrote all the first drafts of our stories. First, I felt it was my responsibility to do as much of the work as I could, especially since I didn't really know at the time what I wanted to (or what we could) produce from our collaborative efforts. Jerry assumed that this was primarily my project and thus looked to me to figure out how to proceed, though he had many questions and suggestions about the writing process. I tried to make it clear to Jerry that he was welcome to do as much of the writing as he wanted, and I would have been delighted to have had him structure the stories. But I also wanted to make sure I didn't burden him; it was enough that he was willing to participate in the ways he did. Second, to be quite candid, it might have been difficult for me to relinquish control and share authority to that degree, though I would be open to giving that a try in the future.

Co-Constructing the Analysis

Initially, I thought that Jerry would be more responsible for the stories and I would be more responsible for the analysis. I was surprised, then, when I asked Jerry, "What, do you think is the moral of this story?" and, with no hesitation, he answered.

> JR: Oh, well, the moral of the story, I think, is ... which is characteristic of many other stories, is we – and I say that when I talk to people at the groups, whether adults or children – we have acquired another sense, an animalistic sense, you know, like ... I love Discovery Channel and you see these animals
>
> CE: They sense danger
>
> JR: Yes, or they, or they sense danger and then when they are, you know, like the wildebeests and all that, how they have to, they know that they are trapped because there is a hyena or those fast animals, cheetahs, or something after them. And they know they are, they don't have a chance, and they run and some of them, they use all their cunning to to to kill it, to save their lives, and so was I. And we all develop these things. It was almost a, we felt like an animal, like a a hunted animal, and we had to ... This is a human, I think you know, any human in a situation like this will develop something like this. I don't think I was special or anything like this but – and you hear stories or read stories from the Holocaust that maybe they are different. Not particular, not this particular one that, but people use their cunning. It's not their cunning, it's this special, what is it, gift or feature...
>
> CE: Intuition that got developed in that situation
>
> JR: Yes, yes, and it happens immediately because it's something
>
> CE: It's a survival instinct
>
> JR: Yes, simple survival instinct. You know, I think it triggers something in your brain that ... from the ethnographic point [of view]...[22]

The conversation in this transcript is halting and disjointed, as conversations can be when two people are deep in dialogue about something that excites them. What is missing in this transcript that would make our words more understandable and our ideas more meaningful is a portrayal of our enthusiasm in our discoveries: how we leaned towards each other, listened closely, gestured wildly to make a point, and laughed together like two friends celebrating a successful venture. While it is difficult to reproduce that excitement in written text, we have created a dialogue from this and other conversations we had that more coherently shows the ideas we shared about how Jerry survived this episode. This conversation follows:

"Your yelling, 'There's a Jew running' was brilliant. How did you know to do that?" I ask Jerry.

Jerry responds, "This man was chasing me through the streets and this was unusual enough that I knew bystanders would pay attention. If they joined with the blackmailer, I wouldn't have had a chance. Given the anti-Semitism in Poland, the best way to get attention off me was to direct them to where an imaginary Jew was running. I figured repeating 'there's a Jew' in the middle of Warsaw would electrify people. They'd wonder, what's a Jew doing here? If I'd said, 'there is somebody running over there,' nobody would have paid any attention, but the word 'Żyd' [Jew] was like the plague, something dirty and repugnant. I used the worst word I could because I was posing as an anti-Semite."

I say, "You were able to figure out how to make that identity work. You knew what you had to do to pass and how to implement it."

Jerry responds: "Thankfully, I could pass as non-Jewish because of my appearance and non-accented Polish speech. Most Jews could not have passed as I did. But there was more. I also had to be *willing* to appear as anti-Semitic. Many Jews, even those who could pass, would not have been willing to act in those ways."

"You actually used their anti-Semitism against your enemy."

"I did, but this makes it all sound too planned out and rational," Jerry argues. "Much of what I did seemed to be the only choice I had at that moment. For example, with the blackmailer, I didn't decide that I should start yelling, 'there's a Jew running,' I just did it. You had to be mindful and in the present to figure out what to do next. Survival during this minute and the next was what mattered."

"You understood danger and were able to instinctively react on the spot, figuring a way out of the situation."

"I had this acquired sense of danger," says Jerry, "like the wildebeests you see on the Discovery Channel, and I used my cunning to save my life. I felt almost like a hunted animal."

"That's amazing."

"I think any human in a situation like this will develop a sixth sense," explains Jerry. "I don't think I was special; many people in the Holocaust learned to use their cunning to get themselves out of situations."

"Yes, a wildebeest doesn't count on luck," I say. "A wildebeest depends on instinct. Yours became more developed and kicked in more quickly than it might have in less dangerous situations."

"Yes, and then my actions triggered the endorphins in my brain and made me feel capable of doing things that normally I wouldn't have been able to do, like running fast enough to escape the blackmailer."

"The amygdala kicks in when you are in danger," I say. "You react before you think about what to do. Then the cognitive part of the brain provides more information. You were in so many dangerous situations that these neural pathways may have become more developed."

"Yes, oh yes," Jerry agrees, excited by our conversation. "It's like evolution speeded up. Under normal circumstances it might have taken years to deepen some of these responses."

"This makes me think about how the Nazis accused the Jews of being non-human animals and did everything they could to turn their victims into animals," I say. "But in taking on the role of wildebeest, as you did, and 'acting like an animal' in the ways we're discussing, you then developed a more refined capacity to survive. Just as you said that many Jews couldn't act in anti-Semitic ways, they probably also couldn't bear to think of themselves or act as non-human animals. Thus they might not have developed the adaptations you did."

Jerry nods, then frowns. "This conversation makes me look pretty smart and capable."

"You were," I say. "For example, you had to know that a courtyard had two openings and was a good place to hide. You acted quickly and smartly to save yourself."

"Yes, but most of the time, as I've told you before, I acted out of fear. Often I had no idea what I was doing. I just wanted to stay alive. Yes, I did things to save myself, but really I survived because others acted to save me. Mostly, I was lucky."

"Luck and agency can go hand in hand," I say.

Honouring Collaborative Relationships

Jerry's analysis of how he survived by acting anti-Semitic and developing and using animalistic instinct was incredibly insightful and evocative. His was not an analysis I would have come up with on my own. In another article that Jerry and I are co-authoring, we have included more of these stories and further developed an analysis of survival that includes other aspects of the agency that, in his case, intersected luck.[23] Though Jerry went along with a focus on how luck and agency can co-exist, from his constant questioning of the term "agency" and his return to events he felt could only be explained by luck, I think he would have been content ending the article the way he had begun it: "I survived because of luck, pure and simple." Sometimes I felt I was trying too hard to persuade him of my position, and I had problems figuring out how to reconcile that with the sharing of authority.

This issue dramatically pointed out to me some of the difficulties that Valerie Yow mentions in trying to co-construct analysis with narrators who might have goals and audiences different from a researcher's.[24] Obviously, Jerry had different "voices" in his head than I. For example, Jerry's family members who were murdered in the Holocaust were a more important audience for him than were the ethnographers and Holocaust researchers I sought to reach with our expression of the dialectic of agency and luck. Similar to most survivors, Jerry wanted to ensure that nothing we wrote would insinuate that he had special skills or powers for survival or imply that those who died were lacking in any way. Luck as an all-encompassing explanation of survival was a way out of that morass.[25] Although I strongly shared Jerry's concerns and understood why he saw things as he did, the researcher in me still wanted to deconstruct "luck" to show how relying on it as an all-encompassing explanation of survival reinforced the unfounded stereotype of Jews as passively failing to resist. I thought we could develop that idea without the accompanying insinuations about those who had died.

In my ongoing work with Jerry, we continue to consider the methodological and interpretive challenges raised by our collaboration.[26] As Shopes, Yow, and other oral historians discuss,[27] and we demonstrate here, it is difficult to figure out procedures for how to work together; when to relinquish and take control; ways to honour multiple goals, voices, and interpretations; and how to devote the time necessary for sharing authority to take place. Collaboration requires "a certain tolerance for ambiguity and uncertainty about how a project will work out."[28] That thought comforts me as I think about how to honour each other's interpretive authority and blend the scholarly voice of the researcher and the experiential voice of the storyteller without losing either.

I would like to talk more about all this with Jerry before completing the article we are working on about luck and agency, but, unfortunately, this may be a matter I will have to figure out on my own. Jerry's wife has advanced pancreatic cancer, and he has become a full-time caregiver with concerns more immediate and personally compelling than thinking about the role of agency in his survival almost seventy years ago. His thoughts are focused on his wife's survival and the survival of an "us" as he cares for her. Though we continue to e-mail many times each week, our article is not our primary concern. At this moment, my friendship and stance on collaboration calls for supporting Jerry in any way I can. In the end, resolving these intellectual issues, drawing conclusions, and helping readers understand the role of luck and agency in survival may not be as important as being a good friend to Jerry.

What is important is to continue communicating with Jerry now through e-mail and again in person when he is available. The relationship Jerry and I have built is sufficiently strong, vital, and meaningful that I feel sure our collaborative conversational work will continue.[29] I believe that Jerry feels his stories have been heard and his experience has been honoured. In turn, I have felt deeply with Jerry and learned much about the strength of human character from his experiences in the Holocaust and, now, from how he is coping with the illness of his wife. Indeed, as Greenspan and others suggest, the aim of collaborative conversation may be to listen compassionately and to have even deeper collaborative conversations.[30]

Jerry and I share a calling – that of the storyteller.[31] We seek to share stories that can be carried to future generations. We believe it is vital that future generations continue to contemplate the moral and meaning of the Holocaust as they try to imagine both its horrors and its lessons about justice, evil, and the kind of societies we aspire to create. At this late date, when soon we will have no survivors to talk with, I believe it is important to form relationships with survivors, to collaboratively and compassionately work with them to tell their stories, and to convey these stories in ways that can be remembered and retold, no matter how difficult this process might be.

Notes

Thanks to Arthur Bochner, Chris Patti, Henry Greenspan, and Steven High for their insightful comments on this chapter; and the University of South Florida Libraries and College of Arts and Sciences, and Florida Holocaust Museum for their support of this research. I acknowledge the National Endowment for the Humanities for the 2010 Summer Stipend that helped support my work on Holocaust testimonies. The views, findings, conclusions, or recommendations expressed in this publication do not necessarily reflect those of the National Endowment for the Humanities.

1 Michael Frisch, *A Shared Authority: Essays on the Craft and Meaning of Oral and Public History* (Albany, NY: SUNY Press, 1990). Frisch claims that oral history is co-created by narrator and interviewer. Steven High suggests that we employ "sharing authority," a more expansive concept that requires co-creation, authenticity, and consideration of narrators, interviewers, and the relationships they form at every stage and in every aspect of the research process. See Steven High, "Sharing Authority: An Introduction," *Journal of Canadian Studies* 43 (2009): 12–34; Michael Frisch, "Sharing Authority: Oral History and the Collaborative Process," *Oral History Review* 30, 1 (2003): 23–26. See also the Montreal Life Stories Project (http://www.lifestoriesmontreal.ca/); *Oral History Review* 30, 1 (2003), an issue dedicated to sharing authority; and the personal stories about oral history collaboration included in *Journal of Canadian Studies* 43, 1 (2009).

2 Linda Shopes, "Sharing Authority," *Oral History Review* 30 (2003): 104. Shopes calls for greater attention among oral historians to the actual talk in which authority is shared. She wants examples of how the views of the interviewer and interviewee play off each other in back-and-forth talk; how their relationship affects questions, answers, and the content of the interview; and how the narrative context helps to understand the material quoted.

3 Jerry reads history and memoirs about the Holocaust. He speaks often to students at the Florida Holocaust Museum and in classes, and he has attended and participated in classes I have taught on the Holocaust.

4 See, for example, Carolyn Ellis, *Final Negotiations: A Story of Love, Loss, and Chronic Illness* (Philadelphia: Temple University Press, 1995); Carolyn Ellis and Arthur P. Bochner, "Autoethnography, Personal Narrative, Reflexivity: Researcher as Subject," in *Handbook of Qualitative Research*, 2nd ed., ed. Norman Denzin and Yvonne Lincoln, 733–68 (Thousand Oaks, CA: Sage, 2000); Carolyn Ellis, *The Ethnographic I: A Methodological Novel about Autoethnography* (Walnut Creek, CA: Left Coast Press, 2004).

5 Arthur P. Bochner and Carolyn Ellis, "Personal Narrative as a Social Approach to Interpersonal Communication," *Communication Theory*

2 (1992): 165–72; Carolyn Ellis, Christine Kiesinger, and Lisa Tillmann-Healy, "Interactive Interviewing: Talking about Emotional Experience," in *Reflexivity and Voice,* ed. Rosanna Hertz, 119–49 (Thousand Oaks, CA: Sage, 1997).

6 See http://digital.lib.usf.edu/ohpi/?doi=F60-00003&packageid=SFS0021979.

7 Jerry Rawicki, "High Holy Days" and "That Night," in *We Were There: Memories of the Holocaust*, ed. Urszula Szczepinska, Shelly Mizrahi, Lane DeGregory, and Jeff Klinkenberg (St. Petersburg: Florida Holocaust Museum, 2007); Jerry Rawicki, *Sins and Sorrows* (Santa Ana, CA: Seven Locks Press, 2007).

8 Jerry Rawicki and Carolyn Ellis, "Lechem Hara (Bad Bread) Lechem Tov (Good Bread): Depravity and Nobility during the Holocaust," *Qualitative Inquiry* 17, 2 (2010): 155–57; Carolyn Ellis and Jerry Rawicki, "Collaborative Witnessing during the Holocaust: An Exemplar of Relational Autoethnography," *Qualitative Inquiry* 19, 5 (2013): 366–80; Carolyn Ellis and Jerry Rawicki, "More Than Mazel? Luck and Agency in Surviving the Holocaust," *Journal of Loss and Trauma: International Perspectives on Stress and Coping* 19, 2 (2014): 99–120 doi:10.1080/15325024.2012.738574.

9 See, for example, work on interpretive interactionism and biography by Norman Denzin, *Interpretive Interactionism* (Newbury Park, CA: Sage, 1989); and Norman Denzin, *Interpretive Biography* (Newbury Park, CA: Sage, 1989); work on narrative by Laurel Richardson, "Writing: A Method of Inquiry," in *Handbook of Qualitative Research*, 2nd ed., ed. Norman Denzin and Yvonne Lincoln, 923–48 (Thousand Oaks, CA: Sage 2000); and work on the interpretive and narrative turn in social sciences by George Marcus and Dick Cushman, "Ethnographies as Text," *Annual Review of Anthropology* 11 (1982): 25–69.

10 Valerie Yow and many other oral historians discuss the "paradigm shift" that occurred in oral history in the late 1980s and early 1990s when the oral history interview began to be seen as a collaborative effort in an interactional context. This shift reflected the changes in the 1960s and 1970s stimulated by the women's movement, the civil rights movement, and recognition of various ethnic groups in American society. See Valerie Raleigh Yow, "'Do I Like Them Too Much?' Effects of the Oral History Interview on the Interviewer and Vice-Versa," *Oral History Review* 24, 1 (1997): 55–79. See also Rebecca Sharpless, "The History of Oral History," in *Handbook of Oral History*, ed. Thomas Charlton, Lois Myers, and Rebecca Sharpless, 19–42 (Lanham, MD: AltaMira Press, 2006); Eva McMahan and Kim Rogers, *Interactive Oral History Interviewing* (Hillsdale, NJ: Lawrence Erlbaum, 1994). A parallel shift occurred in interpretive social science, particularly among qualitative methodologists.

11 Henry Greenspan, *On Listening to Holocaust Survivors: Beyond Testimony*, 2nd ed. (St. Paul, MN: Paragon House, 2010), 217–18. See also Arthur P. Bochner and Joanne B. Waugh, "Talking-With as a Model for Writing-About: Implications of Rortyean Pragmatism," in *Recovering Pragmatism's Voice: The Classical Tradition, Rorty, and the Philosophy of Communication*, ed. Lenore Langsdorf and Andrew R. Smith, 211–33 (Albany, NY: SUNY Press, 1995).

12 Agi Rubin and Henry Greenspan, *Reflections: Auschwitz, Memory, and a Life Recreated* (St. Paul, MN: Paragon Press, 2006), xix.

13 Greenspan, *On Listening*, 221 (emphasis in original); Dori Laub, "Bearing Witness or the Vicissitudes of Listening," in *Testimony: Crises of Witnessing in Literature, Psychoanalysis, and History*, ed. Dori Laub and Shoshana Felman, 57–74 (New York: Routledge, 1992).

14 Greenspan, *On Listening*, 236; Rubin and Greenspan, *Reflections*, 169, 217.

15 Greenspan, *On Listening*, 217–18 (emphasis in original).

16 Rubin and Greenspan, *Reflections*, 220. See also, Laub, "Bearing Witness."

17 Henry Greenspan and Sidney Bolkosky, "When Is an Interview an Interview? Notes from Listening to Holocaust Survivors," *Poetics Today* 27, 2 (2006): 431–49.

18 Yow, "'Do I Like Them Too Much?'"; Mark Klempner, "Navigating Life Review Interviews with Survivors of Trauma," in *The Oral History Reader*, 2nd ed., ed. Robert Perks and Alistair Thomson, 198–210 (New York: Routledge, 2006).

19 Lisa Tillmann-Healy, "Friendship as Method," *Qualitative Inquiry* 9, 5 (2003): 734.

20 Transcript of interview with Jerry Rawicki, 1 July 2009, 23–24, at http://digital.lib.usf.edu/ohpi/?doi=F60-00003&packageid=SFS0021979.

21 Rawicki transcript, 18 May 2010, 40–41.

22 Ibid., 41–43.

23 Ellis and Rawicki, "Collaborative Witnessing during the Holocaust."

24 Yow, "'Do I Like Them Too Much?'" See also Ronald Grele, "Listen to Their Voices," in *Envelopes of Sound*, 2nd rev. ed., ed. Ronald Grele (Chicago: Precedent Publishers, 1985), 213, 216.

25 For example, see Primo Levi, *The Drowned and the Saved*, trans. Raymond Rosenthal (New York: Vintage), 49–50; see also Brian Schiff, "Telling Survival and the Holocaust" (PhD diss., University of Chicago, 1997). As well, luck seemed the only explanation that made sense in a situation in which Jerry was constantly overwhelmed by moments in which he could have died, saw others die around him, and knew that any time death might happen to him as well – no matter his skills and talents.

Thanks to Henry Greenspan for pointing out this idea, which Jerry and I develop further in Ellis and Rawicki, "More than Mazel?"

26 See Ellis and Rawicki, "More than Mazel?"

27 Shopes, "Sharing Authority"; Yow, "'Do I Like Them Too Much?'"

28 Shopes, "Sharing Authority," 106.

29 Greenspan, *On Listening*, 234. Jerry's wife died on 8 June 2012, several months after we submitted this chapter for publication. After a period of illness, Jerry resumed working with me.

30 Greenspan, *On Listening*, 248. See also Chris Patti (Chapter 7, this volume).

31 Arthur Frank, *The Wounded Storyteller: Body, Illness and Ethics* (Chicago: University of Chicago Press, 1995).

7 | Sharing "A Big Kettle of Soup"

Compassionate Listening with a Holocaust Survivor

CHRIS PATTI

Beginning at the End

Monday, 20 February 2012, 8:45 AM, Sandy calls to tell me that Sal's been in the hospital for two days and his health is declining. For the past year Sal had been dealing with colon cancer, but I did not know how much he had deteriorated recently. Sandy says Sal wants to see me, and I tell her I'll be there as soon as I can, at 3:30 PM, after I finish teaching my interpersonal communication class. After I hang up the phone, I don't feel right. A few minutes later I follow my instincts, cancel class, and head immediately to visit Sal at St. Joseph's Hospital, in Tampa, Florida. As I walk out of the elevator on the fifth floor, Sandy is at the end of the hall waiting. She smiles as I get closer and says, "We're so glad you're here."

"I'm honoured to be here," I reply.

She looks strong but drained and says warmly, "Sal brightened up when we told him you were coming."

Her words fill my heart. I say, "I want you and Sal to know what a profound effect our time together has had on me, how much talking with him has changed my life."

Two Years Earlier

Monday, 1 March 2010, 9:30 AM. Location: Wainberg residence.

It's a beautiful spring day in Tampa, Florida. I am headed to meet Salomon and Sandra Wainberg for the first time. After Carolyn Ellis, my dissertation supervisor, interviewed Mr. Wainberg for our Holocaust survivor oral history project with the University of South Florida

Libraries and Florida Holocaust Museum (FHM),[1] she sensed that he and I would connect. She had a feeling he might make a good collaborator for my dissertation research on cultivating a compassionate, ethnographic approach to working with Holocaust survivors. Having conducted eleven videotaped and archived oral history interviews for the FHM project, I seek in my dissertation to collaborate more conversationally with three survivors in particular in order to form ongoing relationships and to hear things not traditionally heard in oral history interviews.[2] Thoughts swirl in my mind as I drive into a charming, upper-middle-class community on a golf course in the semi-rural Tampa suburb of Lutz.

I arrive early and Sal is still out, but Sandy takes me in and shows me their immaculately kept home. Lovely art and artefacts from their travels adorn the walls and display cases: traditional Jewish pieces – paintings and richly coloured glasswork – as well as Hindu prints and Asian brass items. I sit with Sandy at her white kitchen table, which matches the white curtains drawn open on the window beside. We start chatting, my audio recorder already on.

Sandy listens as I explain my project. "I want to find people who would like to connect, where it's hopefully rewarding for the survivors as well as me. I think that's something that's missing in the documentation of the Holocaust."

"I agree," she says with a smile.

I add excitedly, "In the standard 'tell-me-your-life-story' interview, they don't broach topics like 'What's your opinion on how the Holocaust is thought about today, and all of these movies about the Holocaust?' Starting in the '70s there was a miniseries called *Holocaust* on NBC, and then there's *Schindler's List* in 1993."

Sandy responds, "Well the interesting thing about the movies is that my introduction to the Holocaust – being I was born in the United States and not having the experience myself – was with *Judgment at Nuremberg*."

"Wow," I say, drawn to her openness and how she words things. Just then, Sal arrives home, entering through the garage door, situated next to the kitchen where Sandy and I are seated. Without a break he sits down, and his jovial presence takes centre stage.

"Have you started without me?" Sal jokes. I fumble a bit and explain that we can talk about whatever we want with no thought about beginning and ending, and I give him the Institutional Review Board release form for our project. He seems wary of me at first. His laboured breathing, audible on the recording, indicates slight agitation. *I've accosted him*, I think – already being there talking with Sandy, not allowing him time to arrive home peacefully or collect his thoughts. We begin anyway.

I reiterate: "I'm hoping that we can have a conversation that seems interesting to you. Do you have any questions?"

"No, go ahead," he says.

"That makes sense?"

Sal's response is quintessential: "Well, I'll find out if it makes sense as it progresses. But I'm willing." Sandy and I laugh at his directness.

Soon after my awkward start, Sal begins to see what Sandy already felt. By twenty minutes into our first conversation, we are connecting. Sal clarifies his motive to tell: "Whatever I can do regardless of how silly it is, how disgusting it is, how wonderful it is, how terrific it is – I will go to any length to let one more person find out about the Holocaust." Sandy laughs.

I respond, "I really appreciate your willingness to talk with me, and also I hope that through this process – and this is kind of a selfish hope – that our time together is meaningful to you."

"It is," he reassures me.

"Absolutely," says Sandy. "Every time he speaks it makes it more comfortable for him to say."

Over the next two years our conversations flowed, circling around many topics. We talked about his experience, memory, and history; about his and Sandy's relationship as it related to his telling; about popular culture; and about why and how it was that we feel called to share his story. I audio-recorded five of our meetings, totalling more than ten hours in length. We also left many of our meetings as friendly, unrecorded conversations. Our relationship and discussions deepened with each meeting, leading to our final interaction.

My goal here is to show some of "the meat" (to use Sal's words) of our time together – what happened between us, the distinct nature of our collaboration, and the heart of what we have to share. I do this by highlighting four key themes, or moments, from our interactions, using our conversational voices as recorded. First, I show how Sal came to tell his story, initially to Sandy and then to the world; second, I note in Sal's words what telling has brought him; third, I demonstrate the relationship and connection we formed; and fourth, I answer the question, "Why do we tell?"

These dialogues provide the context for my ethnographic telling of our final conversation, which expresses the life-and-death heart of our work. My method focuses on cultivating compassion, a risky motive for academics and oral historians, adding particular, humane voices to the collaborative witnessing approaches demonstrated in this collection, complementing work done by Greenspan; Greenspan and Bolkosky; High; Rawicki and Ellis; Rubin and Greenspan; Sheftel and Zembrzycki; and the Montreal Life Stories project.[3] Instead of adopting a distanced, critical perspective on my relationship with Sal,[4] I offer it as an intimate, vulnerable work of love. As High points out, authors in this lineage are "not only self-aware, continually reflecting on their location in the research process; they are writing deeply personal articles."[5] This is a deeply personal chapter about my relationship with a Holocaust survivor. It goes beyond traditional categories of interviewer-interviewee and diverges from traditional modes of scholarly representation. I begin with a condensed version of Sal's experiences during the Second World War to provide context for the conversations that follow.

The Wainberg/Boruchowicz Family during the Second World War

Sal (pronounced "Saul") is a seventy-four-year-old Jewish Holocaust survivor born on 15 April 1936 in the small, Eastern Polish shtetl of Zelechów. His name at birth was Sholom Wainberg (spelled "Szulim Wajnberg" in Polish). His father Chaim Meyer and mother Perla were successful merchants, selling goods at their regional wholesale store, which had been passed down over generations on Sal's mother's side of the family – the Boruchowicz side. The family store had a monopoly on sugar, cigarettes, and herring, and their house was across the street. At the time of the war, Sal had two older sisters, Riwka and Sara, and a younger brother, Abraham.

His first vivid childhood memory has a specific date – 1 September 1939 – the day Germans invaded Poland. It was the first time he had seen an airplane. As Sal marvelled at the planes overhead, he was hoping to see a helicopter, something he had learned about from his sickly, bookish cousin but could not imagine. That night, Sal's family fled, hiding first in the attic of his mother's sister's fianceé's bicycle and sewing machine shop with thirty-nine others. There they stayed for sixteen days as their town was destroyed.

Sal's father, mother, and siblings moved by cover of night eleven kilometres away to Wilczka. There they hid in the cellar of the Sokols, a Polish family the Wainbergs paid to feed and hide them. Mr. Sokol was the brother-in-law of a family friend, Edward Turek, a man Sal called an "angel." For two years during the war, Sal and his family hid in that cellar – what Sal called "the *grub*" (meaning "grave," "dungeon," or "pit" in Yiddish), eating "nothing soup" – with another Jewish family, the Popovskas. Mr. Sokol also allowed a wounded Russian soldier to hide with the families. Having no rapport with the adults (because he was another mouth to feed), the Russian man connected with Sal and the bored children. He taught Sal Russian songs and they carved a chess set together out of branches that Mr. Sokol brought for the Russian. The man demonstrated to Sal what each chess piece looked like by moulding it out of bread first. Once healed, the mysterious man left and was never heard from again.

Time became meaningless as the months and years passed until bandits found Sal's family. Sal's mother and father believed that Edward Turek's brother, Vladislav, had given the family's location away. The bandits murdered Sal's aunt Gitel Schiffman, his sister Riwka, and two young men hidden with Sal's family – "the Popovska boys." Facing death, Sal's father improvised a *bubbe-meise* (a fictional story) to spare the lives of his family by promising to lead the bandits to what they were after – the supposed Boruchowicz fortune. After years of paying to hide, there was no fortune left, but Sal's father's story allowed him and his family to escape just before dawn.

The Wainbergs spent the next few months wandering and hiding in rye and wheat fields; nearly dying of thirst, hunger, and exposure; surviving on cunning and the hard kernels from the fields. Before sunrise on 2 August 1944, they heard Russian voices in the distance. Sal acted as the tiny translator for his family, telling the soldiers, "We're Jewish – we're Jews: *Yevreyski*." The Wainbergs were liberated. Soon after, Sal's family immigrated to Costa Rica and opened a new store. By sixteen, Sal moved to Detroit to study at a Yeshiva, nearly becoming an orthodox rabbi, before he became "unorthodox." Years later, as Sal got his start in finance and studied at the University of Miami, he met Sandy, a pretty Jewish-American girl, and in 1965 they wed. Sandy knew Sal's family had a "dark secret," but she loved him enough not to pry, even though she felt like an outsider.

I. Coming to Tell Sandy and the World

During our first interview, I ask Sal if he feels telling his story publicly has changed him. He says: "Our life definitely has changed because I think Sandy understands a lot of my shortcomings now, my bad habits. I realized how, I guess, irritating I can sometimes be."

Sandy responds, laughing, "How, your 'coming out' has changed?" We join in laughing at her wording. She continues: "You can't imagine. We were married in 1965. I knew he was a survivor, but I never asked him anything about his survival. I did that knowingly and with respect, because I saw that if I would bring up something like that it would hurt him. We were married for ten years and his being a survivor was only something in his life. It didn't impact mine, except that there was a whole lot of my husband that I didn't know about. Anyway, one of the joys we share is the love of travel. We were going on one of our many trips. This time we were going to Eastern Europe. This was back in '73, right?"

"Yeah," Sal says at a whisper, letting her continue.

"Early on in being able to visit communist Russia, Poland, and East and West Berlin, it wasn't a common place to go. So we were very excited. I was excited for the cultural experience. But it didn't occur to me that Sal had another purpose. He had made contact with the family in Poland that saved him. He was going over there to make contact, to see them."

Sal adds, "To visit and to show her where I was born."

"To show me – " she says.

Sal finishes her sentence in a deep, gravelly voice, "where I came from."

"Yeah," I say, amazed, saying as little as I can to allow their co-telling to continue.

Sandy goes on: "I was totally unaware of this. So we got on the long plane ride. In those days Sal couldn't read on an airplane. He would get airsick. So what else can you do?"

"They didn't have movies then," he jokes.

"Talk to your partner," Sandy says. She adds: "So, after ten years of marriage, he told me his survival story. I was dumbfounded. I could not absorb everything that he was telling me. It was too painful, too shocking, so unexpected, and he told me we were gonna' meet this family. I was amazed. We had travelled to many places in the world before this. And Sal is a very strong, independent, unafraid, know-it-all kind of person. Very, very self-confident. When he got off the plane in Poland he became a child. He held on to me. He was shaking. I've never seen him like this. I said, 'What's the matter?' He couldn't put it into words. But it occurred to me, finally, that he was frightened. I said, 'What are you frightened of?' You know this is so many years later, twenty-five years later. He said to me, which I didn't realize, it didn't occur to me at all, that he was of draft age and he was carrying a passport that said he was born in Poland. He was afraid that the Polish government was going to capture him and put him in the army."

"Wow," I say.

"There was no sense to what he said," she clarifies.

"Well, no," he admits. Sal explains: "When you listen to my story, you might realize that the way we finally left Poland was running away."

Sandy adds, "The shame or the fear – "

"The fear," Sal emphasizes.

She continues, "Or whatever he felt at that point was transferred into this feeling of utter desperation."

Sal repeats once more: "Fear. I was walking on glass."

When I ask Sal how he became involved with telling his story publicly, he says: "It wasn't really 'till the [Florida Holocaust] Museum got me to speak out that I started – and like I said before, the first few times were murder. I would come home exhausted. Whereas now I come home and feel satisfied that perhaps I changed the life of one of the kids. 'Cause, when I talk to the kids, I do include some preaching of tolerance."

I respond, "Yes, I think that's so important coming from someone who has been through that experience. I think that for me it's not only your story – "

"No," Sal agrees and sees where I'm going.

I continue, "that we can learn from but your perspective – "

"Right," Sal says.

I add, "living with that story. I think that's wisdom." I ask Sal to clarify how telling has shaped him: "You say, 'Telling brings me more than relief, it washes my soul.' That's really interesting to me."

He runs with the thought: "There's two things that have happened to me since I started talking at the museum. I think the most important part is that I don't dwell on it like I used to, on the bad parts and stuff. It almost has become a story as far as I'm concerned. As a matter of fact, one of the problems I have with the museum now is they want to restrict my time. And I refuse. Because I say I have to tell the story. I can't just, you know, do like this [chops his hand in the air three times]. But more importantly, there are a lot of things, a lot of names, a lot of places that have become clearer in my mind."

Sal tells me a few moments later: "But I think the other thing is, and I say this to the kids a lot of times, when you first start talking about the Holocaust you'll say, 'This should never happen again.' But it's happening again almost every day. And I think that's what we have to realize, too. So until everybody knows and realizes that it happened and that it could happen again, I think it will. And that's the sad part." Later he adds: "And before that [telling publicly], whenever I would have an inclination to tell, nobody wanted to listen. Now I was in a crowd that wanted to listen, so it's very different. Really, it was *Schindler's List* and Spielberg. I think he should be canonized because he brought the awareness."

"He made it okay to want to know," I say.

"He made it okay to want to know and he made it okay to want to tell. It wasn't until the museum found me that I started to tell. And, Chris, I'll guarantee you I'm not the only one."

"Pretty much every survivor I've spoken with has a similar story of becoming a storyteller, having an audience to tell to," I agree.

Sal reasserts, "If you want to thank somebody – Spielberg."

"It's interesting that you say that. As I've been reading more about this, academics are pretty critical of Steven Spielberg and the film.[6] They say the story was from a German perspective, that the Holocaust is the backdrop. And you're shaking your head."

"That's not true," Sal says. "Yes, he had to use that venue, but look what he did!"

"It doesn't make it any less important," I agree. "Actually, one of the things that historians will admit is that the facts of that movie are very accurate."

"That is important to the historians," he tells me. "To me that's not important at all. What's important is he brought the awareness, where people actually started asking. Then, when they ask, people feel better about telling. So to me it's – " Sal pauses for a moment and then continues, now directing his thought towards our project. "And you should probably use that idea in your dissertation. You're welcome," he smiles.

Stunned and pleased that he is concerned with my dissertation and explicit about including this thought, I respond: "I, I, I will. I will."

II. What Telling has Brought Sal: "A Big Kettle of Soup"

Reviewing Sal's different phases of memory and telling over his life, I say: "So, you're a young man, you're very busy. Then when you retire things changed, the museum comes into play, speaking comes into play. Now when you think about your memory, it seems like there are some memories that are still as vivid as if they happened yesterday. You're following images in your mind when you're telling them."

"Right," Sal says softly.

I ask, "What is that like?"

Here Sal shares with me what has become my model for the mind and what motivates us to remember and tell our experience. His insight also speaks to how we might be able to share, through deep telling and listening together, more of the complex mysteries of our human experiences. Sal says: "Somehow, I have a feeling, if I continue telling, there are going to be other discoveries that I make in my mind. Some of the stuff that I remember are quite – I don't know what to say – quite alarming details. Like, I could almost see [Mr.] Popovska spitting up blood right in front of us. On the other hand are the things that I try to remember that I can't remember. My mom had five sisters, and I can only remember one of them dying. This little cousin of mine, same name as mine, six years younger than me – I don't know when he died. It's something that I've tried to get my sister to tell me and she either doesn't know or doesn't want to know. Unfortunately, there you go again, I didn't think of asking when my mom could have told me. And that bothers me. I'm hoping maybe someday it will – "

Sandy finished his thought, "It'll come."

I agree, "It'll come. I think it's in there."

Sal explains, "Oh, I'm sure it's in there. It's just a question of how to get it out. *The mind is like a big kettle of soup*."

"Mm-hmm," I say, marvelling at his metaphor, reflecting on the "nothing soup" he ate in the *grub*.

He continues: "In that, if you dig long enough, you'll find the meat, and you'll find the stuff that you like. And that's why I'm digging." Sandy and I laugh at how enlightening his statement is.

Sandy says, "There you go! Ah, boy."

"That's one of those quotes," I say, still laughing. "I love that. You make my job so easy when you say things like that." We all laugh.

III. Our Connection and Relationship

As our interviews progressed over the years, our friendship blossomed. Sal, being a kind man and generous host, always asked if I wanted anything to eat or drink while we spoke. Each time I happily accepted his offers, and we shared grilled cheese sandwiches, coffee with a little hot chocolate mixed in, and, on one occasion, the "Sal special" (scrambled eggs mixed with steamed cauliflower and onions). By an hour and thirty-five minutes into our second conversation, it's clear to me that Sal, Sandy, and I are becoming friends. Sandy tells me: "The grandkids know that whatever needs to be fixed, whatever problem they have, to go directly to their grandfather. They know that he'll have the answer, and he does, or he improvises. When he's improvising to make something better, I know it's gonna' be horrible. But, for the few minutes that he's doing it for the children, they love it," she laughs. "Right?"

Sal responds, "That's what counts."

"Yep," she laughs.

I say, "That's good to know. Next time I have a problem I'll know where to go." Sandy and I get a big kick out of this.

Eight minutes into our third recorded interview, this time out to dinner at a Thai restaurant in Tampa, Sal tells me: "I have been interviewed I don't know how many times. And I know that each time I am interviewed something new comes out. Sometimes it's just a memory. And sometimes it's the way people ask questions that it comes out. When people ask questions that I really have to think about, the things that came out would have never came out another way."

I say, "Yeah, that's what's so exciting to me."

Sandy jumps in: "Right, it's probing questions and the way to do a good interview. And you do the same thing," she tells me.

"Thank you," I reply.

Sandy continues, "You talk around it. So this is what we're talking about."

I pick up an earlier thought: "That's why it's so exciting to work with you two. I can see Sal making sense of things newly each time he thinks about it. How do people make sense of any life, let alone a particularly compelling life that speaks to a whole historical issue? Watching you make sense of these issues is to me more interesting than even reading philosophies about how to have meaning in life. I think we can learn more through talking – to any individual, but particularly to one who's looking to find meaning for himself."

Sandy adds, "And the friendly, safe atmosphere that we feel with you. I think that's more important than anything else."

Sal: "Yeah."

Sandy: "Because other people ask maybe the same questions but it won't be the same response. It won't be the same hearer. They ask it – "

"With a different spirit," Sal says, finishing her thought.

To clarify that I understand, I ask, "Is it an openness, a vulnerability?"

Sal responds, "Yeah, a vulnerability. But also – "

"A disinterest," Sandy inserts, "asking a question but not being interested."

About an hour and a half into our fourth interview, Sal gave me a compliment that has stuck with me. I now mention it when I teach and talk about my research and perspective on interviewing. Sal said, "You know what, you're a good interviewer. You elicit answers. They said it about Barbara Walters."

I respond, "Mm-hmm. Well that's – "

Sal continues, "Maybe you're in the wrong profession?"

This leads me to talk to him about Carolyn Ellis's and my perspective on interviewing and compassionate qualitative methods. Sal is happy that I will teach my students this approach and that, in turn, they will improve in their own ways on what I teach them.

By our last recorded interview, Sal's become like a grandparent-friend-guide to me. I mark this by the fact that he wants to know what I think of his "Sal Special." He asks, "Are you really enjoying it? Tell me the truth."

"The book?" I ask, thinking he is talking about the draft of the book he is having written about his history, which he let me read to get my opinion. He was clear that he only let me and Sandy read it, not even his brother.

"No," he says.

Seeing what he means I say, "Oh, this [the eggs and cauliflower]? For sure! And the book as well. I did enjoy it."

He asks, "How's your, eh, thesis going?"

I tell him, "It is challenging, definitely challenging."

Sal gets a big kick out of this and says, "Listen, anything worthwhile is challenging. That I learned."

"I definitely felt, through listening to you, I understand how much work you've done throughout your life, how hard you work. I grew up having a lot of privileges that you didn't have, that even my parents didn't have. I think it's because of that that my generation takes a little longer to mature."

"Yeah," Sal agrees.

I elaborate: "I'm almost thirty but I'm still, you know, maybe where you were when you were six years old, something like that, in terms of maturity. So this has been a big maturation process. I think that's what I'm learning, the day-in-day-out effort that it takes to do anything worthwhile."

He shares with me: "I had to make a lot of decisions which at the time people might have said were the wrong decisions. But history said that they were the right decisions."

At forty minutes into our last recorded interview I say to Sandy, "Something that's been interesting for me to experience is, since I met Sal, our interactions have been pretty open and emotional."

"Mm-hmm," Sandy nods in agreement.

"Yeah," Sal says, almost as if to say "no question."

"I feel like I've seen a side of you that not many other people have," I tell him.

Sandy says, "Yeah, you have definitely seen a side of Sal that nobody else has." She quickly adds, "I mean I have."

"I hear the stories about how when you say something it happens, and it's the law. But in my experience you seemed like a softy," I tell him with a warm smile. They both laugh – Sandy's is a belly laugh, I imagine because she's never heard anyone refer to Sal as a "softy."

Sal explains to me: "A lot of people, including that class that we were in with your people [Dr. Ellis's graduate class that we visited together], they were asking, 'Well, why is that?' It's because I don't throw out my opinions. And that's what makes something different." I take this as a compliment that perhaps Sal saw our time together as something different, as a place to share openly the wisdom that took him a lifetime to come to terms with.

IV. Why Do We Tell?

I ask Sal, "So as we move into the future, what's essential that we remember from your experience and from survivors' experiences?"

"Let me tell you something before I can develop that answer," Sal tells me.

"Yeah, sorry," I say, adding, "The questions I don't know the answer to I ask you."

He says, "I, as well as I think any Holocaust survivor that understands, are very, very grateful to you, to Dr. Ellis – people who basically, the way I see it, dedicate your lives to the remembrance of the Holocaust. We never had that. All we had was deniers. So that to me is tremendous. I think if there's one thing that you should strive for – you and Dr. Ellis and everybody else – it's that somehow it shouldn't stop with you. Because at the museum whenever Sandy Mermelstein [tour director for the FHM] introduces me she says to the kids, 'You're very privileged because your kids probably will never be able to hear a survivor.' That's the very truth. So if you can develop a cadre of students who follow you, they're gonna' take your course, read your thesis, take the time to go to the library and hear me. I think that's probably the biggest thing you can accomplish."

"You just made things very clear for me," I say. "One of my big questions is, 'Why remember? Why retell these stories?' We tell these stories to communicate, to connect one person to another, one generation to another." I ask again in a different way: "What do we learn? What do you hope I learn from telling these stories, listening to these stories, struggling with the burden of it?"

"I'm glad you asked me that," Sal says, "because you have to understand that we really weren't cowards. We really were brave to have the will and the strength and the cunning to survive. A coward would have said, 'Here, run me over with the tank.' And a lot of 'em did. To me they're cowards because as long as you live you must have – and this is what I was trying to tell my daughter the other day – the desire to live." Here Sal strikes something deep inside me, something that's taken me thirty years to realize, something I had to learn by studying stories and communication and their limits in human experience.

"The will to live!" I say.

Sal jumps in, "It's not only the will to live. The ambition – the fortuitiveness to do whatever is necessary to do."

I ask, "So would you say that life itself is the meaning? Like when somebody says, 'What's the meaning of life?' Would you say, 'Life itself'?"

"Life! Life," Sal says. "The artefacts will tell you the appropriation."

I add, "Again, that's kind of a passing-things-on. Stories are a kind of symbolic appropriation, a symbolic lineage."

"Absolutely, absolutely," Sal says.

"This is blowing my mind," I say.

"Hope it doesn't do it here," he jokes.

So what, you might be asking, is the breakthrough in these simple words? It's a breakthrough that in some senses Viktor Frankl and many in the field of communication overlook.[7] It is not "man's search for meaning." It's the will to *experience and express life itself*. The experience of life, this is a "beyond" that is larger than the human symbolic capacity and from which our stories emerge. Sharing experience is the messy, interconnected, relational, and always incomplete process – as Leon and Greenspan note – of "making a story" of what is "not a story."[8] Sitting in awe and wonder at the vastness of life itself, magnified beautifully and complexly in an individual life story, is a big part of what my time with Sal was about – it's a big part of the wisdom I take from this experience. But that was not all.

Through telling and retelling his story, Sal was forced to reflect on his own prejudices – namely, his hatred of Polish people. Both he and Sandy showed that, through thinking about and telling his story, Sal had indeed transformed his thinking. Sal explained to me: "That was a definite hatred you could say [i.e., Sal's feeling towards the Sokols as a young man]. I hated the Polish people, in general because my immediate family died at the hands of Polish people, not the Germans. So I had that for the longest time. As part of telling I guess I realized that people are people. You can't blame a whole population for what some bad guys did. So I went, and I'm still going, through that."

Sandy says, "Sal has come to the realization of not to generalize."

"Because you have to take the example," he interjects.

"Right," she says.

I'll end this section with one final example of why we are telling this particular story. It comes from what Sandy thought would make a good title for Sal's book: "I Don't Have a Number, I Have a Story."

Sal says, "With all the kids asking about my number."

I add, "I think that that is a powerful title because, for a long time, we defined a Holocaust survivor as someone who's in a camp, someone with a number, and other people were disavowed as survivors."

"Right," Sandy says. "They're not real survivors."

Sal explains, "Everybody asks, 'What camp were you in?'"

"People don't understand that a survivor is not just a camp survivor," Sandy says.

Beginning (to "Really" Listen to Sal) at the End[9]

Sandy opens the door and I follow her into Sal's bright hospital room, illuminated with natural light pouring in from the large window on the right side of Sal's bed. Robyn, Sal's daughter, and Andrew, his son, are in the room. We briefly exchange quiet introductions. Robyn, a paediatric physician, sees me notice that the permanently affixed crucifix in the upper right corner of the room is covered with a sheet. She informs me, "The crucifix is a standard fixture in most rooms at St. Joseph's. They attach them so people can't take them home." We both smile. Sal's act of resistance makes me happy, yet my eyes fill with tears.

"Hey, buddy. How are you?" I say to Sal, still standing next to Robyn.

"Chris, Chris, you're half the man you were since I saw you," Sal jokes, referring to my thinness.

"Oh, no, you're just used to seeing me dressed up. I look bigger in formal clothes," I say.

"Okay," he says, moving on. "So nice to see you. Come, sit." He motions with his left hand to the two chairs on the left side of the bed. Robyn allows me to sit closest to Sal for the moment and takes the seat to the left of me, and I place my hand on Sal's forearm. Andrew sits in the corner behind us. Sandy is on the other side of the bed holding a Styrofoam cup filled with water that has a straw sticking out, ready whenever Sal wants a sip.

Sal's hair is still thick and curly, despite nearly a year of aggressive chemo. *Stubborn and strong, just like Sal*, I think. Except it's no longer dark grey. The front is snow white and the back light grey. His skin is ashen and yellow. Bathed in the natural light, Sal's eyes glow a pale and bright blue-green. His unnatural thinness exaggerates his enormous hands, which still look powerful – like I'm used to seeing the rest of him. Sal's booming voice is quiet today but still low, slow, and full of character and rasp. When he is hit periodically by acute pain, he simply closes his eyes for a few seconds, breathes, and continues on, not letting it interrupt his train of thought. "Sal, I can see that you're in pain, and still you're so generous with your conversation," I tell him.

"This is more important," he responds. "*Listen*." Sal looks me in the eyes: "Chris, I will be at peace if I feel one person has *really listened*, has *really tried to understand*. You have."

Chills race through my body as I am overwhelmed and honoured. For a moment I'm speechless, break my intense focus on Sal, and notice Sandy and Robyn smiling at me reassuringly. I finally manage, "Sal, that is a lot of responsibility, and I'm humbled." I take a breath and continue, "I can tell you that, through listening and re-listening to our conversations, I finally feel like I'm beginning to listen to what you're saying. This is the main theme in all our conversations. They always come back to our struggle to listen and to tell."

"Yes," Sal whispers.

"I imagine that you must feel profound satisfaction, having shared your story with so many," I add. "I think you've changed many lives. You've changed mine. Sal, you've helped me to mature, to become a man."

"*Yes*, Chris. This is *it*. Don't confuse it. Life, even after the Holocaust, even with all I've seen, even now, is about *learning to love one another and love ourselves* – to learn to *really listen to each other*."

"I'll do my best to pass this message on," I tell him.

"I know you will. I have the highest hopes for you."

Just then more people arrive to visit Sal – a few friends, one also a Holocaust survivor, and two rabbis. The energy in the room shifts to something less intimate and busier, the work of hellos. I stand up, move to the back, and try my best to get out of the way.

Tears that have been welling up all this time fall freely. I'm left looking down in silence. When I look up I can see Sal is agitated with all the people in the room. Sandy gives me a look that I can't quite make out, a half smile and a sigh, which I interpret as meaning that my presence is still welcome. Everyone in the room is talking to one another at once and the volume is getting louder. I see Sandy lean in to Sal as he says, "Tell everyone to leave."

Sandy announces confidently and calmly: "Okay everyone, thank you for coming. Sal is tired and needs some rest." We all file out of the room. I take a moment to reflect in the hallway. Almost immediately the door to Sal's room opens and Sandy peeks out. "Oh, good, you're still here," she says in a chipper voice. "Sal wanted the others to leave so he could talk more with you," she adds with her infectious laughter. I smile and stick around for the next two hours talking with Sal, Sandy, Robyn, and Andrew, until it's time for some of Sal's treatments.

Two days later I visit again. But, just minutes before I arrive, Sal is moved to the Intensive Care Unit. I can't see him, so I stick around and talk with Sandy, family, and friends in the waiting room. After Sandy and Robyn are called back into the ICU, I say goodbye to Sal and Sandy's friends. Later that evening, I get a call from a family friend telling me that Sal waited for his brother to arrive before he died.

Two days later, I attend Sal's funeral, held graveside at Gan Shalom Cemetery in Lutz. More than a hundred family, friends, and synagogue and community members are in attendance. It is a traditional, conservative Jewish funeral in which we all have a hand filling in the grave, a ritual I experience as profound. Sal's rabbi comments that he considered himself a conservative Jew but that he was his own kind of conservative, that he had a unique moral compass. He is buried between two old oaks on a hot and windy day.

Epilogue

Commitment to sharing authority is a beginning, not a destination.

– Michael Frisch[10]

The goal of this piece is to share, in an intimate way, some of the "meat" of the process of "digging" through the "big kettle of soup" of my time with Sal. I refrain from taking a critical stance on our relationship and the moments I tell here because, for this particular chapter, that would take away from what our voices have to say. Instead, I choose to see the Wainbergs as intellectual authorities and to maximize the space I give to Sal's and Sandy's voices and our relationship. I am not advocating that researchers ought to get involved with our participants in the way that I became involved with Sal and Sandy. Rather, we should abandon simple notions of the boundaries of research with individuals and instead listen closely to our instincts and to those with whom we work in order to collaboratively negotiate – in always-ongoing ways – the most compassionate and appropriate ways to go about our work together.

Through talking with Sal and Sandy and digging through our conversations, it becomes ever clearer how much of this story is omitted and remains silent and untold: for Sal, there are mysteries he never found out about in his life; for Sandy, as well as she knew and loved Sal, parts of him remain a question mark; and for me, as an ethnographer,[11] I feel a near-crippling sense of not being able to do justice, in this or any representation, to the man I knew. To deal with this dilemma, in Robert Coles' words, I "err on the side of each person's particularity,"[12] attempting to show the compassionate "spirit" of this work. Instead of working from a priori theory or traditional methods of "researching" survivors, I, inspired by Greenspan,[13] respond to Sal and Sandy as unique individuals in order to hear more of what it is they have to tell. In struggling

FIGURE 7.1 Sal and Sandy Wainberg on their 2008 trip to Thailand, Vietnam, Laos, and Cambodia. *Photograph courtesy of Sandy Wainberg.*

to represent Sal meaningfully, I have crafted two hundred pages of conversational dialogue, a tiny fraction of which is included here. I privilege the voices of Sal and Sandy, even while knowing more is absent than shared. And I write about our relationship with tenderness and love, as I would if I were telling the story of a family member.[14]

The core of my ethic is inspired by Sal's, as well as Greenspan's and Agi's, "moral of the story"[15] – engaging compassionately with survivors of mass atrocities is a significant scholarly justification, one that tests the limits of oral history and responds to the vastness, complexity, and relational ethics inherent in *coming to terms with* and sharing any life.[16] This piece, therefore, is an attempt to encourage myself and others to listen with more heart to the individual paradoxes of life and death,[17] love and loss, lost and found that emerge from life histories, especially the life histories of Holocaust survivors at the end of life. Beyond that, this chapter is a step towards sharing with others the wisdom cultivated through listening with a friend who had a lifetime of experience coming to terms with life in the wake of the Holocaust.

Notes

This chapter is dedicated to my friends Sal and Sandy Wainberg. I cannot express the depth of my gratitude for their open willingness to share their experiences and time with me. I also must acknowledge Carolyn Ellis for the central role she plays in this work and thank her for her guidance and compassion in helping me realize it. In addition, I thank Steven High and Henry Greenspan for their close readings and sage advice on revisions as well as for their encouragement to show more of Sal's voice and the "in-between" of this story. Last, this chapter is dedicated to the lost lives and stories of the Holocaust universe and those dedicated to sharing as much as they can, as uniquely as they can, before it's too late.

1 For those interested in the formal oral history of Salomon Wainberg, you can learn more from his interviews with the Shoah Foundation Institute (1995) and the Florida Holocaust Museum/University of South Florida Libraries (FHM) (2010). His FHM interview can be found at http://guides.lib.usf.edu/ohpi#doi=F60-00021.

2 My dissertation research consists of three years of casual audio-recorded ethnographic interviews with three Holocaust survivors and their closest family: Salomon "Sal" and Sandra "Sandy" Wainberg, Manuel Goldberg and his wife, Rachel Rivlin, and Sonia "Sala" Wasserberger. I focus only on my work with Sal and Sandy in this chapter.

3 Henry Greenspan, *On Listening to Holocaust Survivors: Beyond Testimony*, 2nd ed. (St. Paul, MN: Paragon House, 2010); Henry Greenspan and Sidney Bolkosky, "When Is an Interview an Interview? Notes from Listening to Holocaust Survivors," *Poetics Today* 27, 2 (2006): 431–49; Steven High, "Sharing Authority: An Introduction," *Journal of Canadian Studies* 43, 1 (2009): 21–34; Jerry Rawicki and Carolyn Ellis, "Lechem Hara (Bad Bread), Lechem Tov (Good Bread): Survival and Sacrifice During the Holocaust," *Qualitative Inquiry* 11, 2 (2011):155–57; Agi Rubin and Henry Greenspan, *Reflections: Auschwitz, Memory, and a Life Recreated* (St. Paul, MN: Paragon House, 2006); Anna Sheftel and Stacey Zembrzycki, "Only Human: A Reflection on the Ethical and Methodological Challenges of Working with 'Difficult' Stories," *Oral History Review* 37, 2 (2010): 191–214; Montreal Life Stories Project at http://www.lifestoriesmontreal.ca/.

4 Critically reflexive approaches to practices of history and oral history are important, and this anthology contains powerful examples of this tradition. So, too, is reflecting on the ethics of "compassion" in academic work with human beings. For reasons of space and in order to offer what I sense is the spirit of Sal's and my conversations, however, I risk telling a raw, vulnerable story of what erring on the side of forming personal, boundary-blurring, family-like relationships with those with whom we work can create. I explain more why I do this in the conclusion.

5 High, "Sharing Authority," 15.

6 Omer Bar Tov, "Spielberg's Oskar: Hollywood Tries Evil," in *Spielberg's Holocaust: Critical Perspectives on Schindler's List*, ed. Yosefa Loshitzky, 41–60 (Bloomington: Indiana University Press, 1997).

7 Viktor E. Frankl, *Man's Search for Meaning*, 60th anniversary ed. (New York: Pocket Books).

8 Greenspan, *On Listening*, 3–4, 20. I am thankful to Henry Greenspan for bringing back to my awareness the complex, relational process of his and Leon's formulation of "making a story." He details this process and the different, relational paradigm it represents on page 234.

9 The story here is constructed based on detailed ethnographic field notes I took immediately after leaving the hospital. I do my best to represent, as accurately as possible, the words and actions of the characters and situation.

10 Michael Frisch, "Sharing Authority: Oral History and the Collaborative Process," *Oral History Review* 30, 1 (2003): 112. Also cited by High, "Sharing Authority," 12 and by Sheftel and Zembrzycki, "Only Human," 198.

11 Lyall Crawford, "Personal Ethnography," *Communication Monographs* 63, 2 (1996): 158–70.

12 Robert Coles, *The Call of Stories: Teaching and the Moral Imagination* (Boston, MA: Houghton Mifflin), 27. I cite Coles' words with deep gratitude to Arthur Bochner, who assigned this book in his narrative theory doctoral seminar and whose work shows the value of personal stories.

13 Greenspan, *On Listening*.

14 Chris Patti, "Split Shadows: Myths of a Lost Father and Son," *Qualitative Inquiry* 18, 2 (2012): 53–61.

15 Ibid., 211. Here, I refer to Greenspan's humane justification to listen to survivors for the purpose of listening and Agi's understanding of compassion.

16 Carolyn Ellis, "Telling Secrets, Revealing Lives: Relational Ethics in Research with Intimate Others," *Qualitative Inquiry* 13, 1 (2007): 3–29.

17 Ibid., 41–73.

8 | "Questions Are More Important than Answers"

Creating Collaborative Workshop Spaces with Holocaust Survivor-Educators in Montreal

ANNA SHEFTEL | STACEY ZEMBRZYCKI

I am the youngest, and the newest, speaker. [Laughter.] Since 2004 I have had only twenty-four engagements, four thousand students. My name is Leslie Vertes. Unfortunately, I came from Hungary. [Laughter.]

– MHMC Survivor Workshop, Montreal, 2009[1]

When asked to briefly introduce himself to the group of forty Holocaust survivors gathered around the large table before him for the first collaborative workshop that we co-organized at the Montreal Holocaust Memorial Centre (MHMC) on 30 November 2009, Leslie Vertes stood up, pushed his chair aside, and uttered the above words. Although he knew many of those in attendance, this was our first introduction to Leslie and to most of the men and women in the room – the group of Montreal Holocaust survivors who frequently give public testimony and whom we have come, over time, to characterize as a "boisterous extended family."[2] Like everyone else, we laughed and moved on when we heard Leslie's remarks, thinking little about their cheeky nature. Upon reflection, however, we realized that they were loaded with meaning, speaking to the shared commitment we have to Holocaust education and to the reasons we created the collaborative workshop spaces that are the topic of this chapter.

Leslie's words were sarcastic, serious, and playful; he used humour to move beyond the awkwardness inherent in introducing oneself in the context of one's "work" as a Holocaust survivor. As a man in his late eighties who has spoken to thousands of students, he was by no means the youngest or newest speaker in the room; rather, he was playing with the bizarre idea that one could be newer, or more experienced, at recounting the most horrific moments of one's life. By numerically citing his engagements, he also stressed the pride he takes in his role as a survivor-educator and the value he places on testimony and his connections to young people.[3] In referring to his Hungarian origins, he simply echoed the sorts of introductions made by others. Each person mentioned their place of birth and the unfortunate circumstances that landed them all in that room on that day – as people who lived through the Holocaust, immigrated to Montreal, and now use their memories to educate young people about the horrors of anti-Semitism, genocide, and intolerance. Leslie's introduction also toyed with the idea that this was "work"; many of these survivors speak in classrooms a couple of times a week during the school year, lead museum tours as well as trips to Poland, and organize and participate in a host of public commemorative events. As a result, some call themselves "professional survivors," another tongue-in-cheek way of articulating just how central their role as survivor-educators has become.[4] However they refer to themselves, all of the survivors we met at our first workshop were there to discuss ways that they could improve upon and deepen their ability to give testimony. We, on the other hand, were there to understand how they do such taxing and complicated work. The intersection of these two goals is explored throughout this chapter.

Our project grew out of the education working group, one of seven groups that made up the Montreal Life Stories project at Concordia University in Montreal.[5] Its goal was to explore how to integrate the life stories of those who survived mass violence into Quebec's high school curriculum. For our part, we turned to local Holocaust survivors who frequently give testimony in public and educational spaces, hoping to learn from the vast individual and collective experiences they have had throughout the region since the early 1980s.[6] Employing loosely structured, in-depth life history interviews, we created reflective spaces where survivors could talk about their Holocaust experiences and their lives as a whole, and how they have constructed, communicated, and shaped their narratives in the years since.[7] In total, a team of interviewers conducted multiple-session life history interviews with nineteen Holocaust survivor-educators, out of an estimated forty or so who regularly bear witness.[8] Members of this group of Ashkenazi Jews, both child and adult survivors, have a range of Holocaust experiences and descend from a variety of European countries. Although this is just a small community (of educators) within a community (of survivors) within a community (of Jewish Montrealers),[9] these people are committed to Holocaust education and firmly believe that they can make the world a better place by sharing their horrific experiences.

While we learned a lot from these encounters,[10] they were just a starting point for us. Forging relationships with this incredible group of survivors led us to recognize the limitations of the individual interview approach. First, although all of our interviewees have recounted their Holocaust narratives many times, they have rarely spoken publicly about or reflected on more recent aspects of their lives. Taking interviews in this direction required more effort on everyone's part. Second, reflecting on survivors' educational roles is necessarily tied to the complicated and interconnected contexts in which they do this difficult work. Giving public testimony does not occur in a vacuum. It takes place within community organizations, such as the MHMC, where survivors routinely interact with other survivor-educators they have known for years. Since Holocaust education is immersed in questions of community, we sought alternative approaches for understanding these experiences. Organizing collaborative workshops presented us with one way to gain access to survivors' stories and the meanings therein.

Methods and goals constantly shift when researchers make a conscious effort to "share authority" with their interviewees.[11] As Alicia Rouverol eloquently states:

> Collaboration requires that we continually reassess our understandings and differences in dialogue, straight through to our desired end. The beauty of collaboration is that the ending isn't always what we have in mind, that our own goal isn't always the best one. Sharing authority also means sharing control of the outcomes.[12]

Given that recounting publicly is a social process, which is difficult to capture in a life history interview, this chapter explains how we developed methodological strategies to meet the challenges outlined above. Specifically, by creating mutually beneficial collaborative spaces, we learned a great deal more than would have been possible had we insisted on sticking to our original research agenda. Committing to a collaborative model means that the goals of those with whom we work have to be given as much space and attention as our own.[13] This suggestion is not just an ethical one. It also leads to more fruitful research that engages with the real and contemporary concerns of our interviewees. In describing what occurred during the three workshops we co-organized with survivors and staff members at the MHMC, this chapter continually returns to the centrality of questions and of creating environments where they can be asked and explored. The tension between questions and answers – and what the relationship between the two is and should be when recounting the Holocaust – came up constantly in our workshops. We employ it here as an illustration of the nuanced and thoughtful discussions that our collaborative approach inspired.

Conceptualizing Collaboration

Our collaborative research approach emerged out of the Montreal Life Stories' methodology. Founded in 2007 through partnerships between various community activists and local scholars, this project used a foundational ethic of community-university collaboration to collect five hundred life stories about displacement due to violence and to facilitate a wide range of creative, academic, and community initiatives so as to make sense of those stories and to communicate them to the public. The project functioned in a deliberately decentralized manner, allowing each of its seven constituent working groups, made up of community and university researchers, to set its own agenda. What united these diverse actors was a humanistic approach to oral history interviewing and related endeavours: we were all attempting to close the distance between researchers and the researched while looking for the larger meanings of violence in life course narratives.[14]

This strong focus on collaboration came out of interconnected ethical and methodological concerns. Ethically, we emphasized building trust with interviewees and local communities so that the context in which these survivors of mass violence found themselves, especially when sharing their difficult stories, was comfortable and not disempowering. We did not want to just "collect" stories and then leave; rather, we tried to make meaningful connections with our interviewees before, during, and after the interview process so that they felt respected and understood.[15] Our multiple interview approach demanded that we spend a lot of time with our interviewees. Ideally, conversations were organic and interviewee-led, which encouraged depth, texture, and reflections on the meanings of the recounted experiences.[16] We, along with the Montreal Life Stories project, believe that the more equitable and just interviewer-interviewee relationships are, the more chance there is for profound "long-haul work" to occur in the interview space.[17]

This ethic was the starting point for our work with Holocaust survivors, which began in 2008. We connected with an enthusiastic group of survivors and covered much chronological and thematic ground through repeat visits to their homes. Nevertheless, we often left our interviewees' homes feeling anxious about the so-called "benefits" of the interview experience. We learned a great deal but we constantly wondered whether our survivors – people who have spent years speaking about their Holocaust experiences – were just doing us a favour.[18] It was hard to gauge whether they found our exchanges interesting or useful, and sometimes we felt guilty asking people to discuss such sensitive topics solely for our benefit.[19] And so we wondered whether there was a way to give something back to our generous interviewees.

At the same time, we realized that discussing survivors' involvement in Holocaust education within the intimate confines of their living rooms was very different from the community context in which it occurred. Since testimony is a public phenomenon, we have, from day one, supplemented our interviewing by attending and participating in community meetings and events. We regularly attended MHMC speakers' meetings, during which survivors and employees discuss the practical and policy issues related to their work; community events, such as the MHMC's annual Holocaust Education Week; and public testimonies given by our interviewees. Stacey was also a survivor chaperone on the 2010 March of the Living trip, an international Holocaust education program that sends Jewish teenagers, accompanied by community leaders and survivors, to Poland and Israel. This experience allowed Stacey to get to know two of our interviewees better and in a different context.

Our role changed from attending to organizing events after a conversation with Batia Bettman, one of our interviewees. As a career educator herself, Batia told us that she harboured a long-held desire to organize a "professional development" series for speakers so that they could discuss their experiences, improve their practice, and strategize about how best to deal with some of the challenges they face in their educational work. Speaking to other genocides and the Israeli-Palestinian conflict, which are outside of survivors' personal experiences, were particularly difficult issues for many. Most survivor-educators know each other quite well because they spend a considerable amount of time together, due to their personal friendships and the staggering number of commitments they make to various committees in a range of local Jewish organizations. Yet, despite this, Batia said that they had never had a space to talk about the nitty gritty of their work.

Our interest in this idea, as researchers whose very goal is to understand how survivors turn their stories into educational tools, was obvious. With Batia's permission, we aligned with the MHMC and co-organized and co-facilitated three "speaker workshops," as they were called, with Batia; Olga Sher, a survivor who chaired the MHMC speaker's committee; and Brunhilde Khandanpour, who worked as the MHMC's survivor liaison at the time.[20] These short, loosely structured meetings were open to survivors who volunteered as speakers for the MHMC.[21] Although the subsequent sections in this piece detail how the workshops evolved, it is important to state, up front, that our initial purpose was simply to facilitate spaces in which survivors could share, listen to, and learn from each other's experiences. These workshops were meant to be productive for survivors, enabling them to explore the challenges they face in the classroom. If we could learn from them and come to better understand how they shape their narratives and inform their practices, then all the better. We tried to make these spaces mutually beneficial for all of us, even if our goals were not always directly connected.

The Evolution of the Workshops

We were both extremely nervous on the morning of our first speaker workshop, which took place on 30 November 2009. Because they are inherently unpredictable, facilitating collaborative spaces is a challenge on the best of days; attempting to do so with an opinionated group of older people when you yourself are a mild-mannered junior female scholar is especially terrifying. We had no idea whether anyone would attend the workshop or if those who came would be interested in the agenda we had prepared with Batia and Bruni. We also worried about what participants would think of the relatively unstructured format. The workshop, which took place in a meeting room in the same building as the MHMC, was scheduled to begin at 2:30 PM, but it only got under way a half hour later, leaving us with just an hour to get through our agenda.

We began with a *tour de table*, asking everyone to introduce themselves. To our amazement, the group was surprisingly large – around forty people – and while many knew each other, some were strangers.

As we went around the room, speakers gave brief statements about who they were, what their basic Holocaust experiences had been, and how long they had been involved in Holocaust education. Their introductions spoke richly to the organizational and social history of Holocaust commemoration in Montreal. Introductions were in a similar vein to Leslie Vertes's remarks, which opened this chapter. Susannah Kohn declared: "My name is Susannah Kohn, I was born in Yugoslavia, and I'm coming to speak to students, since Krysia Starker [the first director of the MHMC] was, I don't know how many years is that." And Mayer Schondorf stated: "My name is Mayer Schondorf, I'm from Slovakia, I think I've been involved now for maybe fifteen years or more, my main experience of speaking is, I've been, together with my wife, on the March of the Living seven times [...] So this is my contribution."[22] Survivors' familiarity with each other meant that introductions were friendly and full of exchanges, comments, and even laughter amidst reminders of everybody's difficult origins. This atmosphere set a good tone as we turned to the agenda, which consisted of breaking into small groups to discuss six different sets of questions related to participants' work as speakers. We asked each group to talk about their topic and then bring their reflections back to the larger group for discussion towards the end of the hour. We sought to ensure that everyone, not just those who were especially vocal, had an opportunity to speak about their assigned topic. Anna, Bruni, and Stacey circulated among the small groups unobtrusively to provide help if any was needed.

Although we used suggestions from the last speakers' meeting to formulate our questions, it quickly became clear that they were comically ambitious. Each group was assigned one of the following questions:

1. *Conditions of speaking:* How much time (ideally) do you need to tell your story? Why? What kinds of tools do you use (artefacts, technology) when telling your story?
2. *Telling your story*: While your story never changes, do you always tell it the same way? How do you adapt it to different audiences, settings? What do you tell? What don't you speak about? Bear in mind that there are several kinds of situations in which to give testimony: after an MHMC visit, at schools, during the education series, and to the Canadian Jewish Congress and other delegations.
3. *Context:* How much general history do you tell listeners before getting into your story and while you tell your story? How do you explain

the ways that your story relates to what others went through and to the general forces of history of the period?

4. *Educational aims:* What is your message? If your audience takes away one thing, what would you like it to be? What do you do to ensure that listeners get this message?
5. *Questions:* What is the best question you have gotten? What's the most challenging question you have received? Have there ever been questions that have come up that you wish you had had a better answer for? What kind of preparation or tools would help you better answer these questions?
6. *Speaking to Related Topics:* How do you address questions about other genocides or political situations when they come up? Do you bring them up, or do your listeners? Do you want to talk about them? If yes, why, and if not, why not? What is your role, as a survivor of the Holocaust, when speaking of related topics?[23]

After the groups returned to the table, we only had time to touch on the first two sets of questions. That said, each question related to the other and so survivors rarely stuck to any one in particular. The discussion progressed naturally as people weighed in, and we, as facilitators, wondered whether the conversation, which jumped quickly and frequently between topics, was problematic. While the immense breadth of the discussion kept things general, participants touched on various topics that were central to their work as speakers: namely, the amount of time there is to speak; the preparedness of teachers and students; issues of respect when speaking to students; the challenge of connecting to students and relating to them; and strategies to help students feel comfortable asking questions. Statements about the importance of flexibility came up frequently. For example, Sidney Zoltak stated:

> I want to just mention here that there are so many different ways of how to speak to a group, depending on the age, and depending their maturity, and depending their intelligence. I can only tell you my experience, I was speaking in a [...] sixth grade [class ...] and I was told that they were very intelligent, and instead of me making a half an hour speech about my story, I was asked to do the following: give them a brief introduction of who I am, where I was born, how old I was when the war broke out, the whole thing didn't take more than ten minutes, and the rest, the rest of the hour, was done in questions. And that was as exactly like

> they do in a class, and I tried it, I [...] the first hour I was a little bit [...] scared, because I'd never done it before, and it worked very, very well. Because, you answered their questions, their concerns [...] every one of them wanted to know, and what you did was answer their questions, and they were not bored, they did not fall asleep, they did not do anything, they were satisfied, I think.[24]

According to Sidney, questions encouraged engagement and built a relationship between him and his listeners. One participant immediately responded to Sid's remark, noting that this was an exceptional experience in that the students were talented and well prepared, while another asked about the size of the group, implying that this model was less realistic for big audiences. This is how we continued during our hour: one participant shared her or his experiences and what she/he learned from them, and others responded, either agreeing with or challenging her/him before turning to their own reflections. It was clear that the speakers saw their contributions as work, which many explicitly stated, and that they were concerned with questions around creating a sort of "best practice" for survivor-educators. For example, Leslie broke down an ideal testimony into percentages, making suggestions for how long a speaker ought to spend on any given part of her or his experience, while Liselotte Ivry emphasized the importance of speaking, rather than reading, one's testimony.

Several problems cropped up during this first workshop. Our ambitious agenda and narrow time frame meant that we barely moved beyond generalities. Recognizing this, we emphasized that this exchange represented the start of a longer and larger conversation, something that we could better direct given that we now understood the issues that participants deemed worthy of follow-up in subsequent workshops. To this end, Anna plainly stated that our priority for the next session was to have a narrower focus. We also asked participants to share their goals in our feedback forms. Another unforeseen issue was the large mix of people in the room – ranging from experienced speakers of several decades to survivors just beginning to share their stories – and the challenges that some had when it came to recounting and communicating the past. In one incident, a survivor, who still had difficulty recounting the past, unintentionally made others in his group feel uncomfortable and even distressed when he insisted on sharing his memories of the Holocaust in graphic detail. As one participant emotively declared: "I'm afraid that after [our initial discussion], we all broke off into our own stories, and we went totally off the page. [Laughter from group.] And it was extremely emotional, and I'm ready to leave. I'm serious, it was really, it was really, um, I mean we're all speaking all the time, but [...] that's what happened."[25] Those involved in this incident asked us to use a heavier hand when facilitating in the future.

This reality, that survivors could be distressed by other survivors, came as a surprise to us and flew in the face of our approach to this workshop. In particular, we intentionally relegated ourselves to the background so as to avoid being perceived as authority figures. After all, who were we, as young Canadian women who have experienced little hardship in our lives, to tell survivors how best to communicate their difficult pasts to various publics? As we left the room that day another survivor approached us and asked if, in subsequent workshops, we would teach them the "right" way to give testimony; we were shocked and concerned that this person thought that this had been our goal. Developing strategies for clearly communicating our intentions and dealing with tensions when they arose became a daunting but necessary task for us.

These considerations preoccupied us when planning the second workshop, which took place on 21 June 2010. At the end of the first workshop, a participant reiterated one of our initial topics: the question of message. Specifically, she stated that her main role as a speaker was to leave students with a coherent message. This topic had great potential – narrowing things down while still allowing us to have a conversation about a "big picture" issue – and so we decided that this would be the focus of our next meeting. Unlike our complicated first handout, this one simply asked participants to consider the following: "If your audience could only take one message away after hearing you speak, what would you want that message to be? What is the most important thing that you want people to learn from listening to your story?"[26]

Scheduled to last a full two hours, those in attendance – about twenty – broke into smaller groups once again. This time, however, Anna, Stacey, Bruni, and Olga each facilitated a group.[27] Every group also received a flip chart so that its members could record their reflections and then easily share them when it came time for the larger discussion.

These small changes were fruitful. Each group approached the main question differently, but the presentations and discussion that followed were more coherent and profound than they had been in the previous

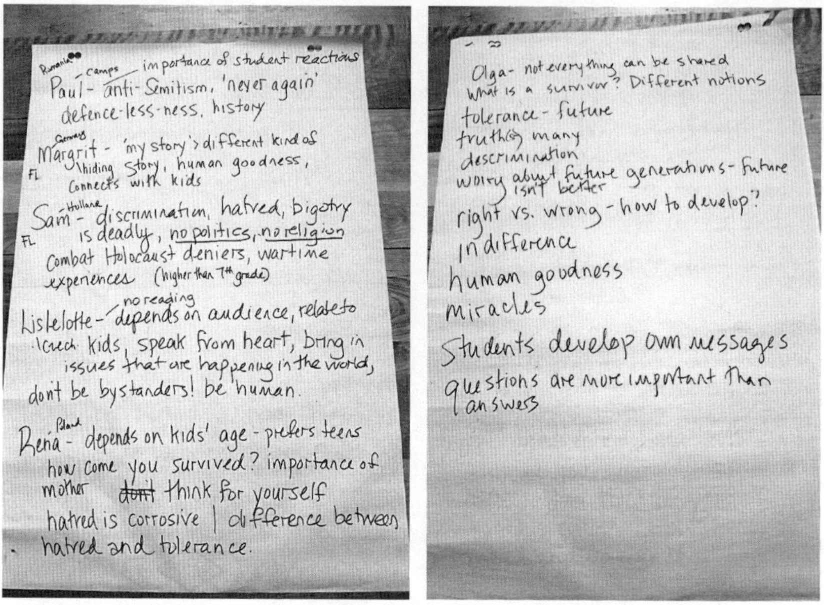

FIGURE 8.1 Two of the flip charts from the 21 June 2010 workshop. *Photographs by Stacey Zembrzycki.*

workshop. Conveying the ideas that came out of each group forced us to find ways to make space for all of them. There was a fascinating balancing act in place as speakers negotiated the various messages that they deemed to be important. For example, there was a dual emphasis on demonstrating the specificity of the Holocaust and anti-Semitic violence, and teaching young people about the dangers of racism, human rights, and social justice more generally. Although this relates to larger debates within Holocaust studies about the appropriateness of using the Holocaust as a larger, more generalized, lesson about humanity,[28] here survivors seamlessly navigated such competing messages in their own narratives. They melded theoretical discussions with how one addresses such quandaries in day-to-day contexts, when contradictions are more easily managed. Another tension arose when we discussed student questions. In particular, speakers talked about their anxiety around questions pertaining to forgiveness, declaring that there was no easy response to this issue. Were they meant to forgive their aggressors – Nazis, Germans, or Poles? Did they have to forgive Poles of a certain generation or Poles today? Survivors shared multiple stories about their encounters with forgiveness, as well as continued animosity, and discussed how hard it is to reduce these difficult subjects to an easily digestible answer in the classroom.

Survivors spoke about their personal experiences in one breath, and the educational strategies they employ in another – the two went hand in hand. For instance, the following exchange took place between several participants, upon the presentation of one of the group's flip charts:

> OLGA: My personal conviction is, I survived because of the good people, you always find them, not a large group, not many, but you need sometimes one or two, if they stretch their hands, and they are heroic enough to help you under difficult circumstances, you are blessed. And I believe in miracles. You know what Ben-Gurion said about miracles? "If you don't believe in miracles, you're not a realist." [Laughter from group.]
>
> ANNA: Does anyone have anything to add, from that group?
>
> LESLIE: Can I have a question for her? What is the answer for the question?
>
> ANNA: I think this was the answer, that these are the sort of things you're trying to get across –
>
> LESLIE: For a student to take home?
>
> OLGA: Oh. Well, I don't think we have an answer for the students, I think they have to find their own answers, from all the testimonies that we present –
>
> UNNAMED SPEAKER: They write you letters and they tell you –
>
> OLGA: I think that was my answer.
>
> ANNA: But the point is you're trying to speak to them about these sorts of topics, right?
>
> UNNAMED SPEAKER: But they write letters to you and they tell you the answers, how they felt, and what they brought [...]
>
> OLGA: I think they should have questions, instead of answers.
>
> UNNAMED SPEAKER: I also believe that miracle, because I had measles in Auschwitz, and for several, for ten days I didn't have

anything in my mouth, no food, no water, and for the goodness of my friend and honesty [. . .] and that was a miracle.

LESLIE: Oh, surviving is a miracle. [Agreement from group.][29]

Olga raised the issue of questions to challenge the concept of communicating a pre-formed "message," showing how survivors could help students explore what they needed to get out of their encounters. Not all agreed, but they engaged with each other. Conversations like the one above were organic. Participants interrupted, contested, listened, and laughed as they tried to make sense of their Holocaust experiences and those they had in local classrooms; they discussed content and form at the same time. For our part, we tried, with limited success, to have a heavier hand in moderating the discussion as people made connections between their experiences.

Our strategy of having more of a presence as facilitators both helped and hindered this process. On the one hand, participants were satisfied with the space they had both within their groups and in the larger discussion, and they believed they accomplished a great deal together. Unlike the first workshop, participants had many opportunities to speak to one another and to build on each other's ideas. On the other hand, in some groups, facilitators walked into rather tense conversations that required intervention. Stacey, for instance, found herself in the middle of an argument about who counted as a survivor and whose stories were legitimate, and again, as a young woman with no personal experience of the Holocaust, she struggled to find ways to help participants speak to each other in a less explosive manner. While the first workshop made clear that the small groups needed more support, we realized that facilitators required support too. Overall, however, participants left the workshop happy, and, in hindsight, it went a long way towards building a sense of good will between the participants and facilitators.

When planning the third workshop, we once again reflected on the lessons we had learned in our previous sessions. Although participants deemed the process thus far to be productive and relevant to their needs, the workshops had nevertheless still been structured largely around our own research interests. As we searched for our next theme, our feedback forms made one thing clear: survivors wanted to know what students and teachers thought of their work. They demanded practical feedback, even criticism. This is easier said than done – no one wants to criticize a Holocaust survivor.

As a way of meeting in the middle, we invited three teachers (elementary, secondary, and university-level educators), who regularly bring survivors into their classrooms, to give brief five- to ten-minute presentations that spoke to their needs and expectations when teaching their students about the Holocaust. Since survivors were interested in the finer details that make for a successful lesson, we also asked teachers to address the following:

- Please describe where you teach and the age group that you work with.
- Why do you bring survivors into your classroom?
- What would you like survivors to talk about? (e.g., general history of the Holocaust, personal experiences, moral lessons, contemporary human rights issues)
- What would you like your students to get out of these visits?
- How do you prepare your students for a survivor's visit to the classroom?
- What are some of the practical considerations that must go into planning a visit? (e.g., time limits, class size, students' attention span, students' understanding of historical context)
- In your experience, what kinds of tools complement survivors' stories (e.g., photos, artefacts, maps, PowerPoint, books, films)
- Can you describe an experience, either positive or negative, in your classroom when you felt that a survivor's visit has left a lasting impression on your students? What was it about this visit that was so memorable?[30]

Everyone was excited about this format, and so we scheduled our third workshop for 18 November 2010.

After the teachers finished their brief presentations, an exchange between them and the twenty survivors in attendance ensued. Although survivors had asked that this workshop focus on concrete suggestions about practice, we quickly moved on from this and discussed, with a surprising lack of tension, such controversial topics as the appropriateness of bringing up issues like the Israeli-Palestinian conflict in classrooms. The teachers' presence, as well as the respectful tone of the room, meant that these conversations were far less hostile than had been the case in previous workshops and MHMC spaces. The group was also quite small and clearly committed to the process. The following exchange between Batia and one of the teachers – about how best to deal with students who are too nervous or hesitant to ask survivors questions – is a good example of the dialogue that took place:

> BATIA: So, people tell the story and then say, "Are there any questions?" Thomas in the white shirt [referring to one of the teachers] prepares water, and he says, "Go ahead, have a drink." You are allowed to stop to catch your breath, it's called a dramatic pause [laughter from group]. You can take a little sip, it refreshes you, it gives them a moment to process the, the things, it could be adults or children. You have finished a certain chapter, it's before, let's say it's before the war. I heard Yehudi [another survivor] do this years ago, very instinctively. He spoke to a group of children in a cinema, and he said to them, "I will tell you my story," and he told them his story, when he was a little child, before the war, and then, the war started. He said, "Before I tell you what happened during the war, are there any questions about what I just told you?" So they said, "So how did you go from here to there?" [...] And they asked a few questions about that time, so that you can stop a few times and say, "Okay, I am now finished this," and you can go to that. So, questions are not just for the end. You can also use questions by saying, um, "This is what happened, we went to such and such a place, what do you think happened?" [...]

> THOMAS (HIGH SCHOOL TEACHER): And you know, I had a survivor, I don't know if you know him, who used humour, because, you know the students, when they get to the auditorium, they're very stressed, they don't know what to expect, and you know they're impressed, like you said, they're very impressed. So they sit down, and you know, you sense that they don't know what to say, they don't even want to approach a person, so, you know, if you want to use humour, whatever it is, if it works for you. He used to, you know, open up a bottle of water, and say, "One minute, I have to drink my vodka" and I had students who would come and see me after and say, "Was that really vodka?" [Laughter from group.] And I said, "Come on," I said, "Come on, he opened up the bottle of water in front of you!" Now, for the questions by the way, and you said for the pause, it's an excellent point, uh, I prepare them with questions before, and I usually tell them, I say, "You know, there's no, obviously no wrong question, but, if you don't know what to ask about the

> past, ask the survivors about the present." Because I'm sure if they ask you about your grandchildren, your children, you will want to answer this. And I said, "You know, they will feel very much at ease to talk to you about what's going on, today."[31]

Here the focus on questions concerned transforming them from a source of anxiety for awestruck students into something that could be productive in their learning process. It was also about demystifying the Holocaust survivor, a problem that had, until now, kept a workshop like this from happening. The teachers spoke with enormous deference to the survivors, but they also felt comfortable enough offering them ideas about how best to approach their students. People waited their turns to speak, much more so than in the previous workshops, and participants built off of, and responded to, each other's ideas. The exchange above shows how this workshop served as a space to not only talk about practice but also to show the other how much they were appreciated and respected. Both were valuable outcomes.

Indeed, this workshop's greatest accomplishment was the trust it generated, allowing each side to discuss its hard work, its respect for the other, and its hopes for Holocaust education. It certainly helped that all of the teachers were individuals who, so to speak, "got it," and thus there was little divergence of opinion between those in the room. Unfortunately, this sort of atmosphere meant that the larger question, of how survivors can successfully navigate classrooms in which teachers and students are less seriously engaged with the Holocaust, could not be meaningfully addressed. We also found that survivors and teachers really just wanted to thank and be thanked for their many years of work, and they took this opportunity to do so. By this point, we were so used to things never going as planned that we did not fight this shift; instead, we viewed it as a timely and welcome way of wrapping up our workshop series. It was also an apt conclusion to the concerns, articulated by survivors, that initiated this process: they felt like they were rarely heard, understood, or taken seriously. And so, in a sense, this third workshop was crucial to addressing their needs, even if it was less about our own goals as researchers.

Learning from the Process

These three workshops drove home the importance of flexibility. In some instances, despite our fears of being seen as either authority figures or people who have all of the "answers," we tried to adopt a dominant and hands-on model; and, at other times, we created a welcoming space and then watched from the sidelines. This process forced us to be attentive to the dynamics of each setting and how people interacted with each other within them. Although we always had a "game plan," responding to people's needs and expectations demanded flexibility.

Flexibility applied not only to our mode of facilitation but also to our objectives. As we state above, the goal of the workshops was to find ways to satisfy our own interests, as researchers focused on Holocaust education, and those expressed by survivors who, it must be stressed, have always had multiple agendas. In the end, the first workshop was modelled more upon our own interests, the second was a bridge between the two, and the third really became about them. This balance was crucial.

This experience forced us to move beyond oral historians' vague and frequently utopian ideals and to seriously consider what it means to "build trust." Getting *them* to trust *us* – wherein the hope is that hard work will make people feel comfortable enough to reveal their deepest darkest secrets to us – is not enough. Building trust must also be a means to its own end. For us, this meant ensuring that our work truly benefited our interviewees – people who had already generously given their time and shared their stories with their community and countless researchers. This is not just about "getting better stuff." It is about making an ethical commitment to the idea that we should not be engaging in this work if it does not add something, big or small, to the lives of the amazing people with whom we work.

Academics have a difficult time ceding control. However, trusting the process and its natural evolution was invaluable in this context. Community-implicated research is often characterized in terms of its many compromises; we tend to talk about giving up autonomy when we connect ourselves with communities. While compromise is an inevitable part of the process, it is important to point out that what we learn far outweighs what we give up. Sometimes a true collaborative process forces us to put our own goals and agendas aside for a moment. This does not make us less rigorous researchers. These workshops deepened the relationships that we forged with our interviewees, and they also continue to serve as points of reference in discussions we have witnessed ever since. For instance, when we run into survivors at public events, like those in which they give testimony, some now refer directly to their "message," articulating it with a new and certain confidence.

Many have come to see what they do in new ways, and this is reflected in how they tell their stories. Testimony, we realize, is always contingent upon what has taken place and what is presently occurring in survivors' lives. We hope, again, that the exchanges we helped to facilitate have been useful not only for our understanding of the work that survivors do but also for their own understandings of themselves.

Furthermore, this focus on survivors' "research agendas" led us to arrive at new ways of conceptualizing our own thinking. We used to worry about the fact that the workshops rarely stayed on track – the topic of education – for long. For example, the discussion of forgiveness during the second workshop shifted between notions about how best to address questions pertaining to forgiveness in classrooms, real-life experiences of being asked to forgive, and instances of how, when faced with contemporary anti-Semitism, one felt prohibited from doing so. After making a few attempts to bring things back to "education" more generally, it occurred to us that we were observing an invaluable lesson: namely, survivors do not separate their perspectives on education and how to speak from their lived experiences – they negotiate the various quandaries involved simultaneously.[32] In short, we came to trust the chaos that necessarily accompanies any kind of fruitful and serious discussion.

Balancing individual interviews with collective workshops was also invaluable. Survivors do not live in bubbles. They are friends with each other, some are related to one another, others have worked together, and there is even a group that spends an hour every Tuesday morning in an aquafit class together. These relationships were evident in how often we laughed together while discussing their difficult stories. To this end, survivors have come to understand who they are, what they have been through, and what the world wants from them through this myriad of interactions. Survivors are not alone in this regard. To understand our interviewees' stories, we must try to gain access to their complex social webs. For us, our collaborative workshops were the most effective spaces in which to watch these larger contexts unfold. By its very nature, giving testimony requires a difficult merging of the personal and the public, and so creating spaces that demanded a similar set of negotiations was the only way for us to understand the complicated work that our interviewees do.

Olga Sher, our co-organizer, insisted both in the workshops and in the conversations we had before and since them that "questions are more important than answers" when it comes to Holocaust education.[33]

Preoccupations with how to encourage and utilize questions emerged out of all of our encounters, and, in many ways, this call for an inquisitive and critical spirit has been equally applicable to our research process. By balancing our priorities, being flexible in our approaches, and creating spaces for diverse exchanges, we learned far more than we could have if we had stuck to a more structured methodology. By putting our own questions aside, we came to better appreciate the questions that our survivors raised, and everyone benefited from this intersection of objectives. The purpose of asking a question is not only to look for an answer; it is also about framing a conversation, connecting ideas, and inviting the person next to you to share their views. This is how we approach our work with survivors, whether it is within interviews, workshops, or our writing. Collaboration is an ongoing personally and intellectually demanding process that requires nurturing and critical reflection.[34]

Notes

This chapter originated in the authors' postdoctoral research at Concordia University; Sheftel was funded by the Fonds québécois de recherche sur la society et culture (FQRSC), and Zembrzycki was funded by the Social Sciences and Humanities Research Council of Canada (SSHRC) between 2009 and 2011. The authors also thank the Montreal Life Stories project (www.lifestoriesmontreal.ca) and the Montreal Holocaust Memorial Centre (MHMC) for their generous support. In addition, this work would not have been possible without the help of Batia Batman, Olga Sher, Brunhilde Khandanpour, and members of the MHMC's speaker committee.

1 MHMC Survivor Workshop, Montreal, Quebec, 30 November 2009. Audio recordings of the three workshops that we co-organized are in the authors' possession. All quotations are from these recordings.

2 Anna Sheftel and Stacey Zembrzycki, "Professionalizing Survival: The Politics of Public Memory among Holocaust Survivor-Educators in Montreal," *Journal of Modern Jewish Studies* 12, 2 (July 2013): 210–31. This "boisterous extended family" reminds us of the fascinating motley crew of characters who play a central role in Barbara Myerhoff's *Number Our Days* (New York: Dutton, 1979).

3 MHMC Survivor Workshop, 30 November 2009; Leslie Vertes, interview by authors, Montreal, Quebec, 17 June 2010. We have also gotten to "know" Leslie through these resources: "It is me Leslie," Leslie Vertes' Blog, http://itismeleslie.blogspot.com/; Leslie Vertes, *Can You Stop the Wind? An Autobiography* (Montreal: Montreal Institute of Genocide Studies,

n.d.), at http://migs.concordia.ca/memoirs/Vertes/leslie_vertes_intro.htm.

4 Sheftel and Zembrzycki, "Professionalizing Survival."

5 Undertaken with Montreal's Rwandan, Cambodian, Haitian, Jewish, and other diaspora communities, Montreal Life Stories (http://www.lifestoriesmontreal.ca/) was a five-year project funded by a Social Sciences and Humanities Research Council of Canada (SSHRC) Community-University Research Alliance (CURA) grant; the project ended in July 2012.

6 The MHMC has been a second home to local survivor-educators since its creation in 1979. See Franklin Bialystok, *Delayed Impact: The Holocaust and the Canadian Jewish Community* (Montreal and Kingston: McGill-Queen's University Press, 2000); Stacey Zembrzycki and Steven High, "'When I Was Your Age': Bearing Witness in Holocaust Education in Montreal," *Canadian Historical Review* 93, 3 (2012): 408–35.

7 Our approach responded to the vast literature on the difficulty of capturing and properly comprehending the experiences of Holocaust survivors. See, for example, Primo Levi, *Survival in Auschwitz: The Nazi Assault on Humanity* (New York: Simon and Schuster, 1996); Charlotte Delbo, *Aucun de nous ne reviendra* (Paris: Editions de Minuit, 1965); Giorgio Agamben, *Remnants of Auschwitz: The Witness and the Archive* (New York: Zone Books, 1999); Henry Greenspan, *On Listening to Holocaust Survivors: Beyond Testimony*, 2nd ed. (St. Paul, Minnesota: Paragon House, 2010); Cathy Caruth, *Unclaimed Experience: Trauma, Narrative and History* (Baltimore: Johns Hopkins University Press, 1996); Dominick LaCapra, *Writing History: Writing Trauma* (Baltimore: Johns Hopkins University Press, 2000).

8 Although this project's team of interviewers included six other people, we became the principal researchers due primarily to our own research interests and the relationships we forged with our interviewees. That said, we are indebted to Steven High, Jessica Silva, Sandra Gasana, Luis van Isschot, Philip Hamon, and Matthew MacDonald for the interviews that they conducted.

9 This sense of community is developed in Zembrzycki and High, "'When I Was Your Age,'" 411.

10 See Anna Sheftel and Stacey Zembrzycki, "'We Started Over Again, We Were Young': Postwar Social Worlds of Child Holocaust Survivors in Montreal," *Urban History Review* 39, 1 (2010): 20–30; Anna Sheftel and Stacey Zembrzycki, "Only Human: A Reflection on the Ethical and Methodological Challenges of Working with 'Difficult' Stories," *Oral History Review* 37, 2 (2010): 191–214.

11 See Michael Frisch, *A Shared Authority: Essays on the Craft and Meaning of Oral and Public History* (Albany: State University of New York Press,

1990); Michael Frisch, "Shared Authority," *Oral History Review* 30, 1 (2003): 111–13; Katharine C. Corbett and Howard S. Miller, "A Shared Inquiry into Shared Inquiry," *Public Historian* 28, 1 (2006): 15–38; Steven High, Lisa Ndejuru, and Kristen O'Hare, eds., "Special Issue of Sharing Authority: Community-University Collaboration in Oral History, Digital Storytelling, and Engaged Scholarship," *Journal of Canadian Studies* 43, 1 (2009); Stacey Zembrzycki, Erin Jessee, Eleanor Beattie, Audrey Bean, Mireille Landry, and Sandra Baines, "Oral History and Adult Community Education: Notes from the Field," *Oral History Review* 38, 1 (2011): 120–35.

12 Alicia J. Rouverol, "Collaborative Oral History in a Correctional Setting: Promise and Pitfalls," *Oral History Review* 30, 1 (2003): 82.

13 Our inspirations include: Daniel James, *Doña María's Story: Life History, Memory, and Political Identity* (Durham, NC: Duke University Press, 2000); Jürgen Matthäus, ed., *Approaching an Auschwitz Survivor: Holocaust Testimony and Its Transformations* (Oxford: Oxford University Press, 2009); and the life work of Alessandro Portelli, especially *They Say in Harlan County: An Oral History* (Oxford: Oxford University Press, 2011).

14 Sheftel was the project's training coordinator between 2008 and 2009, and thus had a hand in fleshing out its training process: http://lifestories-montreal.ca/en/oral-history-training. See also Afsaneh Hojabi, "Methodology, Ethics and Training in the Montreal *Life Stories* CURA," 2008, at http://lifestoriesmontreal.ca/files/Methodology,%20Ethics%20and%20Training_Afsaneh%20Hojabri.pdf.

15 See Valerie Yow, "Ethics and Interpersonal Relationships in Oral History Research," *Oral History Review* 22, 1 (1995): 51–66.

16 Much of the inspiration for our approach can be found in Greenspan's *On Listening*; Henry Greenspan and Sidney Bolkosky, "When Is an Interview an Interview? Notes from Listening to Holocaust Survivors," *Poetics Today* 27, 2 (2006): 431–49; Henry Greenspan, "Collaborative Interpretation of Survivors' Accounts: A Radical Challenge to Conventional Practice," *Holocaust Studies: A Journal of Culture and History* 17, 1 (2011): 85–100.

17 Linda Shopes, "Commentary: Sharing Authority," *Oral History Review* 30, 1 (2003), 105.

18 Feminist oral historians have long worried about the unequal power dynamics in oral history interviews: Sherna Berger Gluck and Daphne Patai, eds., *Women's Words: The Feminist Practice of Oral History* (New York: Routledge, 1991).

19 Many scholars have questioned whether speaking about one's difficult past constitutes a positive, healing experience. See, for instance, the

literature critiquing the impact of truth and reconciliation commissions: Christine Bell, "Dealing with the Past in Northern Ireland," *Fordham International Law Journal* 26, 4 (2002): 1095–147; Yazir Henri, "Reconciling Reconciliation: A Personal and Public Journey of Testifying Before the South African Truth and Reconciliation Commission," in *Political Transition: Politics and Cultures*, ed. Paul Gready, 262–75 (London: Pluto Press, 2003).

20 The scheduling of these workshops largely depended on survivors' yearly migration pattern, as many spend six months in Florida and six months in Montreal.

21 The majority of survivors who speak in schools or other community spaces are sent there by the MHMC, which serves as the main point of contact for such requests. Part of the survivor liaison's job is to match survivors with the organizations that have requested their presence. Some survivors, however, have formed strong connections with particular teachers or schools and so they communicate directly, rather than going through the MHMC.

22 MHMC Survivor Workshop, 30 November 2009.

23 Handout circulated to participants at the first MHMC Survivor Workshop, November 2009.

24 MHMC Survivor Workshop, 30 November 2009.

25 Ibid.

26 Invitation to second MHMC Survivor Workshop.

27 Many of the first workshop's forty participants thought that it was a regular speakers' meeting, not a new event. Those who came to the second workshop were more self-selecting, clear on its content, and devoted to learning from it.

28 See, for instance, Daniel Levy and Natan Sznaider, *The Holocaust and Memory in the Global Age*, trans. Assenka Oksiloff (Philadelphia: Temple University Press, 2006); Daniel Levy and Natan Sznaider, "The Institutionalization of Cosmopolitan Morality: The Holocaust and Human Rights," *Journal of Human Rights* 3, 2 (2004): 143–56; Gavriel D. Rosenfeld, "Reflections on the Recent Polemical Turn in Holocaust and Genocide Scholarship," *Holocaust and Genocide Studies* 13, 1 (1999): 28–61; Lissa Skitolsky, "The Case for Comparison between Nazism and the War against Terror: A Study in Bio-Politics," *International Studies in Philosophy* 38, 2 (2006): 159–77.

29 MHMC Survivor Workshop, Montreal, Quebec, 21 June 2010.

30 Invitation to teachers for the third MHMC Speaker Workshop, November 2010.

31 MHMC Survivor Workshop, Montreal, Quebec, 18 November 2010.

32 This point is developed in Sheftel and Zembrzycki, "Professionalizing Survival."

33 In addition to the workshops, Stacey interviewed Olga (with Steven High) on four other occasions; we videotaped these exchanges and they are currently held at the Centre for Oral History and Digital Storytelling (COHDS) at Concordia University.

34 This echoes the remarks made by Shopes in "Commentary," 106.

9 | On Tour with Mapping Memories

Sharing Refugee Youth Stories in Montreal Classrooms

MICHELE LUCHS | ELIZABETH MILLER

> Three days, three months, three weeks. So much has changed. I have found myself alone. I am the only survivor of my family ... but I am a survivor and today am 22 years old and I am no longer alone. I have a new family. I am the mother of this family, and I have 16 children – girls and boys. Some of my children are older than me. You may ask yourself how is this possible? ... My family is made up of orphans, of students at my school who are also trying to fight loneliness.
>
> – Leontine Uwababyeyi[1]

The small classroom at L'école Internationale is silent as students pause to reflect on the digital story they have just watched, created by a young woman who lost her family during the Rwandan genocide. The author of the video, Leontine Uwababyeyi, is presenting in front of a high school audience for the first time ever. Leontine tentatively invites students to ask questions. A first hand is raised: "How did you get here?" Leontine pauses, unsure of what the student is really asking: What was her means of transport? Who helped her? She cautiously answers, "I got here on a plane." The student continues: "But in your story, you said you were eight when the genocide occurred. Where have you been since then?" Leontine uses an answer she has practised often with us: "That is a long story for another time." This is followed by a string of other questions that range from the personal to the more political, including: "How old was your brother when he was killed?" and "Did you ever try to pretend you were a Hutu?" As project coordinators, we (Michele and Liz) stand in the back of the classroom anxiously observing, wondering if we should intervene. Although the students' questions are well intentioned we worry about the nature of this exchange. As Taylor, Sollange, and Rwigema ask in Chapter 3 (this volume): Are the students simply categorizing this survivor and her testimony into an object of study, a way to verify "facts" they had read about the genocide? While we watch the presentation, more questions are running through our minds. What is the emotional cost on Leontine and other presenters in sharing these difficult stories in a school setting? Have we done enough to support the youth in answering these difficult questions?

Leontine's experience in front of the class was quite different from ours at the back. Although she found the question period stressful, she was energized by the positive feedback she had received from the students after the class and surprised at how strongly many of them connected with her short video and presentation.

The complex emotions and questions of this first visit stayed with us as we joined Leontine and two other youth, Stephanie Gasana and Ayanda Dube, on their visits to thirty high schools in the Montreal area. The tour was the final stage of our five-year participatory media project, Mapping Memories, intended to help youth with refugee experiences use a variety of media tools to tell their own stories and share them with audiences of peers. For us, this meant not simply helping the youth to produce their stories but showing them how to create solid presentations and guiding them to become strong public speakers who were able to present in different settings to a variety of audiences. The tour was a collaborative effort with these three young people and with our main partner, the Canadian Council for Refugees (CCR), a national non-governmental network that advocates for the rights of refugees. Through peer-to-peer sharing we wanted to address stereotypes about refugees and challenge the notion of survivors as one-dimensional heroes or victims. Mapping Memories was also the youth arm of Life Stories of Montrealers Displaced by War, Genocide and Other Human Rights Violations – a collaborative oral history project that brought together community activists and scholars to document and disseminate life story interviews.

In this chapter we address what was involved in extending our participatory media process into the outreach stage to contribute to the broader discussion about the benefits and challenges of disseminating survivors' narratives. We describe our ethical framework, the different roles we assumed, and the questions we constantly faced regarding engaging survivors' accounts in schools. We explore our efforts to create a meaningful encounter around testimony, where student audiences connect to the people in front of them and not simply to the traumatic events in their stories. Influenced by playwright and scholar Julie Salverson's thoughts on staging an encounter in theatre, we wanted audiences to rethink assumptions, become implicated, and, ideally, be changed by the experience.[2] We also examine the impact of our school tour on the youth presenters and on each other – on our own understanding of how digital life stories and peer dialogue about refugee experiences can be ethically engaged in the education of students.

Back Story

The Mapping Memories project that we – Michele Luchs and Liz Miller, documentary makers and educators – have coordinated for five years helps youth with refugee experience use a variety of media tools to create digital stories. Our approach has been to share life stories through media workshops in which youth work together in a supportive environment to engage with the complexity of sharing and representing difficult personal stories on their own terms. Educator and scholar Gerald Campano suggests that "storytelling is one way in which students can begin to understand and perhaps gain a degree of control over past experiences that may not have been fully intelligible at the time of their occurrence."[3] Collaborative creative processes do facilitate spaces to reflect, to remember, and to construct meaning and narratives of past events. Reshaping those stories to share them with diverse publics is a further means of gaining clarity and understanding.

Creating a safe environment was key to our process, and this meant offering youth the chance to tell any personal story in the workshop, not just a story about a past traumatic event. To facilitate this, we led a series of exercises to solicit stories about food, music, and contemporary events in their lives. For Leontine and other group members this was their first time sharing personal stories with a wider public, and, as a result, our group grappled with complex questions around revisiting and representing traumatic events: When are you ready to take a personal story public? How much of a story do you share? Is there a message and who should hear it? As facilitators, our role was to understand the motivation of each individual in sharing a difficult story, give feedback during the writing process, and offer technical experience in using media to tell stories.

The three youth who became involved in the school tour had different motivations and challenges in shaping their stories during our collaborative workshop. For Stephanie, it was not her family but her Grade 8 history teacher who first informed her that her country of origin, Rwanda, had survived genocide. Stephanie interviewed family members to fill in the gaps of past silences and then had to incorporate these interviews into a personal narrative. In her digital story, "My Sister Solange," she compares her own life to that of her sister, fifteen years her senior, who experienced the immediate impact of the genocide.

> The president of Rwanda once suggested in one of his speeches that the Tutsis should put their memories in a box, lock it and put it away, move on, look forward and focus on the future [...] Is this the answer? Is there a way to connect the past to the present? Without your past, who are you? And does it matter if anyone knows? (Stephanie Gasana)[4]

We helped Stephanie explore how incorporating reflexive questions into a narrative could help build complexity, engage audiences, and suggest the difficulty of communicating a traumatic past event.

Ayanda had left Zimbabwe as a teenager, when his family decided that as a politically engaged student he was no longer safe in his own country. In the workshop, Ayanda's first instinct was to seek out other Zimbabweans' stories. Through group discussion, he became motivated to explore how his arrival in Montreal on his own at age eighteen could shed light on the bigger picture of refugee rights and the treatment of newcomers in Canada. In his story "YUL-MTL," Ayanda also uses reflexive questions to explore themes like family, home, and adapting to a new country. "After a number of years of being in Canada, I reflect: What is home? Is Canada my home or is this a temporary refuge? Have I made friends and connections that will last a lifetime? Do I have people I can call family? Did I endure those cold winters in vain?" (Ayanda Dube).[5]

Leontine was eight years old when she lost her family to the Rwandan genocide and twenty when she applied to become a refugee to Canada during Rwanda's truth and reconciliation process. As with Ayanda, Leontine first suggested writing other people's stories. She explained: "At the beginning it wasn't easy to tell a story. I had many stories in mind. But, after I started writing, once upon a time there was a little girl [...] If I wasn't alive, who could tell my story? Who could remember my family?"[6] Leontine's initial motivation for telling a difficult story was to honour her family. When she later revealed in a writing conference that she had two families, we began to discuss how these two stories could work together. In her video, *My Two Families*, Leontine describes how she lost her family to the genocide and how she later created a second family with students who were also survivors of the genocide. By finishing her narrative with the second account, Leontine challenged audiences to move beyond a traumatic event and to understand what happened after she lost her family: to acknowledge both the atrocity she went through and the new "family" she was able to create. We spent time discussing how Leontine's expanding of her story might challenge readers to go beyond any simple classification of a youth survivor as either "hero or emotional wreck."[7]

To celebrate the narratives produced in the workshop and share them with a wider public, we developed a bus tour, created in collaboration with the youth from the project, who also guided the tour. As the bus travelled through Montreal visiting sites that were significant to the guides – the YMCA, St. Joseph's Oratory, and so on – the audience listened to recordings of the stories and asked the authors questions. Between stories, we played music from each of the countries represented: Congo, Zimbabwe, Syria, Rwanda, and Palestine. At one point, while we listened to a rousing Palestinian folksong, Rania, one of the group members, danced down the bus aisle with her father. At another point, we stopped in Old Montreal to honour those who had died in the Rwandan genocide by joining Stephanie and Leontine in throwing rose petals into the harbour. The intimacy of our story-mobile was striking. It was powerful to move from story to story, from one significant place to another, and to embrace the range of emotions evoked on the tour – from quiet contemplation to collective celebration.

The tour helped us identify some key elements in presenting personal stories in such a public way. For one, it was critical to present the stories as a group, which provided a supportive environment for the youth and also helped present the diversity of experiences to our audiences. And, as Leontine explained, rehearsal was important: "In the beginning, I couldn't look people in the eye, I was so shy, I had never stood in front of more than three people. Practice helped me, and working with others. They help you to do something you can not do alone."[8]

Playing recorded stories helped to alleviate performance anxiety. As their stories played, the youth were able to both listen and watch audience reactions. Several mentioned how happy they were that audience members laughed at the humorous parts of their stories or seemed moved by the painful sections. The distance a recorded story provided also helped us move the discussion on the bus beyond the specifics of a single traumatic event to a deeper reflection upon integration and belonging in Montreal. We were able to create conditions for what Taylor, Sollange, and Rwigema encourage: a more embodied, reflexive, and critical response to testimony.[9]

Involving Participants in Outreach

When we initiated Mapping Memories we were familiar with inspiring initiatives that used photography and video with newcomer youth, including the two projects entitled (1) the Documentary Project for Refugee Youth and (2) Towards a Promised Land.[10] Both of these used creative expression and media production to foster new relationships and understandings among youth groups, which they then shared with the public in a variety of ways (in art galleries, on DVDs, and as books). But in most cases youth participation in a media project ends with a project's launch. It is not easy to extend a participatory youth project beyond a final launch. In many cases, projects do not have the resources for an extensive outreach strategy. The project may have emphasized process over final products and the resulting work may not be appropriate for larger audiences. An additional challenge is that youth participants may be ready to move on to other projects or activities.

In her filmmaker-in-residence manifesto, documentary maker Kat Cizek writes that artists working in community collaborations should spend 10 percent of the time making a piece and 90 percent of the time getting it out into the world.[11] While her breakdown seems extreme, following through on a dissemination strategy does involve substantial time, energy, and resources. So why move beyond a launch (in our case our bus tour) and why involve participants? What specific challenges do youth media projects face in extending participation into outreach?

Our own motivation in involving the youth participants as co-creators in a city-wide school tour was to expand the mandates that had shaped our production workshops and the Montreal Life Stories project: collaboration, shared authorship, and a careful navigation of public and private into the realm of outreach.[12] We felt it was critical for the young authors to participate in how their stories would be used in classrooms. We hoped it would be exciting for them to see the impact their digital stories could have on youth audiences. We knew that Leontine, Ayanda, and Stephanie would gain important skills in presenting, which could contribute both to their confidence in sharing and framing the stories and would be useful in their studies and in their work lives.

Furthermore, we shared the concerns expressed by Marie-Jolie Rwigema: if survivors only appear as witnesses and never as authors/filmmakers or experts with moral and intellectual authority, sharing testimony may not only disempower them but also translate into an emotional commodity.[13] Rwigema also suggests that, when survivors direct how their testimony is used, "their position as victim is transformed and the process of social change begins."[14] We hoped that a peer-to-peer model of dialogue would benefit youth audiences and empower the presenters.

The Complexity of Using Testimony in Schools

Through discussions with teachers involved in the Montreal Holocaust Memorial Centre (MHMC), we knew that field trips and guest visitors offered rewarding experiences for students and were often what they remembered most from their education.[15] We were also aware of the complexity of these interactions for the presenters. Life Story of Montreal collaborators Anna Sheftel and Stacey Zembrzycki coined the term "professional survivors" when attempting to describe the range of ways people share their testimonies in the public realm. As they explain: "Professionalism is a useful way to not only think about survivors' commitment to this work, but also understand how they handle some of its challenges, such as grappling with the institutionalization of their narratives. How does this dynamic influence survivors' narratives, memories and identities?"[16]

Taking these complexities into account, we wondered about the long-term impact on the youth presenters. Unlike the "professional survivors" of the Holocaust, who had years to reflect on and distance themselves from their stories, some of the individuals in our group were still actively excavating stories that, in some cases, were raw and delicate. How and what would we be contributing to the phenomena of "professional" survivors and what would this mean for the youth involved? Would sharing recorded stories, instead of "speaking" their stories over and over, shift the risks inherent in presenting sensitive testimony (as it seemed to on the bus tour)? Our questions accompanied us early in the morning and late at night, and became an ongoing means of personal and collective inquiry before and after each presentation.

Preparing for the Tour

We developed the presentation materials for school visits over a period of several months, and a big part of our preparation was leading training sessions with the youth. As facilitators we had three considerations. First, how could we responsibly and ethically help the youth prepare to take their stories into schools and feel confident to respond to a range of questions? None of the presenters had attended secondary school in Canada, and only Ayanda had any previous experience speaking to groups. Second, how would we bring complex issues like genocide into the classroom and avoid perpetuating stereotypes or responses based on guilt or pity? Scholars Erica Leher and Cynthia Milton address the complexity of responses to violence, explaining: "More difficult than regarding other people's suffering may be scrutinizing our own habituated responses to it."[17] Critical pedagogy scholar Lisa Taylor adds: "As educators we have to think how that initial emotional response to the humanity of another person can be channelled into culturally conditioned habits of feeling sorry for – seeing someone as a victim – seeing myself as somehow not implicated in whatever caused this suffering, seeing myself as the hero who will save this person from their suffering."[18] And third, how could we structure a presentation to create at least some small fissure in conditioned responses to trauma and genocide? We knew we couldn't control audience reactions, but could the presentation facilitate a meaningful connection between the presenters and the student audiences?

Articulating Goals

Our first step in working with the youth was to help presenters to articulate not only personal goals for working with the school tour but also the messages they wanted to leave with the student groups. Ayanda, who had arrived in Montreal at eighteen, alone but hopeful and carrying one suitcase, attributed his success to those who opened their hearts and homes to him. He wanted students to do the same for other newcomers in their schools or communities. For Stephanie, who now felt closer to her family and her cultural heritage, the goal was to encourage youth to become curious about their family stories. For Leontine, sharing her story had lifted some of the weight she carried being the only survivor in her family. She wanted students to gain courage to tell their own stories. Her second goal was more political. She saw the students as future leaders and wanted the school tour to help them understand the personal impact of genocide so that they would not stand by when a genocide took place, as most of the world had done during the horrors perpetrated in Rwanda.

Articulating our collective goals was critical to gaining confidence. The exercise also helped us to share and name our collective anxiety over making public presentations about such personal and complex issues. In his book *On Listening to Holocaust Survivors,* oral historian Henry Greenspan discusses the disappointment of Holocaust survivors who, in the aftermath of the Second World War, also wanted to use stories to prevent future atrocities, what scholars often refer to as the "never again" phenomenon. These individuals quickly became frustrated and depressed when they realized how difficult it was to find engaged listeners.[19] We still did not know how student audiences would engage with the stories and whether our lofty goals might need to be revisited once we had encountered real audiences.

As a group, we determined that, in order to engage listeners, the audiences needed to see the presenters as young people whose goals and dreams were similar to theirs but who had survived very difficult situations. To establish this connection, each presenter would share something from her or his current life, such as being a counsellor at a Quebec sleepover camp, working for the local phone company, or taking classes at university. Presenters also contextualized their stories so that audience members could identify commonalities. For instance, Stephanie described how she first heard about the Rwandan genocide during a unit on the Holocaust. When she told her mother what had happened: "She told me I was too young to know about that yet. And, you know what happens when you tell a thirteen-year-old that she is too young? I started asking questions and I never stopped."[20] Stephanie's narrative introduced the idea that history is both dynamic and disruptive. Young audience members, especially those with refugee or recent immigrant experience, identified with Stephanie's curiosity and her desire to find out more about what her family had been through.

Defining goals was also important in determining how much context we needed to provide and the larger framework of the presentation. For example, we realized that, in order to frame the personal stories, we needed to introduce the concept of genocide within a historical framework that addressed colonialism so that students could understand violence as a structural issue and not a result of violent individuals. As well, our presenters were from Rwanda and Zimbabwe and we didn't want students to understand genocide as something that primarily happens in African nations. Presenting complex ideas for student audiences in a mere seventy-five-minute slot required extensive discussion and planning.

Another challenge was how to frame the stories within the larger context of immigration and refugee rights in Canada. The Canadian Council of Refugees (CCR), our partner in the project, hoped that personal stories could help counter the message communicated by the government, which focused on refugees being a burden to the system. We also wanted student audiences to understand that accepting refugees was a legal obligation for those countries who had signed the refugee convention of 1951: it was not an act of charity. Sheftel and Zembrzycki explain how Holocaust survivors who speak in schools are not always comfortable when non-profits connect their personal stories to larger human rights frameworks.[21] Would the youth feel comfortable as spokespeople for these bigger issues? An ideal scenario was to have the CCR involved at each presentation, but the enormous time commitment made this unfeasible. In the end, along with the CCR, we designed a ten-minute PowerPoint that represented our collective interests.

Encouraging Engagement

A critical aspect of the rest of the training was to help presenters field complex questions. During the bus tour, we were concerned when audience members asked such questions as: "How *exactly* did you get here?" or "Who did you live with after you lost your family?" We emphasized to the youth that not answering a question was also an option. We even rehearsed how to evade questions. Still, after the bus tour, the youth had explained to us that the desire to please and the anxiety of the presentation had made it hard if not impossible to avoid answering questions. Although the questions offered audience members a chance to clarify issues, they put the presenters in awkward positions, triggering past emotions or even security concerns.

Critical pedagogy scholar Roger Simon writes about the value of airing questions, even "obscene questions," as a first step in critical learning.[22] Lisa Taylor, however, adds that not all questions have to take place in front of the survivor: "There are questions we may need to work through before the survivor comes, and I need to ask myself why am I asking this question."[23] When we were initially planning the school tour, we debated at length how to incorporate a question-and-answer period into the presentation. We could not be certain how much time a teacher would have had to help students prepare questions or what might come up. Our first instinct was to "protect" the youth presenters even if it meant altogether eliminating a question-and-answer period from the school tour. However, by eliminating questions we would be removing our main chance for interaction.

To test out our presentation structure, we planned a rehearsal with Leontine and Stephanie with the class of a teacher who worked with the Montreal Life Stories project. During the Q&A period one student asked: "What is the physical difference between a Hutu and a Tutsi?" What seemed a logical question to the class was far more complicated for the presenters. The last thing they wanted was to precondition fifteen-year-olds to analyze slight physical characteristics and, in effect, code them as murderers or victims. Together they found a way to explain how Rwandans were trying to move beyond these divisive and damaging classifications. Watching Leontine and Stephanie gracefully negotiate this complex moment together confirmed to us the value of presenting in pairs and the pedagogical potential of these interactions.

During our debriefing, Leontine and Stephanie further explained that they did not want to come off as anti-Hutu or to burn bridges in the Rwandan community. Sharing a personal story is one thing, but becoming spokespeople on a sensitive issue like ethnicity in a post-genocide context is something else entirely. The girls decided to consult with senior Rwandan community members to look into this further. It was not the first time the wider support of the Montreal Life Stories project was essential in finding our way.

After several other school visits, we started to see that the questions were, in fact, beneficial for the presenters. By working out answers to recurring questions, the youth presenters were able not only to feel more in control of the experience but also to see how the questions helped them to further develop their narratives. For example, initially, the question, "How did you get here?" raised anxiety for Leontine. Over time and with support and consultation, she was increasingly comfortable explaining Rwanda's reconciliation process as well as what happened to her between the Rwandan genocide and her arrival in Montreal: "I was nervous to share that part of the story because it's a political matter [...] I no longer have that fear, I am proud of what I did. By discussing it with people they said, 'You said nothing wrong, it's all about your story, so you don't have to be afraid,' and that is true."[24]

The audience's questions also let the presenters know that they were being carefully listened to. After one presentation Stephanie wrote: "As for yesterday [...] there was no other place I would have wanted to be; it was as if I was meant to be there, and so was Leontine. I really enjoyed the presentation and I cannot stop thinking about those kids and how they were listening to me so attentively and being so interactive, truly one of the best moments of my life."[25] Henry Greenspan writes: "Whatever the specific motives in retelling – to remember the dead, to warn the living, to indict the killers, to document the crime – every act of recounting, really by definition, is premised on the possibility of responsive listeners."[26] The presenters' interactions with attentive student audiences were empowering. Whatever fears the youth originally had about sharing their stories fell to the side as they started to see themselves as knowledgeable spokespeople with important stories to tell, as people who were making a difference. In the end, the question period, while risky and frightening for all of us, offered a unique opportunity for important transactional encounters.

Thirty Schools, Many Challenges

Every presentation offered new challenges. Until the fourth or fifth school, we were still working out kinks with the PowerPoint, the order of the stories, and timing. As well, since each presentation took place in a different school with students of different ages who had varying amounts of experience with the subject, each visit felt like starting from scratch. This was complicated by the fact that the youth were giving presentations in both French and English. We had spent a lot of time reflecting on the emotional complexity of the tour and very little time worrying about the complexity of scheduling, which was a challenge in itself. For example, we had planned to meet with the presenters in between school visits but realized that this was impossible given all of our busy schedules; instead, car rides to the visits became coaching sessions in which we would review any changes to the presentation, have presenters practise framing their story, and check in with each other. Initially, we imagined that we would accompany the presenters for the first few visits, but once we recognized the difficulty of equipment set up, and the sheer complexity of the presentation itself, we made sure at least one of us was present for each of our thirty school visits.

At the end of each presentation we had students respond through a writing exercise about something that particularly struck them, or that they found confusing, or about ideas to take the experience further in their own schools. The speakers collected and reviewed the student responses in order to better understand which aspects of the presentation were "sticking" and which needed more clarification. In addition, the feedback provided them with the needed affirmation that what they were doing was important. Through the audiences' comments, they could see themselves in a new light as mentors, educators, even heroes.

Peer assessment and support were also critical elements in further developing the presentation. Because we had decided to have Leontine, Stephanie, and Ayanda present together, the group developed strong affinities by providing emotional support and by modelling different ways to present the material. Ayanda, who was a very confident presenter, had the easiest time adding personal anecdotes and adapting the presentation to audiences of different ages. For example, at an adult education centre where most of the audience members were newcomers, Ayanda focused on Canada's responsibility to refugees and the difficult treatment they often receive upon arrival here. At a rural Quebec school, he asked students to imagine not being able to see their mothers or fathers for ten years. Ayanda's anecdotes helped students connect empathetically to the presentation. At times, students would collectively sigh and ask if they could give him a hug or if he could be their teacher. Leontine and Stephanie observed Ayanda's approach and, over time, discovered their own style of engaging audiences.

While mostly positive, presenting together posed challenges as well. For example, Ayanda engaged the audience to such a degree that he occasionally lost track of time and had to be reminded to leave the others enough time to present. Stephanie often shared the stage with Leontine and found the latter's story of surviving the genocide as an eight-year-old girl heartbreaking. She explained how presenting together raised some difficult questions, including: "How valid is my story next to Leontine's story of survival?" Stephanie, who had grown up outside of Rwanda, protected by her family from the immediate impact of the genocide on their lives, was in the midst of processing questions that many children of survivors have to face. The tour brought all of these into play. Creating spaces for individual and group reflections helped us take into account all of the positive and more sensitive aspects of the presentation.

When we set up the initial school visits, we had hand-picked teachers whose classes had read novels or texts addressing human rights abuses and who provided contextual information to their students and helped them to develop questions for the presenters. We also gave each teacher and her/his school library a copy of our book/DVD, *Mapping Memories: Participatory Media, Place-Based Stories and Refugee Youth,* to offer additional context and follow-up exercises.[27] As the tour developed momentum, we received requests from several teachers who were working with this material for the first time or who viewed the refugee experience through a very different framework. We encountered one teacher, for example, whose students had some understanding of the Rwandan genocide but who seemed, herself, to lack an analysis of structural oppression and questions of power. When she began to discuss "those other refugees who were trying to cheat the system in Canada," Stephanie and Leontine stood speechless, in part because of what she was saying and also because she was the authority in the room. This was one occasion upon which we jumped in to help facilitate the discussion. While we disagreed with the teacher's framework, we could not undermine her authority, so we invited her and the group to further explore the issue. Following the visit, we discussed with the youth how to frame rebuttals and build dialogue in a classroom. We also gathered additional resources we might provide for teachers that presented refugee rights within a larger framework of race, oppression, and human rights.

Another complication that came out of moving beyond our initial group of hand-picked classrooms involved dealing with the appropriate venue for our presentations. Because the schools paid the youth speaker fees, they often wanted the largest number of students possible to benefit from the visit. We went from presenting in classrooms to auditoriums of up to five hundred students. Although it was thrilling to imagine we could reach so many young people, we had lost the intimacy of the bus tour and our initial school presentations. Over time we began to insist that we would only present in classrooms. Even though teachers would sometimes fill the classrooms with as many as one hundred students, those presentations felt more intimate and, for the young people, were the most meaningful.

Group Reflections

After thirty school visits, we had a lot to talk about at our end-of-summer meeting with Ayanda, Leontine, and Stephanie. The tour had been extremely well received. Schools where we had presented were requesting dates for the upcoming school year. As well, with the release of the French version of the *Mapping Memories* book/DVD, we expected more requests from the French schools. We explained that if Ayanda, Leontine, and Stephanie wanted the tour to continue, we hoped they would take over its organization. They were ready: our role on the tour was no longer necessary.

Our meeting was also an important chance to reflect on what the tour had meant to each of us. For Ayanda, the tour was a powerful confirmation that he was not only a skilled presenter but that young people were drawn to him. Educators in several of the schools told him what a gifted teacher he would make. Because Ayanda had been in Canada for over ten years, he was able to take a more political stance during presentations and make links between his story and Canadian policy towards refugees. At the meeting, Ayanda expressed his desire to continue to present in the schools as he felt the tour opened students' eyes to difficult and important issues. As well, Ayanda was being contacted independently to present in larger forums, such as at the national conferences of the CCR and World University Service of Canada (WUSC). He also shared his plans to start a WUSC chapter at his university.

Through this school tour and with her work with the Montreal Life Stories project Stephanie embraced her history in a new way – not simply by telling her story but by becoming a representative of the Rwandan community. Stephanie and Leontine had been asked by Rwandan elders to create a storytelling workshop for Rwandan youth living in Montreal, and they discussed putting their efforts into this work. They both recognized they had something significant to contribute to an ongoing effort to build sensitivity within the community and in schools, but they also wanted time to reflect on what this might look like.

Leontine seemed to have travelled the farthest through the Mapping Memories project. But the process was not without complications and concerns. Being a spokesperson was both exhilarating and unsettling. Although she was very happy with presentations after they were finished, Leontine was shy and, like Stephanie, still found speaking in front of large groups difficult. Public presentations helped Leontine realize the impact of her story on diverse audiences. She was always surprised at the enormous outpouring of empathy and positive feedback she received when students crowded around her after each presentation. While initially worried that her story would overwhelm students, she realized that students wanted to grapple with the complex issues her story raised. Over time Leontine found a way to name the complex political circumstances around her story and to stay true to her original intention, which was to encourage others to share their stories.

She also explained that, by sharing her story, over time she was beginning to remember more details about that turbulent phase of her life, and she was ready to embrace these previously suppressed memories. She added: "Difficult stories, they are not easy. But after sharing it, you feel free. You can see what the future would be. But when you don't tell your story, you only stay in a circle, you don't move. You only see the past, and you don't see the present or the future."[28] As a result of this experience, Leontine hopes to go back to Rwanda to share her story with her adopted family and to lead them through a process of writing and sharing their own stories.

Stepping Aside but Staying Present

As facilitators, we have also reflected on what we have learned. Our roles with Leontine, Ayanda, and Stephanie were multifaceted, many of them behind the scenes, an ever-shifting combination of manager, coach, mentor, documentarian, and friend. Because the youth were so close in age to our own children, we may have also occasionally stepped over those boundaries into a more parental role by giving the occasional "wake up" call, bringing breakfast snacks for an 8:00 AM presentation, or worrying about things (in some cases unnecessarily). The tour was a meaningful way to collaborate with this group regarding how their stories were framed and circulated and providing opportunities to reflect on the experience. And, in most cases, this meant stepping aside but staying present.

There were many unique circumstances in play to make the school tour possible. For example, being part of the larger Montreal Life Stories project permitted us to draw on experience and networks and to learn with the Rwandan working group and the education working group as we navigated complex issues. Michele's network of teachers made it easy to gain access to Montreal high schools. And, most important, because the project took place over five years, we were able to develop relationships with each other built on trust and friendship. We are not sure any of us would have taken the risks we did or invested so much time and energy if we had not developed these close friendships. We also learned the value of articulating goals, presenting in pairs whenever possible, and being available to each other as complex emotional and analytical issues surfaced.

We did not have a similar opportunity to work with student audience members or teachers over time. Although the response to the tour was overwhelmingly positive, what became obvious to us was that presenting material regarding genocide and human rights merits an in-depth, time-based approach. This was especially true for students and teachers who were encountering this information for the first time. We were all excited to read inspired student responses – such as, "Our class should raise money for refugees through a bake sale" – but we also knew that a desire to "help others" was most useful when connected to a more critical analysis of structural violence and oppression. More steps were necessary to move beyond these well-intentioned "gut responses." In this way, as Lisa Taylor suggests, the stories could have also been used to encourage a deeper self-reflection, to look at how we are all "implicated in the causes of systemic violence."[29]

Many teachers expressed the importance of the presentation for their newcomer students with regard to creating a safe space within which to discuss difficult issues. The question was whether the teachers *had* used that space in the days and weeks that followed the presentations and what additional resources we could have offered to help them to do this. The *Mapping Memories* book was helpful in introducing the project, offering classroom project ideas and additional stories, but teachers might also have benefited from material linked directly to the school visits. We have since had numerous conversations with educators who have offered constructive feedback about pre-visit activities and ideas for follow-up projects. And, with the knowledge we have now, were we to re-imagine the tour, we might consider visiting ten schools three times rather than visiting thirty schools once. Through this exercise in praxis, we learned a great deal about working with sensitive stories as well as ethical and pedagogical frameworks that help move digital life stories beyond trauma and into a space of self-reflection and dialogue in classrooms. A process like this requires multiple forms of support, space for reflection, and, of course, lots and lots of time.

Notes

1 Leontine Uwababyeyi, "My Two Families," in *Mapping Memories: Participatory Media, Place-Based Stories and Refugee Youth, Montreal*, ed. Michelle Luchs and Elizabeth Miller (Montreal: Self-Published, 2011), 70. See also www.mappingmemories.ca.

2 Julie Salverson, "Anxiety and Contact in Attending to a Play about Land Mines," in *Between Hope and Despair: Pedagogy and the Remembrance of Historical Trauma*, ed. Roger I. Simon, Sharon Rosenberg, and Claudia Eppert (Baltimore: Rowman and Littlefield, 2000), 77.

3 Gerald Campano, *Immigrant Students and Literacy: Reading, Writing, and Remembering* (New York: Teachers College Press, 2007), 52.

4 Miller, "Creating a Memoryscape," 74. See also www.mappingmemories.ca.

5 Michele Luchs and Liz Miller, "Tell Me a Story," in Luchs and Miller, *Mapping Memories,* 36. Book is available at www.mappingmemories.ca.

6 Liz Miller, *All I Remember* (documentary film, 2013).

7 Henry Greenspan, *On Listening to Holocaust Survivors: Recounting and Life History* (New York: Praeger, 1998), 64.

8 Miller, *All I Remember.*

9 Lisa Taylor, Umwali Sollange, and Marie-Jolie Rwigema, "The Ethics of Learning from Rwandan Survivor Communities: Critical Reflexivity and the Politics of Knowledge Production in Genocide Education" (Chapter 3, this volume).

10 *Towards a Promised Land* is a documentary project for refugee youth, by Global Action Project and Wendy Ewald; see *Towards a Promised Land* (UK: Steidl and Partners, 2006).

11 Kat Cizek, *Filmmaker-in-Residence Manifesto*, ONFB, at http://www.nfb.ca/film/manifesto_animation_bonus_material/.

12 Liz's commitment to exploring these issues was influenced by her past experience developing outreach for documentary films and through her work with human rights organizations. Michele, who has worked for over fifteen years training teachers around Quebec, was aware of what it takes to get teachers to engage with new materials and tools, and she knew how stories from this project could fit into Quebec curricula. Her expertise influenced our mandate to define our primary target audience as students and educators.

13 Taylor, Sollange, and Rwigema (Chapter 3, this volume).

14 Ibid.

15 The Holocaust Education Series Program is run by Montreal Holocaust Memorial Centre and brings together teachers to discuss how to integrate difficult issues into the classroom.

16 Anna Sheftel and Stacey Zembrzycki, "Professionalizing Survival: The Politics of Public Memory among Holocaust Survivor-Educators in Montreal," *Journal of Modern Jewish Studies* (forthcoming).

17 Erica Lehrer and Cynthia Milton, "Witnesses to Witnessing," in *Curating Difficult Knowledge*, ed. Erica Lehrer, Cynthia E. Milton, and Monica Eileen Patterson, 1–20 (Basingstoke, UK: Palgrave Macmillan, 2011).

18 Video interview of Lisa Taylor by Liz Miller, 2012.

19 Greenspan, *On Listening,* 64.

20 Miller, *All I Remember.*

21 Sheftel and Zembrzycki, "Professionalizing Survival."

22 Roger Simon, "The Touch of the Past: The Pedagogical Significance of a Transactional Sphere of Public Memory," in *Revolutionary Pedagogies: Cultural Politics, Education and the Discourse of Theory*, ed. Peter Trifonas (New York: Routledge, 2000), 69.

23 Taylor, video interview.

24 Miller, *All I Remember.*

25 Stephanie Gasana, e-mail correspondence with authors, 2012.

26 Greenspan, *On Listening*, 49.

27 Luchs and Miller," Tell Me a Story," 36.

28 Leontine Uwababyeyi, interviewed by authors, 2012; Miller, *All I Remember.*

29 Taylor, video interview.

PART 3:
Acts of Composure and Framing

10 | Economic Violence, Occupational Disability, and Death

Oral Narratives of the Impact of Asbestos-Related Diseases in Britain

ARTHUR McIVOR

They made us work with poisonous materials that were killing us, and never told us.

– Scottish asbestos insulation engineer[1]

That employment did something wrong to me.

– Owen Lilly, asbestos cement factory worker with asbestosis, Clydebank, Scotland[2]

Mass violence is usually associated with warfare, genocide, and terrorism. However, it also occurs within modern corporate capitalism and the employment relationship. Pierre Bourdieu developed the concepts of symbolic, physical, and economic violence to explain patterns of elite behaviour and the exercise of authority and power.[3] Economic violence occurs when the pursuit of profit and production is prioritized at the expense of workers' bodies, resulting in injury, disability, premature death, and psychological harm (including through lay-offs and stress from overwork). Much of this was and remains preventable. The collective *intentional* exercise and abuse of power by corporations, employers, and managers for economic gain is at the heart of this.

The concept of economic violence has been applied in a number of ways – including through more aggressive employer behaviour and managerial styles associated with the shift to neoliberal globalization in the later twentieth century.[4] Economic violence has a long history among capitalist enterprises and can clearly be witnessed in the historic victimization of labour activists ("troublemakers") and in the corporate neglect and irresponsibility that lay behind the carnage of industrial injuries and deaths that characterized industrialization.[5] Robert Storey makes a beautifully eloquent and persuasive case for this in Chapter 2 (this volume) and in his ongoing research on the workers' injury movement in Ontario.[6] Along with these individual traumas (commonplace in most industrial workplaces) went more insidious, chronic, long-term damage to health and well-being, evident in the modern-day epidemic of workplace stress and repetitive strain injuries, and in the exposure of workers to dust, fumes, chemicals, toxins, and carcinogens. The plague of asbestos-related disease (ARD) provides one of the clearest examples of economic violence and corporate crime.

This chapter explores how oral history approaches elucidate the cultures in which economic violence flourished and provides insight into the impact of ARDs upon people's lives. It attempts to get beyond the body counts to explore the outcomes of this economic violence and what it signified for those at the receiving end of it – what chronic disease linked with exposure to asbestos meant to individuals, to families, and to communities. It draws upon personal narratives from oral history interviews to try to comprehend prevailing work-health cultures, what being diagnosed with a life-threatening disease and encroaching disability signified, and how this affected people's lives. These are "trauma narratives," relating how people made sense of working lives when their or their loved ones' existence was disrupted by contracting entirely preventable disabling and fatal diseases. References to being "killed" (as expressed in this chapter's first epigraph) and to "murder," or "mass murder" feature in these ARD narratives, especially those of bereaved relatives.[7]

My argument builds on oral history fieldwork undertaken by myself and my colleague Ronnie Johnston and that resulted in the publication of our monograph, *Lethal Work: A History of the Asbestos Tragedy in Scotland* (2000). This chapter is part of an ongoing critical process, conducted over the past couple of years or so, which involves revisiting these oral testimonies, collecting some new material, and reviewing similar testimony-based work by other researchers in the field (such as Helen Clayson) as well as ruminating on oral history theory and practice. It reflects my evolving interests in the historical meanings of work, the significance of work-health cultures, and the impact of profit-oriented Fordist production regimes upon workers' bodies.[8]

The focus here is primarily, though not exclusively, upon the lived experience of ARD victims and survivors in the United Kingdom, particularly drawing upon our case study of the Clydeside industrial conurbation centred in Glasgow from the 1930s to the present. An oral history approach enables us to construct a refocused history centred on workers' bodies and emotions. This methodology is capable of enriching our understanding of these encounters between work and the body, what this signified to workers, and how workers were affected by and reacted to risk and danger and to ensuing disability and loss. It enables us to locate those affected by chronic occupational diseases within the specific socio-cultural spaces they occupied at that time. While oral interview material requires critical and sensitive treatment (necessitating the reflective evaluation of how memories are constructed and the past recalled), they nonetheless provide a wide range of insights into the employment-health interaction.

Asbestos and the Body

The asbestos tragedy is a story played out across the globe, first in developed, early industrialized nations in Europe and North America, then in developing and more recently industrializing countries, such as China, Brazil, and India. Beginning in the late nineteenth century, asbestos was extensively mined and its mineral fibres processed and manufactured to be used as an insulating product and fire retardant. Indeed, asbestos found its way into a startlingly wide variety of commodities and was used heavily in engineering, in shipbuilding, in construction, and in many other places – not least in the construction of high-rise flats and office blocks built from the 1940s on.

Inhaling asbestos fibres is associated with several deadly incurable diseases. *Asbestosis* usually results from prolonged exposure in the workplace and consists of a clogging up and resultant scarring and distortion of the lungs, leading to severe and disabling breathlessness and strain on the heart. Malignant *mesothelioma* is a tumour that usually develops on the outer lining of the lung (pleura) but that also appears on the surface of the abdominal cavity (peritoneum). Mesothelioma can be caused by low levels of exposure to asbestos and is an extremely aggressive cancer. Those diagnosed with mesothelioma suffer higher levels of pain than do most cancer victims and frequently have fluid build-up drained from their lungs (pleural effusions). They also experience intense breathlessness and weight loss – becoming emaciated and physically wasting away. Patients rarely live beyond eighteen months after diagnosis. *Asbestos-related lung cancer* is the most common malignancy among individuals exposed to asbestos, and both lung cancer and mesothelioma can be caused by occupational or environmental exposures. The total number of deaths from asbestos is not known. However, the World Health Organization has recently estimated that asbestos is responsible for more than 107,000 deaths every year and that, across the globe, an estimated 125 million people are currently being exposed to the deadly mineral through their occupations.[9] According to one medical expert, the final death toll from asbestos will top 5 million and may be as high as 10 million.[10]

The culpability of negligent employers and production-oriented managers, bolstered by the collusion of some governments, is now well established in the asbestos tragedy, though industry continues to mount a rear-guard defence of its toxic product in some places (not least in Canada and in Russia). The weight of evidence unequivocally indicates that, despite knowledge of the dangers of asbestos, industry continued to manufacture and use the product for economic gain, to withhold or destroy documents proving prior knowledge, to influence or curtail new research and knowledge dissemination, and to use its resources to delay regulation, fight compensation cases, and minimize financial losses. Among landmark studies exposing the economic violence of multinational asbestos companies are Paul Brodeur's scathing critiques of the US asbestos industry and Tweedale's seminal work, which makes use of internal company documents of the main UK-based asbestos manufacturing company, Turner and Newall.[11] In *Defending the Indefensible* (2008), Jock McCulloch and Geoffrey Tweedale present a similarly convincing case for the industry globally.

Those who spoke out against the economic violence of asbestos interests risked retaliation – as in the case of the UK activist Alan Dalton and his publishers, who were forced to pay crippling costs and damages as a result of legal action taken against the publication of *Asbestos: Killer Dust* in 1979.[12] Government regulations passed to control asbestos use (such as the first Asbestos Regulations in the United Kingdom in 1931) were limited, subverted, diluted, widely flouted, and ineffective, and, in the United Kingdom, workers' bodies continued to be exposed, *despite knowledge of the risks*, for a further four decades or so. This was the pattern across Western industrial nations in the twentieth century and prevails in many countries across the globe today. Mostly, those directly affected by workplace exposure (and family contact) are vulnerable low-income individuals and families, and in some countries the pattern is for immigrants or ethnic minorities (as with the Irish Catholics in asbestos insulation work in Clydeside, Scotland) to be employed in such work. However, asbestos also constitutes a wider public risk, contaminating the environment not only in the vicinity of asbestos plants but also when it is unsettled, as occurs in natural disasters such as earthquakes or in human-made disasters such as wars or terrorist attacks.

When governments were forced to take action (pressured by campaigners, trade unions, progressive politicians, and media exposure) and to impose strict(er) regulations – and eventually to ban asbestos – multinational corporations in Western economies either closed and set up elsewhere or used subcontractors, exporting the risk to underdeveloped and developing nations (e.g., in South America and Asia). This has been the pattern over the past fifty years or so as regulations tightened in Europe and North America from the 1960s onward. However, because of the long time-lag between exposure and cancer outbreak – from thirty to fifty years – there is an enormous legacy of disability and death, with mesothelioma mortality set to peak in Europe and North America in the 2010s and 2020s. This "asbestos time bomb" is currently ticking in the developing, recently industrialized, and industrializing nations, with astronomical death rates predicted over the coming decades in Russia, India, Africa, South America, and Asia.[13] In some communities, mortality rates from asbestos-related cancers outstrip all other causes of death. In the infamous Wittenoom blue asbestos mining and milling district in Western Australia, mesothelioma death rates are running at 40 percent of the employed workforce.[14] The mine continued to be worked with few precautions against the carcinogenic dust for two decades after management was aware (in the 1940s) of the risk to health, only closing in 1966 and leaving a grim legacy of disability and death.

Oral History and Historiographies of the Body in the Workplace

This chapter puts workers' bodies at centre stage in this story and privileges the testimonies of those directly affected. This dovetails with a turn towards the patients' perspective and the personal in medical and health history, to some extent bringing occupational health in line with a historiographical trend towards a focus on the "lived experience" and the emotional journeys associated with trauma, ill-health, and premature death. Oral history has featured in this, for example in the work of Joanna Bornat and Lucinda McCray Beier.[15] As Michelle Winslow and Graham Smith recently argue: "It is a mark of the contribution of oral history to the history of medicine that studies located within living memory are open to criticism if they fail to include oral history."[16]

The history of occupational health has been dominated by studies that focus on corporate irresponsibility and neglect, in some notable cases forensically exposing the prior knowledge of hazards, neglect, and abuse that resulted in epidemics of industrial disease – such as "black lung" (coal workers' pneumoconiosis) and ARDs. A range of interpretations exists within what is a hotly contested terrain, from those at one end of the spectrum (who make a case for economic violence) and those at the other (who defend industry, shift the blame elsewhere, and castigate left-orientated historians and other researchers for inappropriate use of hindsight and failing to contextualize the issue within the period and the prevailing state of knowledge and existing work-health cultures).[17] Company records, court files, and state inquiries were among the core source materials for such studies. As Walker and LaMontagne argue, the asbestos story has been "dominated by medical, scientific, legal and government perspectives," while "the voices and perspectives of those most directly affected – exposed and diseased workers, their families and communities – are ... relatively rarely heard."[18] With some exceptions, the debates tended to pass over or neglect the lived experience of disability and disease and to gloss over the agency of victims and their individual and collective responses. The shift towards the personal and to discourses, influenced by postmodernist ideas, has begun to change this landscape, with a clutch of recent studies focusing on lived experience and how people directly affected articulated their stories and shaped their narratives.

What, then, can eye-witness oral testimony bring to the field and how can it add to our understanding? By providing a view from the workplace we gain valuable insights into the limited effectiveness of regulatory frameworks while also getting a sense of the complexity of work-health and body cultures, the interplay of identities (such as gender and class), and the agency of workers negotiating paths through the prevailing exploitative social relations and managerial, productionist work cultures. A number of studies turn to oral evidence to elucidate work and occupational health. These include Bloor, Perchard, Walker, Clayson, and McIvor and Johnston, who focus on the United Kingdom;

Walker and LaMontagne, and Di Pasquale, who interview asbestos workers in Western Australia; Storey, who focuses on injured workers in Canada; and Portelli, who interviews coal miners in Harlan County, in the United States.[19] The latter provides a model oral history project, comprising over two hundred interviews undertaken in fieldwork in Harlan County over more than twenty years. Multiple aspects of economic violence, health, and the body are explored in Portelli's sensitive, panoramic, and seminal monograph. Another exceptional oral-history based investigation is Suroopa Mukherjee's *Surviving Bhopal* (2010), which focuses on the stories of female survivors of the infamous Union Carbide gas leak in India.

These investigations have taken place and have been influenced by concurrent developments in the discipline of oral history. Partly in response to criticisms about the unreliability of memory and partly in order to make its position more robust, oral history has morphed from what has been termed "reconstructive" oral history – in which, typically, testimony was uncritically accepted at face value – towards more "interpretative" approaches. The latter was influenced by the postmodernist turn and by the influential work of Italian oral historians, notably Luisa Passerini and Alessandro Portelli.[20] What emerged was a phase of introspection in the discipline, and the outcome was a more theoretically informed and methodologically rigorous oral history. Ideas were borrowed from a wide range of social science and other disciplines (including sociology, anthropology, psychology, and linguistics) and tested against the empirical evidence. Memory studies basically confirmed the fundamental reliability of memory, and the subjective nature of the evidence – formerly criticized as a weakness – became recognized as a strength. Silences in life stories and misremembering were identified as being significant in their own right and were judged to be full of meaning. Intersubjectivities also became a focus. Testimonies were observed to be composed and shaped both by the interviewers' subjectivities (such as gender and class) and in a dialogue with the interviewee as well as by the prevailing wider media and culture – what has become known as "the cultural circuit."[21] It was established that repetitions, metaphors, and anecdotes in oral testimonies have significance and that personal storytelling is subject to prevailing narrative structures and "rules" within particular societies and cultures. There is a process of adaptation here as narrators gauge their immediate audience (the interviewer) and imagine their wider perceived audience (the end users and readers of the archived final product). In recalling their past in an interview context, narrators are filtering and sieving memories, constructing and composing their stories, and mixing factual evidence with their own interpretations as they try to make sense of their lives in an active, dialogic, and reflexive process of remembering.[22]

So, oral history scholarship and methodologies have become more sophisticated and have contributed to a widening understanding of the body in work and working bodies. The unique nature of oral evidence is now widely accepted and its veracity recognized. Oral historians are now much more reflexively critical of their material and acknowledge the influence their own subjectivities have upon the interview and how narrators position themselves in the narrative, using the encounter as a way of projecting a sense of self. The "new oral history" that has emerged has been influenced by postmodernist ideas, which have challenged and been fused into the radical tradition of oral history. This tradition was pioneered by an earlier generation of socialist and feminist oral historians who were driven by a desire to give marginalized people a voice and a place; their agenda for history was concerned with both equality and democratization. Oral historians postulate that *what* is remembered and *how* it is recalled is significant in its own right and reveals much about how people derive meaning from the past and gain composure in the telling.

Power, Structure, and Agency: Prevailing Workplace Cultures and the Body

How, then, did the participants in the asbestos tragedy – the victims, witnesses, and survivors – make sense of their experience and articulate their stories? What can oral testimonies tell us about the cultures in which such economic violence was incubated and how individuals and families felt, responded, and navigated their way through diagnosis, encroaching disability, and death?

The first point I would make is that such eye-witness testimonies lay bare the realities of irresponsible and abusive power relationships – economic violence – at the point of production and the limited resources that workers could bring to bear upon their situation. The space in which workers toiled and the environment in which bodies were located was frequently vividly recalled, with dust, death, and disability as recurring motifs in asbestos workers' work-life narratives. Such workers in the United Kingdom (and elsewhere) recalled asbestos dust suspended like a "fog" or falling like "snow" in their workplaces in the 1950s, 1960s, and 1970s, and of *playing* with the material – for example, making "monkey dung" (asbestos cement paste) "snowballs."[23] Either information was withheld from workers or only selective (and sometimes misleading) information about hazards was leaked out (such as the benign nature of white compared to blue and brown asbestos). While workers had some intuitive and lay knowledge, they were ignorant of the *extent* of the dangers. They recalled feeling pressured to work with the toxic material, to "cut corners," ignore safety regulations, and maximize productivity because of wage or bonus systems – or simply because there was no alternative employment (as, for example, was the case for the Italian migrants who worked in the Wittenoom mine in Western Australia from the 1930s to the 1960s). An unskilled machine operator who worked at the Turner and Newall Clydebank (Scotland) asbestos factory for eight years in the 1960s commented: "I knew it was dangerous before I went in there 'cause there was people complaining, but when you have two of a family to bring up it was better than walking the streets. I never was idle in my life."[24] In this sense these workers were victims of a Fordist, productionist culture that exalted hard graft and the maximization of earnings at all costs. The problem was primarily a structural one, the product of an exploitative system pivoting around profit maximization and the abuse of economic power. Also relevant here is the persistence of insecurity of the postwar generation of workers who could recall the mass unemployment of the interwar economic depression. The prevailing postwar economic context of deindustrialization in the heavy industries in the United Kingdom (and elsewhere) and the decline of manufacturing in general, with widespread factory, yard and mine closures, provided the backcloth to this unfolding tragedy.

This has to be understood, however, within a cultural framework – a milieu that facilitated the tolerance and persistence of abusive economic violence. Men were habituated to undertaking dangerous work, to accepting a high-risk threshold, and to being part of a fiercely independent working-class culture that frowned upon those who complained or "made a fuss." A dominant (or hegemonic) mode of "hard man" masculinity was forged in such heavy industry workplaces. Stakhanovite grafting was exalted within working-class communities in the United Kingdom (and elsewhere), where the "top producers" and highest earners were lauded and praised. One Clydeside sheet metal worker who started work in 1942 reflected upon his life in a 1999 interview:

> Being a man with no education, the only thing you had was the muscle in your arm and what experience you got with metal, and a very willingness to work. I would go in and say to people, "Yes I'll do that in that time." And whatever it took to do that [job] I would do it. Silly now, looking back through the years, you know.[25]

Those who sought to protect themselves could be pilloried as lesser men, subject to peer pressure to take risks, to compete, to conform, and to maximize earnings. This was what was expected of men in the performance of their "provider" and "breadwinner" roles, and it lay at the very core of mid- to late twentieth-century working-class masculinities. This high-risk threshold culture and behaviour was invariably condoned by employers and management; however, to a surprising degree, it was also accepted as an integral, immutable part of working-class life. Workers were socialized into this. Such risks were part of the fabric of manual working lives and were rarely questioned. As Portelli argues in his recent oral history of coal miners in Harlan County, there was "a cultural disposition" among miners to embrace managerial profit maximization through a culture of hard graft.[26] Risk was influenced intimately by the wider context. In "Third World" and developing nations, poverty and short life expectancy came into play. As one young Indian asbestos factory worker commented in an interview: "I am not going to die immediately. Who knows what my future is."[27] In India, the casual and contract workers were the most vulnerable and were forced to accept risks. Mangabhai Patel worked insulating boilers in Ahmedabad until his asbestosis forced him to quit the job. He recalls: "As a casual worker you cannot even ask for anything, your job is very insecure. Casual workers are treated very badly, given low wages and the most dangerous kinds of jobs."[28] Moreover, while not powerless, workers lacked the capacity (provided by capital) to change things, even in the developed economies where trade unions were more entrenched. As one Clydeside worker put it: "It was like fighting an atomic war with a bow and arrow, you know. You had nae a chance."[29]

Trade unionism partly embraced and reflected such machismo attitudes. Again, the oral testimonies elucidate a range of behaviour from the militant rank-and-file activists who campaigned relentlessly against asbestos exposure (such as Ron Todd in Clydeside beginning in the 1960s) to the indifference of trade union officials and union hierarchies sensitive to job insecurities and the need to prioritize wages and jobs within a precarious employment environment. This might be understood where the threat to jobs and, concomitant with this, the capacity to perform the traditional male provider role was at stake. Increasingly, over time, trade unions in the United Kingdom came to challenge the economic violence associated with asbestos, to question prevailing high-risk work-health cultures, and to nurture an alternative health and safety conscious workforce. Somewhat belatedly, perhaps, the trade unions edged towards a more progressive policy that combined prevention as well as compensation.[30] They developed into a pivotal countervailing force against economic violence, coming to challenge the entrenched masculine culture that had been socialized into accepting high levels of risk, with shop stewards playing a key protective role at the point of production.

That said, there were tensions and conflicts, and it cannot be said that British workers automatically followed union policies, especially when this clashed with their proclivity to maximize earnings in industries dominated by payments-by-results wage systems and subcontracting (as with asbestos insulation). This could lead to vertical "alliances" between management and men against the "health and safety bureaucracy." Thus the factory inspectors, and sometimes the unions, might be distrusted as interfering bureaucrats despite their key role in challenging and campaigning against economic violence. For example, at the Red Road building construction site in Glasgow in the early 1960s, joiners (carpenters) told their trade union official to "get to fuck" and not to interfere when he warned them of the dangers of sawing asbestos insulation boards.[31] Tragically, many of these "white mice" working on the Red Road job subsequently died of mesothelioma and lung cancer.

Workers were enmeshed within the dual exploitative pressures of a productionist culture and gendered ideologies that exalted the tough, risk-taking, competitive, hard-grafting worker. The unions might challenge this, but, at times, they also tolerated and legitimized it – as, for example, in their support for the system of extra payments (sometimes referred to as "danger money" or "dirt money") for working in dust. At the point of production there was a tension between protecting the body and conserving labour power, on the one hand, and taking risks and pushing bodies to the limit in order to maximize production (and hence earnings) and to fulfill managerial expectations, on the other.

In some of the interviews conducted among Scottish asbestos workers the tone fizzes with bitterness, resentment, and anger; in others, it reveals a quiet stoicism and fatalistic acceptance of one's lot. The discovery and confirmation that employers or managers were aware of the risks long before workers were told of them were repeated narratives in the oral testimonies, as was the perception that what had happened constituted intentional killing predicated upon prior knowledge of the deadly nature of the mineral being processed or handled. Clearly, evidence and knowledge that have accumulated since exposure have influenced the way people remember and recount workplace conditions and trauma. While this did not register with us as clearly as it should have in the late 1990s, when we were trying to interpret the oral testimonies of Scottish asbestos workers for *Lethal Work*, in retrospect (and in the re-reading of these interviews) there is much evidence of what has been called the "cultural circuit." Memories were framed with reference to later media and trade union exposures of the deadly risks of working with asbestos and were influenced by knowledge accumulation that had occurred since the personal experiences being recalled (some of which had occurred forty or more years previously). One landmark TV documentary that clearly made an impact (and was mentioned by several interviewees) was *Alice: Fight for Life,* the story of a woman's lingering death from mesothelioma that screened on British TV in 1982. This hard-hitting, prize-winning, ninety-minute film made for harrowing viewing, particularly the interview footage from Alice Jefferson's deathbed. As McCulloch and Tweedale acknowledge: "It was recognized as a path-breaking work that had put Britain (and other countries) on notice that asbestos was a major hazard. No one would ever look at asbestos in quite the same way again."[32]

Living with Disability and Death

Economic violence destroyed lives, leaving in its wake a legacy of disability, premature death, and deep psychological distress not unlike that found in other post-traumatic stress disorders. As a sixty-four-year-old electrician with mesothelioma reflected: "Until now I thought trauma was a fad imported from America and reserved for the middle classes. I am now wiser."[33] Oral interviewing methodologies enable us to explore and to elucidate this experience, to get behind the sterile body counts to the human dimension, the lived reality. Oral testimonies of those suffering from ARDs illuminate a hidden world of private grief, sadness, anger, frustration, disappointment, pain, and suffering. In *Lethal Work* we report on the "blighted lives" of ARD victims in Scotland and argue that people were invariably marginalized by their illness.[34]

Narrators recalled the encroaching social isolation (with the focus of disabled and ill men's lives shifting from the workplace to the female-dominated and feminized space of the home) and restricted social and physical activities (such as walking, sports, and dancing). They spoke of relative economic deprivation associated with income reduction, of the trauma associated with being diagnosed in a GP's office or at a hospital, and of living and coping strategies as they struggled to adapt to the news that they were going to die from an incurable cancer. We suggest that Blaxter's argument that disability triggers social exclusion applies to these occupationally disabled and dying people, although with important caveats.[35] As Castleman and Tweedale show, the majority of mesothelioma victims did not get any financial compensation – even in industrialized countries with statutory Workmen's Compensation systems in the 1980s and 1990s (including the United Kingdom and Canada).[36]

Speaking directly to participants – to those directly implicated – enables us to provide a refocused history that reveals much about the emotional journey (in what was often a hidden and personalized space) involved in the transition from fit and able worker to disabled and dependent person, with all that this represents for gendered identities. What is being recalled is frequently an intimate, personal story of damage, loss, pain, adjustment – and of mutating identities. If the traditional heavy industries provided an environment in which working-class masculinities were forged, they also had the potential to *emasculate* as encroaching disability curtailed men's capacity to perform as men – as providers and breadwinners, as sexually active partners, as supportive parents and grandparents. Lives invariably became narrowed as individuals, partners, and families had to readjust as workers who were disabled by injuries or chronic disease. Male workers found it difficult to sustain consumption patterns commensurate with male identities, such as heavy drinking and smoking. Such disruptions could lead to tensions within the family. This threatened a loss of work identity and the package of intrinsic and extrinsic rewards that was associated with work (such as camaraderie, pride in the job, self-esteem). Again, however, there was agency here, albeit operating within the constraints of having to earn a living. For example, some workers with severe asbestosis chose to hide their disability and to continue to work for as long as they could, despite knowing this could further damage respiratory function. The economic and cultural imperatives to act as men and to provide for families influenced such decisions.

What we perhaps failed to see and to convey adequately in *Lethal Work* is how dying a premature and unnatural death, one that was preventable and that was caused by an outside party, increased psychological distress and discomposure. In a recent interview Phyllis Craig (Welfare Rights Officer for Clydeside Action on Asbestos since 1995) was asked about the impact of mesothelioma on the lives of her clients:

> I think the physical and mental go together; the mental is torment; that's the only word. It's torture. They have severe breathlessness to the point they feel they are suffocating. And they can't breathe. And the fear and anxiety brings it on more. And they try to do things, and they can't walk; they can't do anything. They need somebody to do it all for them. The physical side is terrible.
>
> There's fear; there's pain; there's suffering; there's all sorts of anxieties; there's coping, there's worrying and if you add to that that someone else did this, such an anger because they are taking that person away from their partner; their children [...] Their careers are ended; everything ends because they know they are going to die. I think it's ten times worse, or a hundred times worse if you know someone else has done this. And the families feel it too; they feel a hundred times worse because their personality does change. They are angry.
>
> It's devastating [...] It's horrendous for them. They think about their family; they think about their own mortality and they think about the anger inside them because someone else has caused that [...] If you think that someone in your work [has] done something and caused you to be terminally ill and have a horrific death and you're thinking that's what I'm facing because of someone else and because of greed [...] People have terrible anxiety and difficulty coping because this was not something natural that's happened to them. Someone did this to them.
>
> So the physical pain for them is torture but this is intertwined with the mental picture, losing their family, losing their life and not because they have a cancer that has come and they know that's what happens to everyone [...] but that someone else has killed them; that someone else has taken my life.[37]

To me – a professional eye-witness who has worked for almost twenty years with ARD victims – in Craig's heart-felt narrative the repetition (eight times) of the point that an outside agent was responsible serves to emphasize the significance of this issue.

Recently, in a mixed methods doctoral dissertation that incorporates oral interviews of patients dying of mesothelioma, Helen Clayson (a GP and hospice manager) undertakes the most comprehensive study in the United Kingdom to date of the effects of this incurable cancer. She refers to the "complex emotional turmoil" that diagnosis with a fatal asbestos-related cancer induces and comments: "Bereaved relatives' emotional accounts reflect witnessing severe suffering, express anger and blame around the potentially avoidable asbestos exposure, and present the deaths due to mesothelioma as 'mass murder.'"[38] Clayson emphasizes the prevalence of stoic reactions in the face of severe breathlessness and pain and how "the disease burden is high" even compared to other forms of cancer, usually necessitating multiple visits to GPs, hospital outpatient clinics, and hospital admission in the last year of their lives.[39] Dyspnoea (severe breathlessness) and pleural effusions (lung draining) to release fluid build-up are common and often distressing symptoms. There is also a stigma attached to having a malignant disease and much "anticipatory anxiety" about the cancer risk among those without any symptoms, or with pleural plaques or pleural thickening, who are aware of their exposure to asbestos throughout their working lives.[40] Joe Cowell, a trade union activist and asbestos worker in the United Kingdom, comments: "I started with 25 [fellow workers]. There's two of us left. The others are dead with asbestos. The graveyard is full of my [trade union] members. I have a black tie I constantly wear, attending funerals of asbestos cases."[41] But the overwhelming reactions that Clayson finds in her investigation are those of stoicism and fatalism, with respondents emphasizing how they are coping with their terminal illness. A fifty-five-year-old woman diagnosed with mesothelioma reflects, "I've been perfectly healthy up to 55, so I've had 55, a lot of people don't get that long."[42] A sixty-six-year-old shipbuilding millwright comments: "I've had my upsets, I've had my tears [...] and after that I just said, 'Sod it, I'll just take each day as it comes.' I even go back to work once a fortnight."[43]

Another issue that we did not understand or sufficiently emphasize in *Lethal Work,* and that seeps out of the oral testimonies, is the impact that serious chronic occupational disease has upon what are distinctly gendered identities. We seriously neglected the effect on women's lives either of directly contracting mesothelioma or of having to support and care for loved ones with this cancer or asbestosis. Mesothelioma challenged women's femininity, corroding their capacity to act as nurturers, carers, mothers, and wives – quite apart from the obvious economic ramifications associated with any loss of their earnings (dual-income families were increasingly the norm from the 1960s onwards). Phyllis Craig reflects:

> Women even if they are working are generally still the home-maker; generally still the person who the family comes to; the Dad usually goes along with it [...] And to have that missing, or for her to know that's going to be missing for them would be the biggest concern. For the man it's more financial. They want to make sure they are financially stable. That's the difference. The other one is emotional stability. They [women] fear for their children.[44]

While statistically women were less prone than men to contracting ARDs (given the sexual division of labour and dangerous work "taboo" that existed within working-class culture), as Gorman's and Clayson's work shows, a significant number of them did, and their lives were blighted in similar, if somewhat different, ways than were those of male ARD victims.[45] The proportion of female ARD cases being diagnosed is currently increasing.

For men, ARDs could be deeply emasculating. The oral evidence brought to light the existence of a macho, individualist element in workers' culture that coexisted, sometimes uneasily, with the collective, mutual, class-conscious character of traditional working-class communities. This was notable in relation to the Glasgow area, which had a reputation associated with militancy – hence the tag "Red Clydeside." As one shipyard trade union activist (Jimmy Reid) said in the early 1970s, "We didn't only build ships on the Clyde, we built men."[46] Heavy manual work forged masculinities and men developed a complex relationship with dangerous, health-threatening manual work, to some extent embracing the very processes that consumed their bodies – as Connell argues – in order to fulfill manly roles.[47] Peer pressure determined that men should act in certain ways, including taking risks or taking work to fulfill the breadwinner role even when this work was known to be dangerous. Those unwilling to take risks to maximize earnings might be castigated and pilloried – as effeminate, "cissies," "glundies," and needing "iron jelloids" – as a Yorkshire miner recalled in his autobiography.[48] Portelli also finds this in his study of

Harlan County. It is tied to a powerful, pervasive, and enduring work ethic. Fulfilling the breadwinner role conferred status in working-class communities, as Wight's important ethnographic study, *Workers Not Wasters* elucidates.[49] The "sacrifice" of men's bodies could, in turn, legitimize male power within the home and family. Bodily damage in this productionist and competitive work culture was economically *and* culturally incentivized.

Men responded less directly to health education and hazards-awareness campaigns than did women and were generally more reluctant to admit they had a health problem and to seek medical intervention. And, when they became ill, they would refuse to allow help or to admit that they needed it.[50] The wife of a quantity surveyor with mesothelioma reflected, after his death, that "he never made a fuss [...] I was the one that used to see him sitting on the edge of the bed with his arms around himself rocking back and forward in pain."[51] A sixty-one-year-old shipyard engineering worker with mesothelioma commented: "A lot of it's my own problem. Too macho to be shouting out when I should be, you know, when I'm in pain."[52] Diseased and disabled workers unable to compete and to perform as "men" invariably felt like lesser men. Those affected narrated how this was lived in their everyday lives and how it felt to them. A Glasgow sheet metal worker reflected: "I've had no social life since about 1980. Eh, people unfortunately don't want to know you when you're ill like y'know."[53] Another reflected, "I'm buggered,"[54] and a Clydeside asbestos sprayer quite aptly described ARD victims as "industrial lepers."[55] Emotions might be controlled by many men, except in private moments, as the wife of the quantity surveyor cited earlier recalled:

> You do your best to bolster them and keep going for them and make light of things. And he took my hand and said: "I'm not going to see xxx as a bride." Then we went up to bed together and we just cuddled and we both cried. And it's the one and only time that I saw my husband crying.[56]

She told of how her husband insisted on driving the car out of the drive "and then we would pull in and stop and I would take over." "Men, eh," she pondered, "don't like to give in." A pleural plaques sufferer related: "The depression's bad. You get that something terrible. You just want to greet your eyes out and everything, you know [...] You can get a violent one. You just flash up stuff."[57] Of course, coping capacities and strategies ranged widely, but the oral testimonies consistently referred to the psychosocial distress and disruption to lives, commensurate with trauma, experienced by ARD victims and survivors.

From Adversity to Advocacy: Building an Occupational Disease Movement

Looking back over the thirty-one interviews conducted for *Lethal Work* I was struck by the diversity of impacts and responses. These ranged across a wide spectrum, from stoic acceptance and withdrawal from society at one extreme (with "cancer fatalism" much in evidence), to intense frustration, bitterness, and both private and publicly vented anger at the other. In a recent interview, Phyllis Craig (of CAA) observed: "Men [with mesothelioma] are *consumed* with anger."[58] This could be channelled into activity through the mobilization of advocacy groups and through campaigning for more effective preventative measures, fairer compensation, and better palliative care (for a Canadian parallel, see Storey [Chapter 2, this volume]).

The first known asbestos victims advocacy group was established in London in 1978 by Nancy Tait, the wife of a mesothelioma victim.[59] Tait was a tireless advocate for ARD victims' rights and, until her death in 2003, an outspoken campaigner against the asbestos lobby. At least thirty-five such ARD victims groups exist across the world today.[60] Clydeside Action on Asbestos, formed in 1986, was created by a group of volunteer ARD sufferers who had previously worked in the shipyards, on construction sites, and in asbestos factories around the city. One of the founder members, William Harkness, had, for twelve years, been refused any state compensation benefits for his advanced asbestosis. He embodied the mutual help ethos of the diseased workers' movement in the United Kingdom in the 1980s and 1990s. In 1988, he commented:

> I am half dead. I can't walk anywhere. I have to get taxis all the time and I have a machine at home I have to use every day to help me breathe. Clyde Action on Asbestos have been a great help to me over the years and I am determined to be part of the group and help others in the same condition caused by that filth.[61]

This mobilizing capacity of injury, harm, and a burning sense of injustice has been evident across the globe. The story of the Jonckheere family in Belgium provides another good example. The Jonckheeres had a family tradition of working for the multinational Eternit asbestos cement factory in the small town of Kapelle-op-den-Bos in Flanders. In a recent interview, Eric Jonckheere recalled that his grandfather had been employed in the plant since 1936 and rose to become a director and plant manager before retiring in 1956. A great uncle also set up the Eternit plant in the Congo, while Eric's father, Pierre, worked at Eternit as a mechanical engineer beginning in the early 1950s. Pierre died of mesothelioma in 1987, aged fifty-nine. In the village, Eternit had a reputation as a caring, welfarist employer, and Eric commented on the isolated community's attachment and loyalty to the company, and the "pride" that his father and grandfather had in their work. They were deferential "company" men. Eric's father refused to believe the company was culpable for ARDs or that it was withholding information. He accepted the company's reassurances and the company doctor's misdiagnosis of his mesothelioma (which was initially treated with antibiotics). "My father didn't want us to panic [...] I never realized the suffering he went through," Eric recalled, "he died in great pain."[62]

A decade or so later, in 1999, Eric's mother, Francoise, was diagnosed with mesothelioma due to environmental exposure in the area around the Eternit factory.[63] Gardens in the vicinity of the plant were covered in white dust. She insisted that her five sons be examined, and it was found that they all had asbestos contamination in their lungs. Eternit offered the standard sum of forty-two thousand euros as compensation, with the proviso that this entailed no admission of blame and that acceptance of the money gave the company immunity from further damages claims. Francoise refused and subsequently became an asbestos campaigner and activist, and a cause célèbre, receiving much media attention in Belgium. Before she died in 2000 (aged sixty-five) she was influential in the formation of the Belgian asbestos victims group (Association Belge des Victimes de l'Amiante [ABEVA]). This advocacy and campaigning work has been continued by Eric Jonckheere, who has been president of ABEVA since 2007. "We started to take the side of the victims," Eric commented. "We were aware we could be next [...] These days I cannot answer: will I be the next? Will my brothers be the next?"[64] To date, two of Eric's brothers have also died of mesothelioma: Pierre Paul (aged forty-three) in May 2003 and Stéphane (aged forty-four) in January 2009. Both had young families.

Eric Jonckheere's interview testimony and his family experience raise many issues. One that stands out is the power and control that Eternit exercised over the community, where, for decades, its reassuring pronouncements and paternalist strategy of ad hoc compensation (combined with control over the local labour market) ensured virtual silence on the economic violence it was perpetrating. The Jonckheeres were for some time the only family who stood up against Eternit: "No-one was talking in the village; nobody was raising awareness [...] or challenging the pro-asbestos lobby, very influential in Belgium [...] You were bound to keep quiet," Eric noted, "they were able to silence the people."[65] Another theme evident here is that of agency – how the family's devastating experience marked the transition from deference and denial to organizing and mobilizing a diseased workers' movement.

Oral History and Mobilizing against Asbestos

Lethal Work and the oral testimonies that inform it entered the public domain in 2000. These have subsequently become part of the body of knowledge and, in turn, have had some influence in shaping ideas and deepening our understanding of the cultures that underpinned economic violence relating to asbestos (and the impacts of those cultures) and have played a small part in forming policy and practice. The oral histories provide an alternative discourse, and frequently a critical one, in which what Michael Bloor describes as the "bump of irreverence" is much in evidence.[66] These often powerful and frequently moving narratives (with the interpretation that developed around them) challenged medical orthodoxies and official explanations and placed everyday personal experience at centre stage.

This had an effect on some politicians, encouraging radical reformers like the Clydebank member of the Scottish Parliament Des McNulty, for example, to campaign for more extensive compensation in Scotland, including pleural plaques. *Lethal Work* continues to be featured on the CAA website, and an article written by the authors has had a permanent presence on the International Ban Asbestos Secretariat (IBAS) website since 2002.[67] The IBAS coordinator, Laurie Kazan-Allen, has attested to the importance of *Lethal Work* in shaping her ideas, as have other asbestos researchers, medics, and campaigners (e.g., Helen Clayson, cited previously). Upon Kazan-Allen's request I assisted with providing witness testimony in compensation litigation. In one case, for example, we located two oral history interviewees who worked on the *Queen Mary* refit in Southampton in 1946–47 and similar jobs around that time. Sam Irvine and Hugh Cairney were flown to San Francisco (at the lawyer's expense), where they gave oral evidence in a mesothelioma damages case (March 2001) that resulted in a $1 million settlement.[68] Unfortunately, the plaintiff, Tom Wilmot, never regained consciousness to learn of the outcome of the litigation. Oral history can thus contribute to disease movement mobilizations and compensation struggles – not least as such witness testimony is an established part of evidence accumulation in damages litigation to corroborate product placement (in the Thomas Wilmot case, this was established by asbestos sacks and packages stamped with manufacturers' logos).

While neoliberal economics and the return to mass unemployment across developed Western economies from the 1980s onwards undoubtedly operated as degenerative forces with a negative impact on the body at work, in some places a cluster of countervailing forces co-existed in parallel with them. In Scotland, for example, these included a more distinctively proletarian and leftist culture (exhibited in the strength of the Labour Party vote in that country in contrast to much of England); more dynamic, well-organized advocacy groups (such as CAA); the formation of a new devolved Parliament in 1999 that is more sympathetic to the plight of ARD victims; and the growing influence of European Union Directives on employment rights, including health and safety. In contrast to Canada (see Storey, Chapter 2, this volume), in Scotland these prevailing circumstances and mobilization capacities helped to neuter some of the worst excesses of economic violence, at least by the early twenty-first century. Among the outcomes are that civil law damages tend to be higher in Scotland than in England, and, over the past decade, the Scottish Parliament has passed compensation legislation that covers pleural plaques, giving Scotland one of the most progressive welfare regimes in the world (at least with regard to ARDs). However, this is no reason to be sanguine. While this may have somewhat eased the economic burden of ARDs in Scotland, relatively little has, or can, be done to reverse or relieve the pain, the suffering, and the utter devastation caused by the economic violence associated with the asbestos epidemic in the United Kingdom and elsewhere. The damage has been done.

Conclusion

The argument advanced here is that the ARD story and the economic violence that underlies it can be elucidated through an oral history methodology. This approach has much potential for the development of a refocused history of work and the workplace and the multifarious impacts employment has upon the body. Oral interviews provide workers' and survivors' perspectives on economic violence, enabling the latter to be understood within the prevailing and mutating cultures of time and place. In once again looking over our asbestos project interviews, what stands out is the frequency of stories about bodies – fit and honed bodies; diseased, disabled, and injured bodies; dead bodies. Not surprisingly, bodily damage is a recurring motif. Portelli remarks on this, too, in relation to coal mining in Harlan County.[69]

Why are we, as oral historians, told these stories? In the process of disclosure we were clearly told things that our narrators wished to relate – memories were sieved and anecdotes selected, and there was much digression from the questions asked. Our interview cohort of Scottish workers was not shy in setting the agenda and exerting control over the interview. They were interpreting their past and framing it. The stories we were told had meaning to the respondents. Many of our narrators were constructing and composing their stories in order to highlight social injustice, mistreatment, and inequality – as Doña María did in Daniel James's beautifully crafted biographical oral history.[70] Bitterness and anger frequently seep through. And, directly or by association, our respondents were advocates for policy change – urging us to recognize the lessons of the past, to inform in order to prevent a repetition of this carnage, or to better regulate or more comprehensively compensate victims. There were certainly morality tales about "villainous" bosses pitted against exploited workers represented by "heroic" trade unions – while "activist" narratives expressed the interviewee's rage and frustration.[71] However, not all respondents conformed to one way of storytelling. Other narrative styles were also evident in the cohort, including the "macho" narrative – individualistic, placing gender over class identity, stoically accepting danger and hazards, relishing toughness and the capacity to earn big money while tolerating unhealthy working conditions.

The dignity of labour oozes through these multilayered narratives. What is evident is that, in their storytelling, workers are constructing their identities: these are hard grafters, cooperative work colleagues, good trade unionists, and "real men" who emphasized the work ethic and manliness in the face of tough, dangerous, and health-sapping conditions. The language deployed is colourful and clear – for example, the use of "slavery" and "hell" as metaphors for working conditions. The selection of words and expressions is indicative of what work signified to the narrators – irrespective of whether it objectively describes such employment. In part this was influenced by the "cultural circuit": narrators were locating their working lives in the past in light of their subsequently accumulated knowledge of improved conditions in the present. To varying degrees they were also trying to counteract the dominant ideological representation of workers under 1980s Thatcherism: the worker as work-shy, compensation-dependent, and lazy, relying upon corrupt and overly powerful trade unions. Where workers' narratives are constructed within this frame, they are predominantly crafted to refute its overt and/or covert message by developing alternative discourses emphasizing their and their fellow workers' credentials as grafters, "workers not wasters" (to borrow Wight's phrase).

Narrative analysis is increasingly popular in the oral history field, and Catherine Riessman is among those who have applied this to what she calls "illness narratives." Riessman persuasively argues that, while it is important to decode messages in the text and to deconstruct disability and illness narratives through "deep listening," (1) they must be located in actual lived experience and (2) gender, social class, and historical context are important in their composing.[72] Perhaps, in the oral interview encounter, there is a need to shift from a focus on the "essentialist" self to a recognition of what Riessman terms a more "performative" self. Nonetheless, we can become too preoccupied with language, narrative, and intersubjectivity. In relation to blatant economic violence in health and safety cultures (largely imported from the United States) in the North Sea Oil industry, which culminated in the Piper Alpha oil rig explosion in 1988 that killed 167 workers, Brotherstone and Manson argue: "Oral historians, as they make use of evermore sophisticated analytical techniques must not lose sight of the bigger picture, the way in which personal life stories can challenge orthodoxy and demand the construction of alternative critical narratives about the recent past and its significance."[73] In their eloquent and earnest articulation of their work-health experiences in oral interviews, workers reveal something of themselves and much about how their bodies are affected – directly and indirectly – by the productionist ethos and cultural norms of their workplaces. "Each of us has only one body," Carol Wolkowitz notes, "and it feels the pinch."[74] In common with other trauma victims and survivors of mass violence, those with disabling and terminal ARDs feel the need to have those responsible admit their blame and recognize their role in economic violence. This is crucial for reconciliation, social healing, and making sense of their working lives.[75] Whether one's interest lies in the narrative discourse or the material reality, oral testimony is revealing on many levels. In our (academic) interpretations of such oral testimony (in itself collaboratively constructed in the encounter between interviewer and narrator) we run the risk of perpetuating a form of colonialism (see Taylor, Sollange, Rwigema, Chapter 3, this volume) and of coming into conflict with the victims' own understandings of their experiences. On the other hand, it is to be hoped that our analysis facilitates a better understanding of survivors as complex actors with a range of identities (e.g., in the way masculinities come into play). Developing a dialogue with those directly involved and affected deserves to be employed more widely (and sensitively) in our attempt to explore and understand economic violence and its impacts upon the bodies of workers.

Notes

I would like to thank my long-standing research collaborator and friend, Ronnie Johnston, for his work on our asbestos in Scotland research project and subsequent partnership research up until his retirement in January 2011. Also many thanks to Helen Clayson for permission to cite from her PhD dissertation and interviews, to Laurie Kazan-Allen of IBAS for providing fruitful contacts and leads, and to Phyllis Craig and Eric Jonckheere for talking to me in new interviews while I was preparing this chapter.

1 Interview with Arthur McIvor and Ronnie Johnston, 1 December 1999, SOHC/016/A23. SOHC refers to interview material deposited and archived in the Scottish Oral History Centre, University of Strathclyde, Glasgow, Scotland. Where no names are given the interviewee is anonymous.

2 Owen Lilly, interviewed by Ronnie Johnston, 1 February 1999, SOHC/016/A19.

3 See Pierre Bourdieu, *Language and Symbolic Power* (Cambridge, UK: Polity, 1991); Pierre Bourdieu, "Foreword," in *Dealing in Virtue*, ed. Y. Dezalay and B.G. Garth, vii-ix (Chicago: University of Chicago Press, 1996); Pierre Bourdieu et al., *The Weight of the World: Social Suffering in Contemporary Society* (Cambridge, UK: Polity, 1993).

4 See Sarah Robinson and Ron Kerr, "From Symbolic Violence to Economic Violence: The Globalizing of the Scottish Banking Elite," *Organization Studies* 33, 2 (2012): 247–66.

5 See, for example, Arthur McIvor, *Organised Capital* (Cambridge University Press, 1996), esp. chap. 4, 92–117.

6 Robert Storey, "'They Have All Been Faithful Workers': Injured Workers, Truth and Workers' Compensation in Ontario, 1970–2008," *Journal of Canadian Studies* 43, 1 (2009): 154–85.

7 Helen Clayson, "The Experience of Mesothelioma in Northern England" (MD thesis, University of Sheffield, 2008), 4.

8 See Arthur McIvor, *Working Lives: Work in Britain since 1945* (Basingstoke: Palgrave Macmillan, 2013). Especially relevant in this context is chap. 5, 149–200.

9 World Health Organization, *Asbestos: Elimination of Asbestos-Related Diseases* (Geneva: WHO, 2010), at http://www.who.int/mediacentre/factsheets/fs343/en/index.html.

10 Laurie Kazan-Allen, *Killing the Future: Asbestos Use in Asia* (2007), 6, at http://ibasecretariat.org/ktf_web_fin.pdf.

11 Paul Brodeur, *Expendable Americans* (New York: Viking Adult, 1974); Paul Brodeur, *Outrageous Misconduct* (New York: Pantheon Books, 1985); Geoffrey Tweedale, *Magic Mineral to Killer Dust: Turner and Newall and the Asbestos Hazard* (Oxford: Oxford University Press, 2000).

12 Alan J. Dalton, *Asbestos: Killer Dust* (London: British Society for Social Responsibility in Science, 1979). See also Tweedale, *Magic Mineral*, 248–49; Clayson, *Experience of Mesothelioma,* 55.

13 Kazan-Allen, *Killing the Future*; David Allen and Laurie Kazan-Allen, eds., *India's Asbestos Time Bomb* (IBAS, 2008), at http://ibasecretariat.org/india_asb_time_bomb.pdf.

14 Angela Di Pasquale, "Western Australia's Wittenoom Gorge Blue Asbestos Mine: 'Se l'avessimo saputo, non ci avremmo mai portato i figli,'" *Italian Studies* 66, 3 (2011): 374.

15 Joanna Bornat, Robert Perks, Paul Thompson, and Jan Walmsley, eds., *Oral History, Health and Welfare* (London: Routledge, 1999); Lucinda McCray Beier, *For Their Own Good: The Transformation of English Working Class Health Culture, 1880–1970* (Columbus: Ohio State University Press, 2008).

16 Michelle Winslow and Graham Smith, "Ethical Challenges in the Oral History of Medicine," in *The Oxford Handbook of Oral History*, ed. Donald A. Ritchie, 372–92 (Oxford: Oxford University Press, 2011), 372.

17 See Peter Bartrip, "Too Little, Too Late? The Home Office and the Asbestos Industry Regulations, 1931," *Medical History* 42 (1998): 421–38; Peter Bartrip, *The Way from Dusty Death* (London: Athlone Press, 2001); Tweedale, *Magic Mineral*; Jock McCulloch and Geoffrey Tweedale, *Defending the Indefensible: The Global Asbestos Industry and Its Fight for Survival* (Oxford: Oxford University Press, 2008).

18 Hannah H. Walker and Anthony D. LaMontagne, *Work and Health in the Latrobe Valley: Community Perspectives on Asbestos Issues. Final Report*

(Melbourne: Centre for the Study of Health and Society, University of Melbourne, 2004), 1.

19 Ronald Johnston and Arthur McIvor, *Lethal Work* (East Linton, UK: Tuckwell Press, 2000); Arthur McIvor and Ronald Johnston, *Miners' Lung* (Aldershot: Ashgate, 2007); Alessandro Portelli, *They Say in Harlan County: An Oral History* (New York: Oxford University Press, 2010); Clayson, *Experience of Mesothelioma*; Walker and LaMontagne, *Work and Health*; Michael Bloor, "No Longer Dying for a Living," *Sociology* 36, 1 (2002): 89–105; Andrew Perchard, *Aluminiumville* (Lancaster: Crucible Books, 2012); David Walker, "'Danger Was Something You Were Brought up Wi': Workers' Narratives on Occupational Health and Safety in the Workplace," *Scottish Labour History* 46 (2011): 54–70.

20 See, for example, Luisa Passerini, *Fascism in Popular Memory* (Cambridge: Cambridge University Press, 1987); Alessandro Portelli, *The Death of Luigi Trastulli and Other Stories: Form and Meaning in Oral History* (Albany: SUNY Press, 1991).

21 For the development of this idea, see Alistair Thomson, *Anzac Memories: Living with the Legend* (Melbourne: Oxford University Press, 1994); and Penny Summerfield, *Reconstructing Women's Wartime Lives* (Manchester: Manchester University Press, 1998).

22 On this, see Lynn Abrams, *Oral History Theory* (London: Routledge, 2010); Paul Thompson, *The Voice of the Past*, 3rd ed. (Oxford: Oxford University Press, 2000); Robert Perks and Alistair Thomson, eds., *The Oral History Reader*, 2nd ed. (London: Routledge, 2006).

23 See Johnston and McIvor, *Lethal Work*, 63–111.

24 Interviewed by Arthur McIvor, 1 June 1999, SOHC/016/A26.

25 Interviewed by Ronnie Johnston, 1 February 1999, SOHC/016/A9.

26 Portelli, *Harlan County*, 139, 143.

27 Cited in Allen and Kazan-Allen, *India's Asbestos Time Bomb*, 34.

28 Ibid., 7. Indian casual workers were also not given the regular medical check-ups that permanent workers received.

29 Interviewed by Ronnie Johnston, 3 February 1999, SOHC/016/A18.

30 On this, see Vicky Long, *The Rise and Fall of the Healthy Factory* (Basingstoke: Palgrave Macmillan, 2011).

31 Interviewed by Arthur McIvor and Ronnie Johnston, 1 December 1999, SOHC/016/A23. The interviewees' father died of an ARD.

32 McCulloch and Tweedale, *Defending the Indefensible*, 118.

33 Interviewed by Ronnie Johnston, 15 March 1999, SOHC/016/A13.

34 See Johnston and McIvor, *Lethal Work*, chap. 6, 177–208.

35 Mildred Blaxter, *The Meaning of Disability* (London: Heinemann, 1976).

36 Barry Castleman and Geoffrey Tweedale, "The Struggle for Compensation for Asbestos-Related Diseases and the Banning of Asbestos," in *Dangerous Trade: Histories of Industrial Hazard across a Globalising World*, ed. Christopher Sellers and Joseph Melling, 181–94 (Philadelphia: Temple, 2012), 187.

37 Interviewed by Arthur McIvor, 28 January 2013, SOHC/016/A35.

38 Clayson, *Experience of Mesothelioma*, 4, 30.

39 Ibid., 131–67.

40 Ibid., 30, 135–36, 252–53. A diagnosis of pleural plaques, or pleural thickening, provided evidence of asbestos exposure and was the cause of much "anticipatory anxiety." However, it was rare for compensation systems to provide any benefits for these conditions in their own right.

41 Cited in Allen and Kazan-Allen, *India's Asbestos Time Bomb*, 5.

42 Mrs. T, cited in Clayson, *Experience of Mesothelioma*, 149.

43 Mr. J, cited in ibid., 149.

44 Interviewed by Arthur McIvor, 28 January 2013, SOHC/016/A35.

45 Tommy Gorman, "Women and Asbestos," in *Clydebank: Asbestos, the Unwanted Legacy*, ed. Tommy Gorman, 127–37 (Glasgow: Clydeside Press, 2000).

46 Cited in Martin Bellamy, *The Shipbuilders* (Edinburgh: Berlinn, 2001), 199.

47 Robert W. Connell, *The Men and the Boys* (Cambridge: Polity Press, 2000).

48 Joe Kenyon, *A Passion for Justice* (Nottingham: Trent Editions, 2003).

49 Daniel Wight, *Workers Not Wasters* (Edinburgh: Edinburgh University Press, 1994).

50 Clayson, *Experience of Mesothelioma*, 253.

51 Interviewed by Ronnie Johnston, 22 March 1999, SOHC/016/A20.

52 Mr. I, cited in Clayson, *Experience of Mesothelioma*, 140.

53 Interview, SOHC 016/A9.

54 Interviewed by Ronnie Johnston, 22 December 1998, SOHC 016/A2.

55 Tommy Nelson, interview on *Hidden Hazard, Forgotten Victims* (CAA video, 1995).

56 Interview, SOHC/016/A20.

57 Interviewed by Ronnie Johnston, 25 January 1999, SOHC/016/A4.

58 Interviewed by Arthur McIvor, 28 January 2013, SOHC/016/A35 (emphasis in original).

59 This was the Society for the Prevention of Asbestosis and Industrial Diseases (in 1996, renamed Occupational and Environmental Diseases Association). See W. McDougall, "Pressure Group Influence and

Occupational Health, SPAID/OEDA, 1978–2008" (PhD diss., Glasgow Caledonian University, 2013).

60 Castleman and Tweedale, "Struggle for Compensation," 188.

61 Cited in *Scotsman*, 15 January 1988, 6.

62 Eric Jonckheere, interviewed by Arthur McIvor, 21 February 2013, SOHC/016/A36. Significantly, the same Eternit company doctor, Dr. Lepoutre, also later died of mesothelioma. See Salvator Y. Nay, "Asbestos in Belgium: Use and Abuse," *International Journal of Occupational and Environmental Health* 9 (2003): 287–93.

63 This was one of many such environmental, family, or "bystander" fatalities from asbestos. Fibres were transferred into the home on workers' overalls and dispersed widely on air currents from work sites and waste dumps.

64 Jonckheere interview.

65 Ibid. For a parallel in which a single company controlled the community through paternalist policies with a wide range of impacts on workers bodies, see Perchard, *Aluminiumville*.

66 See Bloor, "No Longer Dying."

67 See Ronnie Johnston and Arthur McIvor, "Oral Histories of the Asbestos Tragedy in Scotland," at http://ibasecretariat.org/eas_rj_am_scotland.php.

68 The full story is told in Ronnie Johnston and Arthur McIvor, "Oral History in Asbestos Investigations," in *The Asbestos Legacy: The Sourcebook on Asbestos Diseases*, Vol. 23, ed. George A. Peters and Barbara J. Peters, 3–35 (San Francisco: LexisNexis, 2001).

69 Portelli, *Harlan County*, 147.

70 Daniel James, *Doña María's Story* (Durham, NC: Duke University Press, 2001).

71 See, for example, interviews, SOHC/016/A18; A22; A23.

72 See Catherine H. Riessman, *Narrative Methods for the Human Sciences* (London: Sage, 2008).

73 Terry Brotherstone and Hugo Manson, "Voices of Piper Alpha: Enduring Injury in Private Memory, Oral Representation and Labour History," *Scottish Labour History* 46 (2011): 71–85.

74 Carol Wolkowitz, *Bodies at Work* (London: Sage, 2006), 117.

75 See Clayson, *Experience of Mesothelioma*, 53.

11 | The Frames We Use

Narratives, Ethnicity, and the Problem of Multiple Identities in Post-Conflict Oral Histories (Bosnia-Herzegovina)

CATHERINE BAKER

> To frame is to select some aspects of a perceived reality and make them more salient in a communicating text, in such a way as to promote a particular problem definition, causal interpretation, moral evaluation, and/or treatment recommendation for the item described.
>
> – Robert Entman[1]

The starting point for this chapter is the idea that speakers often consciously or unconsciously emphasize certain themes and interpretations, and downplay others, in their speech. One metaphor for illustrating this idea is that of a "lens," which filters certain content into or out of focus: speaking about politics through a gender lens, for instance, means drawing particular attention to the gender dynamics of whatever one observes.[2] Another metaphor that I use is that of a "frame" or "framing." To frame a narrative in a certain way is to organize its content or structure around a particular theme or interpretation.[3] In oral history interviews, interviewees and interviewers both apply particular frames to what they say, depending on how they want to talk about what is being narrated. Any other intermediaries who are involved with a narrative will apply frames of their own to the narrative that is eventually presented: How, for instance, does a translator decide whether to choose one contested place name over another in translating a narrative about a disputed political boundary?[4]

The example of the narrative with a contested place name in need of translation reminds us that the politics of translation necessarily affects interviews that are conducted across languages, where at least one participant will have to work through these issues of representation and meaning either when speaking during the interview or when representing its content afterwards. Working across languages is never easy, and if a language intermediary is involved (such as an interpreter during the interview or a translator of the transcript) then the web of "mediation" between languages becomes even more complex and difficult.[5] These concerns, and the implications of choosing one term with political significance over another term with different significance, are even more sensitive in narratives about conflict and mass violence. In presenting a narrative about postwar Sarajevo, for instance, should I use the name "Srpsko Sarajevo" (Serb Sarajevo) or "Istočno Sarajevo" (Eastern Sarajevo) to denote parts of Sarajevo now in the Republika Srpska (the political entity whose name translates as the "Serb Republic")? Either choice implies a particular attitude on the speaker's part towards Serb political control of that territory; it sets the narrative within a particular frame.

Thinking about framing in this kind of context also brings up another implication: that there are frequent disputes over how to represent an event or issue (we can say that its representation is "contested") and that, when certain frames are selected, other frames, which are incompatible with it, are silenced.[6] How some frames win out over others is affected by the power relations between the speakers. The framing of an oral history narrative, then, can often become contested if the interviewee and interviewer are trying to apply different frames. Struggles over which frame(s) to apply to the narrative are therefore a frequent part of the interviewing process.

Conceiving of the interview as a struggle for the power to interpret and represent is uncomfortable for oral historians, who often regard their work as participatory or emancipatory. An awareness of framing makes clear, however, that interviewing involves at least negotiations, and sometimes outright confrontations, between interviewer and interviewee over what frame to use for narrating events. This chapter discusses some instances of these negotiations but also points out that previous stages of framing within project design also affect the course of the interview, especially in collaborative projects in which partners' diverse backgrounds and interests produce multiple potential frames for questioning.

This chapter both presents and does not present oral histories of mass violence. It presents them in the sense that the focus of the project it discusses – peace support operations in 1990s Bosnia-Herzegovina

– would never have come about if the break-up of Yugoslavia had not been followed by violence against populations defined as ethnic and if that violence had not produced a foreign humanitarian and diplomatic response. It presents them in the sense that the political, economic, social, and interpersonal effects of this violence structured the experiences about which interviewees spoke, whether they were part of Bosnian society or whether they enjoyed the privilege of leaving Bosnia after a tour of duty (with no lasting obligations to the country). It presents them in the sense that the interview extracts I choose to highlight reflect direct consequences of mass violence and the post-conflict division of the Bosnian state into one Serb entity (Republika Srpska) and one non-Serb entity (the Federation of Bosnia-Herzegovina), which was further subdivided into ten Bosniak, Croat, and officially "mixed" cantons.

In another sense, however, oral histories of mass violence are not presented here, and this is because the questions that produced these histories highlighted different frames. They could perhaps more accurately have been called "oral histories of translator/interpreter training" or even "oral histories of employment." The participants whose accounts feature in this chapter – former locally employed interpreters who had been hired by foreign forces to work in besieged enclaves during the Bosnian conflict or to routinely cross Bosnian front lines – were not necessarily participating in interviews "about" mass violence. What these interviews turned out to be "about" was determined by the frames within which interviewer and interviewee both sought to speak and listen. By reflecting on processes of framing within these interviews, I hope to show how acts of questioning produce – or sometimes impede – meaning. I do so by discussing a frame that so often becomes relevant within the study of mass violence: the frame of ethnic conflict and identity.

Framing Languages at War

The interviews discussed here took place during a UK-based research project entitled Languages at War: Policies and Practices of Language Contacts in Conflict. Led by a historian (Hilary Footitt) and a linguist (Michael Kelly), it sought to explore official language policies regarding military organizations, the foreign language experiences of people involved in conflict, and how those experiences related to military organizations' policy frameworks. It did this by comparing two conflict and post-conflict situations in twentieth-century Europe: the Allied liberation and occupation of Western Europe (1944–47) and the peace support operations in Bosnia-Herzegovina (1995–2000).[7]

Besides the two universities, a non-academic institution – the Imperial War Museum (IWM) in London – was also involved. The IWM was aiming to expand its mission to "understand human behaviour through the lens of war and conflict" by exploring ways of representing a topic that had previously been considered all but impossible to exhibit: that is, conflict participants' and museum visitors' linguistic encounters with foreignness.[8] Its participation in Languages at War built on experiences of representing foreign-language material in its permanent Holocaust Exhibition (opened 2000) and an intergenerational learning project entitled Their Past, Your Future (2004), in which "students would look at historical events and British involvement in those events through the prism of foreign cultures and sites of memory."[9] This institutional partner's motivations and experiences would influence the academic interviewers' questioning and framing strategies.

I joined the project in 2008 as a post-doctoral researcher whose PhD was on nationalism and popular music in another Yugoslav successor state, Croatia, and in which I explore the difficulties of defining separate national cultures during and after the break-up of Yugoslavia.[10] My approach to ethnicity is not to study fixed ethnic identities so much as the processes by which people come to understand that they have ethnic identities and what those identities are (this is often called "ethnicization"). In writing about the Yugoslav wars, I associated myself with the research of those who have studied strategies of nationalist ethnicization in the media of successor states.[11] I came to Languages at War with this theoretical background and with the experience of having interviewed in a former Yugoslav language, a skill sought by the project leaders (although, in fact, I was rarely to use it).

Both Languages at War case studies used oral history interviewing as an important source of information. The 1944–47 case study, hosted at the University of Reading, drew on existing interview holdings at the IWM Sound Archive and combined these with extensive use of Foreign Office, War Office, and army documents from archives. One researcher at Reading, Simona Tobia, also conducted new interviews concerning language intermediaries' experiences with languages. These were often second interviews with people whom the Sound Archive had already interviewed but whose original interviewers had taken no interest in language. This re-interviewing was itself an exercise in framing and produced striking results: "Interviewees who had barely mentioned languages in the original recordings became voluble about their language experiences and the role which languages had played in their war activity when someone was actually asking them how languages were involved in the jobs they had been given to do."[12] This observation suggests that framing in interview design and questioning has profound effects on the narrative in ways that will not be apparent when, as in many projects, there is only one interview for one purpose.

Unlike the 1944–47 case study, the 1995–98 study, at the University of Southampton, had far less access to archive material because its operations were too recent for documents to have been declassified.[13] The IWM also had far fewer interviews relating to Bosnia than to the Second World War, and these addressed languages only fleetingly or not at all. Relatively speaking, therefore, the Bosnia study made much more use of new interviews. I conducted fifty-two interviews with fifty-one people whose experiences were relevant, including foreign military personnel (linguists and non-linguists), locally recruited language intermediaries (often referred to as "interpreters," although their duties could often also include written translation), and foreign civilian linguists. The research team's interests and backgrounds suggested multiple frames through which to approach interview design.

One important frame, new to me as a researcher, was language policy. States, international bodies, and institutions all attempt to modify practices and ideologies about language through exercising policy in areas concerning such issues as which languages to teach or to use for official purposes.[14] One can often find documentary sources that contain explicit policy statements; however, since these were not available, how could oral history interviews and questions get at the language policy frame? One option was to interview participants in policy-making: here, the value of testimony as historical data would be limited by the unreliability of memory and the potential for different actors to give irreconcilable accounts. Thus, oral history could provide insight into the making of policy but could not, for instance, lead to precise reconstructions of policy wording.[15] Further ways of using oral history to study language policy involved collecting narratives of implementing policy and narratives of experiencing policy being implemented on oneself. We theorized this by incorporating Michael Lipsky's notion of "street-level bureaucrats" – public service workers who have direct contact with the public – into our understanding of policy: the officials' exercise of discretion in applying policy *becomes* the policy as it is understood by service users.[16] Interviewees who could be considered to have made policy in this sense, such as foreign military linguists who set up local interpreter teams on UN bases, were thus asked to narrate how they had identified and responded to the problems they faced.[17]

Another interviewing frame, which provided an ordering principle for interviews with local language intermediaries in particular, was that of working identities. This framed the interviewee as an employee who had performed certain functions – mediation between the language(s) of foreign troops and local residents – in the course of her or his work. Having solicited interviewees through announcements seeking current and former interpreters, translators, and language assistants, I as interviewer was constructing their role as deserving of scholarly interest. This often appealed to prospective interviewees (some expressed pleasure that scholars had bothered to ask about interpreters' experiences), although, in fewer cases, this meant that I needed to reassure participants who were not sure that they fit the criterion (e.g., because they had "only" worked as a field interpreter not as a highly professionalized conference interpreter).

Approaching interviewees as workers raised questions about working conditions, workplace environments, management relationships, experiences of operational security and other policies, and contractual arrangements. The theme of contractual arrangements took on greater importance during a two-week visit to Banja Luka. After several interviews there that highlighted this theme, I began to ask more in-depth questions about it, amplifying the framing effect. Framing the interviewee as a worker or employee and the interview as a narrative of working experiences helped me to engage with research in international relations and global development on socio-economic transformation after humanitarian intervention as well as on the "unintended" (i.e., adverse) consequences of peace operations, including the effects of foreign forces hiring local employees on well-paid but insecure contracts.[18]

A refinement of this frame, highlighting what was specific about work with languages, was to approach interviews through a frame of translator/interpreter training. We consulted with interpreting practitioners and researchers in devising the questions for this frame, identifying key themes in the professionalization of interpreter training and transforming these into questions that would elicit narrative (e.g., "What was it like the first time you interpreted at a meeting?"; "What were you able to learn from your supervisor about how to interpret?"). Apart from one group of interpreters at the NATO headquarters organization, the interpreters had rarely received formal training. These questions therefore produced narratives of improvisation, and, like any other question, could generate results in a different frame from that intended by the interviewer. In one interview, the "first time you interpreted at a meeting" question elicited a narrative of crossing the Inter-Entity Boundary Line (IEBL) shortly after the Dayton Peace Accords and visiting a military headquarters associated with the "other side." As the narrative unfolded, the speaker's focus was on the significance of ethnic identity in that encounter rather than on her building-up of interpreting experience.

Further frames for interviewing and questioning arose as a result of collaboration with the IWM. As part of its collections development strategy, the IWM aspired to collect more interviews with people corresponding to profiles traditionally underrepresented in its sound archive, such as those involved in contemporary conflict, non-British narrators, and civilian narrators. Early in the research design I therefore examined Sound Archive question guides for earlier projects. These had been designed for groups of interviewees, usually soldiers, with something in common (such as a service branch, a war, or an area of operations). Their strategy was to identify moments that would be shared by all group members' narratives (e.g., "entering basic training" for military personnel) and then to develop questions based on these. The guides also included everyday life topics ("What was the food like on the base?") that might help future museum staff construct displays. I found that I kept these questions in reserve as space-fillers or tone-shifters for when an interviewee indicated, either verbally or non-verbally, that she/he would welcome a change of subject.

In contrast to these other frames, the frame of genocide, ethnic cleansing, and mass violence was not in the foreground of designing the Languages at War interviews. Given the case studies' subject matter, however, this frame was always implicit. The post-conflict situations discussed in many of our interviews – whether occupation, post-liberation transitional administration, or peacebuilding – were also situations that constituted the immediate aftermath of violence in which people had been collectively targeted for killing.

Before discussing this frame further, I would like to explain some of the language I choose (not) to use in writing about conflicts such as the war in Bosnia-Herzegovina. In particular, I prefer to avoid the term "ethnic conflict" and to talk about ethnicity in a more "processual" way. Because I have studied how people come to identify and be identified as people with ethnic identities, I avoid language that suggests that ethnic identity, or ethnic rationales for conflict, exist independently of these processes. Indeed, I would concur with Jan Nederveen Pieterse's observation that "the terminology of ethnicity is part of the conflict and cannot serve as a language of analysis."[19] Pieterse argues that the perpetrators of ethnic cleansing themselves depend on hardening the ethnic identities of their own group and their opponents, and on eliminating non-ethnic options for social identification. There is a serious implication here for the language that observers use to talk about a conflict: interpreting a conflict like Bosnia solely through the frame of ethnic difference uncritically reproduces a frame that the conflict participants have *worked to construct* in the service of their objectives.[20] This is not to dismiss the significance that interviewees may attach to ethnicity in the course of making sense of their own biography. It is, however, to observe that the frame of ethnic conflict or mass violence needs to be thought about critically during interviewing and research.

Both Languages at War case studies produced new oral histories with people who could be considered members of survivor groups. The Second World War case study contains a set of interviews with German/Austrian Jewish refugees who had become investigators and interrogators for the British Army due to their native-speaker competence in German, their identities as subjects of Nazi oppression, and their loyalty to the Allies, which they had proven during the war. Their interviews contain (and constitute) narratives of how they had used language choice in "performing a British identity and hiding their German (or Austrian) former self."[21] In the Bosnia case study, there are some interviewees who have not experienced the conflict first hand because they spent the war years outside the country. There are also others who had worked in besieged enclaves during the war (the interview collection contains narratives from Sarajevo, Bihać, Goražde, and Tuzla) or who had routinely crossed ethno-political front lines in the course of their duties. Depending on when they worked, their line-crossing could have been during the war (accompanying United Nations humanitarian convoys or liaison missions) and/or after the signing of the Dayton Peace Accords in December 1995 (enabling NATO troops to enforce local armed forces' withdrawals from the so-called Zone of Separation along the new Inter-Entity Boundary Line).

When Did Interviewees Narrate the Conflict?

Mass violence was necessarily one of the project's interests. A visiting consultant to the project, Louise Askew, who had interviewed a cluster of interpreters working for foreign institutions in Bosnia-Herzegovina during her doctoral research, dealt directly with whether linguistic fragmentation during the ethno-political conflict in the former Yugoslavia had brought Serbo-Croat to an end as a language, and so I did not concentrate on this question.[22] In my own research design, I chose to employ the frames of language policy, working identities, translator/interpreter training, and everyday life as prompts for questions and to let narratives of ethno-political conflict and its consequences emerge as and when the narrator chose to include them rather than framing interviews around these narratives as such.

This was an obvious difference between the approach of Languages at War and that of oral history projects that approach narrators specifically as survivors of genocide or mass violence, such as the work of Montreal Oral Histories or the US Holocaust Memorial Museum.[23] It is also an obvious difference between the Bosnia case study and a number of other interview-based projects on Bosnia that specifically approach interviewees as members of minorities,[24] victims and survivors,[25] perpetrators,[26] exercisers of war memory,[27] or "ordinary people" living in a society in need of post-conflict reconciliation.[28] For two reasons, my awareness of this body of research on Bosnia informed my decision to approach the topic of mass violence obliquely. Not only was it a well-trodden path but, since the interview had not presented itself as being primarily about the effects of ethnic conflict on interviewees, I perceived an ethical obligation to give interviewees the space to keep this topic private. Interviewees provided their narratives of the ethno-political conflict and their experiences of it not in response to direct questioning but, rather, as part of the "connective tissue" of their responses, providing context for the interviewer and our imagined audiences.

Interviewees might give their interpretation of the conflict in a "scene-setting" passage in order to introduce the beginning of their work as interpreters, as in this extract from an interview with Hasan, who describes the handing back of Serb-occupied districts of Sarajevo to the authorities of the "Federation of Bosnia-Herzegovina" entity in February 1996, just before he became an interpreter for the UN International Police Task Force (IPTF):[29]

> So, my first experiences as an interpreter started immediately after the war, when this country was, actually this area of Sarajevo was, still under so-called reintegration, because part of Sarajevo had been still under control of Serb forces and by the Dayton Peace Agreement it's been returned to Sarajevo and Bosnian Federation authorities. So as a member of United Nations International Police Task Force, I believe it was further on abbreviated IPTF, actually dealt with the security situation in those areas where some Serb, local Serb population still wanted to remain, but later on, some of them still remained, but the majority of that population actually unfortunately left, because they sold their properties and they just decided to go and, go outside the Federation and live either in Republika Srpska, the other entity of Bosnia-Herzegovina, or in Serbia.[30]

An interviewee might also provide an interpretation of the wider conflict in order to mark a turning point in the personal narrative. The next extract comes from an interview with Zorica, who had been working for foreign military forces as an interpreter since 1993. She had first worked for the UN in Pale, the wartime capital of Republika Srpska; moved to another office in the Republika Srpska a few years after the war ended; then, after a few more years, returned to Sarajevo. Her explanation of the move away from Pale began with her telling me that her parents had moved away from Sarajevo, and this, in turn, required an explanation of the events of February 1996. This narrative, emphasizing Serbs' fear of Federation authorities, was very different from that of Hasan:

> When the Dayton agreement was signed, my family lived in the Serb-held part of Sarajevo. And most of the people I knew, friends, neighbours, and ... most people decided to leave. There were protests, there were many, many events which made them decide so. [...] And one of the reasons why most people decided at that time in Ilidža, it was not just residents of Ilidža, half of them were refugees from Sarajevo, Serbs who fled Sarajevo somehow. But many Serbs, relatives, friends, who remained in Sarajevo couldn't leave it. So the only fear, the decision of most people from Ilidža, Serbs from Ilidža, was made on the basis of leaving time [i.e., the time to leave]. You can be captured here in Ilidža, as so many people were in Sarajevo. So they were not, they were not ... there were no

> places to go. No accommodation, no nothing. They were just left with ... and this was after four years of fierce fighting. And those who stayed in Sarajevo couldn't even be accused of having done anything wrong. But many, including my relatives, were captured in prisons in Sarajevo, without being, just ... eventually, just, they did something wrong, but they didn't know what. So what could they expect after four years of fighting? That's why most people left.[31]

These accounts are examples of the irreconcilability of public narratives in post-conflict Bosnia: in one, the Serb population of Ilidža "unfortunately left" when the suburb came under Federation control, while in the other, it had felt compelled to leave for fear of retaliatory persecution. Like many other examples visible throughout Bosnian society, these interviews suggest that, in Bosnia, any "thick" reconciliation of communication and trust – rather than the "thin" reconciliation of people's preparedness to live near neighbours with different ethnicized identities and narratives – is a long way from being achieved.[32]

Explicatory narratives of the conflict also occurred when interviewees felt the need to define terminology or to contextualize the implications of a statement. In the extracts below, Sara, an interpreter for various British units between 1998 and 2005, explains an abbreviation she has used to refer to one of the Bosnian armed forces during an account of mine clearance training; whereas Stojan, who worked for Dutch and British units between 1997 and 2007, contextualizes an observation about Dutch soldiers' attitudes towards discussing the conflict with their local interpreters:

> That was also interpretation, mainly, because they organized trainings for deminers. And they had classes every day, showing them how to probe, how to use which part of the equipment, what they should be careful of. They also had some leadership classes, depending on the level of participants. But they were mainly, the participants were members of the VRS. VRS was Army of Republika Srpska. Because at that time there were three warring factions, during the war, actually, let's call them Serbs, Croats, and Muslims. So Serbs had their own army, that was VRS, that was the Army of the Republika Srpska, and since Banja Luka is in this Serbian part, so we had, they had organized classes for them. (Sara)[33]

> It was possible to talk without any anger, without any problems, without any... you know, it was possible to talk. Not with Dutch all the time. Because they had a very negative experience in former Yugoslavia, during the war in former Yugoslavia. Maybe you know that case of Srebrenica massacres. Dutch battalion was responsible for that area, so Serbs were stronger, occupied the pocket of Srebrenica, did war crimes there, and then the Dutch was blamed for that, because actually they prevented those civilians to come into the protected area, so, they had a responsibility to protect them. They were not able to do that. And I still think Serbs were too strong during that time around Srebrenica area, so... for them it was impossible to prevent what happened. But, they had to be more decisive. To try to ... so ... Of course, Serbs, those, should be blamed for that. Because it's a historical fact that happened, and that Serbs ... but they reacted wrongly. Not those soldiers there, those forces, the forces who were there. But I'm talking about their commanders, official politics. NATO is also to be blamed. That had to happen. And, to cause a reaction. But that reaction was, that reaction was bombing, air strikes. Only against Serbs. What again was wrong, according to my, that's my personal opinion. (Stojan)[34]

A few interviewees began their interviews with a stream-of-consciousness narrative, which I did not interrupt (these extended initial answers also resulted in my asking fewer follow-up questions because many of the points in which I was interested had been covered). One long account from Gordana, a part-time interpreter for British forces between 1999 and 2001 or 2002 (she did not remember the precise date she had stopped working), included an explanation of the war in response to an unasked question about whether interpreters had always translated to the best of their ability. This question was not asked, yet she still found it important to address this issue. Gordana appeared to be defending interpreters as a group against an accusation that they might have been swayed by ethnically based loyalties, which might have been an accusation that she or her colleagues had actually faced at work or something about which she and/or they felt insecure:

> A lot of interpreters, I saw myself, and I did it myself, and I think it happened before I started working and after I left, a lot of interpreters did a really good job, and they translated exactly

> what's said, because they knew how important it was, obviously. And, as I said again, a lot of people spoke English very very well. I mean, obviously they had to do certain tests before they get the job. But... because the war, before British came, obviously, the war was basically between Serbian, Croatian and Muslim people, it was a religious war, and we worked mainly in Banja Luka, but there were interpreters who were sent to Sarajevo or some other towns in Bosnia where there is a majority of, like, Muslim people or Croatian people. And I think in general in the whole Bosnia, which was, in general, relationships between interpreters from different ethnic groups were very good. Because they all worked their job, and there wasn't any problems, which unfortunately, after the war there was this gap between these ethnic groups and obviously... in a nutshell, I'll just tell you, I think a lot of people, a lot of people in this country never wanted this war to happen, and it's very complicated to explain how it actually started, and why, because it could take me ten days' non-stop talking to explain all of these things [laughs]. But I know a lot of people were against that. (Gordana)[35]

These interview extracts show that narratives of violence were introduced at different points in the narrative and fulfilled various purposes. Analyzing the speakers' interpretations of the conflict would involve identifying a number of discursive elements in their interviews. How, for instance, did they describe the causes of the war and the actors in it? (Among the options would be identifying a particular collective actor as a guilty party, using the force's official phrasing and referring to "warring factions" without further narrating the causes, or individualizing guilt.) Did interviewees use terms such as "genocide" or "civil war," which aligned with particular collective interpretations of the conflict? Or, indeed, did they deliberately avoid any or all of these? How and when did interviewees use ethnonyms to describe themselves or others? How much detail did they give about what had happened to them and where they had been during the war years before they began working as interpreters? I chose not to incorporate such questions or objectives into my question guide or to systematically collect such responses from each and every speaker. My questioning strategy attempted to avoid addressing Bosnians as ethnic subjects while leaving space for them to do so if they so chose.

Downplaying the frame of conflict could lead to gaps in the narrative. One large cluster of interviewees, for instance, had lived or worked in the vicinity of Banja Luka, the largest town in northwest Bosnia, which had been part of Bosnian Serb territory during the war and became the capital of the postwar Republika Srpska in 1998. Banja Luka had not been on the front line in the sense that armed forces had not fought each other for possession of the city. The Republika Srpska authorities had nonetheless persecuted non-Serbs in Banja Luka, and most of the city's sixty thousand non-Serb inhabitants fled or were expelled between 1992 and 1995 (although some had returned).[36] This was not highlighted in most interpreter narratives from Banja Luka, although one account referred to the dismissal of non-Serb academics from the university. I did not explore this background in as much depth as I could have done since foreign peacekeepers had not been stationed in Banja Luka during the war. However, speakers rarely introduced it of their own accord. By making this observation, I do not want to suggest that interpreters acquiesced in the dominant ethno-political narratives of groups with which they identified. On the contrary, their narratives often expressed disagreements with or direct challenges to these; and for those who had not lived in Banja Luka during 1992–95, the violence and persecution that occurred there during the war was not so important in their individual stories.

Where, then, did interpreters' own experience of the politics of ethnicity come in? At what points did they narrate that their ethnic identity had been made to matter most? Interviewees' narrations indicated that they had varied attitudes about the sense of a collective purpose. Interpreters from the Federation often positioned themselves as having been motivated to become interpreters in order to work towards a collective project of peace, reconstruction, improving the condition of their towns – this was generally very important to them – and establishing a multinational Bosnia. (No interpreters in this collection described themselves as promoting the interests of a single non-Serb ethnic group – that is, the Bosniaks or the Croats – through their work, but that is not to say that this subject position did not exist.) Interpreters from the Republika Srpska were much more likely to describe their motivation as personal, economic, and focused on supporting their families, though a few also saw their work as an opportunity to correct foreign troops' misperceptions of Serbs. An interviewee based in Banja Luka who identified her ethnicity as mixed also spoke at length about her hopes for a reconciled Bosnia. The moment of an interview at which narrating experience would *necessarily* force interviewees to position themselves relative to Bosnian ethno-politics, however, occurred when the narrative turned to assignments that required interpreters to cross ethno-political front lines. These were the narratives of visiting armed forces of the "wrong" ethnicity or, rather, of visiting forces that had declared themselves to be fighting in the name of an ethno-national group antagonistic to the ethnic identity ascribed to the interpreter. The front lines they crossed could thus be called "ethnicized" – that is, they had been made into boundaries between territories inhabited and claimed by distinct ethnic groups.

The last two sentences of the preceding paragraph break down the identity claims that speakers made about themselves and others to an extreme extent. Because they are not expressed in the kinds of terms that are used in everyday speech for talking about mass violence, they may also be difficult to follow – which is a problem I continue to contend with in trying to communicate research about mass violence. Interviewees spoke in much more commonsensical terms about, for example, visiting the "Muslim" (Bosniak) army as a Serb or visiting Bosnian Croat forces as a Muslim or Bosniak. Below, I explore this potential clash of frames by looking more closely at some of the narratives about crossing front lines.

Narratives of Crossing Ethnicized Front Lines

The need to cross ethnicized front lines arose in two main contexts: (1) during the conflict itself and (2) after the Dayton Peace Accords when foreign military liaison visits operated across both sides of the IEBL (between the Federation and Republika Srpska). Before interviewing, we had formed the hypothesis that foreign military forces might have had policies about matching an interpreter's ethnicity to that of the local armed force whom they were visiting, whether for the sake of safety or in order to win the local interlocutor's trust in a context within which people of an "opposing" ethnicity (especially military-age men) were likely to have been viewed as spies or informants. However, interviews with both foreign soldiers and local interpreters did not appear to suggest there had been any such policy at a high enough level to be general. Nor did they suggest that there had been a deliberate policy to take the opposite stand and to choose interpreters regardless of ethnicity in order to demonstrate to local interlocutors that the peacebuilding force expected them to act in an ethnicity-blind way. The foreign force did have policies restricting access to classified information, but, since these related to citizenship and (the lack of) security clearance, they affected all local employees equally rather than applying to some local ethnic identities and not to others. The important decision of whether or not to take an interpreter "across" ethnic lines seems, instead, to have been left to the users of interpreters (creating the potential for an interpreter or onlooker to have experienced the decision as policy when this was not the case), and the interviews contain many examples of both strategies.

Accounts of crossing the IEBL were also significant in interviewees' personal narratives. For them as individuals these line-crossings were also their first time across "the" lines, and even their first contact with the "other side" and its military since the war. Interpreters hired when the foreign force opened new bases in areas of the Republika Srpska after Dayton experienced these situations, which were socially and privately constructed as tense, very soon after starting work. One woman from Banja Luka who identified as a Serb reported that her first interpreting position, in January 1996, had been at a foreign base in a town that had been occupied by the Croatian Army in 1995 and then assigned to the Republika Srpska at Dayton:

> Because my first job was in Mrkonjić Grad, and that was under the Croatian Army at the time, and because I am a Serb, it was like a hostile army. And the town itself ... well, [it] was assigned to Republika Srpska by the Dayton agreement. And they were supposed to withdraw from the town and leave it to Serbs. When we first arrived in Mrkonjić Grad there was nobody there. There was only one granny. She was the only one that was living there, apart from the Croatian Army. And everything was burned down, pretty much. The British soldiers, they have removed corpses from the town. Human ones, but the animal ones were still there. And because I didn't see the war at all until that point it was a bit ... different. But I felt safe. (Slađana)[37]

She went on to relate that her first assignment had been to visit "a Muslim headquarters" – that is, a headquarters of the Army of Bosnia-Herzegovina (ABiH), which had come under the growing control of the Bosniak nationalist political party during the course of the war:

> Anyway, my first job was a visit to the 5th Corps [laughs] in Sanski Most. It was a Muslim army, and I can't say I was happy [laughs]. It wasn't pleasant. But, the British soldiers, they reassured me that they would protect me, because I'm wearing [a] British uniform, and they would be eligible to shoot if somebody wanted to harm me. Because I'm wearing their uniform, and that would be an attack on Great Britain. So we went there, I introduced myself as "Selma" [a typical Bosniak name] [laughs].
>
> CATHERINE: [Laughs.]
>
> SLAĐANA: Yeah, I didn't have the courage to say that my name was Slađana [laughs]. And then, as it happens, I talked to one of the soldiers, and he said, "Where are you from?" And I'm not a good liar, and I don't like to lie. And I said, "Well, I'm from Banja Luka." And I thought, like, my God, now he's going to shoot me immediately. And then he said, "Really?" I said, "Yeah." But I wanted to avoid talking to him, but he was really persistent to talk to me. And then he said, "Oh, right, well, I have a sister down there, she stayed." And I said, "Mm hmm, yeah, well, quite a few people stayed." And then we parted. But I didn't have to translate anything at that meeting because there was another interpreter. This was just, I was just there as a back-up [laughs] interpreter, I didn't interpret anything.[38]

Out of all my interviews, the one in which a speaker was most insistent on narrating his experiences within the frame of ethno-political conflict – to the extent of closing down questions that attempted to establish other frames (such as working identities or translator/interpreter training) – was also about crossing the IEBL. This was an interview with Asmir, who had worked for the Nordic-Polish Battalion in northeast Bosnia between 1996 and 2003. Asmir's narrative began in his home town of Maglaj, which, during the war, had been held by the Army of Bosnia-Herzegovina but shelled by the VRS. He had started learning English by talking to British peacekeepers who had been stationed in Maglaj, but he resisted a question in which I attempted to co-construct a language-learning narrative. His narrative of contact with British soldiers instead emphasized military firefights and noted the greater firepower of Serb forces, positioning both the peacekeepers and the people of Maglaj as the underdogs:

CATHERINE: What did they [the British] do about interpreters at that time?

ASMIR: Their interpreters?

CATHERINE: Yeah.

ASMIR: Well, that was during the war time. I started working as an interpreter some three years after it, when IFOR arrived,[39] so that was in 1996. At that time I think they had one single interpreter. And what I remember from that time, from the war time, when the British UNPROFOR was stationed there [in Maglaj], was that the Serb snipers were often shooting at them,[40] so they shot back at them. So on several occasions I was behind their, together with them as they were shooting back at the snipers. So that's how I experienced them also, firing back at the snipers that were shooting at them, and once they fired lots of rounds back to the snipers that were shooting at them. So the Serb army shot back at them with a tank, and I think one British soldier got crippled, I think he lost his leg. And then they fired with these remote guided missiles back to the tank, but couldn't shoot it down, because it was well hidden in the woods. And it was, obviously, the distance was too big for them to shoot it. And what I heard from them was that they called air support that never came. So they had to be more silent, because the Serb army had more weapon power than they did. So they actually never provoked by shooting back at the snipers again. So they just kept silent at their military base. But the snipers were shooting at us as civilians in those buildings, so, we had to be careful when going to UNPROFOR base to talk to them, because you had two hundred metres' distance where you had to run fast or hide behind a building so the sniper guy wouldn't see you.[41]

Asmir had graduated from high school in 1995 and had begun working as an interpreter in early 1996 at a foreign military facility in Doboj, a nearby town that had been part of Serb-held territory during the war and was now on the other side of the IEBL (while Maglaj was in the Federation, Doboj was in Republika Srpska). Doboj was where our interview took place. His account of starting work again emphasized danger (the risks of mine strikes in military vehicles, armed stand-offs at military sites between local armed forces and foreign troops exercising their post-Dayton powers of inspection) and then arrived at the theme of the interpreter's role in post-conflict reconciliation. Asmir believed that the interpreters' ability to move freely back and forth across the IEBL enabled them to stand as examples to their fellow townspeople and to lead the way in reducing tensions between the two towns and communities. Interpreters had been able to visit old friends who now lived on the other side of the lines. They had been go-betweens for former neighbours who first met each other at the IEBL and had run errands for people who, during the war, had been displaced from one town and moved to the other:

> Maglaj was controlled by the BiH army, so it was the first time for me to come to a Serbian town. And for my Serbian colleague, [an] interpreter from Doboj, to come to Maglaj. And a friend of mine, for example, my colleague, he's from, he's from Doboj, but he was, he had to leave Doboj in '92 because [the] Serbian army took control of this, so he was, throughout the war he was in Maglaj. So he got a job together with me, so it was the first time for him to come to Doboj after four years now as an interpreter and to see his burnt house here in Doboj. So, we interpreters were the first ones to cross the lines. Both Bosniaks and Serbs alike.[42]

Some time later, other people from Maglaj who were not interpreters and who did not visit Doboj in the course of their work began to socialize and shop there, and vice versa. Asmir credited the interpreters with establishing a decisive precedent for achieving a lessening of tensions, though not full ethnic coexistence:

> I think we as a multiethnic team in, as I told you, in IFOR bases, we were the first sign to all the people in these towns that they could get together again and at least talk to each other and work with each other. These towns are still divided somehow, because this [Doboj] is a Serb majority town. You cross the entity line, there's a Bosniak majority town. You go a little bit right, there's a Croat majority municipality. So people still live in certain, in their own towns, and do not visit each other that much, but at least there's not any immediate threat, people don't hate that much each other. There are Serbian people from Doboj working on the Federation side, there are many Federation people working here in Doboj. Returnees return to Doboj, and they are like normal citizens. The main problem here is the economy and the

lack of jobs that we have. And if people had more jobs they would stop thinking about the politics. The politicians still build hatred amongst people. If people had jobs they would be able to get away from the politics, I think. Still, people would mix much more in the future. But thankfully there is no hate among the people. People trust more each other. And for Serbian girls to get, buy some clothes in Tuzla, which is on the Federation side, no problem. I mean, the Serbian girls that I know in Doboj are often in Tuzla, or somewhere else, in Sarajevo. So it's much better. People travel across the lines. But we interpreters crossed first, back in '96. First time for me to enter Doboj was in a huge fifty-ton tank, through the minefields, and it was the first time for me after five years to see Doboj. I was born in Doboj. Because being from Maglaj, mothers would give birth here in Doboj, because Maglaj didn't have a hospital at the time. It was the first time for me to see Doboj here. And as I told you all the stories about. Now it's different. I come to the swimming pool here, spend time, in the summer time, nighttime, and when it's boring in my town I come here with my wife for shopping, et cetera. Many people do so. So, was I helpful?

CATHERINE: Yes, yes! I mean, you know.

ASMIR: I saw your reactions. You didn't expect some of the stories. [Laughs.] Yeah.

Of the fifty-two interviews I conducted for Languages at War, Asmir's now remains in my memory as the interview in which my intentional framing attempts broke down furthest and as the interview in which my embarrassment, incoherence, and slowness to perceive an interviewee's narrative had all been most apparent.

Conclusion

After meeting Asmir, I was annoyed with myself for having taken so long to understand the narrative he wanted to tell – even when he had repeatedly signalled it with illustrations of violence and death, of which the narrative from his home town was only the first.[43] The process of negotiating meaning had failed insofar as I was unable to collect a narrative of his technical work as a person mediating between languages, but it had succeeded insofar as the interview narrative was able to convey the message that his identity as an interpreter had been inseparable from his identity as a non-Serb person from a certain town. Addressing the interviewee primarily as a person who has had a particular professional role does not preclude narratives of ethnic identification from permeating the interview. This held not just for Asmir's interview but also for interviews with a less confrontational dynamic – those in which it could also be seen that interviewees' practices of narration and explaining brought collective narratives to bear on their individual working lives. While interpreters' working identities and experiences created a sense of similarity within the set of narratives, the frame of ethnic (or ethnicized) conflict and its after-effects produced underlying cleavages – a contradiction that interviewees would have been working through for years as members of mixed-ethnicity workplaces and interpreter teams. Within the interviews, the frame of ethnic identity and conflict could not be rendered invisible, despite my attempts to do so.

Insofar as one can say that the conventional form of survivor testimony after the Yugoslav wars is based on the frame of ethnic identity, my interviewing strategy (I now realize) represented an attempt to transgress this form. Asmir – if I read his behaviour correctly – resisted this attempt. Although in some respects my questions and his answers reached common meaning (such as the significance of locally recruited interpreters in building peace), they did not do so for this dimension of the social world. The implications of this impeded attempt to move *beyond* what appeared to me as the conventional forms of narrating the aftermath of the war are broader than the study of the Bosnian conflict. As many of the chapters in this volume show, there is much to be gained by representing mass violence in such a way that it does not reduce those who have experienced it to one simple identity – that of "survivor." This has been amply demonstrated in feminist critiques of "survivor" labelling after sexual violence.[44] Yet, we must also preserve space for narrators to draw meaning, if they wish, from the idea of having survived and from actions they have been able to take because of who, in collective terms, they are.[45] Revising this chapter for publication, I was reminded of Julia Serano's critique of "subversivist" ways of talking about another characteristic – gender identity:

> Subversivism is the practice of extolling certain gender and sexual expressions and identities simply because they are unconventional or nonconforming [...] On the surface, subversivism gives the

appearance of accommodating a seemingly infinite array of genders and sexualities, but this is not the case. Subversivism does have very specific boundaries; it has an "other."[46]

In privileging transgression, subversivism marginalizes those who do identify with the conventional and have had their identity claims invalidated by others. Serano argues instead that "we should turn our attention [...] to challenging all forms of *gender entitlement*, the privileging of one's own perceptions, interpretations, and evaluations of other people's genders over the way those people understand themselves."[47]

What would an approach to representing mass violence that bears in mind Serano's caveats look like? Researchers must resist the temptation to extol only the anti-nationalist, the fluid of heritage, the child of the mixed marriage, the bilingual: such testimonies are no more and no less valuable than are those of people who feel comfortably accommodated within collective identities and narratives. A critical practice in representing mass violence should take as its target ethnic *entitlement* and the use of ethnicity as an instrument in gaining and exercising power rather than simply praising transgression for its own sake. Only then are interviewers most able to fulfill their ethical responsibilities.

Notes

This chapter derives from the project Languages at War: Policies and Practices of Language Contacts in Conflict (funded by the UK Arts and Humanities Research Council), for which I worked as a researcher at the University of Southampton in 2008–12. The methodological reflections are my own but are of course informed by discussions with fellow project members. Thanks to delegates at the Beyond Testimony and Trauma conference, especially Erin Jessee and Anna Sheftel, to Cai Wilkinson, and to the editors of this volume for comments that informed the revision of this chapter.

1 Robert M. Entman, "Framing: Toward Clarification of a Fractured Paradigm," *Journal of Communication* 43, 4 (1993): 52.

2 V. Spike Peterson and Anne Sisson Runyan, *Global Gender Issues in the New Millennium*, 3rd ed. (Boulder, CO: Westview Press, 2010), 37–102.

3 See Erving Goffman, *Frame Analysis: An Essay on the Organization of Experience* (New York: Harper and Row, 1974); Jef Huysmans and Vicki Squire, "Migration and Security," in *The Routledge Handbook of Security Studies*, ed. Myriam Dunn Cavelty and Victor Mauer, 169–79 (London: Routledge, 2009).

4 Siobhan Brownlie, "Situating Discourse on Translation and Conflict," *Social Semiotics* 17, 2 (2007): 140.

5 Bogusia Temple, "Watch Your Tongue: Issues in Translation and Cross-Cultural Research," *Sociology* 31, 3 (1997): 607–18. This important methodological issue cannot be fully discussed here. In my own research, although I spoke fluent Bosnian/Croatian/Serbian, I offered interviewees a choice of language. All (apart from one interviewee in London) chose English, and the responsibility for translation therefore rested with them.

6 Robert D. Benford and David A. Snow, "Framing Processes and Social Movements: An Overview and Assessment," *Annual Review of Sociology* 26 (2000): 625; Pierre Bourdieu, "Rethinking the State: Genesis and Structure of the Bureaucratic Field," in *State/Culture: State Formation after the Cultural Turn*, ed. George Steinmetz, trans. Loic J.D. Wacquant and Samar Farage, 53–75 (Ithaca, NY: Cornell University Press, 1999).

7 Hilary Footitt and Michael Kelly, "Introduction," in *Languages at War: Policies and Practices of Language Contacts in Conflict*, ed. Hilary Footitt and Michael Kelly, 1–18 (Basingstoke: Palgrave Macmillan, 2012).

8 James Taylor, "Exhibiting the 'Foreign' in a National Museum: Imperial War Museum London and Languages at War," in *Languages and the Military: Alliances, Occupation and Peace-Building*, ed. Hilary Footitt and Michael Kelly (Basingstoke: Palgrave Macmillan, 2012), 227.

9 Taylor, "Exhibiting," 233.

10 Catherine Baker, *Sounds of the Borderland: Popular Music, War and Nationalism in Croatia since 1991* (Farnham: Ashgate, 2010).

11 See V.P. Gagnon, Jr., *The Myth of Ethnic War: Serbia and Croatia in the 1990s* (Ithaca, NY: Cornell University Press, 2004); Dubravka Žarkov, *The Body of War: Media, Ethnicity, and Gender in the Break-Up of Yugoslavia* (Durham, NC: Duke University Press, 2007).

12 Footitt and Kelly, "Introduction," 13.

13 Ibid., "Introduction."

14 Michael Kelly, "Issues in Institutional Language Policy: Lessons Learned from Peacekeeping in Bosnia-Herzegovina," *European Journal of Language Policy* 3, 1 (2011): 62–63.

15 Marilyn Collins and Robert Bloom, "The Role of Oral History in Accounting," *Accounting Auditing and Accountability Journal* 4, 4 (1991): 23–31.

16 Kelly, "Issues," 64.

17 I use the concept of "interview" and question the concept of "design" as the latter does not seem to adequately account for how questions are formed within an oral history interview. While I had developed question guides for each occupational profile I expected to encounter within the project (foreign military linguist, foreign military non-linguist, foreign

civilian linguist, local civilian linguist), after the interview phase of the project had begun I rarely referred to them. Despite beginning and ending interviews in a consistent way and using certain questions in every interview, posing other questions as responses to things mentioned in interviewees' narratives made questioning very emergent; occasionally I would even silence or postpone a key question in the interests of maintaining the frame that the speaker had constructed with me and encourage her or him to continue talking within it. Rather like Lipsky's "street-level" policy, made at the instant of the exercise of discretion, question framing is realized at the moment of the interviewer speaking, through the instantaneous exercise of judgment.

18 For a fuller discussion of these issues, see Catherine Baker, "Prosperity without Security: The Precarity of Interpreters in Postsocialist, Post-Conflict Bosnia-Herzegovina," *Slavic Review* 71, 4 (2012): 849–72.

19 Jan Nederveen Pieterse, "Sociology of Humanitarian Intervention: Bosnia, Rwanda and Somalia Compared," *International Political Science Review* 18, 1 (1997): 71.

20 Mel McNulty, "Media Ethnicization and the International Response to War and Genocide in Rwanda," in *The Media of Conflict: War Reporting and Representations of Ethnic Violence*, ed. Tim Allen and Jean Seaton, 268–86 (London: Zed, 1999), 274.

21 Simona Tobia and Catherine Baker, "Being an Interpreter in Conflict," in *Languages at War: Policies and Practices of Language Contacts in Conflict*, ed. Hilary Footitt and Michael Kelly (Basingstoke: Palgrave Macmillan, 2012), 217–19.

22 Louise Askew, "Did Serbo-Croat Die with Yugoslavia? A Different View of Language and Identity in Bosnia-Herzegovina," in *Languages and the Military: Alliances, Occupation and Peace-Building*, ed. Hilary Footitt and Michael Kelly, 217–26 (Basingstoke: Palgrave Macmillan, 2012).

23 See, for example, Joan Ringelheim, Arwen Donohue, Elizabeth Hedlund, and Amy Rubin, *Oral History Interview Guidelines* (Washington, DC: US Holocaust Memorial Museum, 2007).

24 Paula M. Pickering, "Generating Social Capital for Bridging Ethnic Divisions in the Balkans: The Case of Two Bosniak Cities," *Ethnic and Racial Studies* 29, 1 (2006): 79–103.

25 Inger Skjelsbaek, "Victim and Survivor: Narrated Social Identities of Women Who Experienced Rape during the War in Bosnia-Herzegovina," *Feminism and Psychology* 16, 4 (2006): 373–403.

26 Janine Natalya Clark, "Genocide, War Crimes and the Conflict in Bosnia: Understanding the Perpetrators," *Journal of Genocide Research* 11, 4 (2009): 421–45.

27 Anna Sheftel, "'Monument to the International Community, from the Grateful Citizens of Sarajevo': Dark Humour as Counter-Memory in Post-Conflict Bosnia-Herzegovina," *Memory Studies* 5, 2 (2012): 145–64.

28 Janine Natalya Clark, "From Negative to Positive Peace: The Case of Bosnia and Herzegovina," *Journal of Human Rights* 8, 4 (2009): 362.

29 All names used in this chapter are pseudonyms.

30 Interviewed by author, October 2009.

31 Ibid.

32 I owe the distinction between "thick" and "thin" reconciliation to Elissa Helms, "The Gender of Coffee: Women and Reconciliation Initiatives in Post-War Bosnia and Herzegovina," *Focaal* 57 (2010): 17–32.

33 Interviewed by author, May 2010.

34 Ibid.

35 Ibid.

36 Anders H. Stefansson, "Coffee after Cleansing? Co-Existence, Co-Operation, and Communication in Post-Conflict Bosnia and Herzegovina," *Focaal* 57 (2010): 66.

37 Interviewed by author, May 2010.

38 Ibid. See further discussion of this identity performance in Michael Kelly and Catherine Baker, *Interpreting the Peace: Peace Operations, Conflict and Language in Bosnia-Herzegovina* (Basingstoke: Palgrave Macmillan, in press), chap. 6.

39 IFOR stands for International Force (the name used for the multinational peace enforcement force between December 1995 and December 1996).

40 UNPROFOR stands for United Nations Protection Force (multinational peacekeeping force deployed 1992–95).

41 Interviewed by author, May 2010.

42 Ibid.

43 Like Elizabeth Dauphinée, I find myself in the ethically dubious position of obtaining professional advancement – in this case being able to conclude a conference paper and later a publication – off the back of a research participant pointing out a failure of mine. See Elizabeth Dauphinée, *The Ethics of Researching War: Looking for Bosnia* (Manchester: Manchester University Press, 2007), 1–18.

44 See Laura Anderson and Karen Gold, "'I Know What It Means but It's Not How I Feel': The Construction of Survivor Identity in Feminist Counselling Practice," *Women and Therapy* 15, 2 (1994): 5–17.

45 For a thoughtful analysis of "survivor" and "victim" positions in the narratives of Bosnian women who were raped during the conflict, see Skjelsbaek, "Victim and Survivor."

46 Julia Serano, *Whipping Girl: A Transsexual Woman on Sexism and the Scapegoating of Femininity* (Berkeley: Seal Press, 2007), 346–47.

47 Ibid., 359 (emphasis in original).

12 | Memories of Departures

Stories of Jews from Muslim Lands in Montreal

YOLANDE COHEN | MARTIN MESSIKA | SARA COHEN FOURNIER

> Yolande Cohen: We could start with, like we usually do: you could tell us where and when you were born, and a bit of the conditions of life in Algeria, and then we will talk about your departures. Maybe we can start like this if it works for you.
>
> Jean: Oh the "departures," that is quite a euphemism, eh...
>
> – Interview with Jean

An oral history interview involves an encounter between two individuals around a chosen theme. Interviewer and interviewee come together to address an idea. The encounter with this idea can either feel unexpected and give rise to conflict or it can feel normal and almost awaited. In the passage quoted above, Yolande Cohen starts by outlining for the interviewee the expected course of the interview. Jean's immediate reaction is to proclaim his own understanding of the word "departures." Reactions differ according to interviewees, to approaches, and/or to the collective frameworks that shape individuals' perspectives. Yet historical context provides us clues with which to probe various meanings associated with specific outcomes. In this context, Jean is a man in his sixties, reflecting on his life – a life that has led him to leave Algeria, the first of his many departures:

> JEAN: I left um... in secret, and [cough] without telling my neighbours. My parents told me: "And above all, you do not tell anyone, huh, you shut up... you shut up." I had a great friend, an old childhood friend, when I was young; his name was Boris, who lives in Haifa today, well in the suburbs of Haifa. My parents said: "Especially, do not tell Boris." So I didn't tell Boris, and it

> hurt so much to leave without saying goodbye. So I left ... I left like a thief my parents house. We lived in an alley, and my dad backed up the car just in front of the house, and when he arrived at the door [cough], he opened the trunk and said: "Get in." I got in the trunk and I did part of the trip in the trunk. When we were far enough, he opened the trunk, and I got out. He brought me to the airport.

Our questions, inserted within a whole spectrum of departures, reflect the plurality of voices present within a given community of Jews that once lived in Muslim Arab countries and that settled, sometimes temporarily, in Montreal. What are the circumstances that led Jean to feel that the word "departures" was inadequate to his experience? He reacted strongly to its use, showing us that, for him, "departure" meant expulsion, that it was an unpleasant expression. Interviewing Sephardic Jews living in Montreal raised the question of the memories of their departures and of the trauma surrounding them. However, not all narratives were embedded in trauma – on the contrary, many interviewees understood and presented their departures within a context of ease and simplicity. In this chapter we attempt to present the wide variety of perspectives on this massive migration out of Arab-Muslim countries.

We raise the question of how Sephardic Jews coming from Arab-Muslim countries depicted their own departure, which some considered to be a forced exile. What types of narratives did they use? Did they refer to a traumatic moment of their lives? Can we speak of individual resilience or of a collective denial of their particular history? How did they react to the idea of displacement? Indeed, in the present series of interviews and its corresponding methodology, the subjectivity of our informants lies as the centre of an evolving story with varying outcomes.[1]

I. The Research and the Methodology

Among the vast array of Sephardim living in Montreal, we collected data from individuals belonging to different ethno-national groups in order to explore the social memories of trauma and displacement by looking at individual experiences. Aimed at collecting memories of mass violence, the oral history interviews follow the Life Stories methodologies. The interviewees and interviewers explore the migrants' social world, which is embedded in the narration of stories pertaining to the interviewees' newly adopted country.

Within this framework it is easier to question the various aspects of the interviewees' migration within a post-Shoah, postcolonial context. Indeed, the Sephardic migrants' status as a religious minority in their home countries becomes a point of departure for the inquiry. We thus explored the possibilities and histories of "Sephardic Jews," the name given to our subgroup within the group working on the "Holocaust and other persecutions against Jews."

The life stories were collected among Jews who were born in Arab-Muslim countries and who settled in Montreal.[2] We conducted thirty-four interviews with fourteen women and twenty men. The average age of the interviewees was seventy. The majority (twenty-one) came from Morocco, six came from Egypt, three from Lebanon, two from Iraq, and one from Algeria. These interviews were collected in a shared authority perspective.[3]

Could the conditions for massive Sephardic migrations from Arab-Muslim countries be associated with "human rights violations" or with "displacements" (whether coerced or not)? These questions form the core of the present inquiry. The history of Sephardic/Oriental Jews raises a whole new set of substantive questions based on their departure from Arab-Muslim countries in the mid-twentieth century.[4]

Departure in a Postcolonial Context

The departure of most Jews from Arab-Muslim lands occurred suddenly and en masse. In the three decades following the Second World War, almost all Jews from Maghrib (North Africa) and Machrek (Middle East) were leaving countries in which they had been living for centuries. Mapping the specifics of this exodus has led to several findings.[5] However, the question remains as to how this displacement occurred and how the individual and collective stories of displacement contribute to the construction of a new set of narratives not only of Sephardic Jews who settled in Montreal,[6] but also of a Sephardic diaspora.[7]

Montreal is characterized by the presence of a vocal minority of Jews who migrated from North Africa and the Middle East during the period mentioned above. Their presence provides the incentive to further our understanding of their specific trajectories.[8] Furthermore, Montreal offers the ideal "neutral" space in which to analyze this group – a "third" place remote from the initial settings of both colonizer and colonized.

The history of the migration of Jews from the Arab-Muslim world has been at the centre of academic and political debate.[9] Adopting a global perspective, Shmuel Trigano distinguishes between countries where Jews were "excluded" (such as Morocco) and countries where they were "expelled" (such as Algeria, Egypt, Syria, and Iran).[10] Whereas Sami Chetrit considers the migration of North African Jews as a massive population displacement put together by Israeli Zionist organizations,[11] Trigano and Nathan Weinstock understand it against the backdrop of the ongoing humiliation attached to their status as "dhimmi"[12] – as members of a non-Muslim ethno-religious minority recognized as a legitimate religious community but, under Islamic law, subordinate to the Muslim majority.

Coerced or not, the departure of Jews from the Maghrib-Machrek occurred in a context of violence that differed from one country to another. The displacement of Jews from Egypt is especially striking.[13] Of the fifty thousand Jews living in Egypt before the Second World War, forty thousand left the country in 1956–57, and another five thousand departed by 1967. Many factors were at play in the disappearance of Egypt's Jewish community, and the stories collected outline the importance of the question of denaturalization. Jewish legal status moved in this direction as, between 1950 and 1956, new laws were applied to Jews, provoking their massive departure from Egypt. Those who did not hold dual citizenship with another country became stateless. Furthermore, the migration of Maghribi Jews took place after the violence of colonization and during the process of decolonization and of nation building. Of course this was of concern to everyone, not only the Jewish population. French colonization of the Maghrib in the nineteenth century (in the case of Morocco this occurred in 1912) came as a shock and was made possible by colonial wars.[14] Violence during the decolonization period is exemplified by the Algerian War (1954–62), but the political turmoil in Morocco (e.g., a coup against King Hassan II was first attempted in 1971) also provided a feeling of insecurity.[15] Beyond the situation of the Jews, which is generally put in perspective in the interviews, one must consider the general context of colonial and postcolonial violence within which their departure occurred.

Thus, our intention is to analyze how Jews recollected their departure from Arab-Muslim lands, an issue that is still fuelled by political and memory-related issues.[16] The use of oral history allows us to better understand the relationship between memory and the trauma of departure. It raises the question of the type of memories used to express the violence. Beyond testimony and trauma, we found collective and individual resilience: the interviewees recollect their migration and foster a reinterpretation of the past, both collectively and individually. The active memory of the Sephardic community has, since the migrants' arrival to Montreal, undergone a social transformation that has enabled them to better adhere to their new environment.[17] Our inquiry had opened up a new possibility to talk about a silenced history.

II. Analysis of the Interviews

Right from the start, reactions to the question of their displacement induced an interesting dialogue. The use of the terms "persecution" and "Holocaust" came as a shock to most of the people whom we wished to interview. Upon first contact, almost all of our interviewees insisted on questioning the title of our inquiry, "Life Stories of Montrealers Displaced by War, Genocides, and Other Human Rights Persecutions." "Why are we talking about genocide? That's not us." "We are not refugees, we paid for our own fare to come to Montreal." These were among the first comments we received. Both before and during the interviews we noticed a reticence to participate in the project, to reveal names, and to share certain stories. These reactions varied according to the interviewee's native country, but the emotions and fearful reactions played out on a spectrum of discomfort that evoked a collective silence. Perhaps, we thought, our interviewees did not see themselves as having been expelled or excluded from their own countries? But their emotional reactions and fear indicated otherwise. Our straightforward approach uncovered a whole new set of previously undisclosed feelings about their departures.[18]

In the midst of a massive displacement, during which almost all of the members of a group migrate, many individuals – but not the collectivity – might frame their departure as occurring within a forced setting.[19] This, of course, depends on many factors, including historical context, individual stories, collective perceptions, and shared memories. Within many narratives of the Sephardic community, the stoic bearing of a difficult departure is perceived as a powerful force sustaining continuity and coherence.[20] This is exemplified in some of the life stories below. The ability to be an agent of events rather than a victim legitimizes departure as a collective course of action.[21] This narrative enables departees to construct and reconstruct their history, and to show themselves as adaptable and malleable. However, on the other hand, it undermines certain emotions that have been collectively marginalized and that, for individuals, result in inner conflict. The excavation of these emotions, including frustration and residual fear, could allow a reconciliation between the individual's past and the group's history.

Comparing the migrations from Machrek with those from Maghrib sheds light on two types of displacement – coercive and non-coercive. In the case of Machrek, departure is perceived as coerced, as an expulsion. Strong emotions are still present in people's recollections of the events. The fear and angst expressed within the narratives reveal a sense of insecurity with regard to the present as well as a continuing anger towards the past – an anger that could adversely affect any possibility of reconciliation. Hence, it becomes essential to try to identify the factors that affect denial or forgetting. This is a central element in more than one-third of our interviews, with a majority of interviewees who came from Machrek, particularly those from Egypt or from Iraq, emphasizing the forced nature of their departure.

In the case of Morocco, departure is seen as non-coercive: interviewees refused to consider their departure as expulsion. During the pre-interviews, Moroccan interviewees were particularly reluctant to assent to the terminology of the project. They did not consider themselves as displaced "by war" or by "other violations of their rights." Some professed that their departure stemmed from their own will or was linked to something (perhaps familial or professional) that had no relationship to any form of state coercion. Indeed, the situation of Jews in Morocco was entirely different from that of Jews in Egypt. Moroccan independence in 1956 did not lead to discriminatory measures concerning Jewish Moroccan nationality.[22] Nevertheless, triggered by a feeling of insecurity, now well-documented by historians,[23] Jewish departure took place over four decades, beginning with a mass migration to Israel in 1948 and continuing through the 1970s and 1980s, when the last contingents arrived in Canada. In their stories, these people tend to emphasize their freedom to choose their destination, sometimes downplaying the violence of the environment from which they came. In this sense, the plurality of migratory trajectories is quite significant. Furthermore, because these patterns are perceived and presented as "natural," we wanted to find out more about the administrative procedures people had to undertake in order to migrate. In this way, we discovered that either the interviewees did not remember the administrative process involved in coming to Canada or, if they did, they saw it in a positive light. They associated this process with an ease seldom found in the bureaucracy of immigration, thus downplaying the fear of violence that was present in some of their narratives. Analyzing this lack of memory helps us to understand how events are shaped and lived by individuals before becoming historical facts. We now look more closely at these dichotomous narratives.

Trauma and Stories of Forced Migrations

One-third of our interviewees stressed the forced dimension of their departure. We grouped them in order to compare their portrayal of their departures. How were these departures represented in their narratives? Did these subjects consider themselves to be victims? In some cases, they refused victimization. In these cases, what were the elements that enabled them to refuse to be defined as victims? The consequences of forced departures have been analyzed in many studies.[24] These emphasize that forced departure tends to hurt individual development, to accentuate the loss of national identity and citizenship, and, thus, to provoke an internal schism, especially if expulsion occurs before adulthood.[25]

The interview process allowed our subjects to construct and reconstruct their history, but it stirred up emotions that had been ignored collectively. Emotions such as fear, anger, and sadness often emerged in our interviews with people who had been coerced into leaving their country, and fear was present even before the interviews began. For instance, six interviewees chose to remain anonymous.[26] While not all participants opted for confidentiality, seven did, and one person, for example, thought that revealing her/his name might cause retaliation on the part of the Moroccan government. She/he expressed concern that, if the interview fell into the hands of the "Moroccan Police," she/he would be denied entry back into Morocco.

The issue of fear was especially prevalent in the case of Gérard, who was interviewed in 2011.[27] He was born in Egypt and left for France in 1956 after having been expelled. He was a friend of one interviewer's parents and agreed to receive us for an interview. But he refused to sign the consent form, even with an anonymous status. The fact that the project was located within Concordia University increased his doubts. The presence of a strong pro-Palestinian movement at this university, as well as the events of 2002, during which Israeli Prime Minister Benjamin Netanyahu, after a hostile student demonstration, cancelled a speech he was invited to give on the campus, raised the fear that these interviews might "fall into the wrong hands." However, although Gérard did not trust the university, he was willing to share his story because he trusted the interviewers. Several other interviewees expressed the same misgivings.

Gérard's reluctance to participate in the project underlined the way he connected his past to his present preoccupations concerning the situation in the Middle East. This case raises interesting questions about oral history and the attitude of interviewers. What can they do in situations in which procedures meant to protect interviewees are not sufficient to overcome their apprehension? When compared with other working groups,[28] the number of anonymous in our group is high – (seven out of thirty-four), even though we conducted less than one-tenth of the interviews (thirty-four out of 472).

As well as fear, stories of interviewees who left their countries under duress were imbued with anger and sadness. Egyptian Jews expelled in 1956 often recounted their departure in detail. Maryse was born in Cairo and left Egypt with her family in 1956.[29] During the interview, she remembered very clearly when her parents were told that they had to leave. She recalled the "knocks on the door" that she heard before the officials entered the apartment. Gérard, as well, offered a very precise description of his last day in Egypt.

Robert was born in Alexandria, in post–Second World War Egypt.[30] He describes his departure as "a somewhat bitter pill ... an exodus from Egypt, Exodus Two as they say, the second exodus, extremely painful and distressing." Here he reconfigures the traditional image of the Exodus, celebrated during Passover, to describe his own experience. Robert left Egypt when he was seventeen years old under such violent circumstances that he cannot forgive his native country, even fifty years later. His father died a few years preceding the family's departure, a departure that was precipitated by the necessity of getting treatment for his mother's cancer, which was only available in France. When his family members requested permission from the government to leave, they had to wait an entire year for their papers. Robert's recollection of the situation is vivid:

> When we arrived at Cairo airport to leave, my mother had colon cancer, suffering greatly, was in a wheelchair, receiving three injections of morphine per day to control the pain. Well, these barbarians in costumes imposed a complete physical search, and

> I will not go into details. I heard her scream in pain as they made the search to verify if she hadn't hidden jewels in her body. This went against the idea of Egypt as a tolerant country. To persecute a widow afflicted with cancer.

His vivid memories were supplemented by fifty years of retrospection. Robert provided details of his own examination at the airport: "I, myself, was searched in a similar way, as well as my sister too ... so vexatious to the end." He started listing on his fingers: "They withdraw your citizenship, they give you a few dollars, and when you leave they brand you with this indelible memory of molestation with this search for jewelry and money." Showing his ring, he continued: "All they left me with was my Bar Mitzvah ring and that's it ... And bye-bye! We left with a deep disgust for the country where we had lived for centuries and where even our ancestors had been happy for a period."

He considered this treatment an offence to him and to his family, perpetuating as it did the state of disgrace in which the Jews existed, considered thieves of national property, spies working for Israel, or communists. Speaking of the departure of Jews from Egypt he said, "It was a beautiful system, well developed to get rid of its Jewish community and cause a maximum of damage without killing or assaulting people." He drew a parallel between his humiliating rejection by his former country and the loss of his mother, who died a year after their arrival in Paris.

These recollections developed into an obsession. His story is entrenched within memories that he deems "indelible." The Bar Mitzvah ring he wears daily symbolizes his lost youth, an object that links him to the past and crystallizes his sense of self within a context of unfinished forgiving.[31] Robert often mentioned his inability to make peace with his native country. In a sense, he seemed to cherish these difficult emotions as part of his identity. "I do not have fond memories of my homeland and I hate to say that I am 'Egyptian,'" he told us, miming the quotation marks with his hands as he pronounced "Egyptian." "I say that I am a Jew from Egypt, and that's all. I have not made peace with this country because this country has never apologized for what they did, what they did to my family. I do not intend to forget these abuses."

Upon being forced out of Egypt, Robert found himself in a liminal state. He was also frustrated by the non-responsiveness of international caring associations, such as the Red Cross. In France, he was treated as a refugee. In the interview, he reaffirmed: "there will be no peace until there is recognition from the Egyptian government of what happened, but I'm sure I will never see that day." As was often the case in the interviews, the Israeli-Palestinian conflict was also present in his testimony. After describing his departure, he stated: "And we ended up [...] the image on the other side of the problem of Palestinian refugees. Except that we picked up the pieces, restored our life and we tried to pursue a decent life without going to plant bombs left and right and kill people. So this is the story of Jews from Egypt."

Robert seemed to be looking for a sense of closure, a way for his past to be past and not remain a cloud hovering over him. Indeed, he stated during the interview: "the emotions are still here." And later, he said: "We must have been guilty somewhere for the simple fact of being Jewish at fifteen, sixteen." He did not feel capable of inserting the story of his departure into a broader perspective; indeed, he was still blaming himself. In effect, he had replaced other possible perspectives with anger and a complete rupture with his native country. He still hoped for some reconciliation, whereby the story of his stoically endured expulsion would be included in a more all-embracing, collective narrative. However, until this took place, he would continue to lack any personal and collective closure with regard to his past.

The violence of a departure shaped a discourse of trauma that was clearly evident in the interviews we conducted. In a post-Shoah era, when the experience of European Jews became the universal standard for collective trauma,[32] the space for the experience of Arab-Muslim Jews was relegated to the background. Indeed, their mass exodus was not comparable to the experience of European Jews. Thus, the victims of these events are compelled either to stay silent or to advocate for a position as "active players" in the collective memory. This was essentially the case for interviewees who were coerced into leaving Egypt, and Iraq.

From "Natural" Departures to Plural Trajectories

Discourses are plural and are linked to circumstances. Other interviewees, mostly those who came from Morocco, emphasized another dimension of the experience of departure. For them, rupture was felt not as a brutal rupture with their past lives but, rather, as a hazy memory in which they had adopted a diverse number of migratory paths. In these interviews, narratives were built on the decision to leave and were imbued with silence and reticence.

In many cases, narratives of departures of people from Moroccan origins were closely intertwined with work, study, or family necessities. Departees considered such departures as a "natural," neutral move. It appeared as though there were no specific alarming causes for their departure; or, if there were, they had been obliterated from their memory and thus from their narratives.

Arieh is an example of someone whose migratory path had many trajectories. He left Casablanca, Morocco, for Israel in 1969, when he was nineteen years old.[33] He arrived in Paris in 1972 and travelled in Europe before leaving for Montreal in 1974. Although he explained that he left for Israel because of his commitment to Zionism, he did not go into detail about his migratory experience. He indicated that, after being in the Israeli Army: "I turned [j'ai tourné], I ended up in England, and from there I went to Paris." He continued: "I was exploring, I did not know where I was going, I was a bit of a hippie." Going "on the road" at that time was not exceptional. In the 1960s, travelling after a stint in the army was common for young Israelis. However, Arieh's many trips must be put into perspective. He considered his departure from Morocco to be difficult because he had to leave his family behind. However, he had nothing to say about leaving the country itself. Arieh provided few details of his state of mind at the time he left Morocco.

This vagueness and a reticence to develop the details that led to departure were common among Moroccan interviewees.[34] Through their ability to "limit dialogue on specific matters" interviewees exercise their authority and shape their narratives.[35] Sometimes the boundaries between reticence and silence are not very clear. When we asked Arieh if he thought at the time he left that he would perhaps return to Morocco, he only answered, "No, I knew where I was going, even though I was very young, I did not want ... no, I was not quite into it [ça me disait rien]." And in fact, he did not return to Morocco, finally settling in Montreal.

For us, the fact that the interviewees did not want to develop the reasons that led them to leave was a challenge; however, this appears to be part of their narrative. As interviewers we had to engage in "deep listening" in order to delve further into these narratives without "plot." [36] Thus, the interviewees recounted their complex trajectories (Israel, France, Canada, and the United States) in ways that presented their migration as *normal*. They seemed to be in survival mode. The relationships they had with other members of their families were relegated to a secondary role and seemed unimportant, not worth recalling. They did not even tell us whether they discussed their decision to leave with their families. Thus, getting information on their decision to leave was difficult, and the overall impression was that of a quick departure, with no one really in charge of taking care of the details of the actual destination of the family migration.

Pierre, born in Casablanca in 1928, held a managerial position in a bank.[37] In April 1957, he left during the first wave of Moroccan migration to Canada. According to his narrative, he decided to leave Morocco when bank employees went on strike. He recalled an incident that triggered his decision to leave, telling the story of how he ran into his "Muslim best friend" on the way to his office and the conversation they had:

> "Pierre, are you not going on strike? – You know well that I have responsibilities. Well, if you are not afraid for your life, you should be for your daughter's" [...] I said, "Okay, thanks." I left, and I headed directly [to plan my immigration].

Pierre never felt any affiliation with the strikers. He considered his position to be higher than theirs, a position in which one works rather than goes on strike. He understood his conversation with a "Muslim" colleague as a veiled threat against him and his family. Already feeling displaced in his work environment, and though his words may be construed as his reacting as a manager, he interpreted the situation, rightfully or not, as an ethno-religious conflict ("I am threatened as a Jew, so I should leave, now"). However, he did not elaborate on the various aspects of the situation, and, a little while later in the interview, he presented his decision to leave in different terms: "I did not leave because I was scared; I left because I did not like to be told ... well ... I do not like what is mandatory." Pierre did not stress the verbal violence of his friend's words, nor did he express his own emotions. It is possible that he underestimated the danger of the conflict in which he nevertheless felt trapped. Pierre preferred to assert his autonomy. According to him, he was not forced to leave but, rather, decided that he *had* to go. Leaving was not linked to a feeling but to the application of a principle ("I do not like what is mandatory"). Violence, feelings, and fear were not the primary points of emphasis in his interview; on the contrary, he insisted on his ability to make a rational decision to leave, which he did without a second thought.

This "general atmosphere," in which Jews felt unwanted, induced our interviewees to leave Morocco. Paradoxically, if the decision was taken quickly, almost on the spur of the moment, bringing the immigration project to fruition could prove difficult. However, in the midst of the fierce political battles conducted by international Jewish organizations to "save the Jewish community of Morocco," many felt that they had to leave.[38] These experiences led the interviewees to undermine certain aspects of what happened, and this was a challenge for us as interviewers. Analyzing the concrete, administrative steps that had to be taken in order to migrate to Canada can help us to better understand the nature of their departure.

The "Ease" of Immigrating to Canada

Interviewees from Morocco emphasized neither being treated with violence nor the forced dimension of their departure. In these cases, subjects tended to consider migration as a rational decision. At different levels, interviewees stressed the fact that leaving was the result of their own decision and that they were not forced to leave, though at the same time they referred to violent events. But "planning to leave" and the act of "leaving" are very different steps, especially considering the material difficulty involved in getting a visa or a passport.

Interviews with Jews from Morocco would have us believe that getting to Canada was easy. Actually, this process was seldom present in their stories. This is understandable since the interviewees who left with their parents were not in charge of planning the departure. But how did it work for the adults? Viviane, who was married and had a child, arrived in Montreal in 1965.[39] She did not have a strong memory of the procedures her family had to go through to arrive in Canada: "My husband was in charge of it. It was not very difficult, even if it was a bit long, one year or two, but it was not very difficult. [. . .] I do not remember it as a handicap."

Other interviewees mentioned the names of two agencies: the Jewish Immigrant Aid Services (JIAS) and the Hebrew Immigrant Aid Society (HIAS). In their memories, these two associations were often confused. Whereas JIAS was a Canadian, Montreal-based, immigration agency,[40] United-HIAS-Service was a US Jewish organization that worked in Europe and in Morocco.[41] They worked together, but the interviewees were not interested in their specific fields of activity.

Pierre was proud to tell us that he knew an HIAS agent, S. Plasterek, who worked in Casablanca and who was in charge of immigration procedures. His account is more precise than Viviane's but remains ambiguous. The ease with which he obtained his immigration papers was surprising. After his altercation with his Muslim friend at the bank he

> went directly to JIAS [sic] [...] I told Mr. Plasterek, "I'm going to the United States." Mr. Plasterek answered: "You are going to wait a long time to go to the United States. Why don't you go to the anteroom of the United States, to Canada? With your skills, you will be able to enter immediately." I said, "Go on" [allez-y]. [...] Very soon after, he got me a visa.

The vagueness of these descriptions is quite striking. There is no mention of the many forms people had to gather in order to prepare their visa, nor of the role of Canadian immigration officials in this procedure. These descriptions evoke the image of immigration to Canada as being easy, a mere formality. Administrative procedures were imbued with a "magic" dimension.

Jewish organizations were instrumental in enabling Jews from Morocco to come to Canada. But what they saw as a mere formality involving just one person (the HIAS agent in Casablanca) was in reality a project that involved a transnational coalition of associations lobbying the Canadian government to include Jews from Morocco in a special category of immigrants. Our interviewees do not remember being in contact with a Canadian immigration official, but there was contact between them and Jewish agencies. The "ease" enshrined in their discourse does not mean that immigrating to Canada was easy but, rather, that the entire administrative/bureaucratic process, both in Morocco and in Canada, was dealt with by these particular agencies. The project implied strong networking within the state's agencies and staff as well as the ability to work discretely.

Here again, the victimization of the Jews, seen as a vulnerable population in need of rescue by international Jewish organizations, was absent from our informants' stories. Interviews conducted with Jews from Morocco contained no details of the procedures of immigration. If the issue of "papers" arose, it was generally in connection with the Moroccan administration. Little was said about Canadian officials since the Jewish agencies were the main contacts for prospective Moroccan immigrants.

Beyond this example of immigration procedure, the discrepancy between the accounts we receive from oral history interviews and those we receive from other historical sources is clear. The undervaluation of the role of Jewish organizations in this process is quite striking. At some point, subjects were willing to stress the fact that they chose to go to Canada, but they did not link their departure with the proactive roles of North American Jewish immigration agencies.

In the policies they carried out concerning North African Jewry, Jewish international organizations were concerned with the danger these populations faced were they to remain in their respective countries while Israel was at war.[42] At the basis of the deal between Jewish Canadian organizations and the federal government was the idea that North African and Moroccan Jewry were in danger and had to be "saved" by being accepted into Canada. With regard to the interviewees, their refusal to recognize the action of Canadian Jewish organizations (thus minimizing their debt to the mainly Ashkenazi Jewish establishment) in the immigration process conveyed the idea that they were not in need of being saved as they were not in danger. The "magic" process of getting a visa to Canada enabled them to refuse victimhood and to emphasize their freedom to choose their destination.

Conclusion

Stories of the departure of Jews from Maghrib and Machrek countries enshrined memories within a postcolonial context and also reflected contemporary preoccupations and fears. Departures shaped the way interviewees remembered ethnic and religious conflicts in their countries of birth. Some of them had very precise memories of violent events, while others remembered "small events," everyday life conflicts that had a particular value with regard to the way they remembered migration and resulted in their feeling that no future was possible in their homelands. The turmoil and sometimes the violence they experienced during the colonial period and after contributed to shape the way our interviewees apprehended their lives in their countries of birth.

The cases shared in this chapter stress the different departure experiences of Jews who left Arab-Muslim countries. Within various national contexts, these stories provide an idea of the process by which the issue of victimhood is reformulated. We saw that some interviewees expressed strong emotions when recounting the coerced dimension of their migration, while others emphasized the plurality of their migratory trajectories and were reticent about going into details. We can also say that the perceived "effortlessness" of their departure was linked to their desire not to be seen as victims and their desire to understand their migratory trajectories as a matter of choice rather than as an imposition. Whether facing deep political turmoil or being caught up in collective eagerness to leave, individuals from different national backgrounds reasserted their trajectories in strong, autonomous ways.

Furthermore, by comparing these stories with information derived from other sources, we can see how individual memory selects certain elements and participates in the building of a collective memory. These memories help the collectivity to forget the (traumatic) past and to give individuals the wherewithal to act when the situation becomes tense. This continuity reflects the biblical idea of the Exodus, with the narrative being episodic rather than comprehensive and sequential.[43] Hence, by leaving the memory of some aspects of their departure behind, interviewees attempted to construct memories with reference to a specific collective identity, which, in turn, contributed to the construction of the identity of the new diaspora. The resistance displayed by some individuals when confronted with the traumatic events in their lives reveals how much their identity is still associated with survival and dislocation.

Our research on Jews from Arab-Muslim lands living in Montreal reveals a comprehensive picture of their departures. Whether as the result of difficult political situations or through the invisible help of Jewish agencies, these stories are interwoven with the ability to adapt to new situations through departure and the ability of those who departed to reconstitute a collective identity in a diaspora. Through identifying with the ancient Sephardic diaspora, they connected themselves to a rich and venerable history of high culture and transnational networks.

Finally, the conflicting memories regarding whether migrations of Jewish populations from the Maghrib-Machrek were coerced or noncoerced, although largely connected to the specifics of national histories, are embedded within a larger conflict between the religious majority (Arab-Muslims) and the religious minority (the Jews), which came to a head with the Israeli-Palestinian conflict. The post-Shoah and postcolonial contexts have raised this issue to its most extreme level: Jews as the ultimate victim. Paradoxically, during much of the five decades since their first departure from Arab-Muslim countries, our interviewees wanted to erase this history and its image of victimization, replacing it with a plurality of stories typical of postcolonial, free-floating migrations. Others kept their stories to themselves, waiting for their former nations to publicly recognize what happened. In either case, interviewees did not compare themselves with Shoah survivors. Therefore, as it is difficult for them to consider themselves as victims, their stories fit better into a diaspora narrative of the postcolonial type – that of continuous migration. In effect, the departures of Maghribi Jews preceded the mass migration of Maghribi Muslims in the 1970s and thereafter (including those who migrated to Canada from 2000 until the present time).

Notes

We want to thank Steven High for his kind and steady support, and Hubert Villeneuve and Jared Conrad-Bradshaw, who had the difficult task of revising our English. Our thanks go also to Linda Guerry, Myriam Chebat, and Antoine Burgard for their contribution, dedication, and work on our research team.

1 The oral history method often involves a discrepancy between oral sources and social science interpretations of the same events. See Luisa Passerini, "Italian Working Class Culture between the Wars: Consensus to Fascism and Work Ideology," *International Journal of History* 8, 1 (1980): 4–28. Interviews are shaped by various factors, such as the individual being interviewed, the moment of the interview in time, and the direction given by the interviewer. The subjectivity and narrative forms of these sources allow us to analyze these testimonies within their "orality." The narratives are dependent upon the perception of the individual and the boundary between external events involving the group and the subjectivity of the individual's perception. See Alessandro Portelli, "What Makes Oral History Different," in *The Oral History Reader*, ed. Robert Perks and Alistair Thomson, 63–74 (London: Routledge, 2006).

2 We conducted these interviews with no time constraints or other constrictions. The interviewee was free to omit anything from the interview and, in fact, to terminate the interview at any moment. We located the interviewees through various social networks (friends, family, synagogue, holiday services, and word of mouth).

3 "What is most compelling about oral and public history is a capacity to redefine and redistribute intellectual authority, so that this might be shared more broadly in historical research and communication rather than continuing to serve as an instrument of power and hierarchy." See Michael Frisch, *A Shared Authority: Essays on the Craft and Meaning of Oral and Public History* (Albany: State University of New York, 1990), xx.

4 Emily Gottreich and Daniel J. Schroeter, eds., *Jewish Culture and Society in North Africa* (Bloomington: Indiana University Press, 2011); Frédéric Abécassis and Jean-François Faü, "Le monde musulman: Effacement des

communautés juives et nouvelles diasporas depuis 1945," in *Les Juifs dans l'Histoire*, ed. Antoine Germa, Benjamin Lellouch, and Evelyne Patlagean, 815–40 (Paris: Champ Vallon, 2011).

5 Norman M. Stillman, *The Jews of Arab Lands in Modern Times* (Philadelphia: Jewish Publication Society, 1991); Michael M. Laskier, *North African Jewry in the Twentieth Century: The Jews of Morocco, Tunisia and Algeria* (New York: New York University Press, 1994); Shmuel Trigano, ed., *Le monde sépharade* (Paris: Éd. du Seuil, 2006).

6 We use the term "Sephardi" when we are talking about the Sephardic community in Montreal as it is a generic term that was chosen by those Jews who arrived from Arab-Muslim countries. For a discussion of this choice, see Yolande Cohen, "Juifs au Maroc, Séfarades au Canada: Migrations et processus de construction identitaire," *Archives Juives* 43, 2 (2010): 132–44.

7 There is a growing interest in the subject of Sephardic migrations. See Devi Mays, "Playing with Peculiarity: Sephardic Migrations and the Ambiguity of National Identity" (PhD diss., Indiana University, 2012).

8 Jean-Claude Lasry and Claude Tapia, eds., *Les juifs du Maghreb* (Paris/Montréal: L'Harmattan/Les Presses Universitaires de Montréal, 1989); Marie Berdugo-Cohen, Yolande Cohen, and Joseph Lévy, *Juifs marocains à Montréal: Témoignages d'une immigration moderne* (Montréal: VLB, 1987); Norma Joseph, "From Baghdad to Montreal: Food, Gender and Identity in Two Scenarios," in *Migration, Communication and Home: Jewish Tradition, Change and Gender in a Global World*, ed. Tania Reytan-Marincheshka, 92–104 (Sofia: LIK Publishing House, 2011); Yolande Cohen and Linda Guerry, "Mariages et parcours migratoires: Juifs nés au Maroc et mariés à la Spanish and Portuguese Synagogue de Montréal (1969–1981)," *Studies in Religion/Etudes religieuses* 40, 2 (2011): 297–317.

9 Yaron Tsur, *A Torn Community: The Jews of Morocco and Nationalism, 1943–1954* (Tel-Aviv: Am Oved, 2001) (in Hebrew, English translation forthcoming, Stanford University Press); Yaron Tsur, "The Brief Career of Prosper Cohen: A Sectorial Analysis of the North African Jewish Leadership in the Early Years of Israeli Statehood," *Studies in Contemporary Jewry* 22 (2007): 67–72. Yigal Bin-Nun, "Psychosis or an Ability to Foresee the Future? The Contribution of the World Jewish Organizations to the Establishment of Rights for Jews in Independent Morocco, 1955–1961," *Revue Européenne d'Études Hébraïques* 10 (2004): 25–67; Yehouda Shenhav, "Modernity and the Hybridization of Nationalism and Religion: Zionism and the Jews of the Middle East," *Theory and Society* 36 (2007): 1–30.

10 Shmuel Trigano, *La fin du judaïsme en terres d'Islam* (Paris: Denoël, 2009), 9–47.

11 Sami S. Chetrit, *The Mizrahi Struggle in Israel: 1948–2003* (Hebrew) (Tel Aviv: Am-Oved/Ofakim Series, 2004).

12 Nathan Weinstock, *Une si longue présence: Comment le monde arabe a perdu ses Juifs, 1947–1967* (Paris: Plon, 2007).

13 Ruth Tolédano-Attias, "La dénaturalisation des Juifs d'Egypte," in *La fin du judaïsme en terres d'Islam*, ed. Shmuel Trigano, 51–87 (Paris: Denoël, 2009).

14 Daniel Rivet, *Le Maghreb à l'épreuve de la colonisation* (Paris: Hachettes Littératures, 2002).

15 Mohammed Harbi and Benjamin Stora, eds., *La guerre d'Algérie* (Paris: Robert Laffont, 2004); Michel Abitbol, *Histoire du Maroc* (Paris: Perrin, 2009).

16 Yolande Cohen, "The Migrations of Moroccan Jews to Montreal: Memory, (Oral) History and Historical Narrative," *Journal of Modern Jewish Studies* 10, 2 (2011): 245–62.

17 Jean-Luc Bédard, "Mouvances identitaires et restructuration de soi et des autres parmi des Judéo-marocains à Montréal," in *Identités sépharades et modernité*, ed. Jean-Claude Lasry, Joseph Lévy, and Yolande Cohen, 175–90 (Québec: Presses Université de Laval, 2007).

18 Trauma has evolved from "belonging to wounds or the cure of wounds" in the *Oxford English Dictionary* of 1656 to being the "emotional shock following a stressful event." While trauma has permeated the psychiatric field since the 1980s, with the insertion of a diagnostic of "post-traumatic stress disorder" in the *Diagnostic Statistical Manual*, Pierre Janet first observed traumatic memories at the beginning of the twentieth century as "unconscious fixed ideas" lingering in the personal narrative. See Pierre Janet, *Les Névroses* (Paris: Flammarion, 1909). Since then a number of studies have looked at the effects of memory on the physical manifestations of the past. See Marilyn Bowman, *Individual Differences in Posttraumatic Response: Problems with the Adversity-Distress Connection* (Mahwah, NJ: Lawrence Erlbaum Associates, 1997), 23; Richard J. McNally, "Conceptual Problems with the DSM-IV Criteria for Posttraumatic Stress Disorder," in *Posttraumatic Stress Disorder: Issues and Controversies*, ed. G.M. Rosen, 1–14 (Chichester, UK: John Wiley and Sons, 2008); Bessel van der Kolk, Lars Weisaeth, and Onno van der Hart, "History of Trauma in Psychiatry," in *Traumatic Stress: The Effects of Overwhelming Experience on Mind, Body, and Society*, 47–67 (New York: Guilford Press, 1996); Allan Young, "PTSD of the Virtual Kind: Trauma and Resilience in Post-9/11 America," in *Trauma and Memory: Reading, Healing, and Making Law*, ed. Austin Sarat, Nadav Davidovitch, and Michal Alberstein, 21–48 (Stanford, CA: Stanford University Press, 2006).

19 Salman Akhtar, "The Immigrant, the Exile, and the Experience of Nostalgia," *Journal of Applied Psychoanalytic Studies* 1, 2 (1999): 123–30.

20 Rivka Tuval-Mashiach, Sara Freedman, Neta Bargai, Rut Boker, Hilt Hadar, and Arieh Y. Shalev, "Coping with Trauma: Narrative and Cognitive Perspectives," *Psychiatry* 67, 3 (2004): 280–93.

21 Didier Fassin and Richard Retchman, *The Empire of Trauma: An Inquiry into the Condition of Victimhood* (Princeton: Princeton University Press, 2010).

22 Daniel Rivet, *Le Maghreb à l'épreuve de la colonisation* (Paris: Hachette Littératures, 2002).

23 Michel Abitbol, *Histoire du Maroc* (Paris: Perrin, 2009); Susan Gilson Miller, *A History of Modern Morocco* (Cambridge: Cambridge University Press, 2012).

24 Akhtar, "Immigrant."

25 Thien Nguyen Ba and Brigitte Malapert, "Conséquences psychologiques de la guerre et de la migration sur les enfants," in *Réfugiés, les traumatismes de l'exil: Le rôle humanitaire de la Croix-Rouge*, ed. Diana Miserez, 249–86 (Bruxelles: Bruilant, 1988).

26 According to the ethics procedures of the Montreal Life Story Project, each participant could decide that her/his interview be transcribed – with the video and audio material destroyed – and all elements enabling knowledge of her/his identity erased. Nevertheless, people who chose this option had to sign a paper attesting to their acceptance of the project.

27 Gérard did not agree to participate fully in the project and refused to sign the consent form. Nevertheless, he agreed to tell his story given the interviewer's word that he would remain anonymous. He was born in Alexandria in 1946 and he left Egypt to go to France in 1956. He then moved to Montreal.

28 In total, 472 people were interviewed in multi-session interviews conducted in French (202), English (187), Khmer (49), Kinyarwanda (19), Spanish (14), and Arabic (1). Only seventy-eight interviewees chose to place any restrictions on their interviews, with sixty-five limiting access (accessible only in archives, and a pseudonym must be used in quoting from the materials) and thirteen opting for full anonymity. See Steven High, *Oral History at the Crossroads: Sharing Life Stories of Survival and Displacement* (Vancouver: UBC Press, 2014).

29 The interviews were part of the Life Stories of Montrealers Displaced by War, Genocide, and Other Human Rights Violations project. Rules of ethics that the interviewers applied were those adopted by the project. The interviews were semi-structured and were, in most cases, conducted by two interviewers. According to the confidentiality rules of the project, we chose pseudonyms for interviewees who did not want to have their

names published. Maryse was born in Cairo (Egypt) in 1948. See interview with Sara Cohen Fournier/Martin Messika, Montreal, 2012.

30 Robert was born in 1946 in Alexandria. He moved to Cairo before leaving for France. See interview with Sara Cohen Fournier, Montreal, 2011.

31 Vamik D. Volkan, "After the Violence: The Internal World and Linking Objects of a Refugee Family," in *Analysts in the Trenches: Streets, Schools, War Zones*, ed. Bruce Sklarew, Stuart W. Twemlow, and Sallye M. Wilkinson, 77–102 (Hillside, NJ: Analytic Press, 2004).

32 Barbara Tint, "History, Memory, and Intractable Conflict," *Conflict Resolution Quarterly* 27, 3 (2010): 239–56.

33 Arieh was born in 1950 in Casablanca. He decided to leave for Israel with a group of young students in 1969. In 1972 he arrived in Paris, where he had different jobs. He arrived in Montreal in 1974. See interview with Martin Messika/Ruxandra Petrinca, Montreal, November 2012.

34 Lenore Layman, "Reticence in Oral History Interviews," *Oral History Review* 36, 2 (2009): 207–30.

35 Ibid., 210.

36 Anna Sheftel and Stacey Zembrzycki, "Only Human: A Reflection on the Ethical and Methodological Challenges of Working with 'Difficult' Stories," *Oral History Review* 37, 2 (2010): 191–214.

37 Pierre was born in 1928 in Casablanca. He left Morocco to come to Canada in April 1957 with his wife and his child. He first arrived in Toronto but quickly went to Montreal. He started working in a bank. See interview with Martin Messika, Montreal, November 2011.

38 Bin-Nun, "Psychosis."

39 Viviane was born in 1942 in Casablanca into a family of three girls and three boys. She left Casablanca with her husband and her child in 1963. See interview with Martin Messika/Claudia Itzkowich, Montreal, November 2012.

40 Joseph Kage, *With Faith and Thanksgiving: The Story of Two Hundred Years of Jewish Immigration and Immigrant Aid Effort in Canada, 1760–1960* (Montreal: Eagle Publishing, 1962).

41 Ronald Sanders, *Shores of Refuges: A Hundred Years of Jewish Emigration* (New York: Holt, 1988).

42 Bin-Nun, "Psychosis."

43 Nahum M. Sarna, *The JPS Torah Commentary Exodus* (Philadelphia: Jewish Publication Society, 1989).

13 | Finding Meaning in Oral History Sources through Storytelling and Religion

MARIE A. PELLETIER

> I once had eleven brothers and sisters. And in 1975, ten were already married and [...] had forty-one children. On April 17, 1975, all sixty-two plus my mother, that means sixty-three [...] leave Phnom Penh together and after our return [...] after the fall of Pol Pot, among the sixty-three, there were twelve survivors.
>
> – Ven Runnath[1]

When Ven Runnath, a seventy-three-year-old Cambodian refugee, told this story, we were in her daughter's living room in Lasalle, Quebec. She was just beginning to recount her life story. From this opening statement, I could already see that what Ven was recounting was a story of great loss and miraculous survival. I met Ven in the fall of 2009 in the course of my research with the CURA Life Stories project.[2] Between then and August 2010, we had three interview sessions together, for a total of nine hours of interview. Much of her life story revolved around her experience under the Khmer Rouge regime and the impact of this violent time on her life. Throughout her interviews, religious beliefs had a profound influence on the framing of her life story: a devout Buddhist from a very young age, Ven converted to Christianity in 1985.

In themselves, the events of Ven's life are of great historical interest. What she recounts – from her memories of Cambodia before the Khmer Rouge, to her experiences under Pol Pot's regime, to her life as a refugee, to her migration to Canada – provides a variety of personal narratives revolving around historically significant times. However, her life story interview is much more than a simple retelling of events. Along with providing an eyewitness testimony to a genocide, her life story is, before anything else, a story. According to Portelli, through the act of storytelling interviewees "tell us less about *events* than about their *meanings*."[3] More than the number of relatives who fell victim to the Khmer Rouge, what makes Ven's opening story interesting is the importance it holds for her (it is central to her life) and the manner in which she conveys that importance.

Like storytelling, a person's religious framework provides tools to explain, not simply to reflect upon, disparate events and to create links between them throughout one's life. As Clifford Geertz defines it, religion is

> a system of symbols which acts to [...] establish powerful, pervasive and long-lasting moods and motivations in men by [...] formulating conceptions of a general order of existence and [...] clothing these conceptions with such aura of factuality that [...] the moods and motivations seem uniquely realistic.[4]

According to this definition, religion stands above everyday knowledge and experience and can therefore shape the way people perceive and explain their lives.

In the face of genocide, the idea of making sense of events through storytelling is made particularly challenging by overwhelming violence. Michael Jackson argues for viewing storytelling as "a vital human strategy for sustaining a sense of agency in the face of disempowering circumstances."[5] For survivors of genocide, however, finding the words that will properly communicate their experience may be difficult. As Henry Greenspan found in his work with Holocaust survivors, "to recount the Holocaust means most essentially, to try to employ the terms of one world (the world survivors share with all of us) to describe the terms and negation of terms of the other. It is always a translation, and it is always ultimately futile."[6] Whether successful or not, however, efforts at storytelling reflect the individual's attempt to make sense of events and to integrate them into her/his life stories.

In this chapter, I argue that, if oral history analysis goes beyond observing *what* people recount to scrutinize *how* they recount it, we may arrive at a deeper understanding of the subjective experience of interviewees. In this context, religion can provide a uniquely useful window into the meaning interviewees give to events by providing a framework through which they try to explain all aspects of life. When an interviewee's life story must integrate and explain the experience of genocide, a religious framework (assuming there is one) can draw attention to how she/he makes sense of these violent experiences as well as to how these experiences challenge her/his worldview. Thus, we can move beyond treating survivors' life stories only as testimonies to genocide and also look at what they tell us about how survivors experienced and remembered violent events.

The Interview

In his seminal book on oral history, Alessandro Portelli posits that one of the characteristics differentiating oral sources from other historical documents is that it is "always the result of a relationship, of a shared project in which both the interviewer and interviewee are involved together."[7] This feature of oral history adds a layer of complexity to the truism that historical sources are shaped by – and are a reflection of – the context within which they were created. While not meant as a representative sample of the Khmer refugee community in Montreal, Ven Runnath's life story came from a particular social context and she was interviewed for a specific purpose. This context is crucial to understanding her life story.

I interviewed Ven as part of the CURA Life Stories project, whose goal was to collect interviews with Montrealers who had been displaced by war, genocide, or other human rights violations.[8] The project's approach to oral history was based on in-depth interviewing and community involvement. The CURA project was divided into six working groups: Holocaust, education, Haiti, Great Lakes Region (with an emphasis on Rwanda), Cambodia, and oral history performance. All working groups included both university and community partners, but the Cambodian working group had a particularly strong level of community involvement: the role of university researchers – both students and professors – was limited. Most interviews were conducted by members of the Cambodian community, and the activities of the group were shaped by the needs of that community.

The emphasis on in-depth life stories in the CURA project was inspired by Greenspan's work with Holocaust survivors. He declares that a "good interview is a process in which two people work hard to understand the views and experiences of one person: the interviewee."[9] In the CURA project, the phrase "life story interview" is meant to emphasize the idea that interviews with survivors of genocide should not ask only about the interviewee's life under a genocidal regime but should also be open to recording everything that survivor wants to share.

All the interviewees in the Cambodian working group experienced, or were affected by, the Khmer Rouge regime, which ruled Cambodia from 1975 to 1979. At the beginning of its regime, the Khmer Rouge troops evacuated the population of Phnom Penh to the countryside. In the following years, they enforced a strict policy of coerced communal labour and radical communism. The deteriorating living conditions, which resulted in famine and disease, coupled with the systematic execution of former government workers, soldiers, intellectuals, and others considered as enemies, led to the death of over 1.5 million individuals.[10] During these years, many of the social and cultural institutions of Cambodia – including those related to religion, family, and education – were forcibly removed from everyday life. In 1979, Vietnamese forces defeated the Khmer Rouge, but Cambodia's recovery was a long way away. A large number of Cambodians fled to refugee camps in Thailand and Vietnam, and many migrated to Europe, North America, and other regions.

Montreal, with over eight thousand Cambodians, has one of the largest concentrations of Cambodians in Canada.[11] Most of these refugees arrived in Canada between 1978 and the early 1980s, escaping the Khmer Rouge regime and its aftermath or joining family members already in Canada.[12] This refugee population faced a double shock: the impact of the genocide and the need to adapt to a new country.[13] Furthermore, many of the depositories of cultural memory (the elderly, the educated population, and religious institutions) had been destroyed during the genocide, making cultural transmission that much more difficult.[14]

The interviews in the Cambodian working group's collection spanned a wide spectrum of the Cambodian community in Montreal. Most interviewees were middle-aged or senior citizens, and a few were young adults. When I joined the Cambodian working group in 2009, I sought interviewees who were particularly interested in sharing their religious beliefs.

Ven Runnath was referred to me by her daughter Ravann, herself a member of the Cambodian working group. Ven had formerly been a practising Buddhist and was now a devout Christian, and she felt that religion was a very important part of her life story. I listened carefully to the other interviews collected by the Cambodian working group but found that few interviewees spoke openly about religion. This might have been due to their feeling that religious beliefs were too personal to share publicly, to the fact that religion was not important to them, or to the assumption that their interviewers – usually fellow Cambodians – shared their religious outlook and did not need to have it explained to them. Although other interviews provided some extremely interesting stories, I decided to focus my work on Ven Runnath's story in order to put the emphasis on depth of analysis.

I first met Ven Runnath for a pre-interview meeting in mid-October 2009. Our first interview session was held on 27 October and the second session one week later. Our last session came in August 2010, after Ven returned from Cambodia after spending the winter there. We conducted the interviews in Ravann's living room, with Paul Tom acting as my videographer for the first two sessions. In total, we recorded nine hours of interview. Ven usually spoke in English, but many passages from her interview were in French.

Ven recounted her life mostly in chronological order, from her childhood in Phnom Penh to her current life in Canada. Of particular importance in her story was the period of the Khmer Rouge. She described in great detail the difficulties she faced during those years of forced labour and often mentioned the pain of being separated from her family. The Democratic Kampuchea years were also a time of danger, when she felt constantly threatened. She knew she needed to work hard and to keep quiet in order to avoid the threat of execution. She nevertheless often found herself in imminent danger and was seemingly miraculously saved from death. Her faith was always crucial to her, but it was deeply shaken by her suffering during the years of the Khmer Rouge. Her subsequent conversion to Christianity coloured her entire life story, including her explanation of events that preceded it.

Giving Meaning to Events

Viewed as a whole, the life story interview with Ven Runnath tells a tale of survival, crisis of faith, and a new life in Canada. As a linguistic unit, it is a complex narrative with many intermingling stories. More than a simple retelling of events, the stories told by Ven assign meanings to the events of her life. Stories "often contain a message that the narrator wishes to communicate to a wider audience – a message that is moral rather than empirical."[15] For this reason, a deep analysis of how people tell and organize their stories can help us uncover both the role of religion in the life story of interviewees and how people make sense of their lives. If storytelling is an act of giving meaning to events, then how people tell stories can be crucial to an analysis of oral history.

Regarding the link between stories and events, Hayden White writes that, "in historical discourse, the narrative serves to transform into a story a list of historical events that would otherwise be only a chronicle."[16] Interviewees, if considered as historians of their own lives,[17] do the same thing. In his statement, White makes a distinction between events and narratives: events are what actually happened, and the historical narrative arranges these events into a story.[18] He further argues that the narrative form of historical discourse is not an empty vessel through which information about events is conveyed but, rather, a tool that adds information. In fact, he asserts that the narrative form "already possesses content prior to any given actualization of it in speech or writing."[19] He refers to this process as "explanation by employment," by which "the historian arranges the events in the chronicle into a hierarchy of significance by assigning events different functions as story elements in such a way as to disclose the formal coherence of a whole set of events considered as a comprehensible process with a discernible beginning, middle, and end."[20]

My analysis of life story interviews is, therefore, based on the idea that, as Michael Bamberg argues, "narrative is the ordering principle that gives meaning to an otherwise meaningless life."[21] The act of telling a story about one's life takes events and organizes them into a plot in order to underline the meaning assigned to them. Jackson goes further, explaining that it is not enough to say that stories give meaning to events "if by 'meaning' we imply an intellectual grasp of events. For storytelling does not necessarily help us understand the world conceptually or cognitively; rather, it seems to work at a 'protolinguistic' level, changing our *experience* of events that have befallen us by symbolically restructuring them."[22] In this way, storytelling becomes a part of life itself, and, by looking at the stories told during an oral history interview, one can learn not only about past events but also about how these are meaningfully incorporated into the interviewee's ongoing life.

During my first interview session with Ven Runnath, as she was in the process of recounting her life during the first few years of the Khmer Rouge era and expressing how difficult things were for her, she linked the latter to earlier events:

> At night, my tears came because as many people know ... I was very good. I helped the poor, sometimes, someone sick ... I pay for the hospital ... you know ... I tried to be good. But during Pol Pot's time, the people I used to help made worst to me. The poor become chief, the people who have no knowledge become chief.[23]

I would argue that this story concerns what Ven perceived to be the failure of karma. Although she does not use the word "karma," she expresses the expectation that good actions will lead to good results. In other words, she expected that her lifetime of generosity would lead to positive results, and she felt betrayed when it did not.

Her explanation that her life was made difficult by the very same people whom she had tried to help flavours her story with tragic irony.[24] Ven chose to tell her story in this way in order to express the meaning she attributed to the events she had experienced. As White argues, "the best grounds for choosing one perspective on history rather than another are ultimately aesthetic or moral rather than epistemological."[25] Ven told this story in this particular way due to her own perception of the significance of the events rather than because they were inherently tragic or ironic.[26] She used this particular frame to tell the story because it enabled her to emphasize the difficulties she was facing; and, by linking these difficulties to her earlier attempts to gather good karma, she seemed to be preparing the way for her later rejection of Buddhism in favour of Christianity.

In this story, religion provides the standard by which to define the moral meaning of events. It was Ven's belief in Christianity and her rejection of Buddhism that defined the relationship between the events in her story. Through storytelling, she established a moral order that gave sense to her life. As Robert Orsi defines them, religions are not sets of beliefs that individuals accept as they are; rather, they

> provide men and women with existential vocabularies with which they may construe fundamental matters, such as the [...] sources of joy, the borders of acceptable reality, the nature of human destiny [...] It is through these various religious idioms that the necessary material realities of existence – pain, death, hunger, sexuality – are experienced, transformed, and endured, for better or worse.[27]

Through this vocabulary of religious idioms, individuals are often able to make sense of their lives and to create stories that render events meaningful. In Ven's story, the idioms of Buddhism provide the basis for the tragic irony of her suffering under the Khmer Rouge.

Giving Meaning to Life Stories

In his oral history work, Daniel James finds that the construction of a life story that can stand as a whole, coherent unit is of great importance for its narrator: "The wider life story must succeed not only in terms of meeting certain social criteria but in terms ultimately of cohering for the narrator herself. The process of achieving personal coherence, of staving off epistemological crisis, is nearly always far more complex than analysis of a single story would indicate."[28] Although much can be discovered from the analysis of individual stories, our understanding of oral history sources would be limited without a consideration of whole life stories. This analysis enables us to see how isolated events in one's life are linked through storytelling. Going beyond the meaning of specific life events, oral history can further our understanding of how individuals perceive the meaning of their entire lives. Through this analysis, we can observe the narrative tools used to create links within the events of a life story and to create coherence. Like religion, which permeates all aspects of life to explain and give meaning to all things, the coherent life story is the product of an act of synthesis: it integrates all aspects of one's life and leaves no significant event unexplained. Although never perfectly achieved, this goal is apparent in interviewees' efforts to create coherence among the disparate events of their life stories.

One such tool is the "coherence system," which Charlotte Linde defines as a "system that claims to provide a means for understanding, evaluating, and constructing accounts of experience."[29] A set of religious beliefs can function as one such coherence system by purporting to make sense of all aspects of life.

In many of the stories drawn from Ven Runnath's life story, she used her current belief system as a way of establishing coherence. In these stories she did not attribute her survival to her own agency (except sometimes through prayer or wish) or to random luck but, rather, to a Christian god. As she recounted events that occurred near the end of the Khmer Rouge era, when she was heading back to Phnom Penh with her family, she said of one particular instance of seemingly miraculous survival: "God saved me." At that point in the interview, I pointed out that she was not a Christian at the time, to which she answered: "That's right [...] I did not know it yet, but God saved me."[30] Clearly, the meaning that she assigned to this story came long after the story itself had ended. It is apparent that the formation of Ven's life story involved an ongoing process through which she assigned meaning to various events in her life in order to create overall cohesion. Particularly influential in this process was her adoption of a new system of belief as this provided her with an explanation of her life that she was able to accept. Rather than having to live with the failure of her past beliefs, she can now tell the story of how God saved her from difficult circumstances.

In another example of how she used Christianity as an interpretive framework, Ven referred to an isolated incident to make a point about wider themes within her whole life story. Here, she recounts how her difficulties under the Khmer Rouge drove her to try to end her life:

> So all the time I want to suicide, but not alone ... If I die, I like that all my children will die all together ... Because if one of my children still alive, he will be slave to the other. And I don't want that my children be slave to the other. If they still alive, I have to be alive ... to take care of them. And while people told me don't go near that very high tree because a very famous witch is there. Oh, I was very happy because I have a way to die all together. So, I cut trees to build a house near that big tree. And people, "No, not to go." ... I pretend not to know anything about the witch. I pretend not to know.
>
> So I go to build a house ... at last, some people say, "You know, that big tree, the witch of that big tree is very infamous. You will die all together." It's my main purpose [laugh] but I pretend not to know about that and I say, "I don't believe at all." But really I believe ...
>
> After I see that no one near my house, I try to talk with the witch. I say, "Oh witch, everyone told me you are very famous. Me too. I agree. So, now, I give the life of all my family. Take all. But one condition: no one left. If one left, you could not take. If you want to take, all. Me, my husband, all my children. Okay? No one left ... when we sleep take all our soul. Don't let us ... have pain."
>
> Then, after a few days, not the witch of the Indian witch who came ... they came in my own eye. I still awake ... one man, dressed in white and with a white scarf and with a walk stick, he came in front of me. My eyes were still open and he talked

> with me in the language of a king. He said, "Daughter, you want to die. Now have patience. It's not like this forever. And not only you. The whole country ... be patient. You have to be back to your own natal village in three years, ten months and seven days. You will be back to your own natal village."[31]

Later, during my interview with her, she mentioned that the man who had appeared to her was, in her opinion, Jesus Christ. Based on its structure, I believe that this story can be considered as a subset of Ven's overall life story: she tried to use her old beliefs to her "advantage" when faced with difficult circumstances, and when this attempt failed, she was saved by something that, at the time, she did not fully understand.[32]

While the failure of her attempt to bargain with the famous witch can be linked to her later rejection of her old belief system, being saved by a mysterious prophecy (defined later as a Christian prophecy) provided the lead-in to her eventual adoption of a new belief system. This story therefore stands for more than the events it recounts: it is a subset of an important aspect of Ven's life. By linking these events with the overarching theme in her life – her rejection of Buddhism and conversion to Christianity – Ven created a link between this particular story and her life story, thus confirming the coherence of her religious evolution.

Storytelling in a Historical Context

Although the process of life story interviewing is always geared towards the individual subjective experience, the social aspect of the life story interview is ever present. As Mary Jo Maynes, Jennifer Pierce, and Barbara Laslett argue in their work about the role of life stories in social sciences and history: "These stories [...] are individual creations but never simply individual creations; they are told in historically specific times and place and draw on the rules and models and other narratives in circulation that govern how story elements link together in a temporal logic."[33] This is precisely why life story interviews are uniquely useful to historical research: they allow us to glance at the link between the individual and the social.

Paul Ricoeur argues that the process of narrating is also a process of placing oneself in time. According to him, "Time becomes human time to the extent that it is organized after the manner of a narrative; a narrative, in turn, is meaningful to the extent that it portrays the features of temporal experience."[34] More than creating a personal timeline, the narratives of oral history interviewees deal with public time:

> The time of narrative is public time, but not in the sense of ordinary time, indifferent to human beings, to their acting and their suffering. Narrative time is public time in the same sense that within-time-ness is, before it is levelled by ordinary time. Moreover, the art of storytelling retains this public character of time while keeping it from falling into anonymity. It does so, first, as time common to the actors, as time is woven in common by their interaction.[35]

When telling their life stories, therefore, individuals place themselves and the events of their lives on a public timeline rather than on a purely personal one. When we look at how individuals locate themselves in time through narrative, we should not consider time only in its abstract form, where, as Chakrabarty says of historical time, "events happen in time but time is not affected by them."[36] What a personal narrative does is locate individuals in their own experience of time, what Ricoeur refers to as within-time-ness.

This experience of time is especially visible in narrative as it intersects, sometimes simultaneously, with a historical timeline, cultural time markers, and definitive events in the life story. For instance, when she was asked about the evacuation of Phnom Penh in 1975, Ven Runnath situated the event in time in more than one way:

> In 1975, on April 17, it is still Cambodian New Year. So starting on April 13 we were all at home ...After leaving the house, there were crowds ... For an hour we could not walk more than a few metres because all the inhabitants have to leave together ... But we could not go back.[37]

After taking a few minutes to explain the evacuation, she changed the subject:

> I forgot to tell you ... my dad passed away three weeks before the fall of Phnom Penh ... It's a miracle ... My dad helped many people [one week] before he passed away ... He told me that in a week, he will die. I cry, because he loved me the best. He told only me, and he said, "I pray I don't want to see a hard situation. To live in a hard situation." And really, in seven days, he passed

> away. And, so we, for the funeral ceremony [for one week] ...
> And two weeks later, the fall of Phnom Penh.[38]

In this narrative, the events of the fall of Phnom Penh – a defining moment in Cambodian history – are located in a personal timeline (three weeks after the death of her father) and in relation to cultural events (during the New Year festival) as well as in a historical timeline. It is the intersection of the personal experience with the historical/cultural events experienced by the whole country that creates public time in the personal narrative. As Maynes et al. argue, "Historical time contextualizes a life course, even while the narrator's moment in the life course affects how he or she experiences, remembers, and interprets historical events."[39]

A common question in oral history research is: "Where were you when X happened?" This can lead not only to locating the individual within a larger historical event but also to locating this event within an experience of time and events that is deeply personal. As Jackson argues, storytelling gives the narrator some agency: "Storytelling gives us a sense that though we do not exactly determine the course of our lives we at least have a hand in defining their meaning."[40] This agency comes not only from retrospectively redefining the events of one's life but also from locating historical events – those often perceived as beyond personal influence – in a narrative based on one's subjective experience of time.

Although historical time is usually seen as linear, universal, and independent of our subjective experience of it, through storytelling, individuals may modify their timeline to better reflect their own experience. For instance, stories involving premonitions may create a situation in which the future is present in the recounted events. For instance, as Ven Runnath talked about her early encounter with the Khmer Rouge regime, at a time when she was being evacuated from Phnom Penh and was unaware of the difficulties ahead, she told a story about being escorted, along with her family, by Khmer Rouge soldiers:

> [Khmer Rouge soldiers] let us go to live in a Pagoda ... during then ... we were Buddhist ... it's a chance to live in a Pagoda ... But really that Pagoda was a prison. We didn't know that it's a prison ... They order us to go to work. But once, I was in the other room I saw like blood at the door – I saw blood, so tried

> to go to see near and there was ... writing in Cambodian with blood [tries to find the translation] ... suffering ... the worst ... and then I wonder why this is blood ... and "the most suffering, Oh God" it's "hell on earth."
>
> At night, the relation of my husband brought something to let us eat. I remember ... they said that you have to do what they order. Don't go away even one step more than they order. And they say that, don't talk.[41]

These events illustrate not only Ven's experience at the pagoda but also the first signs of the difficulties to come. The full significance of the writing on the door – here translated as "hell on earth" – and the seriousness of the warning she received was only known to her later. This story was made significant by future events and, therefore, shows how Ven manipulated the historical timeline to reflect her experience of the recounted events.

The historical timeline is not simply a blank slate on which interviewees write the story of their lives; rather, the events of history and individuals' roles in them have an influence on the stories told. As Greenspan found, the historical events of the Holocaust affected survivors' narratives; similarly, the quest for coherence and identity in a life story is affected by the nature of the events lived.

Another way in which violent events such as those perpetrated under the Khmer Rouge regime can influence a personal narrative is by turning a life story into a story of disruption. Disruption is characterized by the break it creates in one's projected life: "When expectations about the course of life are not met, people experience inner chaos and disruption. Such disruptions represent loss of the future. Restoring order to life necessitates reworking understandings of the self and the world, redefining the disruption and life itself."[42] More than simply recounting where they were and what they did during these difficult years, interviewees frequently spoke of the impact these events had on their lives, how they disrupted the flow of events that *should* have happened.

In her story of her life under the Khmer Rouge, for example, Ven Runnath explained how the unfolding of the projects she had planned for her family was pre-empted:

> I tried to save money to build villa – big, big villa – so that my children – I planned to have each one one villa. All my children. And I have enough money to let them go to learn abroad, to

> France, to USA. I have enough money ... So I hope that my children will have good knowledge, will be in high rank in the government ... But now, we were in the field and not as good as them ... not enough to eat.[43]

This, again, illustrates the distinction that needs to be made between the "objective" historical timeline and the manner in which individuals experience time and convey it through their life stories. Although survivors may tell their stories in a fairly chronological order, their experience of the Khmer Rouge era as a disruption illustrates that, before this era occurred, they had had an idea of how their lives should unfold. The future, although it may not have been clearly defined, was supposed to follow a certain path, to fall within certain parameters: "People expect stories to have a beginning, a middle and an end; and, in their telling, stories, even when incomplete, anticipate subsequent phases."[44]

Religions often provide the parameters for what ought to happen. For instance, when Ven indicated dismay at the failure of karma to reward her for her past generosity, it was the promise of a predictable future that had been denied her, and she experienced this denial as a betrayal. Similarly, with regard to the difficulty of explaining the Holocaust through religion, Ricoeur explains:

> Should we go so far as to say that unjust suffering is a scandal only for those who expect from God that God be only the source of all good? In this sense, it is the very faith in God that generates indignation. Consequently, it is in spite of evil that we believe in God, rather than we believe in God in order to explain evil. Evil – and by evil I mean exactly unjust, undeserved suffering – remains what is and ought not to be. And what says that it ought not to be, if not the Torah?[45]

Like many survivors of the Holocaust, many survivors of the Cambodian genocide speak of "unjust, undeserved suffering," which they struggle to explain in the face of a religion that, according to the laws of karma, defines suffering as being deserved. It was difficult for people to believe that they had accumulated so much bad karma, even if they allowed for karmic causes to extend into previous lifetimes. The narratives of genocide survivors thus retell not only the timeline of events that happened but also the projected future timeline, which was betrayed by what happened and the gap between it and what ought to have happened.

The subjective experience of time portrayed in Ven Runnath's life story narrative is not limited to placing the events of her life on a timeline. In such narratives consideration for what happened exists alongside what could or should have happened and what would happen in the future. Asking people to tell their stories from beginning to end may create an expectation of linearity for both speaker and listener, but deviations from this are frequent and often telling. When people tell the stories of their lives, they do not retell events in a manner that fits with objective time; rather, what they retell are their subjective experiences of time and events and the manner in which their lives intersected with historical circumstances.

Conclusion

When defining the relationship between oral history sources and historical knowledge, James rejects the idea of treating his interviewee, Doña María, only as a source of historical information: "One reason for the problems, the limit confronted in using this narrative primarily as a source of empirical knowledge, is that it involves a largely passive role for Doña María, as simply a repository of more or less coherent, more or less available, historical data."[46] To mine oral history interviews for historical information is to ignore the agency of interviewees in reflecting their own subjective experience in their retelling of events. Similarly, Portelli argues: "Oral sources [...] become unique and necessary because of their *plot* – the way in which the story materials are arranged by narrators in order to tell the story. The organization of the narrative reveals a great deal of the speaker's relationship to their history"[47] These statements are characteristic of a recent trend in oral history towards a subjective, narrative-based approach. Although, in the last few decades, this view of oral history has become the defining theory of the field, its application to the study of oral history interviews has been slow to take hold.

As this chapter shows, the act of recounting their lives enables interviewees to shape the events of their lives by assigning meaning through storytelling. The role of oral historians is not to extract verifiable information from these stories but, rather, to observe the narrative form for what it tells us about the interviewee and his or her place in history. In order to put this theory into practice, the fields of narrative analysis and linguistics provide many useful tools to aid in our understanding of the meaning conveyed through storytelling.

If storytelling equips interviewees with the means to shape and convey the significance of the events of their lives, religion often provides the ideas through which they understand their world. Like storytelling, religion offers a framework of meaning that contains events within an easily assimilated whole. When looking at oral history as an act of storytelling and meaning-making, an awareness of the narrator's religious outlook may yield a greater understanding of the meaning she or he attributes to her/his life story. Both the religious framework and the structure of storytelling display the interviewees' efforts to recount their lives in a manner that is meaningful to them and comprehensible to the listener. Whether events are explained with reference to the agency of a higher power, to the laws of karma, or to a prophecy is highly significant to our understanding of people's subjective experience of them.

Without rejecting oral history as providing important empirical data – for example, testimonies to the atrocities of the Khmer Rouge – the approach to oral history presented in this chapter underlines the fact that the discipline can provide us with more than historical facts. In my research I have listened to many life stories as told by Cambodian refugees. In this chapter I make no pretence to have represented anywhere near the complexity of the tales told in these interviews; rather, my goal is to show how Ven Runnath's stories of suffering, survival, and religious belief present her as being more than a victim of the Cambodian genocide.

Notes

1 Ven Runnath, interviewed by author and Paul Tom, 27 October 2009. Translated by author.

2 Life Stories of Montrealers Displaced by War, Genocide, and other Human Rights Violations is an oral history project exploring Montrealers' experiences and memories of mass violence and displacement. This project, hosted by Concordia University, divided into six working groups, including the Cambodian working group. See www.lifestoriesmontreal.ca.

3 Alessandro Portelli, *The Death of Luigi Trastulli and Other Stories: Form and Meaning in Oral History* (Albany: State of New York Press, 1991), 50 (emphasis in original).

4 Clifford Geertz, *The Interpretation of Cultures: Selected Essays by Clifford Geertz* (London: Hutchison, 1975), 90

5 Michael Jackson, *The Politics of Storytelling: Violence, Transgression and Intersubjectivity* (Copenhagen: Museum Tusculanum Press, 2002), 14–15.

6 Henry Greenspan, *On Listening to Holocaust Survivors: Recounting and Life History* (Westport: Praeger, 1998), 9.

7 Portelli, *Death of Luigi Trastulli,* 54.

8 Life Stories of Montrealers, "About the Project," at www.lifestories montreal.ca/en/about-the-project.

9 Greenspan, *On Listening,* xvii.

10 Alexander Laban Hinton, *Why Did They Kill?: Cambodia in the Shadow of Genocide* (Berkeley: University of California Press, 2005), 1.

11 Manuel Litalien and Francois Thibeault, *Grimer: Les bouddhistes cambodgiens de Montreal en contexte* (Montreal: UQAM, 2005), 6.

12 Ibid., 5.

13 Frédéric Castel, "Un Memoricide pour Mémoire: Implantation et conditions de vie des Québécois d'origine khmere Cambogienne," in *Le Québec après Bouchard-Taylor: Les identités religieuses de l'immigration,* ed. Louis Rousseau, 33–68 (Montréal: Presses de l'Université du Québec, 2011), 62.

14 Ibid., 63–64.

15 Pamela Sugiman, "'Life Is Sweet': Vulnerability and Composure in the Wartime Narratives of Japanese Canadians," *Journal of Canadian Studies/ Revue d'études canadiennes* 43, 1 (2009): 191.

16 Hayden White, *The Content of the Form: Narrative Discourse and Historical Representation* (Baltimore: Johns Hopkins University Press, 1987), 43.

17 As oral historian Ronald J. Grele explained, it is "necessary to see interviewees, if not as direct voices from the past, as in some manner their own historians, capable of elaborate and sometimes confusing methods of constructing and narrating their own histories." See Ronald J. Grele, *Envelopes of Sound: The Art of Oral History* (New York: Praeger, 1991), 49.

18 White uses the term "narrative" whereas I mostly look at "stories." Although these terms are often used interchangeably in the literature, I consider "stories" to include sequences of events arranged into plots with a beginning, middle, and end.

19 White, *Content of the Form,* xi.

20 Hayden White, *Metahistory: The Historical Imagination of Nineteenth-Century Europe* (Baltimore: Johns Hopkins University Press, 1973), 2.

21 Michael Bamberg, Anna de Fina, and Deborah Schiffrin, *Selves and Identities in Narrative and Discourse* (Philadelphia: John Benjamins Publishing, 2007), 5.

22 Jackson, *Politics of Storytelling*, 15–16 (emphasis in original).

23 Ven Runnath, interviewed by author and Paul Tom, 27 October 2009.

24 Defined in Daniel James's book as "the contrast between the individual and her hopes, wishes, and actions on the one hand, and the working of a dark unyielding power of fate on the other." See Daniel James, *Doña María's Story: Life History, Memory and Political Identity* (Durham, NC: Duke University Press, 2000), 165.

25 White, *Metahistory*, xii.

26 Please note that I use the word "tragedy" to refer to a certain story type. By saying that events were "not inherently tragic," I do not wish to make light of the genocide, only to illustrate how the interviewees tell their stories.

27 Robert A. Orsi, *Between Heaven and Earth: The Religious Worlds People Make and the Scholars Who Study Them* (Princeton: Princeton University Press, 2005), 169.

28 James, *Doña María's Story*, 206.

29 Charlotte Linde, *Life Stories: The Creation of Coherence* (Oxford: Oxford University Press, 1993), 163.

30 Ven Runnath interview, 3 November 2009.

31 Ibid.

32 The story of the spirit (or witch) in the tree is consistent with the belief in spirit described by scholars of Cambodian religion. As Ian Harris explained with regard to *neak ta* (Cambodian spirits associated with a particular place): "They are mundate deities – that is, gods of the realm of men [...] and cannot intervene in the process of final salvation, but they may be induced to bring about significant change in the human and physical realm." See Ian Harris, *Cambodian Buddhism: History and Practice* (Honolulu: University of Hawaii Press, 2005), 55. See also Alain Forest, *Le culte des génies protecteurs au Cambodge: Analyse et traduction d'un corpus de textes sur les* neak ta (Paris: L'Harmattan, 1992).The effect of these spirits can be much more immediate than that of karma. See Nancy J. Smith-Hefner, *Khmer American: Identity and Moral Education in a Diasporic Community* (Berkeley: University of California Press, 1999), 41. The way Ven Runnath tried to use that spirit is consistent with this definition: she was using the spirit to an immediate end and trying to get around the long-term effect of karma, which had brought her to this difficult life.

33 Mary Jo Maynes, Jennifer L. Pierce, and Barbara Laslett, *Telling Stories: The Use of Personal Narratives in the Social Sciences and History* (London: Cornell University Press, 2008), 4.

34 Paul Ricoeur, *Time and Narrative*, trans. Kathleen McLaughlin and David Pellauer (Chicago: University of Chicago Press, 1984), 3.

35 Paul Ricoeur, "Narrative Time," in *On Narrative,* ed. W.J.T. Mitchell (Chicago: University of Chicago Press), 171.

36 Dipesh Chakrabarty, *Provincializing Europe: Postcolonial Thought and Historical Difference* (Princeton: Princeton University Press, 2000), 73.

37 Ven Runnath interview, 27 October 2010. Translated by author.

38 Ibid.

39 Maynes et al., *Telling Stories,* 3.

40 Jackson, *Politics of Storytelling,* 16.

41 Ven Runnath interview, 27 October 2010.

42 Gay Becker, *Disrupted Lives: How People Create Meaning in a Chaotic World* (Berkeley: University of California Press, 1998), 4.

43 Ven Runnath interview, 27 October 2009.

44 Becker, *Disrupted Lives*, 38.

45 Paul Ricoeur, *Figuring the Sacred: Religion, Narrative and Imagination* (Minneapolis: Fortress Press, 1995), 292.

46 James, *Doña María's Story*, 123.

47 Portelli, *Death of Luigi Trastulli,* 50 (emphasis in original).

Afterword

HENRY GREENSPAN

It is said that we live in "an age of testimony,"[1] but the core theme of this volume is that we do not live in "an age of survivors." As Ruth Kluger describes, it is true that survivors are often celebrated in the context of "special occasions."[2] There is no shortage of honorifics. But ceremonial responses to survivors primarily serve to respond to them as *symbols* of what they endured – not as particular people.[3] Meanwhile, working *with* survivors in educational, creative, political, or scholarly partnerships – the kinds of projects described in this volume – happens only rarely. And so the most significant contribution of these chapters may be their demonstrating that the "age of testimony" has, in general, excluded the persons of survivors themselves.

Indeed, and ironically, engaging survivors only as "bearers of testimony" often serves their exclusion. The role of "eyewitness" is a kind of default position to which we assign survivors when we are not equipped – emotionally, politically, or methodologically – to meet them in less limited and limiting ways. Ari Gandsman's chapter on the "ex-disappeared" in Argentina is a wonderful example of this. While these survivors may be called upon to provide testimony in juridical contexts, they remain marginalized more generally, surrounded by a discourse of distrust. One of the ex-disappeared told Gandsman that the disappeared "had never been allowed to 'reappear,' that they were still fundamentally invisible and unrecognized."

Not recognizing survivors has been more the rule than the exception. Thus Robert Storey describes the ways injured workers have been labelled "cheaters, malingerers, and criminals" and rendered "invisible." Marie-Jolie Rwigema cites Innocent Rwililiza on the marginalizing of Rwandan genocide survivors, even within Rwanda itself: "I think everyone would like the survivors to relinquish the genocide, in a way. As if people wanted them to leave the task of dealing with it to others [...] As if we are from now on somewhat superfluous." Despite all their seeming recognition today, Holocaust survivors have fared similarly. Echoing Kluger on the ways that both awe and revulsion have kept Holocaust survivors "at arm's length,"[4] Helen Epstein recalls that the first wave of novels and films about Holocaust survivors portrayed them "either as saints or martyrs, people who had survived the worst and could do no wrong; or alternatively, as little more than shells of their former selves, near criminals, who had stooped to inhuman measures in order to prolong their lives."[5] Henry Krystal, a psychiatrist who is himself an Auschwitz survivor, wrote in 1968 about sexual assault during the Holocaust – the prevalence of which is still debated. Krystal notes that "many women were raped and are reluctant to admit to it." Their reluctance does not stem solely from personal reticence. Krystal continues:

> One woman who at the age of 18 was raped by an SS man in Auschwitz was diagnosed "a prostitute and a psychopathic character." There is hence some justification to the fears that survivors have in relating their experiences in view of the special reaction many people have to survivors – namely, that of suspicion.[6]

The "special reaction" to survivors that Krystal notes complements the "special occasions" that Kluger describes. Suspicion or sanctification both lead to speaking *about* survivors rather than to speaking *with* them: that is, they both lead to patronizing, distance, and sometimes worse.

Most of the chapters in this volume are driven (even haunted) by awareness of this history. The aspiration to go "beyond testimony," conventionally understood, means moving *towards* mutually useful and respectful partnership. The projects described are quite various and include collaboration in activism, in work on public presentations (especially in schools), in creative writing and storytelling, in analyzing the process of retelling itself, in scholarship, and in exploring the meaning of "living after." Still, along with some differences (to which I return), there is a broad consensus, and it is worth summarizing shared convictions:

1. *Sustained acquaintance is essential.* Whatever the hoped-for results of collaborations, they emerge from multifaceted relationships that go far beyond the time needed to accomplish any specific purpose. That may include recorded and informal conversations, phone calls, e-mails, shared meals, and shared laughter (of which the chapters describe a good deal). In other words, results emerge from all that makes relationships relationships.
2. *Process is also product.* Sustained and multifaceted acquaintance enriches – and, indeed, is often required for – intended goals. But collaboration – as actualized in camaraderie, solidarity, or mutual support – is

also an end in itself, no less important than whatever else may be accomplished. Indeed, given the wider history of survivors so often being marginalized, patronized, or silenced, collaborative engagement may be the *most* important consequence of such projects.

3. *Contingency and mutability are real.* Different purposes, different interpersonal chemistries, different questions, different historical and life-historical moments (for all participants), and a mountain of other contingencies will yield different consequences. It is not a question of some being "truer," or inherently "better," than others. Just as we all do, survivors share different versions (with different details, emphases, complexity) of the same essential story, depending on listeners and circumstances. And, indeed, many of the survivors represented in this volume describe the ways their accounts change over the course of multiple retellings and in response to different people and contexts. The idea of a single, definitive "testimony" – while a necessary conceit in juridical contexts – is an illusion.
4. *Collaborative projects require exquisite sensitivity and reflexivity.* In collaborative work – especially work across differences in ethnicity, language, gender, and social status – it is extraordinarily easy not to notice the privileges one takes or inadvertently surrenders. Candour, acknowledgment of uncertainty, and frank description of dilemmas are always required. So also is the awareness that, however attentive one tries to be, a good deal will be missed. In this respect, collaborative work is not unusual. The best scientific articles, for example, include commentary about the limits and uncertainties inherent in the methods and conclusions of the published study. Unfortunately, such reflection is less common in the humanities and social sciences.
5. *Expect the unexpected, and embrace it.* Collaboration means collaboration: if the end of the story (or even a clear idea of what the story is!) was evident from the beginning, then one would not need more than one author. Most of the chapters in this collection tell stories of learning and unlearning – tentative answers interwoven with persisting questions. Collaborative work is always "work in process" in more than one sense and for all participants involved.

These, then, are some of the assumptions shared by most of the contributors to this collection. Needless to say, there are also differences. Here, I would raise a couple of issues in order to encourage collaborative reflection that goes beyond this volume: literally, *after*words.

First, a number of contributors speak of survivors' stories, and they invoke the general process of storytelling (collaborative and otherwise) as an organizing construct. Like testimony, "stories" and "storytelling" are also terms to which I am slightly allergic in the context of survivors. This goes back to the beginning of my own work: most essentially, to a formulation by Leon that emerged while we worked together to understand a particular story of his. About his retelling in general, Leon eventually insisted: "It is *not* a story. It has to be *made* a story. In order to convey it. And with all the frustration that implies. Because, at best, you compromise. You compromise."[7] And so I have spent a lot of time trying to understand the ways survivors do attempt to "make stories" for what is "not a story"; how they contend with their frustration; and how they create, and recurrently re-create, the compromised narratives that emerge. The evolution of Abe's story of his guilt, including his own interpretations of its functions, is one of many such examples.

Understanding stories-as-compromises brings us back to all that is mutable and contingent in survivors' retelling – refuting, once again, the notion of a fixed and finished account. But it is certainly also true, as a number of contributors note, that stories provide meaning and a sense of agency (in the very act of choosing to retell a particular account in a particular way) and that they rescue experiences that *can* be transmitted. Indeed, survivors' stories are themselves survivors of experiences that, if Leon is correct, do not lend themselves to storytelling. The "not-story" to which Leon refers is, in significant part, storytelling's negation. Leon once told me it is even the negation of voice, of sound, itself.[8]

It is my sense that we, who work to engage survivors, speak of their stories and storytelling much more often than do survivors themselves.[9] Important as stories are to retelling particular experiences and memories, what may be more important – and what stories themselves most essentially serve – is not meaning or integration in the abstract but the possibility of communicating with non-survivors: "in order to convey it," said Leon. "*This* they can relate to," said Abe. I also think of what Sal said to Chris Patti: "Chris, I will be at peace if I feel one person has really listened, has really tried to understand"; and that, in the end, life was about learning "to really listen to each other." Stories make listening easier; sometimes stories make listening possible. But I believe that it is the "really listening," and not the stories, that is the core. Not uncommonly, the *dis*integration conveyed through broken or failed stories – including "life stories" – serves "really listening" most of all.[10]

What remains when we have *only* the stories and not the survivors? In the conventional testimony model, survivors themselves become mostly superfluous – not personally, of course, but methodologically. Once the testimonies have been gathered, indexed, and archived, the recounters are no longer necessary. Some have even suggested that survivors "live on" *through* the archive: that, as part of a collection of testimonies, they continue to survive.[11]

The reality, however, is that survivors do not live on; at least not in this way. For those of us who have spent much of our lives engaging survivors as "partners in a conversation," when our partners die, so also do our conversations. Of course, there will still be much to learn and much to remember, just as we learn and remember from many survivors – through their memoirs, for example – who are no longer here. But the change from sustained acquaintance and all that emerges from directly working together to engaging survivors only through recordings, texts, and "testimonies" is a radical one. It is a movement from one methodological universe to another. The change is bearable, but it is also irreparable.

And that is why there is so much work to do.

Notes

1 See, for example, Shoshana Felman and Dori Laub, *Testimony: Crises of Witnessing in Literature, Psychoanalysis, and History* (New York: Routledge, 1992), 53.

2 Ruth Kluger, *Still Alive: A Holocaust Girlhood Remembered* (New York: Feminist Press, 2001), 94.

3 The point is the core theme of my *On Listening to Holocaust Survivors: Beyond Testimony* (St. Paul, MN: Paragon House, 2010).

4 Kluger, *Still Alive*, 94.

5 Helen Epstein, *Children of the Holocaust: Conversations with Sons and Daughters of Survivors* (New York: Penguin, 1988), 177.

6 Henry Krystal, *Massive Psychic Trauma* (New York: International Universities Press, 1968), 87.

7 Greenspan, *On Listening*, especially 181–208 (emphasis in original).

8 Ibid., 200.

9 Exceptions would be survivors, like Elie Wiesel, who explicitly take the role of "storyteller" as their narrative persona. See Greenspan, *On Listening,* 183–85.

10 Ibid., 14.

11 See, for example, *PastForward: The Digest of the USC Shoah Foundation Institute for Visual History and Education*, Autumn 2010. Steven Spielberg is quoted: "And survivors – whether living or gone – will always exist through this Institute [...] They will live on, and they'll all be educators now" (19). The sentiment is obviously generous, but it also reflects the paradigmatic differences between conventional archival and collaborative approaches.

Contributors

Catherine Baker is a lecturer in twentieth-century history at the University of Hull. Her research interests include nationalism, ethnicity, and identity; international intervention; and the politics of language, translation, and interpreting, with a regional focus to date on the former Yugoslavia. Her articles have been published in journals such as *History Workshop Journal*, *Slavic Review*, *Oral History Forum/d'histoire orale*, and *War and Society*, and she is the co-author (with Michael Kelly) of *Interpreting the Peace: Peace Operations, Conflict and Language in Bosnia-Herzegovina* (Palgrave Macmillan, 2013). She is also the author of *Sounds of the Borderland: Popular Music, War and Nationalism in Croatia since 1991* (Ashgate, 2010).

Yolande Cohen is a full professor of modern European history at the Université du Québec à Montréal. President of the Academy of Arts and Humanities of the Royal Society of Canada, she is also Chevalier de l'Ordre de la Légion d'honneur of France.

Sara Cohen Fournier recently started medical school at the Université de Montréal where she hopes to pursue her interest in understanding resilience and memory. She completed a master's degree in oral history, researching resilience and transmission of memory within a Vietnamese-American community in Brooklyn. In the five years of the project, she worked as an active interviewer for Life Stories of Montrealers Displaced by Wars, Genocide and Other Human Rights Violations. From this research, a new project evolved. It looks at the place of food, recipes, and transmission of traditional knowledge in first- and second-generation migrants and is entitled *Dishing up the Past:* http://rootsandrecipes.wordpress.com/.

Carolyn Ellis is Distinguished University Professor of communication at the University of South Florida. Her most recent books include *The Ethnographic I: A Methodological Novel about Autoethnography; Revision: Autoethnographic Reflections on Life and Work; Music Autoethnographies: Making Autoethnography Sing/Making Music Personal;* and *Handbook of Autoethnography*. She has published numerous articles, chapters, and personal stories situated in emotions and interpretive representations of qualitative research, particularly autoethnography. Her current research focuses on compassionate listening to Holocaust testimonies and sharing authority in a collaborative, relational research process with first- and second-generation survivors.

Ari Gandsman is an assistant professor in the Department of Sociology and Anthropology at the University of Ottawa. He received his PhD in 2008 from McGill University and was previously visiting assistant professor at Union College in New York.

Henry Greenspan is a psychologist and playwright at the University of Michigan where he is also chair of the program in social theory and practice. His most recent book is the second and expanded edition of *On Listening to Holocaust Survivors: Beyond Testimony* (Paragon House, 2010). In 2012 he was the Fulbright Visiting Research Chair at Concordia University in Montreal, affiliated with Concordia's Centre for Oral History and Digital Storytelling.

Steven High is Canada Research Chair in Oral History at Concordia University and co-founder of the Centre for Oral History and Digital Storytelling. From 2005 to 2012, he directed the Montreal Life Stories project (www.lifestoriesmontreal.ca), a community-university research alliance recording the life stories of Montrealers displaced by large-scale violence. He has also worked extensively with displaced industrial workers in Canada and the United States. Most recently, he is the author of *Oral History at the Crossroads: Sharing Life Stories of Survival and Displacement* and, with Edward Little and Thi Ry Duong, *Remembering Mass Violence: Oral History, Digital Media, and Performance.*

Michele Luchs is director of English language arts programs for Quebec's Ministry of Education and co-coordinator of the Mapping Memories project. For the last fifteen years she has worked with teachers around the province to develop projects involving media and writing.

Arthur McIvor is professor of social history and director of the Scottish Oral History Centre at the University of Strathclyde, Glasgow, Scotland. His research interests lie in the history of work and the body, and he has published widely in this area, including (with Ronnie Johnston) *Lethal Work* (2000) and *Miners' Lung* (2007). His latest book is *Working Lives: Work in Britain since 1945* (Palgrave Macmillan, 2013).

Martin Messika is a PhD student in history at the Université Paris I Panthéon-Sorbonne/Université du Québec à Montréal. His research deals with North African migration to France and to Canada.

Liz Miller is a documentary maker, community media artist, and professor in the communication studies program at Concordia University in Montreal. Her documentary films, *Novela, Novela* and *The Water Front* have been exhibited and broadcast around the world and are used to inform policy and educational initiatives. Miller has developed participatory media projects with women, youth, senior citizens, and a wide range of human rights organizations.

Chris Patti is assistant professor of communication at Appalachian State University in Boone, North Carolina. His ethnographic research seeks to illuminate intimate, relational processes central to human experience through listening to and representing richly personal stories of love, loss, and transformation. The goal of his work is to explore and cultivate compassion – as an interpersonal scholar and in the broader world.

Marie A. Pelletier is a graduate of the MA history program at Concordia University. She started her oral history research in 2006 as an undergraduate student interviewing homeless Montrealers. Her academic interests are centred on the theory and meaning of oral history. She wrote her master's thesis in collaboration with the Cambodian working group of the Montreal Life Stories project, examining in depth a small number of life story interviews for how meaning is created through storytelling and religion.

Jerry Rawicki was twelve years old when Germany invaded Poland and he was deported from his native city of Plock to the small town of Bodzentyn. Together with his older sister, he made his way to the Warsaw Ghetto, where he became a courier between the budding Jewish resistance and the Polish underground. In April 1943, he fought in the Warsaw Ghetto uprising and escaped its smoldering ruins. With the help of forged identification provided by the Polish underground, he survived the remainder of the war as a Roman Catholic. He arrived in New York in 1949 where he became an optician, and then later retired to Florida. He was married for fifty-six years to his wife, Helene (now deceased), and they have a son, daughter, and seven grandchildren. Jerry is the author of the novel *Sins and Sorrow* and several essays and articles about his experiences during the Holocaust.

Marie-Jolie Rwigema is a community and arts-based educator, researcher, mental health counsellor, and documentary filmmaker (*The Rwandan Genocide as Told by Its Historian-Survivors*). Her work in these capacities includes event organizing, community needs assessment, and workshops on anti-violence, anti-racism, and youth engagement. She is a doctoral student in social work (University of Toronto) with a master's in social work (Toronto) and an honours BA in African studies and international development studies (York University). Her research examines the racialized politics of knowledge production concerning the 1994 Rwandan genocide and resistant knowledge traditions within survivor communities.

Anna Sheftel is assistant professor of conflict studies at Saint Paul University in Ottawa. She completed her doctorate at the University of Oxford where she studied how people in the northwest of Bosnia-Herzegovina construct narratives of wartime violence and grapple with the larger politics of memory in the region. She and Stacey Zembrzycki are currently working with Holocaust survivors in Montreal to understand their wartime and postwar experiences as well as how they recount those experiences publicly. She is also interested in the ethics and practice of collaborative oral history methodology and, to that end, is co-editor (with Stacey) of *Oral History Off the Record: Towards an Ethnography of Practice* (Palgrave Macmillan, 2013).

Umwali Sollange is a popular educator, community-based researcher, community mentor, activist, and advocate. She has over eleven years of leadership experience in the non-profit sector, working with diverse communities and community organizations: her work includes community development/empowerment, community centre directorship, and organizing annual genocide commemorations in Toronto. She was part of a team that was instrumental in getting the City of Toronto to officially recognize April 7 as a "Day of Reflection on the Genocide in Rwanda." Her research interests include notions of citizenship and the role of trans-national politics among African communities residing in Canada.

Robert Storey teaches in the School of Labour Studies and the Department of Sociology at McMaster University. His decade-long research into the lives and political activism of injured workers is an ongoing source of inspiration and a constant challenge to his pessimism of the intellect.

Lisa K. Taylor is full professor of education at Bishop's University in Quebec. Her research and teaching are in the areas of critical literacy, anti-racism, anti-colonial and social justice teacher education, critical global education, pedagogies of remembrance, postcolonial perspectives in TESOL, and transnational feminist literature. She has published in *TESOL Quarterly*, *Intercultural Education*, and *TOPIA: Canadian Journal of Cultural Studies*. She co-edited *Contested Imaginaries: Reading Muslim Women and Muslim Women Reading Back – Transnational Feminist Reading Practices, Pedagogy and Ethical Concerns* as a journal and forthcoming as an edited collection.

Rob Wilson is a professor in the Department of Philosophy at the University of Alberta, Canada, where he is the director of Philosophy for Children Alberta (p4c.ualberta.ca/) and the principal investigator of the CURA-funded project entitled Living Archives on Eugenics in Western Canada (eugenicsarchive.ca). Rob received his BA from the University of Western Australia, and his MA and PhD in philosophy from Cornell University.

Stacey Zembrzycki is an affiliate assistant professor in the Department of History at Concordia University. A modern Canadian oral and public historian of ethnic and immigrant experience, she is the author of *According to Baba: A Collaborative Oral History of Sudbury's Ukrainian Community* (UBC Press, 2014) and its accompanying website www.sudburyukrainians.ca and is co-editor, with Anna Sheftel, of *Oral History Off the Record: Towards an Ethnography of Practice* (Palgrave Macmillan, 2013).

Index